# THE CRITICAL HERITAGE SERIES

GENERAL EDITOR: B. C. SOUTHAM, M.A., B.LITT. (OXON.)
*Formerly Department of English, Westfield College, University of London*

For a list of books in the series see the back end paper

# GEORGE ORWELL

*THE CRITICAL HERITAGE*

*edited by*
JEFFREY MEYERS

ROUTLEDGE & KEGAN PAUL: LONDON AND BOSTON

First published in 1975
by Routledge & Kegan Paul Ltd
Broadway House, 68-74 Carter Lane,
London EC4V 5EL and
9 Park Street,
Boston, Mass. 02108, USA
Set in 11 on 12 pt Monotype Bembo
and printed in Great Britain by
Butler & Tanner Ltd, Frome and London
Copyright Jeffrey Meyers 1975

ISBN 0 7100 8255 X

For
Alfredo and Barbara

# General Editor's Preface

The reception given to a writer by his contemporaries and near-contemporaries is evidence of considerable value to the student of literature. On one side we learn a great deal about the state of criticism at large and in particular about the development of critical attitudes towards a single writer; at the same time, through private comments in letters, journals or marginalia, we gain an insight upon the tastes and literary thought of individual readers of the period. Evidence of this kind helps us to understand the writer's historical situation, the nature of his immediate reading-public, and his response to these pressures.

The separate volumes in the *Critical Heritage Series* present a record of this early criticism. Clearly, for many of the highly productive and lengthily reviewed nineteenth- and twentieth-century writers, there exists an enormous body of material; and in these cases the volume editors have made a selection of the most important views, significant for their intrinsic critical worth or for their representative quality—perhaps even registering incomprehension!

For earlier writers, notably pre-eighteenth century, the materials are much scarcer and the historical period has been extended, sometimes far beyond the writer's lifetime, in order to show the inception and growth of critical views which were initially slow to appear.

In each volume the documents are headed by an Introduction, discussing the material assembled and relating the early stages of the author's reception to what we have come to identify as the critical tradition. The volumes will make available much material which would otherwise be difficult of access and it is hoped that the modern reader will be thereby helped towards an informed understanding of the ways in which literature has been read and judged.

B.C.S.

# Contents

CONTENTS

# Acknowledgments

The editor and publishers wish to thank the following for their permission to reprint copyright material for the extracts quoted:

Edward Arnold Ltd and *Listener* for No. 92; *Atlantic Monthly* for No. 53 (copyright © 1950, by the Atlantic Monthly Company, Boston, Mass.); Georges Borchardt, Inc., *Hudson Review* and Random House for No. 102 (copyright © 1957 George P. Elliott. First published in *Hudson Review*); Georges Borchardt, Inc., and *New Yorker* for No. 107; *Canadian Forum* for No. 67; *Commonweal* for Nos 16, 23 and 49; the late Cyril Connolly for No. 64, and *New Statesman* for No. 18; *Contemporary Review* for Nos 10 and 31; *Current Digest of the Soviet Press* for No. 85 (translation copyright 1950 by *Current Digest of the Soviet Press*); Editions Gallimard for No. 1; *Evening Standard* for No. 62; Farrar, Straus & Giroux and *New Yorker* for Nos 66, 73 and 95; Victor Gollancz Ltd for No. 27; *Guardian* for No. 39; David Higham Associates, *Daily Telegraph* and *Esquire* for Nos 103 (© Anthony Powell, 1968) and 106 (© 1969 by Esquire, Inc., first published in *Esquire*); Irving Howe and *Harper's* for No. 105 (copyright © 1969 by *Harper's Magazine*); *Hudson Review* for No. 26; Hutchinson Publishing Group Ltd and St Martin's Press, Inc. for No. 77; Mrs Q. D. Leavis for No. 60; Golo Mann and *Frankfurter Rundschau* for No. 84; William Morris Agency and *New Yorker* for No. 22; Malcolm Muggeridge for No. 11; *Nation* for Nos 5, 33, 44, 50, 65, 72 and 80; *New Leader* (New York) for Nos 42 and 81; *New Republic* for Nos. 6, 43, 52, 70, 94 and 97; *New Statesman* for Nos 4, 32 and 63; Conor Cruise O'Brien and *Listener* for No. 104; *Observer* for Nos 12, 79, 90 and 99; *Partisan Review* for Nos 61 and 75; A. D. Peters & Co. for Nos 3, 20 and 41; *Philological Quarterly* for No. 108; Henry Popkin for No. 100; V. S. Pritchett and *New Statesman* for No. 89; Peter Quennell and *New Statesman* for No. 14; Herbert Read Discretionary Trust for No. 86; Estate of Philip Rahv and *Partisan Review* for No. 82; Bertrand Russell Estate for No. 91; Mrs Vasiliki Sarant, *Commentary* and *Partisan Review* for Nos 25 and 54; *Saturday Review* for Nos 51 and 71; Secker & Warburg Ltd for No. 87; Society of Authors as literary representatives of the Estate of John Middleton Murry for No. 74;

*Spectator* for Nos 8, 13, 17 and 68; *Tablet* for Nos 40 and 69; Hugh Thomas and *New Statesman* for No. 45; *Time and Tide* for Nos 29, 36, 47, 55 and 96; *The Times Literary Supplement* for Nos 2, 9, 19, 35, 46, 57, 78 and 98; Philip Toynbee and *Encounter* for No. 34; *Tribune* for Nos 7, 28, 48 and 93; John Wain and *Twentieth Century* for No. 101; George Woodcock for No. 76; *Yale Review* for No. 24 (copyright Yale University Press).

It has proved difficult in certain cases to locate the proprietors of copyright material. However, all possible care has been taken to trace ownership of the selections included and to make full acknowledgment for their use.

# Introduction

Before he published his first book at the age of thirty, Orwell's experience ranged from Eton to service in the colonial police, and from short periods as a tramp, dishwasher, hop-picker, tutor and teacher to book reviewer and pseudo-Georgian poet. And during the next twelve years he worked as a book dealer, farmer, shopkeeper, film critic, broadcaster, editor, columnist and war correspondent to supplement his meager income as an author. Orwell deliberately sought out experience to provide material for his writing, and everything he produced is related to the events of his life. His acute eye for detail and passionate desire to inform others of the human and political reality he had discovered made him pre-eminent as a reporter, essayist and satirist rather than as a novelist.

Because his books were critical of society and of governments, of received opinion on the Right and on the Left, they often inspired controversy and were difficult to publish. *Down and Out in Paris and London* was rejected by Cape and Faber. The English edition of *Burmese Days* was refused by Cape and Heinemann, and then delayed for a year when the India Office objected to its anti-imperialism. *The Road to Wigan Pier* carried a Foreword by Victor Gollancz, addressed to the members of the Left Book Club, which attacked Orwell's attacks on Socialism. And Gollancz rejected *Homage to Catalonia* for political reasons before a word of it was written, though he insisted on retaining his rights to Orwell's future books and did not relinquish his contract until 1944. *Animal Farm* was again refused by Gollancz, Cape, Faber and twenty American publishers because of its criticism of Stalinist Russia. *1984* got an icy reception in Left-wing circles and was violently attacked in the Communist press. Though Harper published Orwell's first three works, none of his books appeared in America between 1936 and 1946; and *Keep the Aspidistra Flying*, *The Road to Wigan Pier*, *Homage to Catalonia*, *Coming Up For Air* and 'Such, Such Were the Joys' did not appear in that country until Harcourt Brace, who became Orwell's publisher in 1946, brought them out after his death.

Orwell's books were closely related to the historical events and political issues of his time. *Burmese Days* reflected the decline of British imperialism; *Down and Out in Paris and London, A Clergyman's Daughter, Keep the Aspidistra Flying* and *The Road to Wigan Pier* were published during the Depression and dealt with poverty; *Homage to Catalonia* came out during the Spanish Civil War; and *Coming Up For Air* appeared three months before the outbreak of the war that it prophesied. *Inside the Whale* and *The Lion and the Unicorn* were published during the Second World War, *Animal Farm* a few days after Hiroshima, *1984* at the height of the Cold War, and the *Collected Essays, Journalism and Letters* during the bitter protests against the war in Vietnam.

Though Orwell regularly published a book every year from 1933 to 1941, and edited and contributed to three books of essays in 1941–3, his works were usually published in small editions of 1,500 to 3,000 copies and did not sell well until 1945. Before then he was generally unknown and frequently hard-up, and was forced to undertake the 'quite exceptionally thankless, irritating and exhausting job'[1] of industrious and indiscriminate book reviewing, which brought in a vital three or four pounds a week. His journalistic output was enormous and in less than twenty years he produced more than seven hundred articles in addition to his books. Malcolm Muggeridge relates that Orwell hated the journalistic grind and 'cherished the dream that he would retire to the country and write great literary masterpieces; nevermore sit in anguish over a typewriter with a deadline to meet' (No. 106).

Orwell did far too much reviewing himself to take it very seriously. He had gone from Eton to Burma and, like his hero Gordon Comstock, despised and resented 'those moneyed young beasts who glide so gracefully from Eton to Cambridge and from Cambridge to the literary reviews.'[2] In his witty 'Confessions of a Book Reviewer' he recommended that reviews have a minimum of a thousand words and said, 'The great majority of reviews give an inadequate or misleading account of the book that is dealt with. . . . The usual middle-length review of about 600 words is bound to be worthless, even if the reviewer genuinely wants to write about it' (IV, pp. 183–4). And in his 'As I Please' column of 1944 Orwell condemned the reviewers of the 1930s in a somewhat exaggerated tirade:

The truly shameful feature of literary life before the war was the blurring of the distinction between advertisement and criticism. A number of so-called

2

reviewers, especially the best-known ones, were simply blurb writers. . . . The literary pages of several well-known papers were practically owned by a handful of publishers who had their quislings planted in all the important jobs. . . . A book coming from the right publishers could be absolutely certain not only of favourable reviews, but of being placed on the 'recommended' list. . . .

In America even the pretence that hack reviewers read the books they are paid to criticise has been partially abandoned. Publishers, or some publishers, send out with review copies a short synopsis telling the reviewer what to say. (III, pp. 168–9)

Orwell knew that the facile reviewers did not need a publisher's synopsis to enable them to judge a book without actually reading it and that critics often had to praise trash in order to get their reviews printed.

Yet Orwell, who had to live on his earnings as a writer, was well aware of the connection between criticism and sales, and he took a pragmatic and cynical attitude about reviews. As he wrote in 1938 to Cyril Connolly, who was about to publish *Enemies of Promise* (an autobiography that described the young Orwell at prep. school and Eton): 'I see from the *NS&N* that you have a book coming out sometime this spring. If you can manage to get a copy sent me I'll review it for the *New English* [*Weekly*], possibly also *Time & Tide*. I arranged for Warburg to send you a copy of my Spanish book (next month) hoping you may be able to review it. You scratch my back, I'll scratch yours' (I, p. 309).

Many of Orwell's books were reviewed by friends like Connolly, Richard Rees, Malcolm Muggeridge, Anthony Powell, Julian Symons, George Woodcock, Max Plowman and T. R. Fyvel in periodicals to which he frequently contributed: the *Adelphi* (founded by Middleton Murry and co-edited by Rees in the 1930s), the *New English Weekly* (founded by A. R. Orage of the *New Age*), *Time and Tide*, the *New Statesman* (founded by Sidney and Beatrice Webb), the *Tribune* (the Socialist weekly, edited by Aneurin Bevan, which published Orwell's 'As I Please' column from 1943 to 1947), *Horizon* (edited by Connolly), *Partisan Review* (which published Orwell's 'London Letters' during the war), the *Observer* (which published Orwell's war dispatches) and the *Manchester Evening News* (which published his weekly book review in the mid-1940s).

Though Orwell's books were widely reviewed and well-received, his reputation—which can be divided into four phases—developed slowly and he did not achieve fame until the end of his life. In the early phase, from *Down and Out* (1933) to *Keep the Aspidistra Flying* (1936), his books were often discussed with some other mediocre works, and he received those brief and sometimes superficial 600-word reviews that contained more plot summary than serious criticism. But the reviewers showed more indulgence than discrimination about his early novels, which got surprisingly good notices. In the middle phase, from *The Road to Wigan Pier* (1937) to *The Lion and the Unicorn* (1941), Orwell published his idiosyncratic and unpopular attacks on Socialism and Stalinism, became a controversial but respected and sympathetic figure, and received longer and more perceptive reviews.

Orwell's reputation changed dramatically in the late phase, from *Animal Farm* (1945) to *1984* (1949), when unlike Conrad, Joyce and Lawrence, he became both popular and wealthy in his own lifetime. After the publication of his beast fable Orwell attracted the best critics of the time, received brilliant as well as appreciative reviews on the front page of the *New York Times Book Review*, in the lead review of the *New Yorker*, and in all the prominent periodicals, and was recognized as one of the major writers of the twentieth century. Most of the reviews after 1945 are valuable for their intrinsic interest as well as for what they say about Orwell, and many were substantial enough to be reprinted in books. These reviews, however, did not significantly affect Orwell's attitude to his work. But they contributed to the success that freed him from continuous journalism, and allowed him to buy a house on Jura, in the Hebrides, and concentrate on *1984*. It is ironic that *Animal Farm* coincided with the terminal phase of his tuberculosis and the last years of his life.

In the fourth phase of his reputation, from *Shooting an Elephant* (1950) to the *Collected Essays, Journalism and Letters* (1968), the reviews of his posthumously published books provided a revaluation in the light of *Animal Farm* and *1984*, refined the earlier critical judgments, and distinguished between Orwell's strengths and weaknesses. This posthumous phase was strongly influenced by the splendid obituaries of Victor Pritchett (No. 89) and Arthur Koestler (No. 90), which helped to establish the legend of the tall, lined and shaggy man who shot the elephant in Burma and was shot in Spain, witnessed a hanging and saw the poor die, went in the spike and down the mine, and was perhaps prematurely canonized as a secular saint. It is worth noting, as Orwell would say, that though critics invariably admire the subtle art of his autobiographical writings, they sometimes forget that Orwell's legend is based mainly on his *own* carefully projected self-image.

4

A number of dominant themes emerge from the criticism on Orwell. Critics like Irving Howe (Nos 50 and 105), Q. D. Leavis (No. 60) and Conor Cruise O'Brien (No. 104) mention his lack of imaginative power, discuss the difference between the successful *persona* in his documentary works and the self-pity of his unconvincing fictional heroes, and agree that he is much better as a reporter than as a novelist. Other writers, most notably Isaac Rosenfeld (No. 54) and Henry Popkin (No. 100), analyze Orwell's profound conservatism (he wanted his son to go to Eton), his desire to establish a continuity between the England of the past and the present, and the paradox that he was both a Socialist and a man in love with the pre-war world.

Orwell's personal characteristics: his courage, compassion, honesty, decency, generosity, integrity and responsibility as well as his masochism (West, No. 22), and his stylistic qualities: vigor, clarity, precision, forcefulness, confidence and commonsense, have also received a good deal of attention. But the two most serious criticisms of Orwell, made by T. S. Eliot (p. 20), George Woodcock (No. 76) and Bertrand Russell (No. 91), are his bitterness, pessimism and negativism, and the superficiality and inconsistency of his political ideas.

Critics agree that the early novels are Orwell's weakest books and that he is a superb reporter and critic. His essays on Swift, Dickens, Gissing, Kipling, Koestler and Henry Miller are now considered essential to an understanding of these writers, and both 'Shooting an Elephant' and 'Politics and the English Language' have become modern classics. But there is no consensus about what constitutes his best work. *Homage to Catalonia* is perhaps his most characteristic and compassionate book, *Animal Farm* the most popular and perfect, and *1984*, which created the concepts of Big Brother, Doublethink and Newspeak, the most powerful and influential. It is clear, however, that Orwell's reputation was extremely high when he died at the age of forty-six in January 1950 and has continued to rise since then.

### Down and Out in Paris and London

In an autobiographical passage of *The Road to Wigan Pier*, Orwell explains how the overpowering guilt that resulted from his years as a policeman in Burma forced him to seek expiation among the outcasts at the extreme fringe of society:[3]

I wanted to submerge myself, to get right down among the oppressed, to be one of them and on their side against the tyrants. . . . I could go among these people, see what their lives were like and feel myself temporarily part of their world. Once I had been among them and accepted by them, I should have touched bottom and—this is what I felt: I was aware even then it was irrational —part of my guilt would drop from me.

Orwell's squalid experiences as a tramp and dishwasher during the late 1920s provided the subject of his first book, which was published by Gollancz in January 1933. Orwell's real name was Eric Blair, and his pseudonym was selected from a list that included P. S. Burton, Kenneth Miles and H. Lewis Allways.

Orwell's contrast between the luxury of the grand hotel and the exploitation of the workers, his analysis of the psychology of poverty, and his direct experience and personal involvement in human degradation met the demand for social realism in the 1930s and his book was well received. He was praised for his honesty and sincerity—which were recognized in *Down and Out* and have been commented on ever since—his sensitive social conscience, his practical suggestions for the alleviation of poverty, and his portrayal of the differences in national temperament in the contrasting sections on Paris and London. But the reviewers had little to say about the characterization of Bozo and Boris; and they ignored what many critics now consider the most interesting literary and biographical aspects of the book: the *persona* which revealed his emotional need to share poverty and hardship.

The first review of *Down and Out*, in the *TLS*, rightly emphasizes his sympathy with the underdog and criticism of the casual ward system (No. 2). C. Day Lewis responds to Orwell's vividly presented 'tour of the under-world' by stating, 'if you wish to eat a meal in a big hotel without acute nausea, you had better skip pp. 107–109' (No. 3). But a restaurateur with the unlikely name of Humbert Possenti, writing from the Hotel Splendide in Piccadilly and claiming forty years' experience in the trade, vigorously protested against Orwell's defamations in a letter to *The Times*: 'Such a disgusting state of things as he describes in such places is inconceivable. The kitchens of large and smart restaurants have to be clean . . . are cleaner than those of most private houses.'[4] Orwell took the offensive eleven days later and replied:

M. Possenti seems not to realise that these remarks are quite beside the point. The passages objected to in my book did not refer to Paris hotels in general, but to one particular hotel. And as M. Possenti does not know which hotel this was he has no means of testing the truth of my statements. So I am afraid that, in spite of his 40 years' experience, my evidence in this case is worth more than his. (I, p. 116)

But Orwell's response ignores the fact that he *did* generalize about all luxury hotels from his experiences in one, in order to develop his ideas about the degrading relationship between those who labor and those who consume.

W. H. Davies relates the book to his own experience as a tramp and discriminates between kinds of beggars, praises its truth about real life and says it is 'packed with unique and strange information' (No. 4). Though Herbert Gorman suspects that Orwell's indignation has 'colored the facts a trifle,' he mentions the effectiveness of his 'rough-and-ready styleless style.' He notices Orwell's masochism and shrewdly observes that he 'rather enjoys being down and out.'[5] The reviewer in the *Nation* comments on Orwell's ability to convey a 'powerful sense of destitution and helplessness' and his 'damning indictment of society' (No. 5). The novelist James Farrell mentions that Orwell had been to Eton, stresses the utter degradation and waste of poverty and praises the account as 'genuine, unexaggerated and intelligent' (No. 6). Daniel George discusses Orwell's characterization and, like Gorman, questions some of the facts and raises the important issue of whether the book is fiction or autobiography (No. 7).

In an interview with the *Paris Review* in 1962, Henry Miller, another connoisseur of Parisian low-life, said, 'I was crazy about his book *Down and Out in Paris and London*; I think it's a classic. For me it's still his best book. Though he was a wonderful chap in his way, Orwell, in the end I thought him stupid. He was like so many English people, an idealist, and, it seemed to me, a foolish idealist.'[6] Miller's cynical judgment reaffirms his earlier opinion. For when Orwell met Miller in Paris in 1936 on his way to fight in Spain, the American novelist, who was completely indifferent to the Civil War, told Orwell that he was an idiot. In 'Inside the Whale' and three enthusiastic book reviews Orwell revealed his fascination with and attraction to Miller's astonishing passivity and his total rejection of the concept of decency.

## Burmese Days

Kipling was the first major English writer to deal extensively and seriously with the British colonies. He was the most popular and influential author of his age, and his ideas about colonialism were the ones that overwhelmingly prevailed until the 1930s and beyond. It was Kipling's image of India that inspired the ideological opposition in the novels of empire that followed in the genre he had created. In *A Passage to India* and *Burmese Days*, the English officials who express

Kipling's ideals and values are portrayed in a negative light; and what was serious for Kipling becomes ironic in the novels of Forster and Orwell, who record the decline of British imperialism just as Kipling had celebrated its greatness.

Though Orwell later wrote that the English in India 'could not have maintained themselves in power for a single week, if the normal Anglo-Indian outlook had been that of, say, E. M. Forster' (II. p. 187), critics noticed that *Burmese Days* was strongly influenced by *A Passage to India*, which was published in 1924 when Orwell was serving in Burma. Both novels concern an Englishman's friendship with an Indian doctor, and a girl who goes out to the colonies, becomes engaged and then breaks it off. Both use club scenes to reveal a cross-section of colonial society, and both measure the personality and values of the characters by their racial attitudes. The themes of lack of understanding and the difficulties of friendship between English and natives, the physical deterioration and spiritual corruption of the white men in the tropics, are sounded by Forster and echo through Orwell's novel. But *Burmese Days* is a far more pessimistic book than *A Passage to India* because official failures are not redeemed by successful personal relations. There are no characters, like Fielding and Mrs Moore, who are able to prevail against the overwhelming cruelty of the English and maintain a civilized standard of behavior.[7]

In 'Why I Write' Orwell, who believed that good prose should be unobtrusive, 'like a window-pane,' suggested the limitations of his first novel, *Burmese Days*: 'I wanted to write enormous naturalistic novels with unhappy endings, full of detailed descriptions and arresting similes, and also full of purple passages in which words were used partly for the sake of their sound. And in fact my first completed novel, *Burmese Days*, which I wrote when I was thirty but projected much earlier, is rather that kind of book' (I, p. 3). Gollancz at first rejected the novel when colonial officials complained it would give offense in India and Burma, but after Harper had published it in New York in October 1934 he changed his mind and brought out the English edition in 1935.

Fred Marsh calls *Burmese Days* a 'superior novel' in which 'Orwell has made his people and his background vividly real,' and relates it to Orwell's experience in the Burmese police force during 1922–7.[8] Sean O'Faolain, by contrast, considers it 'very heavy-handed,' dislikes the bitter tone and condemns Flory as a 'misanthropic and unimpressive character' (No. 8). The anonymous pukka-sahib in the *TLS* also criticizes Orwell's 'pen steeped in gall,' recognizes the anti-Kipling bias, and makes a spirited imperialistic defense of the newer type of Burman official and of the higher English officials 'who really run the country' (No. 9). G. W. Stonier comments on the 'glaring realism' and admires Veraswami's ironic defense of English imperialism (No. 10). Malcolm Muggeridge calls it a 'not particularly satisfactory' novel but admires the portrayal of U Po Kyin and the two best scenes: the jungle shoot and the native riot. He compares Orwell's experiences with his own years in India at the same time, and states 'there was a Kiplingesque side to his character which made him romanticise the Raj and its mystique' (No. 11).

*A Clergyman's Daughter*
Orwell was ashamed of *A Clergyman's Daughter*, called it 'bollox' and 'tripe,' and when he finished it late in 1934 wrote to his agent Leonard Moore: 'I am not at all pleased with it. It was a good idea, but I am afraid I have made a muck of it—however, it is as good as I can do for the present. There are bits of it I don't dislike, but I am afraid it is very disconnected as a whole, and rather unreal' (I, p. 141). And Orwell was thinking of this novel when he said in 'Why I Write,' 'Looking back through my work, I see that it is invariably where I lacked a *political* purpose that I wrote lifeless books and was betrayed into purple passages, sentences without meaning, decorative adjectives and humbug generally' (I, p. 7)—the very antithesis of the qualities that normally distinguish his writing.

Orwell was a good critic of his own work and recognized that 'One difficulty I have never solved is that one has masses of experience which one passionately wants to write about . . . and no way of using them up except by disguising them as a novel' (IV, p. 422). In *A Clergyman's Daughter* his experience as a hop-picker, tramp and teacher is 'disguised' too transparently and is reported rather than rendered into a convincing and coherent work of art.

Fortunately, the critics were kinder than Orwell to his weakest book, which was published by Gollancz in March 1935. Like *Keep the Aspidistra Flying* and *Coming Up For Air*, this novel also concerns an attempt to escape from the boredom and triviality of a middle-class existence and the inevitable return to the *status quo*. Though L. P. Hartley finds Reverend Hare 'exaggerated to the point of being a monster,' and the thesis 'neither new nor convincing,' he feels that Orwell's treatment of 'man's inhumanity to man' is sure and bold and his dialogue 'always appropriate, and often brilliant' (No. 12). Victor Pritchett emphasizes the negative rather than the nostalgic portrayal of religion, calls the satire 'a whip for vicarages' and praises the 'immense knowledge of low life.' Like Peter Quennell and Michael Sayers, Pritchett compares the Trafalgar Square episode to the Nighttown scene in *Ulysses* (1922). Though the scene is not really Joycean, his statement that Orwell's Joycean style 'utterly ruins the effect' is still repeated today (No. 13).

Quennell calls the novel 'ambitious yet not entirely successful.' Though the writing is 'uncommonly forceful,' Dorothy 'remains a cipher' (No. 14). Sayers correctly prophesies that Orwell's 'future work is going to be unusually interesting' and he admires his clarity and honesty. Despite Orwell's statement about the purple passages in *Burmese Days* and his angry anti-imperialism, Sayers finds the novel objective, and states there is no local color, 'nor bitterness, nor cynicism, nor contempt' (No. 15). Perhaps Sayers skimmed too quickly through *Burmese Days*, which Jane Southron rightly criticizes as 'too obviously bitter and too savagely prejudiced to be classed as first-rate fiction'—though she goes too far in condemning Orwell's 'apparent contempt for humanity.' Despite the feeble Freudian explanation of Dorothy's behavior, Southron believes that *A Clergyman's Daughter* represents 'a big jump in quality' from his earlier books, and she admires its sympathetic understanding.[9] Geoffrey Stone, on the other hand, emphasizes Orwell's temperamental pessimism (No. 16).

Vincent McHugh's perceptive review recognizes that the book is 'a minor novel in Gissing's tradition,' that Dorothy's school is Dickensian, that the book's greatest weakness is the 'rather loose construction,' and that the main theme concerns the middle-class fear of losing respectability.[10] Considering Orwell's condemnation of his novel as disconnected, unreal, lifeless and badly written, the reviews were remarkably generous.

## Keep the Aspidistra Flying

Orwell was well aware of the weak plot, style and characterization of *Keep the Aspidistra Flying* (1936) but published it anyway because he needed the money. As he wrote in 1946:

There are two or three books which I am ashamed of and have not allowed to be reprinted or translated, and that is one of them. There is an even worse one called *A Clergyman's Daughter*. This was written simply as an exercise and I oughtn't to have published it, but I was desperate for money, ditto when I wrote *Keep the A*. At that time I simply hadn't a book in me, but I was half starved and had to turn out something to bring in £100 or so (IV, p. 205).

William Plomer remarks that Orwell 'spares us none of the horrors of sordid loneliness and a hypertrophied inferiority complex,' but he accepts the rather unconvincing happy ending (No. 17). But the reviewer in *TLS* states that the happy ending evades the final issue of 'whether an educated man could continue to let himself sink as a matter of principle' (No. 19). Cyril Connolly loyally calls the novel 'a completely harrowing and stark account of poverty . . . written in clear and violent language' (No. 18). Richard Rees mentions the influence of Dickens, Butler, Joyce and Lawrence, and enthusiastically praises the 'consistent seriousness and real vigour' of the 'fundamentally honest' book (No. 20). Kenneth Macpherson says it is 'a remarkable and subtle distillation of reality' (No. 21).

The longer and more perceptive reviews of the first and posthumous American edition of 1956, written after Orwell had published all his books and had been recognized as a major writer, provide an interesting retrospective view of both the man and his work. Anthony West's article is one of the most original and stimulating interpretations of Orwell. He sees the seeds of *1984* in *Keep the Aspidistra Flying* —'his mind is already warming to the idea of a universal smash-up'— and relates the later novel to Orwell's autobiographical essay on his sadistic prep. school. West writes that the terrors of *1984* 'are of an infantile character, and they clearly derive from the experience described in "Such, Such Were the Joys". . . . what he did in *1984* was to send everybody in England to an enormous Crossgates to be as miserable as he had been.' West concludes his interpretation by suggesting that 'only the existence of a hidden wound can account for such a remorseless pessimism' (No. 22).

Henry Popkin believes that *Keep the Aspidistra Flying* expresses 'the strange ambiguity of his attitude toward middle-class life,' and his regretful admiration for it; and that the theme becomes even more prominent in *Coming Up For Air* (No. 23). Dorothy Van Ghent emphasizes Orwell's insistent and furious 'satirical energy,' but feels that he is not 'in complete command of his feelings and judgments' (No. 24). This lack of control is also mentioned by Isaac Rosenfeld, who thinks 'he was full of self-hatred, rage, spite and contempt.' Rosenfeld also recognizes the conservative strain in Orwell's radicalism, and finds the conclusion unconvincing: 'the regenerative meaning [of Gordon's marriage] cannot reach him . . . it is too late to save him'

(No. 25). Louis Simpson makes the surprising judgment: 'This may be the best book Orwell wrote,' and says that 'Rosemary is unique as a created character in Orwell's fiction,' though she closely resembles Julia in *1984* (No. 26).

### The Road to Wigan Pier

In January 1936 Orwell was commissioned by Victor Gollancz and the Left Book Club to write a personal report about economic and social conditions in the depressed industrial areas of northern England. He gave up his job in a Hampstead bookshop and spent the next three months gathering material for *The Road to Wigan Pier* in a very deliberate attempt to compensate for the failure of theoretical Socialism to make contact with the working class. He expressed his characteristic commitment when he wrote to Richard Rees from Wigan: 'Have you ever been down a mine? I don't think I shall ever feel quite the same about coal again' (I. p. 164). In the spring Orwell moved to the village of Wallington in Hertfordshire where he finished the book and kept some barnyard animals.

But Orwell's book, which was published by Gollancz in March 1937 in a public edition and as a Left Book Club choice (43,000 copies were printed in the familiar orange cover), was not at all what his backers expected and typified Orwell's attacks on both the Right *and* the Left. Gollancz states that Orwell expresses his 'burning indignation against poverty and oppression,' but that he finds Socialists 'a stupid, offensive and insincere lot.' Gollancz insisted on adding a Foreword that attempts to draw the venom from Orwell's sting and to pacify the outraged sentiments of the members of the Left Book Club, which published works to help in the struggle against Fascism and war, but did not, as an apolitical character in one of Orwell's novels assumes, concern books left in railway carriages.

Orwell's attack on 'pansy-left circles' was a specific jab at the disciples of Edward Carpenter, social reformer and homosexual propagandist, and Gollancz gallantly steps into the breach to dissociate sodomy from Socialism. He anticipates Marxist critics of *Animal Farm* and *1984* by blindly refusing to recognize the brutal methods used by Stalin to achieve industrialization; and he condemns Orwell for committing 'the curious indiscretion of referring to Russian commissars as "half-gramophones, half-gangsters"' (No. 27).

The reviews tend to divide along party lines. Walter Greenwood, writing in the Socialist *Tribune,* notices the dichotomy between Orwell's *reportage* and his vivisection of Socialists. He praises the first part of the book as 'authentic and first-rate' and calls Orwell 'a keen observer with great skill at character drawing.' But he says of the second part, 'I cannot remember having been so infuriated for a long time' (No. 28). Arthur Calder-Marshall, by contrast, agrees that Orwell's criticism of Socialism is essentially valid, and reveals that the book is typical of the 1930s. For in the working class 'Orwell, in common with many writers of his generation, sees the cultural and political hope of the present and future' (No. 29). H. J. Laski notices the influence of *Hard Times* (1854) and *Germinal* (1885), dismisses Orwell's attack as 'an appeal to "better feelings" . . . an emotional plea for socialism addressed to comfortable people,' and concludes with a rather boring lecture (No. 30). But to Douglas Goldring, 'this brilliant, disturbing book' explains why the Socialist party 'has been steadily losing ground during the past ten years' (No. 31). Hamish Miles emphasizes Orwell's 'own conflict with English caste-consciousness' and admires the moving description of the 'human cost' of coal (No. 32).

Robert Hatch's more objective review of the first American edition of 1958 sets the book in its historical perspective and calls it 'an elegy on the spirit of poverty' (No. 33). Philip Toynbee emphasizes Orwell's personal relation to English social problems and characterizes him as the best reporter of his generation. But in an important discussion of Orwell's *persona,* Toynbee writes that he 'sees himself too consciously as the tough and honest man who has really found out the truth instead of simply dealing in high-minded abstractions' (No. 34). In a valuable review in the *New Yorker,* Dwight Macdonald compares Orwell with Engels, Mayhew, Jack London and Trotsky and calls his book 'the best sociological reporting I know.' He particularly commends the exuberant 'rhetoric of abuse' that 'combines indignation with specificity' and Orwell's 'emotional identification with the people he lives among.'[11] The main difference between the contemporary and posthumous reviews is the shift in emphasis from the political issues to the committed man, from the Socialist squabbles to Orwell's personal qualities and self-characterization.

## Homage to Catalonia

Orwell went to Spain in December 1936, five months after the outbreak of the Civil War, to write newspaper articles. But he immediately enlisted in the rather obscure and ill-equipped Trotskyist POUM militia at the Lenin Barracks in Barcelona 'because at that time and in that atmosphere it seemed the only conceivable thing to do.'[12] After a week of so-called training, he became an ordinary soldier in the revolutionary army and fought with the Independent Labour Party contingent on the Aragon front in northeast Spain. He experienced the static trench warfare in a freezing climate until he was shot through the throat by a Fascist sniper on 10 May. When he began to recover from his wound the following month, he volunteered to return to battle. But POUM was suddenly declared illegal in mid-June and Orwell, investigated and hunted by the Communist police, barely managed to escape across the French frontier.

Orwell's experiences in Spain marked the crucial turning-point in his political beliefs. Though he wrote that 'we started off by being heroic defenders of democracy and ended by slipping over the border with the police panting on our heels' (I, p. 279), he nevertheless felt 'no one who was in Spain during the months when people still believed in the revolution will ever forget that strange and moving experience. . . . I have seen wonderful things & at last really believe in Socialism, which I never did before' (I, pp. 287, 269).

In 'Why I Write,' Orwell said '*Homage to Catalonia* is, of course, a frankly political book, but in the main it is written with a certain detachment and regard for form. I did try very hard in it to tell the whole truth without violating my literary instincts' (I, p. 6). Yet Gollancz, who had given Orwell trouble with *Burmese Days* and *The Road to Wigan Pier*, refused to publish *Homage to Catalonia* because of Orwell's attacks on Stalin's Communists, just as Kingsley Martin, the editor of the *New Statesman and Nation*, refused to publish his articles and reviews on Spain. Fortunately, Secker & Warburg said they would take any book Orwell wrote about his experiences and in April 1938, while the war was still raging, they published what is probably his best book. It sold only a few hundred copies during his lifetime.

The reviews of *Homage to Catalonia*, like those of *The Road to Wigan Pier*, were more political than literary. The *TLS* reviewer mentions that in Spain the fighting was amateurish and the equipment poor, and (like Geoffrey Gorer) grasps the essential fact that the Communist influence in Barcelona was not progressive, but reactionary (No. 35). Gorer recognizes Orwell's 'personal and political protestant integrity,' praises his contrast between the fighting on the front and in Barcelona, and his description of the 'emotional atmosphere of a revolutionary militia,' and commends the book as 'a work of first-class importance' (No. 36). John McNair's propagandistic review emphasizes the spirit of comradeship that was so important to Orwell and confirms the reliability of his political reporting (No. 37). Philip Mairet agrees with Gorer that 'The book is likely to stand as one of the best contemporary documents of the struggle,' and notes Orwell's political *naïveté*, 'the heart of innocence that lies in revolution' (No. 38). This review reveals the difficulty of knowing what was really happening in Spain, for the warfare was both ideological and military, and the Anarchists and Socialists were fighting the Communists as well as the Fascists.

The *Manchester Guardian* reviewer finds Orwell's 'defence of the Trotskyist P.O.U.M. convincing,' and realizes that the conflict on the Left was between the Trotskyists who wanted immediate revolution and the Stalinists who wanted to win the war (No. 39). In the end, of course, they achieved neither revolution nor victory. Douglas Woodruff, writing in the conservative *Tablet*, states that Orwell is a romantic who does not understand the Fascist point of view, but who nevertheless 'reached the conclusion that the one thing at stake in Spain is certainly not Democracy, but a choice of dictatorships' (No. 40). Stephen Spender, writing just after Orwell's death, calls him 'one of the virtuous men of his day . . . a man of outstanding courage.' 'He was really classless, really a Socialist, really truthful.' Though *Homage to Catalonia* contains both common sense and crankiness, it is a 'better book than *1984*' and 'one of the most serious indictments of Communism which has been written' (No. 41).

*Homage to Catalonia* was first published in America during the Korean War when—in contrast to the 1930s—Orwell's anti-Communism was particularly persuasive. T. R. Fyvel's propagandistic review calls Orwell a 'romantic, typically English figure' and attributes the poor sales to 'Communist machinations,' though they were really due to the unpopular point of view which characteristically antagonized both the Left and the Right (No. 42). George Mayberry notes Orwell's 'fairness and good temper', and that the war was lost because the Fascists intervened with men and arms while the western democracies kept out (No. 43). Herbert Matthews's review is extremely valuable for the historical background of the book and for Juan Negrín's astute analysis of Orwell's character, and he states that Orwell's 'experience in Catalonia was a turning-point in his life' (No. 44). Hugh Thomas agrees with Matthews that Orwell's book is the best account of the Civil War, but that it is limited to Barcelona and

the Aragon front, gives only the POUM point of view, and is misleading about the war as a whole (No. 45).

*Coming Up For Air*

In March 1938 Orwell became ill with tuberculosis, a recurrence of his
childhood disease, and with the help of an anonymous gift of £300
(from the novelist L. H. Myers) was able to spend the winter in the
mild climate of Marrakesh, Morocco, where he wrote *Coming Up For
Air*. This novel, published by Gollancz in June 1939, a few months
before the Second World War, is Orwell's central transitional work.
It is at once synthetic and seminal, gathering the themes that had been
explored in the poverty books of the 1930s and anticipating the
cultural essays and political satires of the next decade.

Philip Henderson's description of the ambivalence of the Socialist
writer, William Morris, applies with equal force to Orwell's attitude
toward the past in *Coming Up For Air*:[13]

Emotionally he was attached to the past, to an unchanging order: intellectually
he was convinced of the necessity of a new order, and in social revolution he
saw the only hope for the future. He appears now as a Janus figure facing both
ways. His work is that of a traditionalist: as a thinker he was in the vanguard of
the most progressive movements of his time.

Orwell's work concerns an apocalyptic vision that destroys the dream
of childhood; and he was thinking of the nostalgic novels, *The History
of Mr. Polly* (1910) and *Mr. Britling Sees It Through* (1916), when he
wrote of *Coming Up For Air*: 'Of course the book was bound to
suggest Wells watered down. I have a great admiration for Wells, i.e.
as a writer, and he was a very early influence on me' (IV, p. 422). And
in a review of Edmund Blunden's *Cricket Country*, he spoke of 'his
nostalgia for the golden age before 1914, when the world was peaceful
as it has never since been' (III, p. 48).

The *TLS* reviewer characterizes *Coming Up For Air* as a 'cautionary
tale' with 'an impassioned and ruthless honesty of imagination' (No.
46). Winifred Horrabin notes that Bowling takes refuge in fantasy and
fails to find his paradise (No. 48). John Cogley speaks of Orwell's
desperate nostalgia for the pre-war world of security and continuity,
but lapses into a rather fatuous conclusion (No. 49). Margery Allingham mentions the theme of disillusion and rather blandly calls it 'a
fine book, a fair comment on one aspect of life today' (No. 47). Her
criticism of Orwell's use of the first-person narrator anticipates his own
comment on the novel: 'Of course you are perfectly right about my

own character constantly intruding on that of the narrator. I am not a real novelist anyway, and that particular vice is inherent in writing a novel in the first person, which one should never do' (IV, p. 422).

Just after Orwell's death in 1950, *Down and Out in Paris and London* and *Burmese Days* were reprinted and *Coming Up For Air* was published for the first time in America, and the reviews of Irving Howe, Edmund Fuller, Charles Rolo and Isaac Rosenfeld consider all three books. Howe praises the character of Bozo and the description of the different 'kinds of humiliation' in *Down and Out*, but calls *Coming Up For Air* 'completely predictable.' He believes that Orwell does not possess 'the creativity of the true novelist' and convincingly argues that he is best in his essays and reportage (No. 50). Fuller makes two rather surprising judgments. He claims that the 'narrative skill, characterization, and evocation of place [in *Burmese Days*] are of a high order . . . [it] might possibly be Orwell's finest piece of literary art'; and that Orwell, who is frequently praised for his great compassion, 'did not just dislike the human race; he downright despised it' (No. 51).

By contrast James Stern maintains that 'England never produced a novelist more honest, more courageous, more concerned with the common man.' He speaks of the breadth of Orwell's experience but claims, less convincingly, that a 'less subjective writer never lived.' Unlike Howe, Stern considers *Coming Up For Air* 'a masterpiece of characterization, an astonishing *tour de force*' (No. 52); and Rolo, who calls Orwell 'a witness to his time,' also believes that the novel is a 'masterly achievement' (No. 53). Rosenfeld, one of the best critics on Orwell, feels that his characteristic ideas were expressed in his earliest work and that he 'underwent no apparent development,' and he sees the connection between John Flory and Winston Smith. Rosenfeld thinks *Coming Up For Air* 'fails to catch the anxiety of the pre-war days,' but makes the acute and influential observation (which also links Orwell with William Morris) that he was 'a radical in politics and a conservative in feeling' (No. 54).

*Inside the Whale*

Orwell's first collection of essays, published by Gollancz in March 1940 shortly after the Second World War broke out, emphasized a new and extremely important aspect of his work, which was recognized and appreciated by the critics. 'Charles Dickens,' the longest of his essays and one of the earliest critical studies of the novelist, is still valuable for its freshness and vigor as well as for Orwell's suggestive identification with his subject. 'Boys' Weeklies' examines the political implications of those magazines 'sodden with the worst illusions of 1910.' And 'Inside the Whale' uses Henry Miller to exemplify the attractive and comfortable declaration of irresponsibility which Orwell himself was unable to make.

Calder-Marshall's enthusiastic review praises the 'brilliant' and 'superb' essays and patriotically attacks writers who, unlike Orwell, abandon their political conscience (No. 55). Mairet mentions the influence of Marxism on Orwell's sociological thought and states 'He is too sincere to write except when he is interested and too active in temperament to be interested in anything without doing something more than write about it' (No. 56). Victor Pritchett praises the 'lucid revelation of a mind that is alive, individual and nonconforming.'[14] But the *TLS* reviewer, while recognizing the 'blunt and tenacious honesty of mind,' feels that Orwell exaggerates the political significance of boys' weeklies and unfairly criticizes Dickens for his ' "negative, rather unhelpful political attitude" ' (No. 57). Later critics of *Animal Farm* and *1984* often make this same criticism of Orwell. Max Plowman believes the three essays are unified by the theme of political responsibility, and prophetically writes that Orwell is 'a complete critic but essentially a satirist' (No. 58).

Robert Herring feels that Orwell overrates Henry Miller, who lacks political commitment; but he observes that Orwell's 'sharpness and detachment, which is after all merely sanity,' seems brilliant (No. 59). This is a tribute to Orwell's ability to convey partisan feeling in an objective fashion. Queenie Leavis's review in the influential *Scrutiny*, edited in Cambridge by F. R. Leavis, states that Orwell is not essentially an imaginative writer: I 'have read three or four novels by him, and the only impression those dreary books left on me is that nature didn't intend him to be a novelist.' (Orwell confirms this judgment in IV, p. 422, quoted on page 17.) But she was one of the first critics to draw attention to the distinctive qualities of Orwell's non-fiction, which is closely related to his personal experience and based on independent thought: 'he has lived an active life among all classes and in several countries, he isn't the usual parlour-Bolshevik seeing literature through political glasses' (No. 60).

## The Lion and the Unicorn
*The Lion and the Unicorn: Socialism and the English Genius*, the first in a series of Searchlight booklets which offered socialistic solutions to

wartime problems, analyzes the distinctive cultural characteristics and class structure of England at the same time that it attacks the political system from a Left-wing point of view. It was published by Secker & Warburg in February 1941 in an edition of 7,500 copies; and the first section was later reprinted as the title-essay of *England Your England*. Dwight Macdonald mentions Orwell's confident but false prophecies (which continued through *1984*), praises 'the *human* quality to Orwell's political writing' and summarizes his political program as 'nationalization of land, mines, railways, banks and major industries; democratization of education; equalization of personal incomes; freedom for India' (No. 61). Many of these plans were later implemented when the Labour government was elected in 1945.

*Animal Farm*
In his Preface to the Ukrainian edition of 1947, Orwell describes the creative impulse of his barnyard bolshevism:

I saw a little boy, perhaps ten years old, driving a huge cart-horse along a narrow path, whipping it whenever it tried to turn. It struck me that if only such animals became aware of their strength we should have no power over them, and that men exploit animals in much the same way as the rich exploit the proletariat. I proceeded to analyse Marx's theory from the animals' point of view.

And he also states that 'For the past ten years,' that is, since the Spanish Civil War, 'I have been convinced that the destruction of the Soviet myth was essential if **we** wanted a revival of the Socialist movement' (III, pp. 405–6).

*Animal Farm* was written between November 1943 and February 1944, after Stalingrad and before Normandy, when the Allies first became victorious and there was a strong feeling of solidarity with the Russians, who even in defeat had deflected Hitler from England. Orwell was nevertheless shocked when his satire was rejected for political reasons by Gollancz, Cape, and Faber. T. S. Eliot, a director of Faber, softened the blow by comparing Orwell to Swift and praising the literary qualities of the fable. But Eliot, who wrongly assumed that the most intellectual animals are best qualified to run the farm, was unwilling to publish what he considered to be a negative, Trotskyist criticism of the Russian ally:[15]

We agree that it is a distinguished piece of writing; that the fable is very skilfully handled, and that the narrative keeps one's interest on its own plane—and that is something very few authors have achieved since *Gulliver*. On the other hand, we have no conviction (and I am sure none of the other directors would have) that this is the right point of view from which to criticise the political situation at the present time. . . .

My own dissatisfaction with this apologue is that the effect is simply one of negation. It ought to excite some sympathy with what the author wants, as well as sympathy with his objections to something: and the positive point of view, which I take to be generally Trotskyite, is not convincing. I think you split your vote, without getting any compensating strong adhesion from either party—i.e. those who criticise Russian tendencies from the point of view of a purer communism, and those who, from a very different point of view, are alarmed about the future of small nations. And after all, your pigs are far more intellectual than the other animals, and therefore the best qualified to run the farm—in fact, there couldn't have been an Animal Farm at all without them: so that what was needed (someone might argue), was not more communism but more public-spirited pigs.

Orwell was quite naturally frustrated and angry by the rejections, and in July wrote to his agent that if Secker & Warburg did not publish it, 'I am not going to tout it round further publishers, which wastes time & may lead to nothing, but shall publish it myself. . . . I have already half-arranged to do so & have got the necessary financial backing' (III, p. 187). Though Orwell made arrangements with his friend Paul Potts at the Whitman Press, who had the necessary paper despite wartime shortages, *Animal Farm* was in fact published by Secker & Warburg in August 1945, at a crucial moment in world history. In the previous four months, Roosevelt, Mussolini and Hitler had died, Churchill had been voted out of office, Germany had surrendered and, on 6 August, the atomic bomb had exploded over Hiroshima. Of the Big Three, only Stalin still survived.

That month was also a turning-point in Orwell's history, for half a million copies of *Animal Farm* were sold through the American Book-of-the-Month Club and it was translated into thirty-nine languages. Orwell earned about £12,000 from the book by 1950 and became financially successful for the first time in his life. There were BBC radio versions of the satire in 1947 and 1952, it was made into an extremely effective animated cartoon in 1954, and by 1972 sales in hardcover and paperback editions had reached eleven million.

Though one bright American editor at Dial Press rejected *Animal Farm* because 'it was impossible to sell animal stories in the USA' (IV, p. 110), most of the American resistance to it came from Communists and fellow-travellers. As Peter Viereck wrote in a journal edited by a promising young academic called Henry Kissinger:[16]

With the characteristic hatred of literary Stalinoids for genuine democratic socialists (a hatred more frenzied and frothing than any they expend on fascists), [Angus ] Cameron also was among those who after the war prevented Little, Brown from publishing George Orwell's anticommunist satire, *Animal Farm*. Some 18 to 20 publishers, almost all the leading ones, turned down the best anti-Soviet satire of our time. In view of its wit, its readability, its sale-ability, and its democratic outlook, the most likely motive for these rejections is the brilliantly successful infiltration (then, not now) of Stalinoid sympathizers in the book world.

All the evaluations of *Animal Farm* were influenced by the politics of the reviewers and their attitude toward Stalinist Russia. Graham Greene describes Orwell's difficulty in publishing the satire in the face of wartime appeasement and prophesies the animated cartoon of the book (No. 62). The review of the 'Stalinoid,' Kingsley Martin, who had refused to publish Orwell's reports on Spain, gives a distorted view of Orwell's political development, for his criticism of the Soviet Union, which began with *The Road to Wigan Pier*, was not a recent development. Like Eliot, Martin calls Orwell a Trotskyist (the common name for anyone who opposed Stalin), claims that he has 'lost faith in mankind' and that his satire 'is historically false and neglectful of the complex truth about Russia' (No. 63).

Connolly describes Orwell as 'a revolutionary who is in love with 1910' and paints a brighter picture of Stalinist Russia than Orwell would allow (No. 64). Arthur Schlesinger Jr, writing on the front page of the *New York Times Book Review*, calls the satire 'the most compact and witty expression of the left-wing British reaction to Soviet Communism' and 'a wise, compassionate and illuminating fable for our times.'[17] He also anticipates Irving Howe's *Politics and the Novel* (1957) and links Orwell with Silone and Koestler as political novelists. Rosenfeld also compares Orwell with Koestler and admits Orwell's allegiance belongs to an old and honorable liberalism that 'still holds as its dearest thing the right to liberty of judgment.' But he nevertheless feels 'this is a disappointing piece of work,' inspired by a middle of the way imagination that 'cannot seriously deal with events that are themselves extreme' (No. 65).

By contrast, Edmund Wilson, who mentions Orwell's difficulty in publishing *Burmese Days* in England, feels unqualified enthusiasm. Wilson, in a rare accolade, calls the book 'absolutely first-rate,' compares Orwell with Voltaire and Swift, and thinks that he is 'likely to emerge as one of the ablest and most interesting writers that the English have produced' in the last decade (No. 66). Wilson's influential *New Yorker* review praised Orwell's literary qualities just as Schlesinger had admired his political beliefs, and these two authoritative estimates helped to solidify Orwell's reputation in America. Northrop Frye is very perceptive about the inconsistencies of Orwell's satiric allegory. He believes 'The final metamorphosis of pigs into humans at the end is a fantastic disruption of the sober logic of the tale' and that the parallelism of Stalinism and Czarism is 'complete nonsense, and Mr Orwell must know it to be nonsense' (No. 67).

*Critical Essays* (US title: *Dickens, Dali and Others*)
Orwell's second collection of ten essays, published by Secker & Warburg in February 1946, reprinted the earlier studies of Dickens and boys' weeklies and included eight other social interpretations of Kipling, Wells, Yeats, Koestler, Wodehouse, Dali, comic postcards and thrillers. In each of his essays on popular culture Orwell favorably compared the static and old-fashioned view expressed in these works with that of their harsher and crueler successors. His book confirmed the considerable reputation he had established with *Animal Farm* and was greeted enthusiastically by the critics, who saw the originality and importance of Orwell's essays on the political and social implications of popular art. Stuart Hampshire, Evelyn Waugh, Eric Bentley, nearly everyone but Edmund Wilson himself, compared Orwell's essays with those of Wilson, who was generally regarded as the greatest American critic.

Pritchett describes the essays as 'brilliant examples of political anthropology applied to literature by a non-conforming mind' and, returning to ideas that originated in connection with *Coming Up For Air*, says 'His traditions are those of the Right, and he cannot quite forgive the world for driving him to the Left.'[18] Hampshire calls Orwell a 'moralist-critic' with 'enlightened good sense,' commends his 'penetration and integrity' and considers him 'potentially the most authoritative and interesting of English critics' (No. 68). Waugh's essay is valuable for its discussion of Orwell's capacity for clear-sighted analysis and his lack of religious beliefs. He writes that the essays represent 'the new humanism of the common man,' and says: 'he never seems to have been touched at any point by a conception of religious thought and life. . . . He frequently brings his argument to the point when having, with great acuteness, seen the falsity and internal contradiction of the humanist view of life, there seems no alternative but the acceptance of a revealed religion, and then stops short' (No. 69).

Harry Levin places Orwell in opposition to the tradition of English critics from Pater and Arnold through Eliot, Empson and Connolly, and praises his unfashionable yet 'comprehensive grasp and trenchant analysis of the patterns of popular culture' (No. 70). Bentley, like Howe, believes that the essays represent Orwell 'at his best,' compares him to Dickens, and emphasizes the connection between his life and art: he 'has sought experiences which would bring him close to the central events of the time.' Bentley also admires his 'straight-forwardness, generous intelligence, and serious devotion to culture' (No. 71). Wylie Sypher agrees with Orwell's definition of himself as 'a liberal writer at a moment when liberalism is coming to an end.' He praises Orwell's independence and flexibility, and identifies one of his dominant political ideas: the abiding disillusionment with 'the left-wingers who have wished "to be anti-fascist without being anti-totalitarian" ' (No. 72).

Wilson also praises Orwell as 'the only contemporary master' of sociological criticism, though he is surprised that he takes Dali's infantile and self-conscious outrages so seriously. He commends Orwell's 'readiness to think for himself, courage to speak his mind, the tendency to deal with concrete realities rather than theoretical positions, and a prose style that is both downright and disciplined' (No. 73). Middleton Murry considers Orwell and Connolly 'the two most gifted critics of their generation.' Like Waugh, he comments on Orwell's lack of religious philosophy and then presents his own fuzzy and narcissistic beliefs (No. 74). Arvin places Orwell in the commonsensical school of English critics who are free from abstractions, impatient with 'nonsense' and capable of realistic perceptions, and writes that his work is 'humane at the core and salutary in its main effects' (No. 75).

### GEORGE WOODCOCK ON ORWELL

George Woodcock, who knew Orwell in the 1940s, wrote the first serious essay about him in 1946, before the appearance of *1984*. This provides a biographical introduction to and a fair and far-sighted judgment of his work. He describes Orwell as 'an independent socialist

with libertarian tendencies,' writes that his works are 'essentially autobiographical and personal' and that the 'literary merits . . . are much
more consistent and impressive than the political qualities.' Woodcock
also places Orwell in the tradition of the English radical novelists—
Godwin, Dickens, Wells—and makes a fundamental criticism of his
two main weaknesses: the superficial 'failure to penetrate deeply into
the rooted causes of the injustices and lies against which he fights, and
[as Eliot observed] the lack of any really constructive vision for the
future of man' (No. 76).

## 1984

*1984* was begun in August 1946 and finished twenty-seven months
later in November 1948, and Orwell was seriously ill for much of that
time. He was sick in bed in April 1947, ill in May and September, and
forced into bed again in October. He entered a tuberculosis sanatorium
near Glasgow in December 1947 and remained there until June 1948;
suffered a relapse in September and October, and was seriously ill in
November and December 1948. He entered another sanatorium in
the Cotswolds in January 1949, corrected the proofs there, and was
in hospital in Gloucestershire and London for the last year of his life.
In October 1948 Orwell wrote to Fredric Warburg:

I am not pleased with the book, but I am not absolutely dissatisfied. I first
thought of it in 1943. I think it is a good idea, but the execution would have
been better if I had not written it under the influence of T. B. I haven't definitely fixed on a title but I am hesitating between Nineteen Eighty-Four and
The Last Man in Europe. (IV, p. 448)

*1984*, which had a first printing of 26,500, was published on 8 June
1949, during the Cold War, and created some bitter political controversy. Orwell attempted to clarify his position as early as 16 June
and wrote:

My recent novel is NOT intended as an attack on Socialism or on the British
Labour Party (of which I am a supporter) but as a show-up of the perversions
to which a centralised economy is liable and which have already been partly
realised in Communism and Fascism. I do not believe that the kind of society
I describe necessarily *will* arrive, but I believe (allowing of course for the fact
that the book is a satire) that something resembling it *could* arrive. I believe also
that totalitarian ideas have taken root in the minds of intellectuals everywhere,
and I have tried to draw these ideas out to their logical consequences. The
scene of the book is laid in Britain in order to emphasise that the English-
speaking races are not innately better than anyone else and that totalitarianism,
*if not fought against*, could triumph anywhere. (IV, p. 502)

Critics immediately recognized that Orwell's expression of the political experience of an entire generation gave *1984* a veritably mythic power and that it was one of the most important books of the age. It was condensed in the *Reader's Digest* and translated into twenty-three languages, and has sold eleven million copies. In 1956 the novel was made into a film with Edmund O'Brien as Winston Smith.

Fredric Warburg was the first to read *1984*, and his perceptive publisher's report notes the influence of Swift, Dostoyevsky, Jack London and Arthur Koestler. He observes the element of sado-masochism and the unrelieved pessimism, and feels that the brief lyricism merely intensifies the later horrors (No. 77). Julian Symons states that the book is really about power and corruption, and that Orwell is' a novelist interested in ideas, rather than in personal relationships' (No. 78). Orwell agreed with Symons that the novel is marred by the schoolboy sensationalism of the torture scenes.

In a long, brilliant, pessimistic letter, written from California in October 1949, Aldous Huxley praises Orwell's book, suggests that the horrors of *1984* are destined to modulate into the nightmare of *Brave New World* and expresses his fears about a devastating atomic war:[19]

I had to wait a long time before being able to embark on *Nineteen Eighty-Four*. Agreeing with all that the critics have written of it, I need not tell you, yet once more, how fine and how profoundly important the book is. . . .

The philosophy of the ruling minority in *Nineteen Eighty-Four* is a sadism which has been carried to its logical conclusion by going beyond sex and denying it.Whether in actual fact the policy of the boot-on-the-face can go on indefinitely seems doubtful. My own belief is that the ruling oligarchy will find less arduous and wasteful ways of governing and of satisfying its lust for power, and that these ways will resemble those which I described in *Brave New World*. . . .

Within the next generation I believe that the world's rulers will discover that infant conditioning and narco-hypnosis are more efficient, as instruments of government, than clubs and prisons, and the lust for power can be just as completely satisfied by suggesting people into loving their servitude as by flogging and kicking them into obedience. . . . The change will be brought about as a result of a felt need for increased efficiency. Meanwhile, of course, there may be a large-scale biological and atomic war—in which case we shall have nightmares of other and scarcely imaginable kinds.

Harold Nicolson, like many others, compares Orwell to Huxley, writes that 'The Inferno atmosphere of the story is cunningly created and well-maintained,' and finds the book impressive even though the vision of the future is not convincing (No. 79). Mark Schorer praises the 'work of pure horror' and calls it an 'expression of Mr Orwell's moral and intellectual indignation before the concept of totalitarianism. . . . No other work of this generation has made us desire freedom more earnestly or loathe tyranny with such fulness.'[20] Lionel Trilling, who mentions Orwell's connection to the culture of the past and Winston's severance from it, describes *1984* as a 'profound, terrifying and wholly fascinating book' about 'the ultimate threat to human freedom,' and as a work in which 'the nature of power is defined by the pain it can inflict on others.'[21] The influential reviews of Schorer and Trilling virtually guaranteed the success of the book in America.

Diana Trilling speaks of the 'cruelty of its imagination' and believes that Orwell's purpose is to make us 'understand the ultimate dangers involved wherever power moves under the guise of order and rationality' (No. 80). Daniel Bell and Philip Rahv shrewdly observe that the satire is an extreme version of what is actually present today, and Bell agrees with Diana Trilling that Orwell is concerned about how to control the abuse of power (No. 81). Rahv distinguishes Orwell's qualities from the weaknesses of many Left-wing writers and thinks *1984* is 'far and away the best of Orwell's books.' Rahv considers the novel in the context of Utopian fiction and places it in 'the melancholy mid-century genre of lost illusions and Utopia betrayed' (No. 82).

Samuel Sillen's abusive review, entitled 'Maggot-of-the-Month,' dismisses the novel as 'cynical rot' and a 'diatribe against the human race' (No. 83). It is typical of the violent attacks of the Communists, who felt that Orwell, more than any other writer, was the greatest danger to their cause. By contrast, Golo Mann's review in the *Frankfurter Rundschau* is interesting as a liberal German's reaction to *1984* during the Cold War. (Golo's father, Thomas Mann, who had gone into exile and lived in America since 1939, left that country in 1952 during Senator McCarthy's anti-Communist witch-hunt.) Writing from California, Golo Mann warns against the present danger of totalitarian ideology in Germany as well as in Russia, and significantly emphasizes that the novel is not merely an attack on Communism (No. 84). As a historian, Mann is particularly concerned with the importance of historical truth and with the dangers of destroying the past in order to strengthen the present dictatorships, ideas that Orwell had considered in his essays 'Politics and the English Language' and 'The Prevention of Literature.'

Herbert Read compares Orwell to Defoe, analyzes the source of his power and, like Rahv, calls *1984* a utopia in reverse and considers it Orwell's greatest book (No. 86). The anti-Communist Czeslaw Milosz praises Orwell's perception of Russian oppression (No. 87), while I. Anisimov's review conveys the predictable response of *Pravda*, which was enraged by attacks from a writer on the Left. Though Orwell is sympathetic to the proles in *1984*, the Russian insists that he despises and 'imputes every evil' to them, and he condemns Orwell's 'contempt for the people, his aim of slandering man' (No. 85). The Communist James Walsh, who notes the important influence of Zamyatin's *We*, speaks of Orwell's 'neurotic' and 'depressing hatred of everything approaching progress,' and claims that he 'runs shrieking into the arms of the capitalist publishers with a couple of horror-comics' (No. 88).

Sillen, Anisimov and Walsh make the same attack on Orwell and feel that because he criticizes Communism he must be in favor of capitalism; because he depicts the degradation of man he must hate the common people. These reviews are extreme examples of how critics who are blinded by ideology condemn Orwell's work. But Golo Mann's and Czeslaw Milosz's appreciations testify to the power of Orwell's imagination and his ability to interpret political experience in human terms.

## OBITUARIES

Pritchett's sympathetic and insightful obituary, which appeared a week after Orwell had died of tuberculosis on 21 January 1950, was extremely influential in establishing the personal reputation of Orwell: the 'tall emaciated man with a face scored by the marks of physical suffering.' Pritchett mentions his masochism and that he 'had "gone native" in his own country,' and calls him 'a kind of saint': 'His was the guilty conscience of the educated and privileged man' (No. 89). Arthur Koestler, who was so often compared to Orwell, speaks of his friend's 'austere harshness' and 'uncompromising intellectual honesty,' and considers him 'a kind of missing link between Kafka and Swift' and 'the only writer of genius among the *littérateurs* of social revolt between the two wars' (No. 90). Bertrand Russell also compares Orwell to Swift, thinks he will be best remembered for *Animal Farm*, and commends his 'love of humanity and incapacity for comfortable illusion.' But he criticizes Orwell's negativism: 'He preserved an impeccable love of truth, and allowed himself to learn even the most painful lessons. But he lost hope. This prevented him from being a prophet for our time' (No. 91).

*Shooting an Elephant*

Orwell's first posthumous collection of essays was published by Secker & Warburg in an edition of about 7,500 in October 1950. The book included, with the title-essay, 'A Hanging' and 'How the Poor Die,' 'Politics and the English Language' and 'The Prevention of Literature,' interpretations of Swift, Tolstoy, Gandhi and James Burnham, and nine selections from his amusing and idiosyncratic 'As I Please' column. The respectful obituaries and three autobiographical essays encouraged an emphasis on Orwell's character, but critics also began to synthesize and evaluate his literary and stylistic qualities.

Spender writes that his work, which 'contains a maximum of lived experience and a minimum of inventiveness,' is defined by a 'clear sensibility and a disquieting conscience' and by 'a certain apocalyptic fire.'[22] In an extremely important review, later included in *Two Cheers For Democracy*, E. M. Forster describes Orwell's peculiar combination of gaiety and grimness, and says 'He found much to discomfort him in his world and desired to transmit it, and in *1984* he extended discomfort into agony. . . . *1984* crowned his work, and it is understandably a crown of thorns' (No. 92). Though Forster writes that 'Shooting an Elephant' is forceful but flat and without reverberations, the accurate detail of the setting, the moral dilemma of the narrator and the slow death of the elephant present an allegory of imperialism.

Fyvel discusses Orwell in relation to other English radicals and, once again, mentions his honesty and nostalgia for the past (No. 93). Christopher Sykes sees him as 'an essentially paradoxical man,' justly states that 'his understanding of pictures and poetry was negligible' and calls him 'a philosophical writer whose descriptive essays contained almost as much of his thought as did his political work' (No. 94). Edmund Wilson also stresses his uniqueness and his paradoxical qualities, and places him in the tradition of 'middle-class British liberalism that depended on common sense and plain-speaking' (No. 95). C. V. Wedgwood concentrates on the wider implications of his essays on the debasement of language and analyzes the 'powerful, concealed undercurrent of compassion' which gives Orwell's autobiographical essays their 'hard, unemotional power' (No. 96).

*England Your England* (US title: *Such, Such Were the Joys*)
The English edition of Orwell's third collection of essays was published by Secker & Warburg in 1953 in an edition of 6,000 copies. It did not include the title-essay of the American edition which described the horrors of 'Crossgates', his prep. school in Eastbourne, for it was considered libellous and was not published in England until 1968. The reviews develop the idea of Orwell as a heroically honest man who expressed the social and political conflicts of his generation. Spender states that Orwell was 'an extremely English writer' with a passion for 'intellectual freedom,' and that the Spanish Civil War was the 'turning point in Orwell's disillusionment.' He repeats a point from his review of *Shooting an Elephant*—that his main ideas 'have roots in his personal experience'—and makes the connection (later elaborated by West) between Crossgates and *1984* (No. 97).

Like many critics, the *TLS* reviewer sees the book as an expression of Orwell's character and, like Russell, considers *Animal Farm* his best work. He praises Orwell's stylistic powers, zest for the hopeless struggle and denunciation of fashionable intellectual attitudes (No. 98). Angus Wilson mentions the growth of esteem and affectionate respect since the death of Orwell, who has been called a prophet. Wilson discusses the note of hysteria in the 'nightmare vision' of *1984* and his sentimentalization of the working class; and he disagrees with most critics by stating that Orwell lost more than he gained by not going to Oxford or Cambridge. Wilson also suggests that his view of the working class is faulty because he concentrates on the rootless fringe of society and 'lost touch with those in all classes whose lives were in fixed patterns' (No. 99).

Popkin writes that Orwell tried to extend the Edwardian Eden 'by an effort of will' to 1914 or even 1918, that 'he loved everything Edwardian, everything he had first encountered before 1918,' and that his unresolved dilemma was the 'conflict between his socialism and the pessimism that found its fullest expression in *1984*' (No. 100). John Wain, whose work is strongly influenced by Orwell, believes that his 'essays are obviously much better than his novels,' that his portraits of real people are much better than his fictional characters, and that Orwell 'was a man of comparatively few ideas, which he took every opportunity of putting across' (No. 101). George Elliott calls Orwell 'the secular prophet of socialism,' and thinks 'from his experience he wrote what must be the best book likely to be written about the Spanish Civil War.' But, unlike Wain, Elliott feels he is 'a slight artist because he succeeded only in the lesser arts of essay-writing and reporting,' a judgment that fails to account for Orwell's power and influence (No. 102).

*Collected Essays, Journalism and Letters*

The publication of the four volumes of Orwell's collected shorter works was a major publishing event of 1968. It provided a biographical framework, revealed his surprising productivity, and led to a retrospective evaluation of the writer and the man, who was recognized as a classic of English literature and one of the most notable figures of our time. These volumes, which appeared during the fierce controversy about the war in Vietnam, included a number of letters, about a third of his occasional journalism and nearly all his major essays, including 'Such, Such Were the Joys.'

Anthony Powell mentions his old friend's innate eccentricity, agrees with Russell that *Animal Farm* is his 'most accomplished literary work,' and exaggerates Popkin's ideas by stating, 'His love of the past caused one side of him to cling to the idea that nothing ever changed' (No. 103). In an extremely perceptive review Conor Cruise O'Brien sees the volumes as a 'contribution to a cult,' distinguishes between Orwell's reputation in England and America, rejects the simplistic and misleading tag of 'dedicated anti-communist' and describes him as 'a puritan with a lively hatred of intellectual dishonesty,' criticizes his political inconsistencies, and calls him 'a great journalist, pamphleteer and fabulist' (No. 104). Wain, like Elliott, considers *Homage to Catalonia* 'his best book,' and discusses Orwell's running warfare with the intellectuals, his moral values and his personal example.[23]

In a long and influential essay in the radical *New York Review of Books*, Mary McCarthy casts her characteristically cold eye on Orwell. She seems to have started a nasty hatchet job but then admired Orwell too much to complete it. She emphasizes his fear 'that people would become interchangeable parts in a totalitarian system,' and maintains that he is 'not a natural novelist, having no interest in character.' Like Henry Miller, she makes the odd judgment that *Down and Out* is his 'masterpiece,' and that 'surely Orwell's best work is that of the heroic early period' when 'he used himself as an experimental animal in the course of his social researches.'[24] Howe's substantial review has none of McCarthy's reservations and considers Orwell 'the best English essayist since Hazlitt,' the intellectual hero to a whole generation, and 'the greatest moral force in English letters during the last several decades.' Howe writes that Orwell 'was driven by a passion to clarify ideas, correct error, persuade readers, straighten things out in the world and in his mind' (No. 105).

Muggeridge repeats his earlier statement about Orwell's 'sympathy with the mystique of British rule in India,' affirms (like Howe) that 'as an essayist and journalist he was incomparable,' and emphasizes the sad irony of his life: 'everything came true for him when it was too late' (No. 106). George Steiner says the volumes allow us 'to follow the entire development of Orwell's awareness' and his 'total attention to aspects of society and culture ordinarily under the carpet.' Steiner concludes that 'his two most interesting achievements [are] a critique of language and, at the very last, the most telling use of allegory in English literature after Bunyan and Swift' (No. 107). Finally, the first section of my long review-essay 'The Honorary Proletarian' (which analyzes Orwell's four books on poverty), discusses the omissions from the four volumes, the characteristics of Orwell's style and the biographical revelations of the letters and essays. This essay suggests that the dominant pattern in Orwell's life 'is the series of masochistic impulses for a higher cause that testifies to his compulsive need for self-punishment' and that his 'writing is manifest proof of his ability to transcend this personal guilt' (No. 108).

### CRITICS ON ORWELL

Despite some inevitable contradictions, banalities and obtuseness, the numerous reviews give a fair and frequently perceptive appraisal of Orwell's works; and they suggest the basic critical conceptions that are investigated, elaborated and sometimes distorted by later writers. Most of the twenty books on Orwell are competent. Tom Hopkinson's British Council pamphlet appeared in 1953; and the first two books on Orwell were published in 1954 by John Atkins and Laurence Brander, who had known him in the 1940s and who provided basic surveys of his work. Two years later Christopher Hollis, who was Orwell's contemporary at Eton and had met him briefly in Burma, added some biographical information but wrote the same sort of book. In 1961 Orwell's closest friend, Sir Richard Rees, published his book, subtitled 'Fugitive From the Camp of Victory'; and though this contributed some useful ideas about Orwell, it was disappointing as criticism.

In 1961 the first scholarly work on Orwell by Richard Voorhees.

an American professor who did not know him personally and was therefore more objective, analyzed his paradoxical attitudes about rebellion and responsibility, power and Socialism. Edward Thomas wrote an introduction to Orwell for a series of books on modern writers in 1965. The next year George Woodcock published the best book on Orwell, *The Crystal Spirit*, which provided the fullest biographical discussion of the man, and the most careful explication of his fiction, his political ideas and his criticism. B. T. Oxley published another introductory book in 1967, and in 1968 Jenni Calder's comparison of Orwell and Koestler as revolutionaries and prophets provided many valuable insights about their social and political thought. In contrast to this, Ruth Ann Lief's book seemed weak and unsatisfactory. Two more scholarly books, by Robert Lee and Keith Alldritt, appeared in 1969. The former was devoted to Orwell's fiction, and the latter was especially good on his development as a writer.

*The World of George Orwell*, a collection of essays with photographs edited by Miriam Gross in 1971, attempts to see him 'both in terms of what he means today and as a man whose achievement very much needs to be set in the context of his own period.'[25] Though the book contains perceptive essays by William Empson and Malcolm Muggeridge, who knew Orwell, most of the contributions are too short for an extended argument, and lack originality and intellectual substance. Raymond Williams's book, which appeared in the Fontana Modern Masters series in 1971, is a Marxist attack on Orwell as a reactionary and a revisionist who made an unacceptable accommodation to capitalism. It recalls the extreme Left-wing condemnation of Orwell's books from *The Road to Wigan Pier* to *1984*.

David Kubal's *Outside the Whale* (1972) is a rather superficial attempt to connect the two main divisions, literary and political, in Orwell's work. Peter Stansky and William Abrahams's *The Unknown Orwell* (1972) is a biography of the first thirty years and culminates in the publication of *Down and Out in Paris and London*. Though it brings together much useful information about Orwell, it does not fulfill the claim of its title. The authors present a familiar figure and merely fill in the details of a picture that remains substantially the same. The theme of the book, that 'Blair was the man to whom things happened; Orwell the man who wrote about them,'[26] is hardly convincing because they do not show that Orwell changed his personality when he changed his name.

Roberta Kalechofsky's *George Orwell* (1973) is a basic introduction.

Alan Sandison's *The Last Man in Europe* (1974) unsuccessfully attempts to relate Orwell to the center of the Protestant tradition and maintains that the crisis of individualism which for Orwell is subsumed in contemporary political developments is fundamentally and explicitly a spiritual and moral crisis before it is a political one. Alex Zwerdling's *Orwell and the Left* (1975) is less concerned with the evolution of Orwell's political ideas than with his search for a literary form that would serve as an ideal vehicle for his Socialist thought. My *Reader's Guide to George Orwell* (Thames & Hudson, 1975) argues that all his books are autobiographical and spring from his psychological need to work out the pattern and meaning of his personal experience, and that his great triumph is his ability to transform his early guilt and awareness of what it means to be a victim into a compassionate ethic of responsibility, a compulsive sharing in the degradation of others. Orwell's guilt suggests his similarity to French writers like Malraux and Sartre, who see themselves 'responsible in the face of history' for moral awareness and social justice, and whose ethic goes beyond the traditional claims for artistic integrity and personal commitment, and both limits and liberates their artistic powers.

The articles on Orwell fall into two categories: biographical and critical. Beadon, Connolly, Dunn, Fen, Heppenstall, Morris, Potts, Powell, Symons and Warburg have written interesting anecdotal reminiscences; and all but those of Morris and Heppenstall (the latter got drunk and was beaten up by Orwell when they shared a London flat in 1935) were extremely favorable. Powell was the most perceptive about his paradoxical and individualistic character, and Warburg was excellent on the publishing background of *Animal Farm* and *1984*.

Scholars have written on Orwell in Serbo-Croat, Dutch, Norwegian, Finnish, Hungarian and Japanese as well as in French, Italian and German. There have been critical essays on his attitude toward imperialism, Socialism and Communism; on his relation to Dickens, Gissing and Kipling; on his criticism, style, patriotism and nostalgia for the past. Two poems have been written about Orwell; several very thorough bibliographies of his extensive uncollected writings and of criticism about him have been compiled; and in 1950 and 1975 special issues of *World Review* and *Modern Fiction Studies* were devoted to him.

Lionel Trilling's 'George Orwell and the Politics of Truth' (1952), which was written as the introduction to the American paperback edition of *Homage to Catalonia*, was probably the most influential essay on Orwell. Trilling believed that '*Homage to Catalonia* is one of the most important documents of our time. . . . It is a testimony to the nature of modern political life. It is also a demonstration on the part of its author of one of the right ways of confronting that life.'[27] John Wain has written some of the best criticism of Orwell in the review-essays that have appeared during the last twenty years. In his *Spectator* review Wain emphasized the importance of Orwell's campaign for clearer thinking and writing; 'Orwell in Perspective' discussed Orwell's effectiveness as a writer of polemic and the relation of his style to his character; and 'Here Lies Lower Binfield' suggested that the difference between Orwell and ordinary Socialists was revealed in his ambivalent attitude toward the recent past, which he expressed in *Coming Up For Air*.

Between 1966 and 1969 Muste, Benson, Weintraub and Hoskins considered Orwell's contribution to the literature of the Spanish Civil War. His essays on popular culture have influenced sociological critics like Richard Hoggart, who has written a particularly good essay on the contradictions in *The Road to Wigan Pier*, 'between an absolutist and a tolerantly resilient man, out to get things done by communal political action, and a dark despairer; between the one who urged the need for revolutionary changes in our thinking and a man with a deep-seated sense that things would always go on much as they always had.'[28]

Most of the criticism has focused on Orwell's most famous and influential book, *1984*. Spender has discussed the anti-Utopian aspects; West has examined the biographical implications; Isaac Deutscher, the biographer of Trotsky, has discussed Orwell's fear of the future and what he called 'the mysticism of cruelty'; and Irving Howe, in an important essay, introduced the 'nightmare' interpretation. Other scholars have compared Orwell to Swift, Dostoyevsky, Trotsky, Zamyatin, Huxley, Koestler, James Burnham and writers of utopian novels and science fiction; studied his irony, satire, parody, prophecy, psychology, masochism and theory of language.[29]

The phases of Orwell's reputation—as the social critic of the 1930s, the essayist and political satirist of the 1940s, and the austere yet gentle figure whom Trilling called a 'virtuous man' and Pritchett named 'the wintry conscience of his generation' (No. 89) in the 1950s—culminate in a more unified view in the 1960s and 1970s. Orwell is now considered important for his social, political, literary and personal qualities, and has been placed with Johnson, Blake and Lawrence in the English tradition of prophetic moralists.

Orwell's literary legacy is also significant. His novels and concern with the problems of poverty have influenced English writers like John Wain, Arnold Wesker, Harold Pinter and John Osborne; his essays on popular culture, a genre that he virtually invented, have influenced English sociological critics like Richard Hoggart, Raymond Williams and Malcolm Bradbury; and in an age when writers from Norman Mailer to Yukio Mishima are once again committed to political activism, his political essays and *reportage* have provided a form and a *persona* for the passionate and persuasive American works like James Baldwin's *The Fire Next Time* (1963), Mary McCarthy's *Vietnam* (1967) and Mailer's *The Armies of the Night* (1968). Orwell's reputation is now firmly established, and as we approach 1984 he is more widely read than perhaps any other serious writer of the twentieth century.

## NOTES

1 *The Collected Essays, Journalism and Letters of George Orwell*, ed. Sonia Orwell and Ian Angus, IV (London: Secker & Warburg, 1968), p. 183. Subsequent citations to volume and page refer to this edition.
2 George Orwell, *Keep the Aspidistra Flying* (Harmondsworth: Penguin, 1962), p. 13.
3 George Orwell, *The Road to Wigan Pier* (Harmondsworth: Penguin, 1962), pp. 130–1.
4 Humbert Possenti, Letter to *The Times*, 31 January 1933, p. 6.
5 Herbert Gorman, 'On Paris and London Pavements,' *New York Times Book Review*, 6 August 1933, p. 4.
6 Henry Miller, 'The art of fiction,' *Paris Review*, VII (Summer 1962), p. 146.
7 For a thorough discussion of this subject see my book, *Fiction and the Colonial Experience* (England: Boydell Press; USA: Rowman & Littlefield, 1973).
8 Fred Marsh, 'Sahibs in Burma,' *New York Times Book Review*, 28 October 1934, p. 7.
9 Jane Southron, review of *A Clergyman's Daughter*, *New York Times Book Review*, 9 August 1936, p. 6.
10 Vincent McHugh, review of *A Clergyman's Daughter*, *New York Herald Tribune Book Review*, 16 August 1936, p. 8.
11 Dwight Macdonald, 'Varieties of political experience,' *New Yorker*, XXXV (29 March 1959), pp. 137–46.

12 George Orwell, *Homage to Catalonia* (Boston: Beacon Press, 1952), p. 3.

13 Philip Henderson, *William Morris* (Harmondsworth: Penguin, 1973), p. 433.

14 V. S. Pritchett, 'Back to Jonah,' *New Statesman and Nation*, XIX (16 March 1940), p. 370.

15 T. S. Eliot, letter to Orwell, 13 July 1944, in *The Times*, 6 January 1969, p. 9.

16 Peter Viereck, 'Bloody-minded professors,' *Confluence*, I (September 1952), pp. 36–7.

17 Arthur Schlesinger Jr, 'Mr Orwell and the Communists,' *New York Times Book Review*, 25 August 1946, pp. 1, 28.

18 V. S. Pritchett, 'The rebel,' *New Statesman and Nation*, XXXI (16 February 1946), p. 124.

19 Aldous Huxley, *Letters*, ed. Grover Smith (London: Chatto & Windus, 1969), pp. 604–5.

20 Mark Schorer, 'An indignant and prophetic novel,' *New York Times Book Review*, 12 June 1949, p. 1.

21 Lionel Trilling, 'Orwell on the Future,' *New Yorker*, XXV (18 June 1949), pp. 78–83.

22 Stephen Spender, 'A measure of Orwell,' *New York Times Book Review*, 29 October 1950, p. 4.

23 John Wain, 'Orwell and the intelligentsia,' *Encounter*, XXI (December 1968), pp. 72–80.

24 Mary McCarthy, 'The writing on the wall,' *New York Review of Books*, XII (30 January 1969), pp. 3–6.

25 Miriam Gross, ed., *The World of George Orwell* (London: Weidenfeld & Nicolson, 1971), p. i.

26 Peter Stansky and William Abrahams, *The Unknown Orwell* (London: Constable, 1972), p. xiv.

27 Lionel Trilling, 'George Orwell and the politics of truth,' in *The Opposing Self* (London: Secker & Warburg, 1955), pp. 151–2.

28 Richard Hoggart, 'George Orwell and *The Road to Wigan Pier*,' *Critical Quarterly*, VII (1965), p. 80.

29 William Steinhoff's *George Orwell and the Origins of '1984'* (1975) is the first book about Orwell's novel. The second volume of Stansky and Abrahams's book is now in press, and Bernard Crick is writing the authorized biography.

# Note on the Text

The reviews and essays printed in this volume follow the original texts. Quotations from Orwell's works have been retained, and typographical errors corrected.

# DOWN AND OUT IN PARIS
# AND LONDON

1933

## 1. George Orwell, Introduction to
## *La Vache enragée*

1935

*La Vache enragée* (Paris: Gallimard, 1935), pp. 7–9.

In his Introduction to the French edition of *Down and Out in Paris and London* Orwell confirms the authenticity of the book, which was questioned by some reviewers, and feels obliged to apologize for his grim portrayal of Paris and to reaffirm his love for the city.

My loyal translators have asked me to write a short preface for the French edition of this book. Since many French readers may wonder how I came to be in Paris at the time of the events that I relate, it will be best, I think, to begin with some biographical details.

I was born in 1903. In 1922 I set out for Burma, where I entered the Imperial Indian Police Force. It was a most unsuitable profession for me; so in the beginning of 1928, during my leave in England, I resigned in the hope of earning my living as a writer. I succeeded almost as well as most young people who take up a career of letters— that is to say, not at all. My first year of literary work paid me scarcely twenty pounds.

In the spring of 1928 I left for Paris in order to live cheaply while I wrote two novels—which, I regret to say, were never published— and also to learn French. One of my Paris friends found me a furnished room in a working-class quarter, which I have concisely described in the first chapter of this work and which every Parisian, however inexperienced, will surely be able to recognize. During the summer of 1929, after I had written my two novels, which the publishers rejected, I found myself almost penniless and in urgent need of work. At that time it was not forbidden—at least not strictly forbidden—for foreigners staying in France to have jobs, and I found it easier to stay in the city where I was rather than return to England where there were two and a half million people unemployed. So I stayed in Paris, and at the end of the autumn of 1929 the adventures I have related took place.

As for the authenticity of my story, I can affirm that I have exaggerated nothing, except in the sense that every writer exaggerates: in selecting. I did not feel I was obliged to relate the events in the order they occurred, but everything I have described really happened at some time or other. But I refrained, as far as possible, from drawing specific portraits. All the characters that I have described in the two parts of this book represent types of their class in Paris and London, and not individuals.

I should also add that this book does not pretend to give a complete picture of life in Paris and London, but only to describe one special aspect of it. Since all the personal scenes and events have something repulsive about them, it is quite possible that I have unconsciously portrayed Paris and London as abominable cities. This has not been my intention, and if I am misunderstood, it is simply because the subject of my book—poverty—essentially lacks charm. When you haven't a penny in your pocket you begin to see any city and any country in the most unfavorable light; and every human being, or almost every one, appears to you either as a companion in suffering or as an enemy. I have taken care to state this point precisely for my Parisian readers, for I would be hurt if they believed I feel the least hostility toward a city that is very dear to me.

I have promised, at the beginning of this preface, to give the reader some biographical details. So I will add, for those who might be interested, that after I left Paris at the end of 1929 I earned my living mainly by teaching and partly by writing. Since the publication in England of *Down and Out in Paris and London*, the present volume, I have written two other books [*Burmese Days* and *A Clergyman's Daughter*]. I have just finished the second. The first will appear in a few days in New York.

Translated by Jeffrey Meyers

# 2. Unsigned notice, *Times Literary Supplement*

12 January 1933, p. 22

Real life experiences are always more gripping than fiction, and it is not uncommon for real life to be as surprising as the most fantastic novel. Mr Orwell does not get his effects by emphasizing the fantastic, although many of the characters he met on his adventures are as odd as any in Dickens—which is probably responsible for their uncomfortable lives. Living in a Paris slum, starving much of the time, he found work as washer-up in a famous restaurant, gaining there experiences which, he alleges, have made him vow never to eat a meal in a Paris restaurant as long as he lives. Life below stairs in such a place, and in the even worse little 'inn' to which he went afterwards—a place that was all *décor* and possessed no capital, he says, to buy reasonably good food—is a strained and greasy business; in the cramped quarters of the kitchen, melting with heat, slipping on discarded food flung to the floor, the workers found their tempers frayed, their nerves irritated and life became merely a matter of work, bed and drink. One interesting thing the author learnt from his Paris experiences, and that is the pride in their work felt by the most over-worked and ill-paid servants of the restaurant, a pride and honour that surely deserved better opportunity.

His later experiences in England, tramping about from one casual ward to another while waiting for a promised job, make tragic reading. He has great sympathy with the man on the road, since he has discovered, as many observers have, that many of them are not natural tramps at all, but good workmen lacking work and tools and the clothes that would be their passport to a job. He is very critical of the system which spends £1 a week a head on keeping workless men moving from 'spike' to 'spike,' clad in rags, fed on the most meagre food, sleeping in great discomfort and never given the opportunity to work even for the food they are consuming at the cost of the working community. He is critical, too, of some charitable institutions where either a man has to pay as much as he would in a commercially run lodging-house and is subjected to many more rules and regulations than even the 'spike' lays down, or else a hypocritical conformity with religious observances is the price to be paid for a meal. It is a vivid picture of an apparently mad world that Mr Orwell paints in his book, a world where unfortunate men are preyed upon by parasites, both insect and human, where a straight line of demarcation is drawn above which no man can hope to rise once he has fallen below its level. One lays down his book wondering why men living in such conditions do not commit suicide; but Mr Orwell conveys the impression that they are too depressed and hopeless for such a final and definite effort as self-inflicted death.

# 3. C. Day Lewis, *Adelphi*

February 1933, p. 382

Cecil Day Lewis (1904-72), English Poet Laureate 1968-72.

Orwell's book is a tour of the under-world, conducted without hysteria or prejudice, and if the discovery of facts made any real impression on the individual conscience, the body of active informers in this country would be inevitably increased by the number of readers of this book. The writer found himself in Paris without money or work. He becomes acquainted with all the squalid shifts of poverty, the extremities of dirt and hunger. Finally, he obtains a job as a 'plongeur' or scullion in a big hotel; 'plongeurs' in Paris work anything from fourteen to seventeen hours a day and, at the three rush hours, behind-the-scenes is a simple mediæval hell of heat, filth and demoniac activity. Incidentally, if you wish to eat a meal in a big hotel without acute nausea, you had better skip pp. 107–109. Orwell's study of the relations between the different branches of the personnel—head waiters, waiters, cooks, plongeurs, etc., is a model of clarity and good sense. And, as he says, the plongeur's work 'is more or less useless. . . . For, after all, where is the real need of big hotels and smart restaurants?

... They are supposed to provide luxury, but in reality they provide only a cheap, shoddy imitation of it ... what makes the work in them is not the essentials; it is the shams that are supposed to represent luxury. . . . Essentially, a "smart" hotel is a place where a hundred people toil like devils in order that two hundred may pay through the nose for things they do not really want.' From Paris, Orwell goes to London, and lives as a tramp, on the road, in 'spikes' and cheap lodging-houses. The facts he reveals should shake the complacence of twentieth century civilisation, if anything could; they are 'sensational,' yet presented without sensationalism. He has no illusions about the extremely poor; he finds the effects of hunger and poverty upon himself and the rest compelling to shame, lying, servility, self-pity, bestial fatalism, apathy—'Hunger reduces one to an utterly spineless, brainless condition, more like the after-effects of influenza than anything else.'

# 4. W. H. Davies, *New Statesman and Nation*

18 March 1933, pp. 338–40

William Henry Davies (1871–1940), English poet and author of *The Autobiography of a Super Tramp* (1908).

This is the kind of book I like to read, where I get the truth in chapters of real life. . . . In reading these extraordinary confessions, it is very curious to see how London and Paris compete in the making of strange scoundrels. In some instances the same characters could be found in either city, with only a difference in their names. The Rougiers, who sold sealed packets on the Boulevard St Michel, to give the impression that they contained pornographic postcards, could be found in London forty-five years ago, trading under other names. These packets could be bought by any frequenter of Petticoat Lane. London, in this instance at least, appears to have been superior to

Paris; for these pornographic pictures could be bought in Petticoat Lane on the Sabbath day, which the Rougiers probably kept holy nor laboured on. If Mr Orwell has a greater liking for Paris than London, I am sure he will forgive my pride in claiming this superiority for our own capital.

When the writer of this book says, on the last page, 'At present I do not feel that I have seen more than the fringe of poverty,' we make haste to assure him that his book is packed with unique and strange information. It is all true to life, from beginning to end. Perhaps a few important slang words could be added, such as 'scrand' for food; 'skimish' for drink; 'stretchers' for laces; 'sharps' for needles; 'pricks' for pins; 'feather' for bed; 'needy' for beggar; 'clobber' for clothes, and many others. But this is only a small matter, as the list could almost be extended to a full language. Indeed we have heard beggars at the wayside use so many strange words in conversation that it was with the greatest difficulty that we could follow their meaning.

As for the earnings of different beggars, is it not wise to take into consideration which one leads the most interesting and most pleasant life? For instance, who would be a pavement artist, who sits in silence near his pictures, waiting for a stray copper as a poor dog waits for a bone? Who would be an organ grinder, dragging his heavy organ from place to place on a hot summer's day, without even the pleasure of making his own notes? Who begrudges such a man a pound or two a week for doing such hard work? Perhaps the best man, after all, is the Downrighter, who makes no pretence of selling or singing, and goes in for straightforward begging. This man only makes a shilling or two a day, and his food as extra. But his life is a real joy to him, because he is a student of humanity, and a great artist. He eyes his prospective victims as they come along, as a squirrel selects the sweetest nuts, or a robin chooses the whitest crumbs. He fits his story to the special case, and success comes to him time after time. If he begs from a young man who has only just left boyhood, he keeps on calling him 'Sir,' and the boy eventually surrenders his last and only penny.

When this Downrighter sees a woman coming along with a little child he fastens his eyes on the little one; and when he is near enough to be heard he sighs audibly. To the woman this is of deep interest, and a wonderful softness spreads all over her face. It is now that our friend, the Downrighter, apologises for his rudeness in looking at the child, and asks to be forgiven for the sake of his own little one, whom he will never see again. Result, twopence—given with tears and thankfully received.

I once knew another Downrighter, who spent hours in Downing Street, in the hope of begging from the highest official in the land. But this poor fellow's ambition was never gratified, and he died a disappointed man. His lesson of persuasive oratory, that was to extract silver from the Prime Minister of England, is now lost to the world forever.

# 5. Unsigned notice, *Nation*

6 September 1933, p. 279

This interesting and rather painful document has been compared to a 'populist' novel like Eugène Dabit's *Hôtel du Nord*,[1] and indeed, in its vivid, unforced fashion, it is more absorbing than any novel of that sort, since all experience, honestly set to paper, is more interesting than experience derived through the sieve of fiction. The author is, or was, an old Eton boy and ex-civil servant who became a dishwasher in Paris and a bum in his own country. His account of these experiences has attracted great attention in England. Several reviewers have dealt with his book in a semi-autobiographic fashion, commenting that it is rather pleasant to be down and out by the Seine, but not so pleasant by the Thames, and so on. This commentator would state, like Mr Orwell himself, that it is not pleasant to be down and out anywhere. No writer submitting himself for the nonce to a horrible existence, for the sake of material, could possibly convey so powerful a sense of destitution and hopelessness as has Mr Orwell, on whom these sensations were, apparently, forced. If we are correct in this conclusion, if this book is not merely a piece

---

[1] Published in New York in 1931.

of 'human nature faking,' it is a restrained and all the more damning indictment of a society in which such things are possible.

# 6. James Farrell, *New Republic*

11 October 1933, pp. 256–7

James Farrell (b. 1904), American novelist, author of *Studs Lonigan* (1934).

Mr Orwell writes: 'It is altogether curious, your first contact with poverty . . . You thought that it would be . . . simple; it is extraordinarily complicated. You thought that it would be terrible; it is merely squalid and boring. It is the peculiar *lowness* of poverty that you discover first . . . the complicated meanness, the crust-wiping.' And after poverty has become casualized, it is—utter degradation. It begets in people 'a sniveling self-pity.' All their energy is forcibly directed into the satisfaction of primary wants—shelter, no matter how miserable, food, even though it be dug from a garbage can and, less important, sexual gratification, despite the fact that it be brutalized or perverted, and that it exact a toll of disease. Poverty is an unnecessary and disgusting waste of human life; the author makes this point clear.

George Orwell is an Eton graduate. In the beginning, his interest in poverty was impersonal, but he found himself penniless in Paris. He pawned his belongings, foraged for food and work, and was finally employed as a *plongeur* (dish-washer and handy man) in a smart Parisian hotel. There he slaved ten hours a day and longer in a dim and filthy cavern behind the glittering dining rooms of the establishment. His wages merely kept him alive. He escaped, only to be forced for a period, into living a tramp's life in England. Again he met with degradation, hopelessness, squalor.

His account is genuine, unexaggerated and intelligent. Possessing a sense of character, Mr Orwell adorns his narrative with portraits and vignettes that give the book interest and concreteness. In addition, he contrasts poverty in France and England, and his contrasts tend somewhat to reveal the differences between the two nations. And with humility he suggests, as a final word, that his study is only a beginning in understanding this problem. His story permits only a thin trickle of ooze to come to the surface. Orwell has escaped from the depths. There are thousands to whom no door of escape is opened. *Down and Out in Paris and London* will give readers a sense of what life means to these thousands.

# 7. Daniel George, *Tribune*

24 January 1941, p. 13

Daniel George, English critic and anthologist.

And now for a Penguin which also seems to deserve the attention of *Tribune* readers—*Down and Out in Paris and London* by George Orwell. Nothing indicates that it has been published before, but I think it must be an early Orwell. His style has improved.

Labelled as fiction, it is autobiographical in form, recounting adventures of an Englishman (a gentleman, an ex-public school boy, and, it appears later, a journalist) experiencing temporary poverty in the company of queer 'characters.' They and the narrator make this a book of such lively interest that scepticism seldom grows out of surprise.

Much of it is, I should judge, written from first-hand knowledge. There are descriptions of work in Paris hotels and restaurants for which no one but a retired *plongeur* with a ready pen could have been responsible. To read about the kitchen conditions in these places is to be filled with disgust. ('Roughly speaking, the more one pays for food, the more sweat and spittle one is obliged to eat with it.') But the wonder grows that out of such chaos, such filth and mismanagement, so many appetising meals were so punctually created.

The Parisians with whom the writer associates are fascinating creatures. I can't get over Charlie, 'very pink and young, with the fresh cheeks and soft brown hair of a nice little boy, and lips excessively red and wet, like cherries.' You should hear him talk. 'Ah, l'amour, l'amour! Ah, que les femmes m'ont tué!' he declaims. I deplore the necessity which compels him, for the reader's convenience, to continue in perfect English; it mars the effect of his quotation from Byron which has to be rendered thus: 'Fill high ze bowl vid Samian vine. Ve vill not sink of semes like zese.' Judging from his style, one would have said his favourite authors were Georges Ohnet and Marcel Prevost. 'All my savagery, my passion, were scattered like the petals of a rose. I was left cold and languid, full of vain regrets; in my revulsion I even felt a kind of pity for the weeping girl on the floor.' As his historian remarks, he was a curious specimen.

There was Boris, too, an ex-captain of the Second Siberian Rifles. 'I have been night watchman, cellarman, floor scrubber, dishwasher, porter, lavatory attendant. I have tipped waiters, and I have been tipped by waiters.' You will like Boris.

When the narrator gets to London, having been offered the job of looking after a congenital imbecile, he is again thrown on his beam ends in the company of tramps and queer tradesmen, each eager to impart the story of his life. He had often been the prey of bugs in Paris, and in London he has no better luck. 'It is,' he says, 'a curious but well-known fact that bugs are much commoner in south than north London. For some reason they have not yet crossed the river in any great numbers.' I suppose he must have authority other than his own observation for making this statement. My experience suggests the contrary. I am sure, at least, that there are bigger and better bugs north of the river.

His remarks on swear words are interesting, too. 'Twenty years ago the London working classes habitually used the word "bloody." Now they have abandoned it utterly, though novelists still represent them as using it. The current London adjective, now tacked on to every noun, is ——.' (The dash is the author's.) Forgive me if I say that I think this is all ——. (The dash is the editor's.)

There is no doubt that this book is worth sixpence of anybody's money. You come upon the oddest things in it.

One went down an area and through an alley-way into a deep, stifling cellar, ten feet square. Ten men, navvies mostly, were sitting in the fierce glare of the fire. It was midnight, but the deputy's son, a pale, sticky child of five, was there playing on the navvies' knees. An old Irishman was whistling to a blind bull-finch in a tiny cage. There were other songbirds there—tiny, faded things, that have lived all their lives underground. The lodgers habitually made water in the fire, to save going across a yard to the lavatory.

O Gargantua, O Gulliver, what manner of men were these? What kind of fire was this in a cellar ten feet square?

# BURMESE DAYS

## 1934

## 8. Sean O'Faolain, *Spectator*

### 28 June 1935, p. 1118

Sean O'Faolain (b. 1900), Irish novelist and biographer of De Valera (1933) and Countess Markievicz (1934). The other two books reviewed were *This Sweet Work* by D. M. Low and *Follow Thy Fair Sun* by Viola Meynell.

After these two subtle books, *Burmese Days* seems very heavy-handed. But the comparison is accidental and should not be made—Mr Orwell has his own merits and his own methods and they are absolutely competent in their own class. His novel is the story of a man who, because born with an ugly birthmark flung in a blue ugliness across his cheek, is doomed to be a misfit. When we meet him he has been for years buried in Burma, and is already half-rotted there: then an English rosebud comes out to him and life shines again. He is by now, unfortunately, sunk so low as to be a reader of books, a Socialist, a disbeliever in the white-man's burden, and a friend of the natives: and his only virtues in the eyes of the 'Kipling-haunted Club,' where there is 'whisky to the right of you and the Pink 'un to the left of you,' is that he drinks like a fish and keeps a native mistress. The bitter tone of the book will be apparent, and with a savagery that knows only a passing pity and eschews all reticence Mr Orwell depicts the life of this misanthropic and unimpressive character. He gives incidentally so grim a picture of Burmese life that while one fervently hopes he has exaggerated, one feels that the outlines, at least, are true.

As a matter of criticism that is crucial with this type of book, the evidence is too good; it all hangs together too well—the sweat and the drink, the loneliness and the dry-rot, the birthmark and the misanthropy, the misanthropy and the anti-social ideas, the anti-social ideas and the ostracism. Poor Flory hasn't a dog's chance against his author. However, one advantage in weighted dice is that the game is secure, and if one does not perceive that Mr Orwell is being too Olympian then the course of his hero's life will seem natural and ineluctable as Fate, and one will say, 'Yes, it rings true—it had to happen that way.'

# 9. Unsigned notice, *Times Literary Supplement*

18 July 1935, p. 462

The names of the native characters were changed in the English edition: Dr Veraswami was called Dr Murkhaswami and U Po Kyin (the real name of an officer in the Burmese Police) was called U Po Sing.

*Burmese Days*, by George Orwell, is symptomatic of the reaction against conventional portrayals of Burma as a land of tinkling temple bells, gentle charming Burmans, and strong, silent Englishmen. The scene is Kyauktada District during the rebellion period, but there is nothing heroic about it. The English—they number only half a dozen men and two commonplace women—are too aloof, the Burmese too abject. Mind and body alike deteriorate in the heat and boredom. The one man among them who would have liked to take an interest in the people, Flory, the forest manager in a second-rate timber firm, is cold-shouldered for making friends with an Asiatic, the Civil Surgeon, Dr Murkhaswami. The jungle Burmese are attractive enough, but those of the town seem to consist mainly of pimps, professional witnesses and corrupt magistrates. One of the last, U Po Sing, the sub-divisional magistrate, actually wins promotion for suppressing a rebellion he never saw, a rebellion at which, indeed, he had connived for that very purpose; he then proceeds to frame false charges and ruin Dr Murkhaswami simply because the poor little man is honest. As for Flory, environment has been too much for him, for he is not really alcoholic or crapulous by nature, and he regrets it when a girl from England arrives to stay at Kyauktada; she is a poverty-stricken little snob on the look-out for a husband, but he has not seen a spinster for a decade, and he succumbs on the spot whereupon his discarded Burmese mistress makes a scene in front of her and every one else, and he ends by committing suicide.

The book has traces of power, and it is written with a pen steeped in gall. That gall is merited, for these people exist; but a little less would have carried more conviction. The inaccuracies are no worse than in pleasant books which idealize the East—a Burmese husband does not talk with his wife as U Po Sing and his wife are made to talk, there are several mistranslations, and some of the incidents could not happen precisely in the form related. The author entirely ignored the newer type of Burman official, men of high character who resent the U Po Sings even more than we do. And when he writes of their English superiors, that few of them work as hard or intelligently as the postmaster in a provincial town, he shows that he can hardly have mixed with the men who really run the country.

# 10. G. W. Stonier, *Fortnightly*

August 1935, p. 255

George Stonier (b. 1903), English author and translator of
Flaubert and Jules Renard.

Several years ago Mr George Orwell wrote a vivid and horrifying
autobiography called *Down and Out in Paris and London*. His book
was first-hand, surprising and (I seem to remember) ferociously gay.
He relished, as a writer, the squalor of the worst paid jobs, the brutality
of employers, the comedy, in mean lodgings and even meaner outdoor
shifts, of living on the fringe of work. His second book was a novel,
*A Clergyman's Daughter*, which I did not read.[1] *Burmese Days* is another
novel, and I recommend it to all those who enjoy a lively hatred in
fiction.

The Europeans of Kyauktada, eight in number, met at 'the Club' to
drink gin, to exchange dirty stories, deplore the fall of the Raj, and
sniff round one another with grinning suspicion. It suggests the horrors
of a common room in some outlying public school, with the added
discomfort of the climate and the pressure of an indolent native
population. We see the characters of various people, mostly un-
amiable, hardening into premature boredom and decay. Frayed nerves
and a weather-beaten exterior, moral bankruptcy and the need for
keeping a firm hand—it is true, no doubt, of uncongenial lives everywhere; but in the isolation of Burma (conveyed with glaring realism)
the false heartiness and idiotic talk of these exiles become hectically
squalid; pathetic, too, the attempts at decency or bringing off a love
affair, for which drink, *Punch* and *La Vie Parisienne* under the Club
punkah have been accepted as substitutes. For, of course, the great
thing is to keep going—and the 'Bolshevism' of Flory, an English
political black sheep, is as futile as the Conservatism of the others. He
tries to get an Indian doctor into the Club, but his nerve fails in face

---

[1] *A Clergyman's Daughter* was actually Orwell's third book, but it was published in
England before *Burmese Days*.

of the 'dirty nigger' attitude. By an admirable stroke of irony, Mr Orwell makes Flory and the Doctor, a pompous plump little Hindu, argue at cross-purposes. Flory sneers at public schools, British rule and the ideal of the gentleman; Dr Murkhaswami is as contemptuous of his own race, but has a fanatical respect for the English character. Their friendship, the arguments which always take the same course, are excellent comedy; these two, in fact, are the only characters in the book whom one can genuinely like. *Burmese Days* is something of a heatwave in current English fiction, but if you can stand the glare and the revelation of shabbiness and drooping spirits, it is the most impressive novel of the five.

# 11. Malcolm Muggeridge, *World Review*

## June 1950, pp. 45–8

Malcolm Muggeridge (b. 1903), friend of Orwell; English journalist, critic, editor of *Punch* 1953–7, television wit. The *World Review* devoted a special issue to Orwell in June 1950.

George Orwell's *Burmese Days* is based, of course, on his own experiences in the Burma Police in the years after he left Eton—that is in the early twenties. There can be no doubt that this experience played a great part in his life. His family had close connections with India; he was born in Bengal, where his father was an official in the Opium Department. One day an attempt will doubtless be made, coolly and objectively, to analyse the effect on the English of their association with India. It is a fascinating subject, and whoever undertakes dealing with it will have plenty of data in works of fiction, from *Vanity Fair* to *Plain Tales from the Hills* or *A Passage to India*. *Burmese Days* belongs essentially to this tradition. It is a study of the human factor in the British Raj.

Considered simply as a novel, *Burmese Days* is not particularly satisfactory. Most of the characters are stock figures, and most of the dialogue is intended rather to present them as such than to reproduce actual conversation. The hero, Flory, is scarcely convincing, nor is the Deputy District Commissioner, Macgregor. Oddly enough, it is the villain, the fat, wicked, Burmese magistrate, U Po Sing, who best comes to life. In his portrayal there is real zest; his wickedness is presented with almost sensual delight, rather in the manner, though in a very different context, of Graham Greene.

The ordinarily-accepted view is that Orwell was deeply revolted by what was expected of him as a member of the Burma Police Force, and that his subsequent political views were to some extent a consequence of the great revulsion of feeling thereby induced in him. Personally, I consider that this is an over-simplification. It is perfectly true that Orwell was revolted by the brutality necessarily involved in police duties in Burma, as he was revolted by all forms of brutality, and, indeed, to a certain extent, by authority as such; but it is also true that there was a Kiplingesque side to his character which made him romanticise the Raj and its mystique.

In this connection, it is significant that one of the most vivid descriptive passages in *Burmese Days* is of the hunting expedition that Flory went on with Elizabeth. Another is of the attack on a small handful of Englishmen in their club by an enraged Burmese mob. Flory was the hero of this occasion. He, with his defacing birthmark and unorthodox attitude towards the 'natives', saved the situation, whereas Verrall, 'lieutenant the honourable', polo player, handsome and insolent Sahib —a sort of Steerforth as in *David Copperfield* or Townley as in *The Way of All Flesh*—unaccountably failed to put in an appearance.

These two episodes are described with tremendous gusto and vividness, and alone give promise of the considerable writer Orwell was to become. Even Flory's passion for Elizabeth, which has up to that point been difficult to believe in, comes to life when they are hunting together. Their hands meet by the warm carcase of a jungle cock—'For a moment they knelt with their hands clasped together. The sun blazed upon them and the warmth breathed out of their bodies; they seemed to be floating upon clouds of heat and joy.'

On the other hand, the description of the Europeans in their club, of their discussions about electing a 'native' to membership, their quarrels and their drunkenness and their outbursts of hysteria, is somehow unreal. As it happens, I was myself living in India at the same period as Orwell was in Burma. It was my first visit there. I was teaching at an

Indian college in Travancore, and occasionally used to visit a neigh-bouring town where there was a little community of English living rather the same sort of life as the European community in Kyauktada. It is, of course, perfectly true that the general attitude towards Indians was arrogant, and sometimes brutal, and that a European who did not share this attitude was liable, like Flory, to find himself in an embarrassing situation. On the other hand, it is equally true that Orwell's picture is tremendously exaggerated, and even unreal—the sadistic outburst of Ellis, for instance:

If it pleases you to go to Murkhaswami's house and drink whisky with all his nigger pals, that's your look-out. Do what you like outside the Club. But by God, it's a different matter when you talk of bringing niggers in here. I suppose you'd like little Murkhaswami for a Club member, eh? Chipping into our conversation and pawing everyone with his sweaty hands and breathing his filthy garlic breath in our faces. By God, he'd go out with my boot behind him if ever I saw his black snout inside that door. Greasy, pot-bellied little . . .!'

The fact is, it seems to me, that a tremendous struggle went on inside Orwell between one side of his character, a sort of Brushwood Boy side,[1] which made him admire the insolence and good looks of Verrall, and a deep intellectual disapprobation of everything Verrall stood for. Verrall is presented by Orwell as, in some ways, a far more admirable character than Flory, in whom there are, unquestionably, strong autobiographical elements. Verrall is what he is; but Flory is tormented by doubt, finds his secret solace in the companionship of Dr Murkhaswami, an Indian, and, at the same time, repeats to him gross remarks made at the club about 'filthy niggers', and feels bound to sign a defamatory notice about him in connection with a proposal that he should be admitted to the club. The same conflict existed in Kipling, who, however, settled it by coming down very heavily on the Brushwood Boy side. Orwell settled it the other way, and came down heavily on the side of Pagett, M.P.,[2] and 'anti-imperialism'. Yet, in both Kipling and Orwell the conflict really remained unresolved, leading Kipling to make the hero of his best book, *Kim*, a little English boy 'gone native', and Orwell to present Verrall and U Po Sing, the two extremes of European and native callousness, as the most effective, if not the most lovable, characters in *Burmese Days*.

[1] The ideal hero in Kipling's story of the same name (1894).
[2] The ignorant and blundering radical politician in Kipling's article 'The Enlightenments of Pagett, M.P.' (1890).

Orwell had an immense admiration for Kipling as a writer, though of course he deplored much of the content of his writing. His long essay on Kipling is extremely interesting, and far from being wholly denigratory. When I used sometimes to say to Orwell that he and Kipling had a great deal in common, he would laugh that curious rusty laugh of his and change the subject. One thing, incidentally, they indubitably had in common was that they found it easier to present animals than human beings in a sympathetic light; the *Jungle Books* and *Animal Farm* are cases in point. As Hugh Kingsmill remarked of Orwell, he tended only to write sympathetically about human beings when he regarded them as animals.[1]

*Burmese Days*, as I have said, is not on any showing a great novel. It is, however, extremely readable and, in some of its descriptive passages, brilliant. The sense, if not the manner, of living in India is wonderfully conveyed—the boredom, the hatefulness, and, at the same time, the curious passionate glory of it. Anyone who believed that that was literally how Europeans lived in Burma before the country was 'liberated', and relapsed into its present squalor and chaos and misery, would be hopelessly mistaken. There is much more to be said for British rule than Orwell says; much more that was heroic even about those little remote philistine collections of English in up-country stations than he suggests. At the same time, *Burmese Days* has its own verisimilitude, but more in relation to Orwell than to India as such.

Events have moved fast indeed since he wrote the book, and the pretentious clubs, which both U Po Sing and Dr Murkhaswami so passionately desired to be allowed to join, have already for the most part ceased to exist, or become the haunts of brown burra Sahibs not less concerned than their white predecessors to maintain their position of superiority. If the copies of *The Tatler*, *The Illustrated London News*, along with local equivalents, remain where they were, and are still turned over, the Ellises, the Latimers, the Macgregors, the Westfields, have either departed, or adjusted themselves to a position of obsequiousness to their new masters. My impression was very strongly that Orwell was not quite sure how pleased he was about all this. In any case, it makes the scene of *Burmese Days* as much a period piece as Lytton's *Last Days of Pompeii*.

[1] See Hugh Kingsmill, *The Progress of a Biographer* (London, 1949), p. 171.

# A CLERGYMAN'S DAUGHTER

1935

---

## 12. L. P. Hartley, *Observer*

10 March 1935, p. 6

---

Leslie Poles Hartley (1895–1973), English novelist, author of *The Go-Between* (1953) and *The Hireling* (1957).

---

If the Reverend Charles Hare, Rector of St Athelstan's, Knype Hill, Suffolk, had been a character in one of Mr Powys's books, one would not have complained that his portrait was overdrawn; but *A Clergyman's Daughter* is a realistic novel, to be judged by canons of verisimilitude founded on daily life; and therefore we can say unhesitatingly that he is exaggerated to the point of being a monster. The milk of human kindness had completely dried up in him; he treated his long-suffering daughter, Dorothy, like a drudge. The trivial round, the common tasks at the Rectory she might have endured; but not the unkindness, above all not the (quite unnecessary) shortage of money. It is not surprising that, after a *mouvementée*[1] evening with Mr Warburton, the village atheist and reprobate, she lost her memory. Nor are her adventures with the hop-pickers, while she was still unaware of her identity, or tramping the streets of London, when she was aware of it, contrary to probability. The penultimate phase of her exile from Knype Hill, when she was mistress of all work in Miss Creevy's school for girls, does strain one's credulity, though it is so entertaining that every detail is as diverting to the reader as it was irksome, or worse, to poor Dorothy. But it is surely unnatural that her father should not have answered his daughter's letters, however annoyed he might be by the tale of her elopement with the ungodly Warburton, and that she

[1] Full of incident.

58

should not have communicated with her relations instead of spending the night on a bench in Trafalgar-square.

However, Mr Orwell is not concerned with probability in the wider sense, but with exhibiting in the strongest possible light, and with the most vivid illustrations, man's inhumanity to man. The hop-pickers are comparatively amiable; the down-and-outs in Trafalgar-square are patient, and sometimes humorous, in their misfortunes. The disreputable Mr Warburton is good-natured, even when most satyric, and Nobby, who had been to prison four times, is, apart from Dorothy, the most sympathetic character in the story. But give a man or a woman a grain of authority and respectability, and they become, like the Rev Hare and Miss Creevy, fiends incarnate. The thesis of *A Clergyman's Daughter* is neither new nor convincing; its merits lie in the treatment, which is sure and bold, and in the dialogue, which is always appropriate, and often brilliant, although (when Dorothy's humbler friends are speaking) it has to be expressed largely in dashes and exclamation marks.

# 13. V. S. Pritchett, *Spectator*

22 March 1935, p. 504

Victor Sawdon Pritchett (b. 1900), English critic, director of the *New Statesman*, author of *The Living Novel* (1946) and *A Cab at the Door* (1968).

Mr Orwell's manner is not dissimilar, but his is a colder talent. His satire is a whip for vicarages; he is out to make the flesh of vicars' daughters creep and to show the sheltered middle-class women that only a small turn of the wheel of fortune is needed for them to be thrown helpless among the dregs of society. Having said this, he adds that if they are like Dorothy Hare, the daughter of the Rector of St Athelstan's,—and most of them are, according to Mr Orwell—there is no hope for them anyway.

Tyrannized over by her father, slaving for him in his Rectory, his church, his parish, rising before the maid, hardening herself by a penitential cold bath on winter mornings, pricking herself with pins in church every time her mind strays from the sermon or the prayer, visiting the recalcitrant sick, drilling the Girl Guides, calming duns, making costumes for amateur theatricals in an unending effort to raise church funds, and having on top of all this to deal firmly with the cynical advances of the local amorist, the plain, obstinate, stoical and delightful Dorothy at last breaks down. She suddenly finds herself far from the security of Suffolk, wandering in filthy clothes down the Old Kent Road in the company of three down-and-outs. She has lost her memory, been robbed, and is thrown on the world. An appalling life follows. Her companions are going on foot to the Kentish hopfields and an awful journey, made longer by weary detours in search of food, follows. At last, starving and in rags, she and a cheerful young thief, who alone of the party have survived, get jobs picking hops. An excellent account of this sweated trade follows. But her man—he is not her lover; Dorothy has a profound and irremediable horror of what she calls 'All that,' and is condemned by the neurosis to refuse even desirable offers—is arrested, the hop-picking ends, she recovers her memory by recognizing a photograph of herself in a newspaper which has made the utmost of the scandal of her disappearance, and writes to her father. There is no reply. She cannot face the scandal, so she goes to London to find a job. But her class is not trained to meet real emergency and she sinks swiftly to the level of the starving down-and-outs who sleep out on the Embankment and in Trafalgar Square. This scene shows an immense knowledge of low life, its miseries, humours and talk, but has unfortunately been written in a 'stunt' Joyce fashion which utterly ruins the effect.

But the president of the immortals had not finished with Dorothy. She is rescued, but only as her fantastic, scandal-terrified relatives can rescue. And here Mr Orwell's satirical facility has lured him away from his best manner to the glib cruelties of caricature. It is not certain—and Mr Orwell seems uncertain on this point—that Dorothy is a half-wit. Her training has been half-witted; but Dorothy? One does not believe that she would not have put up a more intelligent fight. Still, Mr Orwell's case is a sound one.

# 14. Peter Quennell,
## *New Statesman and Nation*

23 March 1935, p. 422

Peter Quennell (b. 1905), English biographer of Byron (1935), Ruskin (1949) and Pope (1968).

*A Clergyman's Daughter* is ambitious yet not entirely successful. Up to page 93, Dorothy is the mild, repressed, self-effacing daughter of an East Anglian parson. At that point, however, after a distressing episode with Mr Warburton, the local 'bad hat,' she loses her memory, wanders away from home and wakes up to find herself in London. There she joins a group of tramps bound for the hopfields. From Kent, she wanders back again to Middlesex; and in Chapter Three Mr Orwell treats us to an elaborate set-piece, laid among penniless down-and-outs condemned to spend a night shivering on the benches of Trafalgar Square. This passage would be more impressive if it were less reminiscent of the celebrated Nighttown scenes at the end of *Ulysses*. A good deal of the writing is uncommonly forceful; but Dorothy, alas! remains a cipher. She is a literary abstraction to whom things happen. . . . We have no feeling that her flight from home and her return to the rectory have any valid connection with the young woman herself.

# 15. Michael Sayers, *Adelphi*

August 1935, pp. 316–17

This is a composite review of *A Clergyman's Daughter* and *Burmese Days*.

George Orwell is a popular novelist sensitive to values that most other novelists are popular for ignoring. One feels he has ideas about the art of the novel, and that his future work is going to be unusually interesting. At present Mr Orwell appears to be most concerned with presenting his material in the clearest and honestest way. Being a man of considerable and diverse experience this problem naturally comes to him before any æsthetic considerations; yet, in his first book, *A Clergyman's Daughter*, he was already experimenting with new forms when Naturalism seemed inadequate. In the widely praised Trafalgar Square Episode in that book the down-and-outs are characterised by a technical device from the drama (but in this case probably derived from *Ulysses*), which has the effect of enlarging them to immense dimensions, and they seem, not so much a congeries of misfortunate men and women, as a mere undifferentiated mass of human sufferings. The various pathetic, degenerate, irrelevant and comic personal peculiarities of these down-and-outs are remarkably well portrayed, but at the same time Mr Orwell contrives to communicate an understanding of some impersonal misery, some universal communion of wretchedness, in which the individual with his egotisms is tragically immersed:

Charles draws himself up, clears his throat, and in an enormous voice roars out a song entitled 'Rollicking Bill the Sailor.' A laugh that is partly a shudder bursts from the people on the bench. They sing the song through again, with increasing volume of noise, stamping and clapping in time. Those sitting down, packed elbow to elbow, sway grotesquely from side to side, working their feet as though stamping on the pedals of a harmonium. . . .
Once more the people pile themselves on the bench. But the temperature is now not many degrees above freezing point, and the wind is blowing more

cuttingly. The people wriggle their wind-nipped faces into the heap like sucking pigs struggling for their mother's teats.

The quotation is a fair specimen of Mr Orwell's style. The lucidity —so to speak, the *transparence*—of his prose is a necessary quality of the realistic novel, which aims at exhibiting action rather than significant language. Mr Orwell has a story to tell that compels attention on its own account, and he tells it drily and perspicuously, without a trace of sentimentality, and with an occasional, casual comment or aphorism that drops into the limpidity of the narrative like a berry into a pool.

This quality is most noticeable in Mr Orwell's second novel, *Burmese Days*. He is dealing here with the lives of various Imperialist officials and traders, and some native types, in Burma; and the point of æsthetic interest is the way in which Mr Orwell, instead of wrapping his tale in a shroud of 'local colour,' extracts his story and people out of the exotic environment. Again one is struck by the clarity of the style, which presents the scene almost with the vivacity of hallucination. Neither pity, nor bitterness, nor cynicism, nor contempt is permitted to obscure the insidious degradations of Imperialism, acting upon white and coloured alike: the greed, the snobbishness, the injustice, the opacity of alien loyalties and alien hates, the meanness, the bigotry, the despair, the dirt, the consciousness of being an interloper and a despoiler, or a victim, the realisation of incalculable waste—in short, an existence made endurable only by whisky and brutality and fornication. All this is shown, rather than stated, by Mr Orwell, in a novel that deserves the attention of serious readers. But Mr Orwell's career has only begun.

# 16. Geoffrey Stone, *Commonweal*

18 June 1937, p. 220

Geoffrey Stone was a critic on the staff of the *American Review*.
*Commonweal* is a liberal Catholic weekly published in New York.

George Orwell, the Englishman, looks at things most pessimistically; if his book is written to prove anything, it is to prove that life is no fun at all. His pessimism seems more the result of temperament than of a clear view of circumstance, for in *A Clergyman's Daughter* he arranges circumstance so that the pessimistic conclusion will seem inevitable. Whatever the validity of his philosophy in its own right, it effect upon his novel is unfortunate; his characters have not the self-sustaining quality of characters in memorable novels, being conceived as illustrations of the gloomy thesis. Mr Orwell confines his attention chiefly to the young lady of his title. Dorothy is an earnest but not especially bright girl whose life is taken up with attending to the duties her father neglects in his parish. By a strange stroke of fate she is swept, successively, into the hop fields, the resorts of the down-ands outs in London, and a girls' school of more than Dickensian squalor. Her experiences in these places cause her to lose her faith, which has carried her through the horrors of parish visiting and children's theatricals, but they do not rid her of a morbid distaste for marriage, and Mr Orwell, with some satisfaction, though he is not hard-hearted, leaves her 'pasting strip after strip of paper into place, with absorbed, with pious concentration, in the penetrating smell of the gluepot.' One is tempted to believe that her story was written under similar conditions.

# KEEP THE ASPIDISTRA FLYING

1936 (1st American edition 1956)

## 17. William Plomer, *Spectator*

24 April 1936, p. 768

William Plomer (1903–73), South African biographer, poet and novelist; author of *Cecil Rhodes* (1933), his autobiography *Double Lives* (1943) and *Museum Pieces* (1952).

Mr George Orwell's new book, bitter almost throughout and often crude, is also all about money. He opens it with a long quotation from the Epistle to the Corinthians in which he has seen fit to substitute the word 'money' for 'charity.' His version ends: 'And now abideth faith, hope, money, these three; but the greatest of these is money.'[1] The scene is London, the time is the present, and the hero is Gordon Comstock, a seedy young man of thirty who works in a seedy bookseller's shop. Gordon would like to be famous and to be loved. He has vague aspirations in regard to the writing of poetry, and tender feelings towards a certain Rosemary. His heredity and upbringing have been against him. His exceedingly depressing and depressed lower-middle-class family have set, he considers, undue store by money, of which they have seen little. Reacting against their standards, he refuses the chance of becoming 'a Big Pot one of these days' in a red lead firm, deliberately throws away his good prospects in a publicity company, and embraces squalor. The embrace is protracted for some three hundred pages, and Mr Orwell, who is the author of a book called *Down and Out in London and Paris*, spares us none of the horrors of sordid loneliness and a hypertrophied inferiority complex expressing itself in physical grubbiness and stupid debauchery. In the end, after

[1] Orwell's epigraph is from I Corinthians 13.

65

various contretemps, described with what may be called painful realism, Rosemary comes to the rescue and persuades him to return to publicity and bread-and-butter, which is just as well, for there is an unknown child to be considered. Turning over the pages of a magazine he takes a straight look at the world to which he is returning:

Adorable—until she smiles. The food that is shot out of a gun. Do you let foot-fag affect your personality? . . . Only a *penetrating* face-cream will reach that under-surface dirt. Pink toothbrush is *her* trouble. . . . Only a drummer and yet he quoted Dante. . . . How a woman of thirty-two stole her young man from a girl of twenty. . . . Now I'm schoolgirl complexion all over. Hike all day on a slab of Vitamalt!

His rebellion against money has brought him 'not only misery, but also a frightful emptiness, an inescapable sense of futility.' Yet in the conclusion his bitterness is softened by the reflection that although 'our civilisation is founded on greed and fear, in the lives of common men the greed and fear are mysteriously transmuted into something nobler.' He therefore marries and settles down with Rosemary—and an aspidistra, which has to be 'kept flying,' for perhaps it is 'the tree of life.'

# 18. Cyril Connolly,
## *New Statesman and Nation*

### 25 April 1936, p. 635

Cyril Connolly (1903–74), at St Cyprian's and Eton with Orwell; journalist and author of *Enemies of Promise* (1938) and *The Unquiet Grave* (1945).

*Keep the Aspidistra Flying* also brings up the question of material. It is about London. *Burmese Days* was about Burma. Now the reader knows too much of London, and not enough about Burma. He cannot, in fact, be as interested in Hampstead. But the writer of *Burmese Days* was also himself fond of Burma and included many beautiful descriptions of it, while the writer of *Keep the Aspidistra Flying* hates London and everything there. Hence the realism of one book was redeemed by an operating sense of beauty, that of the other is not. It is, in fact, a completely harrowing and stark account of poverty, and poverty as a squalid and all-pervading influence. The hero works for two pounds a week in a bookshop. He has a girl whom he is too poor to marry, and is writing a poem on which he is too poor really to concentrate. It is winter. The book is the recital of his misfortunes interrupted by tirades against money and the spiritual evil it causes. It is written in clear and violent language, at times making the reader feel he is sitting in a dentist's chair with the drill whirring, at times seeming too emphatic and far-fetched. There have been so many novels in which young men and their fiancées sit over the gas fire and wonder where the next shilling is coming from, or go out and hate the streets. This is perhaps the most logical of all of them, but suffers, with an irony which the author would appreciate, from the fact that the obsession with money about which the book is written, is one which must prevent it from achieving the proportion of a work of art.

# 19. Unsigned notice,
## *Times Literary Supplement*

2 May 1936, p. 376

---

If this book is persistently irritating, this is exactly what makes it worth reading; few books have enough body in them to be irritants. Does what most people regard as a rational mode of living and of earning one's way necessarily involve aspidistras and the narrowness of view of which the author uses them as symbols? He seems to think that the possession of wealth is in itself a sufficient guarantee against narrowness and drabness of outlook—which is obviously untrue—and that, lacking wealth, the effort to live in reasonable comfort and decency must imply absorption in money. This may, of course, be so in certain cases, but surely it depends on the individual in the last resort. Admittedly it is easier to lead a noble spiritual life if one is free from material worries, but there is nothing necessarily more noble in arbitrarily accepting a lower standard of life than one could enjoy—lower not only in creature comforts but in interests, in learning and in friends.

This, however, is what Mr Orwell's hero does. Determined to be free from the bondage to money, he refuses what he considers the degradation of a 'good job,' takes drab uninteresting work, and deliberately disintegrates into mental and physical squalor. One may protest that the author has begged the question in making his possible 'good job' a very unelevating one; a more serious objection is that he has evaded the final issue (whether an educated man could continue to let himself sink as a matter of principle) by dragging his hero back to the business world through the need to support the girl whom he has loved for some years in an entirely self-centred way.

Those who know Mr Orwell's other work will know that he writes well and vividly. The more depressing his theme, the more effectively is his skill displayed, and he has dealt unusually convincingly with Gordon's shabby-genteel origins and his gradual descent into a more sordid world.

# 20. R. R. (Richard Rees), *Adelphi*

June 1936, p. 190

---

Sir Richard Rees (1900–70), close friend of Orwell and model for Ravelston in *Keep the Aspidistra Flying*; co-editor of *Adelphi* 1930–6, author of books on Orwell (1961), D. H. Lawrence (1958) and Simone Weil (1966).

---

This is Mr Orwell's third novel and, even more than his two previous ones, it makes clear that he is a good hater. Almost everything in the modern world, from Catholicism to contraceptives, he violently assaults. But beneath a rather loose violence of style there is a consistent seriousness and a real vigour which make him a more promising novelist than many whose observation is subtler and sharper.

He is a fundamentally honest writer, and perhaps that is why one tends in reading him always to compare him, rather unfairly, with the best in whatever kind he is attempting. In *Burmese Days* his theme inevitably suggested comparisons, unfortunate for him, with E. M. Forster and Somerset Maugham; and in his new book, which describes the horrors of London's literary under-world and the struggle of a young writer to avoid selling his talent to Big Business, he challenges comparison with Aldous Huxley. But one has only to compare the conversations in *Keep the Aspidistra Flying* with those in Mr Huxley's novels to see what a lot Mr Orwell has still to learn. Nevertheless, his books have a sufficiently interesting personal flavour to make one hope that he *will* learn. He is old-fashioned in some ways, and proud of it (one might hazard that Dickens and Samuel Butler, rather than Joyce and Lawrence, are his masters; though he has not neglected the two latter) and he has obviously a passion for writing which is quite different from the nauseous literary obsession which afflicts so many reputedly serious modern writers.

## 21. Kenneth Macpherson, *Life and Letters Today*

Autumn 1936, pp. 207–8

Kenneth Macpherson (1903–71), Scottish novelist and editor. The description of Socialism in the quotation from the novel clearly foreshadows *1984*.

Mr Orwell has resurrected the aspidistra. When most pens waver in the air, hesitating to scratch a name so spent to symbolise the crushing drabness of apartment rooms, the author here brings it back with a flourish, very much as Schiaparelli will start the whole town wearing revised versions of discredited fashions of the past.

It is a book about London. It is horribly a book about London. About the kind of London we glimpse as our boat-trains slow down near the terminus. About the kind of London we sense in an overheard remark, a bleached face, washing hanging in the soot, wet streets, and, of course, aspidistras seen in windows where the curtains are a little torn but starched. It is a book about the crushing deadliness of London, not London's seamy side, but London's suit 'turned good as new', its threadbare tie, its ankles inked to hide holes in its socks.

And what a remarkable, what a subtle distillation of reality! The dreadful little underling hero, earning two pounds a week in a bookshop, who hates socialism, (regarding it as 'Some kind of Aldous Huxley *Brave New World*: only not so amusing. Four hours a day in a model factory, tightening up bolt 6003. Rations served out in greaseproof paper at the communal kitchen. Community-hikes from Marx Hostel to Lenin Hostel and back. Free abortion clinics on all the corners.') and yet has declared war on the Money God, a defiant, wailing war, full of longing and repudiation. 'There was the intimacy of hatred between the aspidistra and him. "I'll beat you yet, you b——," he whispered to the dusty leaves.'

It is inevitable that this little man has a girl who doesn't love him.

When they do fix a day in the country and that long desired end is about to be reached, with what shattering precision does Mr Orwell describe the ignoble frustration. With what shattering precision does he describe the spending of ten pounds arriving unexpectedly from an American magazine for a poem accepted, and with what cunning, through stages of disintegration, he leads his hero to marriage and a home and an aspidistra, no longer a poet but a man in a bowler hat with an advertising job.

Perhaps the most extraordinary of Mr Orwell's many talents is his ability to create his characters with complete detachment. This was evident in his two other novels—*A Clergyman's Daughter* and *Burmese Days*—and here again, without betraying sympathy for or against any character in the book, he seems, like a Toscanini, to interpret not to create, to photograph not to paint; and that perhaps, is the highest compliment that can be paid to him.

# 22. Anthony West, *New Yorker*

28 January 1956, pp. 86–92

Anthony West (b. 1914), English critic and staff member of the *New Yorker*; author of *D. H. Lawrence* (1948) and *Principles and Persuasions* (1956).

The publication of *Keep the Aspidistra Flying* in this country twenty years after its first appearance in England, makes most of George Orwell's work available to American readers and provides the occasion for an urgently needed revaluation of it. The novel, which is his second, appeared in 1936, the year he said in his essay 'Why I Write' was the critical one of his career, because he felt that during it he discovered what he had to do. This was to write political books designed 'to push the world in a certain direction, to alter other people's idea of the kind of society that they should strive after.' This throws some light, though not enough, on why *Keep the Aspidistra Flying* is what it is. Taken at its face value, it describes a man's fight to be a poet and a free spirit in a money-ridden society. He loses out because the whole weight of that society bears down on him with all its crass materialism and vulgarity. He has no chance of happiness while he lives by poetic values; as long as he holds to them, he is denied love, creature comforts, and even, it appears, a chance to keep his neck clean:

The money-stink, everywhere the money-stink. He stole a glance at the Nancy. . . . The skin at the back of his neck was as silky-smooth as the inside of a shell. You can't have a skin like that under five hundred a year. A sort of charm he had, a glamour, like all moneyed people. Money and charm; who shall separate them?

This passage has an obvious stylistic echo of D. H. Lawrence, but there is another echo behind that—of F. Scott Fitzgerald and his tormenting feeling that whatever a man was, and whatever he did, he could never capture the glow that emanated from the rich and marked them out as superior beings. In the passage from which I have just quoted, Orwell's hero, Gordon Comstock, looks across the book-shop where he works and sees the Nancy in exactly the same way that the narrator in *The Great Gatsby* sees Daisy, as a talisman that will reveal his own inadequacy. This echo sounds even more strongly in a passage in which Comstock is horrified to find not only that he has the tiny sum of fivepence halfpenny to last him from midweek to payday but that part of it is a threepenny bit. The discovery fires off a remarkable soliloquy:

Beastly useless thing! And bloody fool to have taken it! It had happened yesterday, when he was buying cigarettes. 'Don't mind a threepenny bit, do you, sir?' the little bitch of a shopgirl had chirped. And of course he had let her give it him. 'Oh no, not at all!' he had said—fool, bloody fool!

His heart sickened to think that he had only fivepence halfpenny in the world, threepence of which couldn't even be spent. Because how can you buy anything with a threepenny bit? It isn't a coin, it's the answer to a riddle. You look such a fool when you take it out of your pocket, *unless it's in among a whole handful of other coins.* 'How much?' you say. 'Threepence,' the shopgirl says. And then you feel all round your pocket and fish out that absurd little thing, all by itself, sticking on the end of your finger like a tiddleywink. *The shopgirl sniffs. She spots immediately that it's your last threepence in the world.* You see her glance quickly at it—she's wondering whether there's a piece of Christmas pudding still sticking to it. And you stalk out with your nose in the air, *and can't ever go to that shop again*. No! We won't spend our Joey. Twopence half-penny left—twopence halfpenny to last till Friday.

The phrases I have italicized show that this passage is really not about poverty at all but about the mood of a man who feels inadequate and despised because he is not rich. No such social stigma was ever attached to the Joey, the threepenny bit. When Orwell was writing, it was a small coin, the size and color of a dime, and the easiest one of all to lose. There was consequently a prejudice against it as intense as the dislike some Americans have for the two-dollar bill. But that was the limit of the prejudice. Comstock's feeling about shopgirls is as odd in its way as his feeling about the coin. Why should one be a bitch for giving it to him? And why should another one sense that it was his last coin, and despise him? It is the Scott Fitzgerald mania again, the belief that everybody can tell how rich a man is at a glance.

This feeling comes out into the open when Orwell describes Comstock's education:

Even at the third-rate schools to which Gordon was sent nearly all the boys were richer than himself. They soon found out his poverty, of course, and gave him hell because of it. Probably the greatest cruelty one can inflict on a child is to send it to school among children richer than itself. A child conscious of poverty will suffer snobbish agonies such as a grown-up person can scarcely even imagine.

What follows is another version of Orwell's harrowing essay called 'Such, Such Were the Joys,' which is a description of his own schooling at Crossgates. Subjectively, if one accepts this account of the process, it is a dreadful business: Two horrible people, animated entirely by the desire to make money and to better their social position, set out to break the spirit of a child and to turn it into a performing freak who will win scholarships when a whip cracks. Objectively, one can see the outline of something else. The school in question charged well-to-do parents high fees and used part of them to subsidize the education of promising boys whose parents couldn't afford to give them that kind of schooling. These subsidized boys were forced along to prepare them for scholarship examinations that would get them into the best schools in England, and they were forced hard because the competition was intense. What Orwell represents as an apparatus designed to cripple him was in actuality an attempt to give boys like him a chance to win the best possible start in life. Orwell's hatred of the forcing process, and of the exposure of his parents' financial inadequacy that it involved, was so fierce that he could never admit either the nature of the chance that was being offered or that he was, in fact, offered it. He proclaimed, instead, that he had been given a very bad education and had been maimed by middle-class snobbery. In a sense he had been, and the hurt child's feeling that money is the measure of all things—a notion derived from the experiences at school that are chronicled in 'Such, Such Were the Joys'—is treated as the final truth about the adult world in both *Down and Out in Paris and London* and *Keep the Aspidistra Flying*. The two books have to be taken in parallel, because Gordon Comstock in the novel makes the trip to the squalors of Gorkyland that Orwell made in reality and that he describes in *Down and Out*. Gorky's knowledge of the lower depths was not a matter of tourism; he had no choice about making the exploration. But Orwell, a gifted man, with many friends who were anxious to help him, was never in the grip of real necessity. He sought poverty out in the hope that contact with it would, as he explains in *The Road to Wigan Pier* (1937), purge him of his sense of guilt. Comstock's wretchedness is voluntary, too; all the time he is suffering there is a good job waiting for him at an advertising agency. Orwell, in the following passage, explains the purpose of Comstock's visit in *Keep the Aspidistra Flying* with what seems greater candor than he brings to bear on his own behaviour a year later:

He had finished for ever with that futile dream of being a 'writer.' After all, was not that too a species of ambition? He wanted to get away from all that *below* all that. Down, down! Into the ghost kingdom, out of reach of hope, out of the reach of fear! Under ground, under ground! That was where he wished to be.

Yet in a way it was not so easy. One night about nine he was lying on his bed, with the ragged counterpane over his feet, his hands under his head to keep them warm. The fire was out. The dust was thick on everything. The aspidistra had died a week ago and was withering upright in its pot. He slid a shoeless foot from under the counterpane, held it up, and looked at it. His sock was full of holes—there were more holes than sock. So here he lay, Gordon Comstock, in a slum attic on a ragged bed with his feet sticking out of his socks, with one and fourpence in the world, with three decades behind him and nothing, nothing accomplished! Surely *now* he was past redemption? Surely, try as they would, they couldn't prise him out of a hole like this? He had wanted to reach the mud—well, this was the mud, wasn't it?

The book goes on to explain that the device of degrading oneself to a point beneath criticism doesn't work, and ends up with the poet beating the system by cynically conforming to it and becoming a success as the advertising man he was clearly born to be. But Orwell writes this 'happy' ending without much conviction; his mind is already warming to the idea of a universal smashup. It would destroy the middle class, which had invented the horrible educational machine that had hurt him, and it would destroy the whole world of money values, in which he felt himself inadequate. That Orwell's mind is taking this direction is indicated by a fantasy with which Comstock comforts himself in *Keep the Aspidistra Flying*:

Our civilization is dying. It *must* be dying. But it isn't going to die in its bed. Presently the aeroplanes are coming. Zoom—whizz—crash! The whole western world going up in a roar of high explosives. . . . In imagination he saw them coming now; squadron after squadron, innumerable, darkening the sky like clouds of gnats. With his tongue not quite against his teeth he made a buzzing, blue-bottle-on-the-window-pane sound to represent the humming of the aeroplanes. It was a sound which, at that moment he ardently desired to hear.

This fantasy gets out of hand in Orwell's next novel, *Coming Up for Air*, in which it figures as a secondary theme. The first mention of bombing comes on page 19, and there is a prophecy of doom on page 24:

No guns firing, nobody chucking pineapples, nobody beating anybody else up with a rubber truncheon. If you come to think of it, in the whole of England at this moment there isn't a single bedroom window from which anyone's firing a machine gun.
But how about five years from now? Or two years? Or one year?

This note is struck again and again throughout the book, and the passages that strike it take on an increasingly hysterical tone. At last an R.A.F. aircraft drops a bomb into the main street of the little town the hero is visiting in sentimental pursuit of his recollections of youthful happiness. (Needless to say, he finds everything changed, and for the worse.) The accident is described in a screaming fit:

But the lower rooms had caught the force of the explosion. There was a frightful smashed-up mess of bricks, plaster, chair-legs, bits of varnished dresser, rags of tablecloth, piles of broken plates and chunks of a scullery sink. A jar of marmalade had rolled across the floor, leaving a long streak of marmalade behind, and running side by side with it there was a ribbon of blood. But in among the broken crockery there was lying a leg. Just a leg with the trouser still on it and a black boot with a Woodmilne rubber heel. This is what the people were oo-ing and ah-ing at. . . .

I'll tell you what my stay in Lower Binfield had taught me, and it was this. *It's all going to happen.* All the things you've got at the back of your mind, the things you're terrified of, the things you tell yourself are just a nightmare or only happen in foreign countries. The bombs, the food queues, the rubber truncheons, the barbed wire, the colored shirts, the slogans, the enormous faces, the machine guns squirting out of bedroom windows. It's all going to happen. I know it—at any rate I knew it then. There's no escape. Fight against it if you like, or look the other way and pretend not to notice, or grab your spanner and rush out to do a bit of face smashing along with the others. But there's no way out. It's just something that's got to happen. . . .

The bad times are coming, and the streamlined men are coming too. What's coming afterwards I don't know, it hardly even interests me. I only know that if there's anything you care a curse about, better say goodbye to it now, because everything you've ever known is going down, down, into the muck, with the machine guns rattling all the time.

There are two minor points of interest about this. One is that Lower Binfield, the place of remembered happiness in *Coming Up for Air*, is also the place, in the closing chapters of *Down and Out in Paris and London*, where Orwell is accepted by the tramps as one of their fraternity. The other point is the echo of the phrase 'down, down, into the muck,' from Comstock's reverie about his self-degradation in *Keep the Aspidistra Flying*. But the important one is that this passage, written in 1939, contains the entire substance of a novel written ten years later—*1984*. There is clearly something perverse in this. By then the squadrons of planes had done their worst, and Lower Binfield—which may be taken as a symbol for ordinary England—had not only known the dramatic, apocalyptic terror of concentrated bombing attacks but had experienced the mass impoverishment and long-drawn-out near-starvation that brings on revolutionary crises. The British declined to go to pieces under the strain; the big faces, the colored shirts, and the rubber truncheons never appeared, and no machine guns squirted out of bedroom windows. It would be unfair, perhaps, to say that Orwell was disappointed, but at any rate he felt cheated. Like a number of other writers who had thought themselves ill-used by prewar society and had been unconsciously looking forward to Armageddon and social shipwreck, he consoled himself by constructing a fantasy of universal ruin. *1984* is not a rational attempt to imagine a probable future; it is an aggregate of 'all the things you've got at the back of your mind, the things you're terrified of.' Most of these, in *1984*, are of an infantile character, and they clearly derive from the experience described in 'Such, Such Were the Joys.' At Crossgates, women—the headmaster's wife and the 'grim statuesque matron'— were particularly dangerous; they seemed to be spying on Orwell all the time, and whenever they caught him doing anything they handed him over to 'the head' for physical punishment. This idea crops up early in *1984*:

Winston had disliked her from the very first moment of seeing her. He knew the reason. It was because of the atmosphere of hockey fields, and cold baths, and community hikes and general clean-mindedness which she managed to carry about with her. [This is, of course, the essence of the English private-school atmosphere.] He disliked nearly all women, and especially the young and pretty ones. It was always the women, and above all the young ones, who were the most bigoted adherents of the Party, the swallowers of slogans, the amateur spies and nosers out of unorthodoxy.

But the real horror of Crossgates is that the masters seem, by some kind of magical omniscience, to know what every boy does and even what he thinks. This horror appears in *1984*, and in the first fifteen hundred words:

The telescreen received and transmitted simultaneously. Any sound that Winston made, above the level of a very low whisper, would be picked up by it, moreover; so long as he remained within the field of vision which the metal plaque commanded, he could be seen as well as heard. There was of course no way of knowing whether you were being watched at any given moment. How often, or on what system, the Thought Police plugged in on any individual wire was guesswork. It was even conceivable that they watched everybody all the time.

The whole pattern of society shapes up along the lines of fear laid down in 'Such, Such Were the Joys' until the final point of the dread summons to the headmaster's study for the inevitable beating. In *1984*, the study becomes Room 101 in the Ministry of Love, and the torturers correspond closely to the schoolmasters; in fact, they use some of the tricks Orwell compains of in his picture of Crossgates. Even the idea of Big Brother, which seems to be drawn from a rational examination of the propaganda technique of dictatorship, goes back to the same source. Big Brother, the feared dictator whom everyone pretends to love, is really Bingo, the headmaster's wife:

How difficult it is for a child to have any real independence of attitude could be seen in our attitude towards Bingo. I think it would be true to say that every boy in the school hated and feared her. Yet we all fawned on her in the most abject way, and the top layer of our feelings towards her was a sort of guilt-stricken loyalty. Bingo, although the discipline of the school depended more on her than on Sim [her husband], hardly pretended to dispense justice. She was frankly capricious. An act which might get you a caning one day might next day be laughed off as a boyish prank, or even commended because it 'showed you had guts.' ... Although my memories of Bingo are mostly hostile, I also remember considerable periods when I basked in her smiles, when she called me 'old chap' and used my Christian name, and allowed me to frequent her private library, where I first made acquaintance with *Vanity Fair*. .... Whenever one had the chance to suck up, one did suck up, and at the first smile one's hatred turned into a sort of cringing love.

This passage from 'Such, Such Were the Joys' does a good deal to explain why the opening scene of *1984* ends with the hero committing his hatred of Big Brother to writing in his diary, and why the book ends, when he has had his punishment in Room 101, with his tearful declaration that 'he loved Big Brother.' In between, the hero's spirit is broken by a man called O'Brien, in reality his enemy, who pretends to be his friend and even lends him a forbidden book he wants to read. As these parallels fall into place, one after another, like the tumblers in a combination lock, it is possible to see how Orwell's unconscious mind was working. Whether he knew it or not, what he did in *1984* was to send everybody in England to an enormous Crossgates to be as miserable as he had been.

There is another aspect of *1984* that merits examination: In it, the bombing nightmares that occur in *Keep the Aspidistra Flying* and *Coming Up for Air* repeat themselves with manic violence and a generalized sadism that is clearly beyond control. They begin in the first dozen pages, with an account of a newsreel in which a child is mutilated, and they continue throughout the book, alternating with even uglier fantasies about torture. The pretext is political realism, but it is hard not to feel that what is involved is to a considerable extent a matter of rousing fear for fear's sake. The book is Gothic, in the pejorative eighteenth-century sense of the word, in that it seems to relish the murky and the horrible. But this is not surprising; the mind behind the book is Gothic, and it reveals its characteristic pattern of distortion in the most astonishing contexts, sometimes in ways that are almost touching. While in Marrakech in 1939, Orwell feeds a gazelle:

Though it took the piece of bread I was holding out it obviously did not like me. It nibbled rapidly at the bread, then lowered its head and tried to butt me, then took another nibble and then butted again. Probably its idea was that if it could drive me away the bread would somehow remain hanging in mid-air.

Orwell cannot, or will not, remember that while they are sucklings the young of all such creatures butt their mothers as a signal to let down their milk, and form a habit that they tend to repeat when hand-fed with anything they like. Horses do it gently when you feed them sugar lumps. It is anything but a gesture of dislike. But then, there is nothing in the realm of common or uncommon experience that Orwell cannot stand on its head and interpret in a negative and essentially paranoid sense. There is another revelation of this warping in the first verse of the poem he wrote in 1935, and which he quotes in 'Why I Write':

> A happy vicar I might have been
> Two hundred years ago
> To preach upon eternal doom
> And watch my walnuts grow.

Vicars, as Christian ministers, are supposed to preach a gospel of love, and an offer of salvation, even now. The truth is that if Orwell had been a vicar two hundred years before he composed this verse, he would have been a Dean Swift, flinching from the same things with the same passion, and we would write of him as a French critic has written of Swift, 'He carries the rational criticism of values to a point where it menaces and impairs the very reasons for living.' We would also say of him, as the same critic has said of Swift, that 'his personality is a problem which has not as yet disclosed the whole of its secret.' Bad as Crossgates was, and bad as the state of the world was during Orwell's lifetime, neither justified a picture of a future order in which all children are treacherous and cruel, all women dangerous, and all men helpless unless cruel and conscienceless. Only the existence of a hidden wound can account for such a remorseless pessimism.

# 23. Henry Popkin, *Commonweal*

23 March 1956, pp. 650–1

---

Henry Popkin (b. 1924), Professor of English at the State University of New York in Buffalo; drama critic and editor.

---

Published twenty years ago in England, this interesting, minor early novel of George Orwell's is now appearing here for the first time. The time that has passed since it was written has not quite given it the character of an historical vignette. Chronologically, we may be, right now, almost midway between 1934, when the novel begins, and 1984, the year that Orwell did so much to make famous, but we have not yet achieved nearly half the horrors of that catastrophic year to come. Orwell's hero, Gordon Comstock, has to choose between earning a living and maintaining his integrity; even in the atomic age, such a choice has not become exotic or far-fetched. Witness Clifford Odets' melodramatic restatement of the same issue, *The Big Knife*, filmed only several months ago.[1]

Still, a certain notable development of the last few years has called into question the particular terms in which Orwell has stated Gordon's dilemma. At the beginning of the novel, Gordon has persuaded himself that he is somehow more independent if he clerks in a rather abysmal lending library than if he writes advertising copy. Either way he panders to mass culture, but it takes him the whole length of the novel to discover that it is pointless to insist on the difference between selling out in an advertising agency and staying pure in a bookstore.

But now, in 1956, the various arms of mass culture are amalgamating. Gordon's *bête noire*, the advertising industry, has expanded its operations. Over here, in addition to running election campaigns, it supervises television entertainment for many of the people who used to frequent Gordon's shabby haven, the lowbrow lending library. A Gordon Comstock in our decade would be much more overwhelmed

---

[1] Clifford Odets (1906–63), American playwright, wrote *The Big Knife* in 1949.

by the extensive operations of the advertising world; he would probably find fewer alternatives to sustain him before he fell back into the
waiting arms of the mass media.

The novel dramatizes one of Orwell's chronic dilemmas—the
strange ambiguity of his attitude toward British middle-class life.
Orwell became expert at describing its ugliness, its dullness, its hardships, and yet he could not help expressing a regretful admiration for
it. His hero is a rather eloquent mouthpiece for all the stock com-
plaints against the drab life of the middle classes, against the money
that holds the social structure together, and against the bourgeois
symbol—the aspidistra.

But chance flashes of eloquence are one thing, and the plot is another. As Gordon is drawn further and further into action, it becomes
increasingly apparent that his war on society is self-destructive. Poverty and discomfort prevent him from writing poetry. Life in his
grimy boarding house, under the watchful eye of his nosy landlady, is
in every respect the reverse of *la vie de bohème*.

His job is as false as the rest of his rebellion; arranged for by a
wealthy friend, it consists of lending books he despises to people whom
he equally despises. At times the masochistic side of his revolt can
be seen, when Gordon is savoring the effect of his wretchedness upon
his girl or his wealthy friend. He at last becomes aware of his obligation to life when he feels instinctively that his girl must bear his
child and not have an abortion. In this crisis, his theoretical, academic
misanthropy turns out to be greatly exaggerated. He gratefully
accepts his fate: 'It was what, in his secret heart, he had desired.' Even
the mighty bourgeois symbol looks better to him: 'The aspidistra is the
tree of life, he thought suddenly.'

# 24. Dorothy Van Ghent, *Yale Review*

Spring 1956, pp. 461–3

Dorothy Van Ghent (b. 1907), was Professor of English at the University of Vermont and author of *English Novel: Form and Function* (1956).

In George Orwell's *Keep the Aspidistra Flying* (published in England in 1936, now in its first American publication), the hero makes a valiant effort to live by what he thinks he knows: 'One's got to get right out of it, out of the money-stink. It was a kind of plot that he was nursing. He was as though dedicated to this war against money.' The aspidistra is the symbol of the pretensions and mendacities of the middle-class money-dependent situation Gordon Comstock refuses: he has a secret feud with the aspidistra: 'Many a time he had furtively attempted to kill it—starving it of water, grinding hot cigarette-ends against its stem, even mixing salt with its earth. But the beastly things are practically immortal. In almost any circumstances they can preserve a wilting, diseased existence.' The adaptation of I Corinthians xiii, used as epigraph, expresses the thesis of the greater part of the novel: 'Though I speak with the tongues of men and of angels, and have not money, I am become as sounding brass . . .' and so on, down to 'And now abideth faith, hope, money, these three; but the greatest of these is money.' Orwell hammers on this note so continuously, for so long a time, that he begins to sound like sounding brass himself;

Money and culture! In a country like England you can no more be cultured without money than you can join the Cavalry Club. . . . For after all, what is there behind it, except money? Money for the right kind of education, money for influential friends, money for leisure and peace of mind, money for trips to Italy. Money writes books, money sells them. Give me not righteousness, O Lord, give me money, only money.

There is enough truth in this exasperated satirical campaign to make some of it stick:

It was only now, when he was down to two quid a week and had practically cut himself off from the prospect of earning more that he grasped the real nature of the battle he was fighting. . . . It was not a question of hardship. You don't suffer real physical hardship on two quid a week, and if you did it wouldn't matter. It is in the brain and soul that lack of money damages you. Mental deadness, spiritual squalor—they seem to descend upon you inescapably when your income drops below a certain point.

Gordon sinks, with the courage of his convictions, into slummy apathy, finally becoming less an underground man than an unburied corpse. But at this point the wild truth that the book has so far had becomes a liability, for the action winds up as a romantic comedy of manners. Gordon's sweetheart rescues him by becoming pregnant; he rouses into marital and paternal responsibility, takes his old advertising job writing passions for Q. T. Sauce and Truweet Breakfast Crisps, and buys an aspidistra for the flat. Life is back where it started under the aspidistra, whose shade is no longer malign but salubrious, symbolizing the thrill of the natural struggle, of having babies, of buying furniture on the installment plan. One does not really know what the book is about; the satirical energy which Orwell expends on Gordon Comstock's world is too insistent and furious to be taken as the emotion informing a comedy of manners; Gordon's peace with the aspidistra makes his revolt merely a touchingly awkward and mistaken pose of youth; and the problem of maintaining moral identity in the lower-middle-class is broken in two like a surrealist cadaver with the legs of Don Quixote and the uxorious face of Dagwood, smiling from ear to ear.[1] The action of the novel is humorously pathetic, the characterizations winsome, but one feels that Orwell was not—here, at least—in complete command of his feelings and judgments.

[1] Dagwood is the simple-minded husband in the American comic strip 'Blondie'.

# 25. Isaac Rosenfeld, *Commentary*

June 1956, pp. 589–91

Isaac Rosenfeld (1919–56), American critic and novelist, author of *A Passage from Home* (1947) and *An Age of Enormity* (1962). *Commentary* is a monthly magazine of cultural affairs published by the American Jewish Committee.

It is strange that the fair, bland, decent, fresh-butter wholesome Orwell of the essays should have been such a terror in his fiction. One after another, the heroes of his novels come in for a thorough shellacking, a savage going-over hideous to behold; such, at least, is the lot of the central characters of *Burmese Days, Coming Up for Air, 1984,* and *Keep the Aspidistra Flying.* This violence is quite uncalled for; his Florys, George Bowlings, Winstons, and Gordons are ordinary men, neither conspicuously noble nor *sale type.* As far as I can see, his only grievance against them was that they did not measure up to the old-school definition of a gentleman. This remark may seem a bit unfair, as Orwell was always riding charges against old-school stuffiness—not in the manner of a St George, but in a casual and unpretentious way, flying only the colors of human decency.

But he was ahead of his age in being conservative, and this quality of his went largely unnoticed during his lifetime; he combined the gentlemanly with the democratic, an oxymoron typical of conservatism. Orwell detested the snobbery and class ground on which the definition of the gentleman stood, but the concept itself was a different matter, and in the greater part of his literary career he behaved in perfect accordance with it. Hence the fairness, the unassuming and disarming honesty of the writing, which we have come to regard as characteristic. Nor was the gentlemanly, as Orwell entertained it, such a narrow notion. The gentleman was for him the private citizen and irreducible unit of social life, more or less as John Stuart Mill thought of him, the free man of free mind and cultivation, whose continued existence was essential to the health of a democracy. Taken in this larger sense, the idea was by no means inconsistent with Orwell's socialism.

In *Keep the Aspidistra Flying*, Gordon Comstock, thirty-ish, a poet with a 'slim volume' to his credit entitled *Mice* (good press, bad sales, soon remaindered), chooses the life of poverty and failure in preference to a career in copywriting (for which, unfortunately, he has more talent than for poetry). He makes this choice for the sake of his writing, to keep himself free of the success drive, but in so doing he also stages the usual young man's rebellion against the middle-class expectations of his family. To his disgust, he discovers that it was all in vain. If success is a swindle, so is failure.

Living in furnished bedrooms, under nosey landladies, working at miserable jobs in dusty bookstores, he is too demoralized, too tired and lonely at night to do his writing, and too poor for beer and cigarettes, let alone amusements. His life is in no way more liberal than that of his drab, dull, penny-pinching family, and the same gloom hangs over him as hangs over his self-sacrificing spinster sister, off whom he sponges. Short on principles, he makes himself a martyr for his living conditions, and blames all his misfortunes on money. The literary world snubs him because he is a pauper, women are indifferent for the same reason, and if his own girl, Rosemary, has been holding out on him for years—for what other reason can she refuse him than his poverty? When she finally does sleep with him, it is out of pity and disgust for the hopelessly roach-ridden, torn-shirt, dirty-neck, who-gives-a-damn condition into which he has fallen. But as the result of this single act (and him too poor to buy contraceptives!) she becomes pregnant. Then Gordon, backed into a corner, takes the job in the advertising agency and does right by the girl. But his first official step as a husband is to buy an aspidistra. This house-plant had always been to him the abhorrent symbol of middle-class domesticity—as much as to say, 'He loved Big Brother.'

I have heard it said that this is a false interpretation; that Gordon, far from being the sniveler and weakling I take him to be, must be understood as something of a hero of our time. At the last moment, just as he is teetering on the brink of the inane, with the cliff crumbling away at his feet, he rights himself, comes to his senses, puts away childish things and chooses life, responsibility, and maturity. This is an attractive interpretation, and I am tempted to agree with it because it fits so well my own point about the conservative element in Orwell. Moreover, one of the central symbols of the novel, Rosemary's pregnnacy, does yield up such a meaning (among other meanings, however). But the reasons for withholding consent seem to me too strong to allow such a reading. The preliminary indictment of Gordon is too heavy, and the evidence against him is presented without mercy. We see him in every last, sickening detail of his folly, without a single ambiguous touch that one might interpret to his credit. Nor does Rosemary's pregnancy carry much hope for him. He does the right thing, but his decision is not the result of right thinking—he never has, and never acquires, the courage or intelligence to understand himself. His style of living will improve, he will wear clean shirts and eat well-balanced meals, but the regenerative meaning cannot reach him. He has been presented as the sort of creature who not only invites but deserves his misfortunes; it is too late to save him. The pattern is so well established that the life symbol of the pregnancy is wasted on him—the child is the final springing of the trap. Not only success, not only failure, life itself is a swindle.

I return to my first observation, that Orwell was always mauling his characters. Here, I believe, lay his failure as a novelist; not that he was brutal, but that he did not justify his brutality in fictional terms. There is no good reason for walloping Gordon, or Flory, or the others. Their only offense, as far as I can see, is that they were not gentlemen. They lacked the grace, strength, resourcefulness, dignity, good sense, and clear understanding; neither nature nor society would bend to them or receive them among the elect. Modern fiction is full of such types, but Orwell, evidently, was unable to leave the shabby, poor bloke alone; I suspect he felt put on the spot when he confronted him. The reminiscences which Orwell's friends have published show him forever struggling with, and striving to kill off, his own gentlemanly ideal. The contradiction in himself is matched in the characters. He deliberately chose the bloke, the sniveler, the man who cannot make it, and to hell with the gentleman—and then punished them cruelly for not being gentlemen.

But why pick on Gordon? Many a dead horse has been flayed, this one was skinless to begin with. Because he makes all the better a carcass for his author's self-destructive appetite to feed upon.

Because such a procedure is unjustified in fiction, Orwell soon leads us out of bounds; and I, for one, could never resist speculating on his self-destructiveness. I know very little about him, and I can't say how accurate my impression is, but under the bland, fair, mild, empirical, and fair-minded manner which he perfected in the essays, I feel he was full of self-hatred, rage, spite and contempt. This is no reason for disapproving of a novelist, so long as the personal motive is well covered. In Orwell it was usually uncovered, it showed through the devices of his fiction and called attention to himself when he should have been most in control to direct attention to his characters. Their undoing became an obvious substitute for his own, and one smarted and felt uncomfortable—a relationship to an author which it is hard to pass off as literary.

Even so, this would not have mattered—and in 1984 it was of little importance—if only he had been able, more often, to find an appropriate fictional object to stand in for himself and receive the assault. For there are ways of conducting the flagellation so that the ego, to all appearances, is spared; one can, for instance, turn the self inside out and convert it into a world, or find cause, among public objects, for one's secret discontent. This he succeeded in doing in 1984, where a world is present; Winston goes down, but the totalitarian mystique goes with him. In the other novels, too little of the world is involved in the destruction of the hero. And in *Keep the Aspidistra Flying* he drags down the drain with him nothing more than a few dried pips and peels of a somewhat off-center anti-bourgeois tirade: a desiccated family, a spinsterish sister, a sisterish girl friend, and a wealthy and therefore uneasy socialist and literary patron, one Ravelston, who befriends Gordon and makes him feel all the more disgusted with himself. It is Gordon all the way, and therefore Orwell all the way. And wherever Gordon can't quite completely symbolize his author's *Selbstmord*[1] (after all, Orwell *was* a gentleman, and no Gordon by a long shot), Ravelston fills in for him. Anything that won't fit Gordon will slip easily and without pinch onto Ravelston's foot.

Now this is nonsense, and terribly dated, like the old adolescent rebellion against shoe polish. In a much sounder and more honest investigation of poverty, *Down and Out in Paris and London*, Orwell told the truth about the self in the middle-class world, how one lives in it under the threat of starvation and resorts to devices to outwit the wolf—devices, more often than not, shameful and desperate, but still part of the dirty business of staying alive in a dirty world. He did not have to wear a stinking shirt by way of a Gordon in false pride, and even falser self-punishment, for his ability to come to terms with this world (this is, however, an accurate touch in the characterization of Gordon, since nothing galls the writer in advertising more than the

[1] Suicide.

87

recognition that he's good at it). No, he would have loved a clean shirt, clean linen, a bath, a decent living, and a circle of his peers. But in *Down and Out* Orwell was writing in his characteristic mien of fairness to all, himself included, and he made no bones about his reasonableness. He condoned his own failure to be a gentleman or—it comes to the same thing—managed to forgive himself for being one.

# 26. Louis Simpson, *Hudson Review*

Summer 1956, pp. 306–7

Louis Simpson (b. 1923 in Jamaica), poet and Professor of English at the State University of New York in Stonybrook; author of *At the End of the Open Road* (1963).

Significantly, the hero of Orwell's *Keep the Aspidistra Flying* is employed around books: he works in a London bookshop. The time is before World War II. As Gordon Comstock, 'last member of the Comstock family, aged twenty-nine and rather motheaten already' looks out from the shop, he confronts a hoarding covered with posters:

A gallery of monstrous doll-faces—pink vacuous faces, full of goofy optimism. Q. T. Sauce, Trusweet Breakfast Crisps ('Kiddies clamour for their Breakfast Crisps'), Kangaroo Burgundy, Vitamilt Chocolate, Bovex. Of them all, the Bovex one oppressed Gordon the most. A spectacled rat-faced clerk, with patent-leather hair, sitting at a cafe table grinning over a white mug of Bovex. 'Corner Table enjoys his meal with Bovex,' the legend ran.

As he looks around, Gordon Comstock pieces together lines for a poem about the dreariness of the lower-middle-class life, the clerk's hopes and terrors. He is also working on a long poem called *London Pleasures*, which will never be finished. He is obsessed with the power of money. 'Though I speak with the tongues of men and angels, and have not

money, I am become as a sounding brass, or a tinkling cymball'—
so he adapts First Corinthians. Of course, he could have a better job if
he wanted it, writing advertising copy—but then, he'd have to be a
gentleman. . . . If you cannot get money, he reasons, perhaps the way
to beat the money racket is to give it up altogether—escape from the
clerk's hell by sinking downward. He chucks this job, which has
managed to keep him looking respectable, though never well fed, and
goes to work for a bookseller 'in the desolate stretch of road south of
Waterloo Bridge.' He lives in a slum:

Under ground, under ground! Down in the safe soft womb of earth, where
there is no getting of jobs or losing of jobs, no relatives or friends to plague
you, no hope, fear, ambition, honour, duty—no *duns* of any kind. That was
where he wished to be.

Only a few shillings less a week, but he has crossed a line. He is running down. It no longer seems worthwhile to try; and soon he cannot
try, for want of nourishment. From this hole, deepening into a grave,
he is rescued by his girl, Rosemary, who visits him in his miserable bed
and becomes pregnant. When Gordon realizes that they are going to
have a child, a warm sense of responsibility rises up and animates
him. They will get married. He throws away his unfinished *London
Pleasures*, and with it his artistic ambitions. He will work at advertising
copy or anything else. In his window he will keep and care for an
aspidistra, the rubbery plant that is the symbol of respectability.

This may be the best book Orwell wrote. Here the vision of lower
depths which pervades *Down and Out in Paris and London*, is put to
use. The nightmare terrors of *Nineteen Eighty-Four* are made relevant
to our own everyday lives. But more than this, there is fiction for its
own sake. I do not know of anything better in its way than the account
of the expedition made by Gordon and Rosemary, their day in the
country. The weather lures them on and they get lost. They find an
eating place at last; it is, of course, too expensive—but it's too late to
back out:

It was exactly like an aquarium. It was built entirely of greenish glass, and it was
so damp and chilly that you almost have fancied yourself under water. You
could both see and smell the river outside. . . . The beef and salad were corpse-
cold and did not seem like real food at all. They tasted like water. The rolls,
also, though stale, were damp. The reedy Thames water seemed to have got
into everything.

Yet—and this is where Orwell's unflagging honesty pays off—these poor lovers generate a warmth between them which, because we have descended with them all the way, we too are able to enjoy:

And at this moment the sun burst out again and the dreary aquarium was flooded with pleasant greenish light. Gordon and Rosemary felt suddenly warm and happy. . . . Over their glasses their eyes met. She was looking at him with a sort of yielding irony. 'I'm your mistress,' her eyes said; 'what a joke!'. . . . There was deep intimacy between them. They could have sat there for hours, just looking at one another and talking of trivial things that had meanings for them and for nobody else.

Rosemary is unique as a created character in Orwell's fiction. Gordon we know only too well—he is an Orwell without Orwell's talent. But Rosemary, in her mousey but tenacious femininity, and above all, in the absolutely uncalculating quality of her affection, shows that Orwell had a great potential where a novelist must have it, in the love and understanding of character for its own sake. It is Rosemary, after all, who takes a chance; she is the revolutionary in the story—as is the girl in *Nineteen Eighty-Four*; more revolutionary than Gordon, with his half-baked Marxism, his acerbated vision of suburban houses tumbling down under a rain of enemy bombs. Rosemary loves him just because he has been reduced to absurdity. She is, if you look at her from a conventional angle, a mouse-trap; in a larger view, the view Gordon, to his credit, is able to take, she is a pocket goddess, '*Vénus toute entière à sa proie attachée.*'[1]

[1] 'Venus completely attached to her prey,' from Racine's *Phèdre* (1677).

# THE ROAD TO WIGAN PIER

1937 (1st American edition 1958)

## 27. Victor Gollancz, Foreword

1937

*The Road to Wigan Pier* (London: Gollancz, 1937), pp. xi–xxiv. Victor Gollancz (1893–1967) was Orwell's first publisher.

This foreword is addressed to members of the Left Book Club (to whom *The Road to Wigan Pier* is being sent as the March Choice) and to them alone: members of the general public are asked to ignore it. But for technical considerations, it would have been deleted from the ordinary edition.

I have also to make it clear that, while the three selectors of the Left Book Club Choices—Strachey, Laski[1] and myself—were all agreed that a Foreword was desirable, I alone am responsible for what is written here—though I think that Laski and Strachey would agree with me.

Why did we think that a Foreword was desirable? Because we find that many members—a surprisingly large number—have the idea that in some sort of way a Left Book Club Choice, first, represents the views of the three selectors, and, secondly, incorporates the Left Book Club 'policy.' A moment's thought should show that the first suggestion could be true only in the worst kind of Fascist State, and that the second is a contradiction in terms: but we get letters so frequently —most interesting and vital letters—which say: 'Surely you and Laski and Strachey cannot believe what So-and-So says on page so-and-so of Such-and-Such a book,' that there can be no doubt at all that the misconception exists.

The plain facts are, of course, (a) that the three selectors, although

[1] John Strachey wrote about Orwell in *The Strangled Cry* (London, 1962), pp. 23–32. For Laski see the headnote to No. 30.

91

they have that broad general agreement without which successful committee work is impossible, differ as to shade and *nuance* of opinion in a hundred ways; (*b*) that even if they were in perfect agreement on every point, nothing could be worse than a stream of books which expressed this same point of view over and over again; and (*c*) that their only criterion for a Choice is whether or not the reading and discussion of it will be helpful for the general struggle against Fascism and war. And that brings me on to this question of Left Book Club 'policy.' The Left Book Club has no 'policy': or rather it has no policy other than that of equipping people to fight against war and Fascism. As I have said elsewhere, it would not even be true to say that the People's Front is the 'policy' of the Left Book Club, though all three selectors are enthusiastically in favour of it. What we rather feel is that by giving a wide distribution to books which represent many shades of Left opinion (and perhaps, most of all, by providing facilities for the discussion of those books in the 300 local centres and circles that have sprung up all over the country) we are creating the mass basis without which a genuine People's Front is impossible. In other words, the People's Front is not the 'policy' of the Left Book Club, but the very existence of the Left Book Club tends towards a People's Front.

But we feel that a Foreword to *The Road to Wigan Pier* is desirable, not merely in view of the misconception to which I have referred, but also because we believe that the value of the book, for some members, can be greatly increased if just a hint is given of certain vital considerations that arise from a reading of it. The value can be *increased*: as to the positive value itself, no one of us has the smallest doubt. For myself, it is a long time since I have read so *living* a book, or one so full of a burning indignation against poverty and oppression.

The plan of the book is this. In Part I Mr Orwell gives a first-hand account of the life of the working class population of Wigan and elsewhere. It is a terrible record of evil conditions, foul housing, wretched pay, hopeless unemployment and the villainies of the Means Test: it is also a tribute to courage and patience—patience far too great. We cannot imagine anything more likely to rouse the 'unconverted' from their apathy than a reading of this part of the book; and we are announcing in the current number of *The Left News* a scheme by means of which we hope members may make use of the book for this end. These chapters really *are* the kind of thing that makes converts.

In the second part, Mr Orwell starts with an autobiographical study, which he thinks necessary in order to explain the class feelings and prejudices of a member of 'the lower upper-middle class,' as he describes himself: and he then goes on to declare his adherence to Socialism. But before doing so he comes forward as a devil's advocate, and explains, with a great deal of sympathy, why, in his opinion, so many of the best people detest Socialism; and he finds the reason to lie in the 'personal inferiority' of so many Socialists and in their mistaken methods of propaganda. His conclusion is that present methods should be thrown overboard, and that we should try to enrol everyone in the fight for Socialism and against Fascism and war (which he rightly sees to be disasters in the face of which little else is of much importance) by making the elemental appeal of 'liberty' and 'justice'. What he envisages is a great league of 'oppressed' against 'oppressors'; in this battle members of all classes may fight side by side—the private schoolmaster and the jobless Cambridge graduate with the clerk and the unemployed miner; and then, when they have so fought, 'we of the sinking middle class . . . may sink without further struggles into the working class where we belong, and probably when we get there it will not be so dreadful as we feared, for, after all, we have nothing to lose but our aitches.'[1]

Now the whole of this second part is highly provocative, not merely in its general argument, but also in detail after detail. I had, in point of fact, marked well over a hundred minor passages about which I thought I should like to argue with Mr Orwell in this Foreword; but I find now that if I did so the space that I have set aside would be quickly used up, and I should wear out my readers' patience. It is necessary, therefore, that I should limit myself to some of the broader aspects.

In the first place, no reader must forget that Mr Orwell is throughout writing precisely as a member of the 'lower upper-middle class' or, let us say without qualification, as a member of the middle class. It may seem stupid to insist on this point, as nothing could be clearer than Mr Orwell's own insistence on it: but I can well imagine a reader coming across a remark every now and again which infuriates him even to the extent of making him forget this most important fact: *that such a remark can be made by Mr Orwell is* (if the reader follows me) *part of Mr Orwell's own case*. I have in mind in particular a lengthy passage in which Mr Orwell embroiders the theme that, in the opinion of the middle class in general, the working class smells! I believe myself

---

[1] The quotation from Orwell echoes the last lines of the *Communist Manifesto* (1848): 'The proletarians have nothing to lose but their chains. They have a world to win.'

that Mr Orwell is exaggerating violently: I do not myself think that more than a very small proportion of them have this quaint idea (I admit that I may be a bad judge of the question, for I am a Jew, and passed the years of my early boyhood in a fairly close Jewish community; and, among Jews of this type, class distinctions do not exist —Mr Orwell says that they do not exist among any sort of Oriental). But clearly *some* of them think like this—Mr Orwell quotes a very odd passage from one of Mr Somerset Maugham's books—and the whole of this chapter throws a most interesting light on the reality of class distinctions. I know, in fact, of no other book in which a member of the middle class exposes with such complete frankness the shameful way in which he was brought up to think of large numbers of his fellow men. This section will be, I think, of the greatest value to middle class and working class members of the Left Book Club alike: to the former because, if they are honest, they will search their own minds; to the latter, because it will make them understand what they are 'up against' —if they do not understand it already. In any case, the moral is that the class division of Society, economic in origin, must be superseded by the classless society (I fear Mr Orwell will regard this as a wretched and insincere cliché) in which alone the shame and indignity so vividly described by Mr Orwell—I mean of the middle class, not of the lower class—will be impossible.

Mr Orwell now proceeds to act as devil's advocate for the case against Socialism.

He looks at Socialists as a whole and finds them (with a few exceptions) a stupid, offensive and insincere lot. For my own part I find no similarity whatsoever between the picture as Mr Orwell paints it and the picture as I see it. There is an extraordinary passage in which Mr Orwell seems to suggest that almost every Socialist is a 'crank'; and it is illuminating to discover from this passage just what Mr Orwell means by the word. It appears to mean anyone holding opinions not held by the majority—for instance, any feminist, pacifist, vegetarian or advocate of birth control. This last is really startling. In the first part of the book Mr Orwell paints a most vivid picture of wretched rooms swarming with children, and clearly becoming more and more unfit for human habitation the larger the family grows: but he apparently considers anyone who wishes to enlighten people as to how they can have a normal sexual life without increasing this misery as a crank![1]

[1] Orwell's attack on birth control *is* illogical and contradictory. Rosemary's pregnancy in *Keep the Aspidistra Flying* is the result of similar attitudes on the part of Gordon.

The fact, of course, is that there is no more 'commonsensical' work than that which is being done at the present time by the birth control clinics up and down the country—and common sense, as I understand it, is the antithesis of crankiness. I have chosen this particular example, because the answer to Mr Orwell is to be found in his own first part: but the answers to Mr Orwell's sneers at pacifism and feminism are as obvious. Even about vegetarianism (I apologise to vegetarians for the 'even') Mr Orwell is astray. The majority of vegetarians are vegetarians not because 'they want to add a few miserable years to their wretched lives' (I cannot find the exact passage at the moment, but that is roughly what Mr Orwell says), but because they find something disgusting in the consumption of dead flesh. I am not saying that I agree with them: but anyone who has seen a man—or woman—eating a raw steak (*saignant*, as the French say so much more frankly) will feel a sneaking sympathy.

The fact is that in passages like that to which I have referred, and in numerous other places in this part of the book, Mr Orwell is still a victim of that early atmosphere, in his home and public school, which he himself has so eloquently exposed. His conscience, his sense of decency, his understanding of realities tell him to declare himself a Socialist: but fighting against this compulsion there is in him all the time a compulsion far less conscious but almost—though fortunately not quite—as strong: the compulsion to conform to the mental habits of his class. That is why Mr Orwell, looking at a Socialist, smells out (to use a word which we have already met in another connection) a certain crankiness in him; and he finds, as examples of this crankiness, a hatred of war (pacifism), a desire to see woman no longer oppressed by men (feminism), and a refusal to withhold the knowledge which will add a little happiness to certain human lives (birth control).

This conflict of two compulsions is to be found again and again throughout the book. For instance, Mr Orwell calls himself a 'half intellectual'; but the truth is that he is at one and the same time an extreme intellectual and a violent anti-intellectual. Similarly he is a frightful snob—still (he must forgive me for saying this), and a genuine hater of every form of snobbery. For those who can read, the exhibition of this conflict is neither the least interesting nor the least valuable part of the book: for it shows the desperate struggle through which a man must go before, in our present society, his mind can really become free —if indeed that is ever possible.

I have said enough, I think, to show, by means of one example, the way in which I should venture to criticise the whole of this section of the book. But there is another topic here which cannot be passed over without a word or two. Among the grave faults which Mr Orwell finds in Socialist propaganda is the glorification of industrialism, and in particular of the triumphs of industrialisation in the Soviet Union (the words 'Magnitogorsk' and 'Dnieper' make Mr Orwell see red—or rather the reverse). I have a fairly wide acquaintance among Socialists of every colour, and I feel sure that the whole of this section is based on a misunderstanding. To leave Russia out of account for the moment, no Socialist of my acquaintance *glorifies* industrialism. What the Socialist who has advanced beyond the most elementary stage says (and I really mean what he *says*, not what he *ought to say*) is that capitalist industrialism is a certain stage which we have reached in the business of providing for our needs, comforts and luxuries: that though it may be amusing to speculate on whether or not a pre-industrialist civilisation might be a more attractive one in which to live, it is a matter of plain common sense that, whatever individuals may wish, industrialism will go on: that (if Mr Orwell will forgive the jargon) such 'contradictions' have developed in the machine of capitalist industrialism that the thing is visibly breaking down: that such break-down means poverty, unemployment and war: and that the only solution is the supersession of anarchic capitalist industrialism by planned Socialist industrialism. In other words, it is not industrialism that the Socialist advocates (a man does not advocate the sun or the moon), but Socialist industrialism as opposed to capitalist industrialism.

Mr Orwell, of course, understands this quite elementary fact perfectly well: but his understanding conflicts with his love of beauty, and the result is that, instead of pointing out that industrialism can be the parent of beauty, if at all, then only under planned Socialist industrialism, he turns to rend the mythical figure of the Socialist who thinks that gaspipe chairs are more beautiful than Chippendale chairs. (Incidentally, gaspipe chairs *are* more beautiful than the worst Chippendale chairs, though not nearly as beautiful as the best.)

As to the particular question of the Soviet Union, the insistence of Socialists on the achievements of Soviet industrialisation arises from the fact that the most frequent argument which Socialists have to face is precisely this: 'I agree with you that Socialism would be wholly admirable if it would work—but it wouldn't.' Somewhere or other Mr Orwell speaks of intelligent and unintelligent Socialists, and brushes aside people who say 'it wouldn't work' as belonging to the latter category. My own experience is that this is still the major *sincere* objection to Socialism on the part of decent people, and the major *insincere* objection on the part of indecent people who in fact are thinking of their dividends. It is true that the objection was more frequently heard in 1919 than in 1927, in 1927 than at the end of the first Five Year Plan, and at the end of the first Five Year Plan than to-day—the reason being precisely that quite so direct a *non possumus* hardly carries conviction, when the achievements of the Soviet Union are there for everyone to see. But people will go on hypnotising themselves and others with a formula, even when that formula is patently outworn: so that it is still necessary, and will be necessary for a long time yet, to show that modern methods of production *do* work under Socialism and *no longer work* under capitalism.

But Mr Orwell's attack on Socialists who are for ever singing paeans of praise to Soviet industrialisation is also connected with his general dislike of Russia—he even commits the curious indiscretion of referring to Russian commissars as 'half-gramophones, half-gangsters.' Here again the particular nature of Mr Orwell's unresolved conflict is not difficult to understand; nor is it difficult to understand why Mr Orwell states that almost all people of real sensitiveness, and in particular almost all writers and artists and the like, are hostile to Socialism—whereas the truth is that in several countries, for instance in France, a great number, and probably the majority, of writers and artists are Socialists or even Communists.

All this is not to say that (while this section gives, in my view, a distorted picture of what Socialists are like and what they say) *Socialists themselves* will not find there much that is of value to them, and many shrewd pieces of, at any rate, half-truth. In particular I think that Mr Orwell's accusation of arrogance and dogmatism is to a large extent justified: in fact as I think back on what I have already written here I am not sure that a good deal of it is not itself arrogant and dogmatic. His accusation of narrowness and of sectarianism is not so well grounded to-day as it would have been a few years ago: but here also there is still plenty of room for improvement. The whole section indeed is, when all has been said against it, a challenge to us Socialists to put our house and our characters in order.

Having criticised us in this way (for though Mr Orwell insists that he is speaking merely as devil's advocate and saying what other people say, quite often and quite obviously he is really speaking *in propria persona*—or perhaps I had better say 'in his own person,' otherwise

Mr Orwell will class me with 'the snobs who write in Latinised English' or words to that effect) Mr Orwell joins us generously and whole-heartedly, but begs us to drop our present methods of propaganda, to base our appeal on freedom and liberty, and to see ourselves as a league of the oppressed against the oppressors. Nothing could be more admirable as a first approach; and I agree that we shall never mobilise that vast mass of fundamentally decent opinion which undoubtedly exists (as, for instance, the Peace Ballot showed) and which we *must* mobilise if we are to defeat Fascism, unless we make our first appeal to its generous impulses. It is from a desire for liberty and justice that we must draw our militant strength; and the society which we are trying to establish is one in which that liberty and that justice will be incarnate. But between the beginning in that first impulse to fight, and the end when, the fight won, our children or our children's children will live in the achievement, there is a great deal of hard work and hard thinking to be done—less noble and more humdrum than the appeal to generosities, but no less important if a real victory is to be won, and if this very appeal is not to be used to serve ends quite opposite to those at which we aim.

It is indeed significant that so far as I can remember (he must forgive me if I am mistaken) Mr Orwell does not once define what he *means* by Socialism; nor does he explain *how* the oppressors oppress, nor even what he understands by the words 'liberty' and 'justice.' I hope he will not think I am quibbling: he will not, I think, if he remembers that the word 'Nazi' is an abbreviation of the words 'National Socialist'; that in its first phase Fascism draws its chief strength from an attack on 'oppression'—'oppression' by capitalists, multiple stores, Jews and foreigners; that no word is commoner in German speeches to-day than 'Justice'; and that if you 'listen in' any night to Berlin or Munich, the chances are that you will hear the 'liberty' of totalitarian Germany —'Germans have become free by becoming a united people'—compared with the misery of Stalin's slaves.

What is indeed essential, once that first appeal has been made to 'liberty' and 'justice,' is a careful and patient study of just *how* the thing works: of *why* capitalism inevitably means oppression and injustice and the horrible class society which Mr Orwell so brilliantly depicts: of *the means* of transition to a Socialist society in which there will be neither oppressor nor oppressed. In other words, *emotional* Socialism must become scientific Socialism—even if some of us have to concern ourselves with what Mr Orwell, in his extremely intellectualist anti-intellectualism, calls 'the sacred sisters' Thesis, Antithesis and Synthesis.

What I feel, in sum, is that this book, more perhaps than any that the Left Book Club has issued, clarifies—for me at least—the whole meaning and purpose of the Club. On the one hand we have to go out and rouse the apathetic by showing them the utter vileness which Mr Orwell lays bare in the first part of the book, and by appealing to the decency which is in them; on the other hand we have so to equip ourselves by thought and study that we run no danger, having once mobilised all this good will, of seeing it dispersed for lack of trained leaders—lance corporals as well as generals—or even of seeing it used as the shock troops of our enemies.

# 28. Walter Greenwood, *Tribune*

## 12 March 1937, p. 12

Walter Greenwood (1904–74), English novelist and playwright of working-class life, author of *Love on the Dole* (1933).

This book is an account of a tour made by Mr Orwell in Durham, Yorkshire, Lancashire, South Wales and London. It also provides Mr Orwell with an opportunity to air his views on Socialism, Fascism and the works of some authors.

The first part of the book is a studied account of the conditions of life of the people in the areas mentioned, and it is authentic and first rate.

Mr Orwell has the gift of writing vividly, of creating in the mind's eye a picture of the scene described. He takes you down a mine and you crouch with him in the narrow galleries; he shows you miners on their knees shovelling coal over their shoulders, and your muscles begin to ache—that is, if the miners he happens to be writing about are lucky enough to be working.

He shows you what happens when they are not working: you get vivid pictures of hordes of skilled men scratching the surfaces of the 'slag heaps' (huge deposits of dirt dumped by the pit-head) for bits of coal for their own fires, while, down below, a couple of hundred feet or so, are the coal seams which are 'not economic' to work.

These first three chapters show Mr Orwell at his best as a keen observer with great skill at character drawing. But the chapter on housing ought not to have been marred by the long quotations from Mr Orwell's notebooks.

Most readers, unfortunately, are mentally spineless and, as soon as they see tables of statistics or anything that looks like the report of a sanitary inspector, turn the pages to a more agreeable chapter or lose interest in the book altogether.

Up to this point which takes you half-way through the book, Mr Orwell has the reader at his mercy in a most compelling fashion. Thereafterwards, when he begins to explain himself in relation to Socialism, when he begins to tell you what this and other 'isms' are, he has you with him one moment and provoked beyond endurance the next.

I cannot remember having been so infuriated for a long time than by some of the things he says here. And, since his arguments are tied up with each other in such a manner as to make quotation and criticism either interminable or unfair to the author, the final judgment must be left to Mr Orwell's readers.

For one, at least, it held his interest from cover to cover, which, these days, is an achievement in itself.

# 29. Arthur Calder-Marshall, *Time and Tide*

20 March 1937, p. 382

Arthur Calder-Marshall (b. 1908), English novelist, biographer and critic.

Of Mr Orwell's book, there is little to say except praise. . . . Starting with the usual middle-class public school education, he has attempted to join the [working] class. The first part of his book is a description of life in the North of England. It opens with the most realistic description of a lodging house over a tripe shop, kept by two terrifying people called Brooker. The other lodgers are two old-age pensioners (paying their weekly ten shillings for board and lodging, their lives insured by the Brookers); Mr Reilly, a mining mechanic; a Scotch miner, injured in a pit accident; and a man on the P.A.C.[1] named Joe.

Mr Brooker was a dark, small-boned, sour, Irish-looking man, and astonishingly dirty. I don't think I ever once saw his hands clean. As Mrs Brooker was now an invalid, he prepared most of the food, and like all people with permanently dirty hands he had a peculiarly intimate, lingering manner of handling things. If he gave you a slice of bread-and-butter, there was always a black thumb-print on it. Even in the morning when he descended into the mysterious den behind Mrs Brooker's sofa and fished out the tripe, his hands were already black. . . . I do not know how often fresh consignments of tripe were ordered, but it was at long intervals, for Mrs Brooker used to date events by it. 'Let me see now, I've had in three lots of froze (frozen tripe) since that happened.' We lodgers were never given tripe to eat. At the time I imagined that this was because tripe was too expensive; I have since thought that it was merely because we knew too much about it. The Brookers never ate tripe themselves, I noticed.

Mr Orwell did not spend his whole time in this depressing house.

On the day when there was a full chamber-pot under the breakfast table I decided to leave. *The place was beginning to depress me.* (My italics.)

[1] Public Assistance Committee.

It is in some ways a pity that Mr Orwell has devoted his first chapter to the delineation of a squalor that may be typical of lodging-houses in industrial areas, but lacks the humanity of even the most poverty-stricken working-class homes: a pity, because many tender-minded readers may be deterred from proceeding to the later chapters. These later chapters, devoted to housing conditions and conditions of living in employment and unemployment, are full of accurately observed information (supported by 32 plates, illustrating the condition of villas, schools, etc.), and interpreted by explanatory material of first-class importance to anybody interested in the way four-fifths of the population of this country live.

The picture which Mr Orwell paints is appalling: but from my own experience, I have not the least doubt that it is true. Mr Orwell is detached. He writes of what he has seen. He does not exaggerate. There is no need to. Indeed, to gain credence from the thousands of self-righteous people, whose comfort depends on ignoring the plight of slum-dwellers, it is necessary to dilute the truth.

Having established this picture, Mr Orwell proceeds to explain how he came to undertake his investigation. He describes his childhood, the inculcation of class hatred in himself, his service in Burma as an Imperial policeman, his resignation from the force under an intolerable sense of guilt, his deliberate association with tramps and down-and-outs, and his final identification with the working class. It is impossible, he says with considerable honesty, for any man or woman brought up in the middle class to throw off the traditions of his class and *merge with* the workers. But it is possible (provided the unconscious antagonisms are recognized), to *co-operate* with the working class, in whom Mr Orwell, in common with many writers of his generation, sees the cultural and political hope of the present and future.

What amounts to a third section of the book is the examination of what is to be done to remedy unemployment and the fear of war. Mr Orwell accepts the aims and the programme of socialism without comment. What interests him is, 'Why, given the self-evident superiority of socialism as a social system, socialism should appear still so remote?' His explanation is one-sided. He blames the failure on to the socialists entirely. (1) Socialists accept the ideal of a Wellsian machine age without criticism, whereas the majority of people rightly distrust the advance of science without rigid control. (2) Socialists are cranks. There is no connection between social*ism* and for example vegetarianism. Yet many social*ists* are vegetarians. (3) Too much emphasis is placed on the doctrinaire acceptance of Marxism; whereas the broad aims of socialism should be the basis of the appeal to the public.

There is admittedly much to be said for these criticisms, though both the second and third are not as applicable as they were some time ago. They are criticisms which I should like all socialists and communists to take to heart. Yet they do not explain the failure of socialism during the last ten years. The explanation rests on two factors, one negative, the other positive. The power of right-wing organs of propaganda is colossal, in education, press, radio, films, etc. Yet these organs of propaganda would be powerless in face of a strong Trade Union leadership. Since the General Strike, the leadership of the Trade Union has been concentrated on Co-operation. Until the Trade Unions resume a militant policy, socialism will be thwarted by those very forces which were expected to achieve it. Mr Orwell advocates a United Front. But it is not the Socialist League, the I.L.P., the Communist Party or the Liberal Party which opposes this sinking of differences. It is the mandarins of Transport House. Meanwhile, the hungry sheep look up and are not led.

# 30. H. J. Laski, *Left News*

March 1937, pp. 275–6

---

Harold Laski (1893–1950), Professor of Political Science at the London School of Economics, intellectual spokesman of the Labour Party, co-founder of the Left Book Club. In 'Politics and the English Language' Orwell uses Laski to exemplify turgid language and the 'mental vices from which we now suffer' (IV, p. 128).

---

In a sense, I am not quite certain that this note of mine is not really superfluous. Most of what I think about Mr Orwell's book has been admirably expressed by Gollancz in his Foreword; and the temptation is to let it go at that. But there are, perhaps, certain additional things it is worth while to emphasise, and Mr Orwell's method of approach is a useful basis upon which to say them.

The first part of his book is, I think, admirable propaganda for our ideas. It takes an ugly section of British life, and it forces us to confront it for the ugly thing that it is. Every social observer knows that what Mr Orwell has here so graphically described is true of large parts of not only industrial Britain, but of rural Britain as well. It explains the dreadful picture of a life void of colour and beauty that Mr Beales and Mr Lambert gave us in their remarkable *Memoirs of the Unemployed*. It provides a useful background to the account Wal Hannington has recently given us in his very valuable *Unemployed Struggles*. The men and women who marched behind him with such fortitude and endurance came from just the kind of environment Mr Orwell has made living in all its inherent ugliness.

The value of this part of his work, as I see it, is the kind of value we get from Dickens' *Hard Times*, or from the novels of Zola and Balzac. The danger for all of us is, in these matters, that we tend to make of living and suffering men and women a kind of composite picture, which easily becomes a concept fitting into the habitual mental picture of the world we carry about with us. As soon as that occurs, it ceases seriously to worry us in a way that compels action. It rests somewhere within our consciousness as a thing only awakened when some special experience makes it concrete again. We assume that we can do little about it. It is unpleasant and, so far as we can, we repress it. That is why, for hundreds of thousands of people in this country, the picture Mr Orwell paints is as unmeaning as though it were written in some remote tongue. They have never experienced it, it does not trouble them as reality. I believe that the wide distribution of his book among such people would be the conference upon them of an awareness that a civilisation of which such ugliness is an integral part is unhealthy in its foundations. But having, very ably, depicted a disease, Mr Orwell does what so many well-meaning people do: needing a remedy (he knows it is socialism), he offers an incantation instead. He thinks that an appeal to 'liberty' and 'justice' will, on the basis of facts such as he has described, bring people tumbling over one another into the Socialist Party. People, he seems to say, who have seen ugliness as he has seen it will become socialists if only they can be made to understand that socialists are not 'cranks' but people like themselves. The walls of Jericho, as it were, will tumble down if only the trumpeter has the right accent and the right kind of clothes when he blows the trumpet.

This view is based on fallacies so elementary that I should doubt the necessity of explaining them as fallacies were it not that there are so many people who share Mr Orwell's view. Its basic error is the belief that we all mean the same things by liberty and justice. Most emphatically we do not. If Mr Orwell will reflect for a moment on the mentality implied in the attitude of those who think that socialism is confiscation, or who could not see that our present rule in India is a denial of freedom, he will realise that there is not a common agreement in our society about the content of the ends we ought to seek. And further reflection should convince him that, in a large measure, our differences in the views we take about the content of those ends very closely reflect our class-position in society. Broadly speaking, those who to-day own the instruments of production believe that our system is both just and free on the whole. They may well agree that improvements are wholly desirable. But they are rarely prepared to pay the price for those improvements if paying it means that they are not fully to retain the privileges born of their ownership. Even democratically to legislate them out of that ownership by Act of Parliament leaves them angry in the belief that they have been deprived of 'justice' and 'freedom.'

Mr Orwell ought to consider the implications of John Bright's[1]

[1] John Bright (1811–89), English radical statesman.

hostility to the Factory Acts; but John Bright believed in 'justice' and 'freedom.' Lord Shaftesbury saw the 'justice' of the Factory Acts; but Mr and Mrs Hammond[1] have pointed out that the great landowner regarded the agricultural trade-union movement of Joseph Arch[2] with 'disdainful arrogance.' If he will consider that the Supreme Court of the United States has, in the full belief that it was doing 'justice,' so interpreted freedom of contract as to make it the main barrier against exactly that social legislation he would himself at once recognise as 'just,' he will, I think, be led to see that a campaign for the abstractions he feels so deeply still leaves all the main questions unsolved. For the problem is how to relate the ends upon which, in the abstract, it is so easy to agree (as Gollancz admirably shows) with the means for which men will (as they are doing in Spain) cheerfully kill one another with the profound conviction that 'justice' is on their side.

From this it follows that socialist propaganda must be something far more profound than Mr Orwell has considered. It has to be based not merely on an appeal to the 'better feelings' of people who could associate comfortably with socialists who looked and spoke and behaved like B.B.C. announcers; which is really Mr Orwell's conception of the matter. His kind of socialist propaganda would, no doubt, persuade people in Streatham and Chichester and Cheltenham that socialists are 'really quite nice people'; they might even get invited to the best dinner-parties in the best set in the neighbourhood. But it would not bring the realisation of socialism nearer. It might get a little social amelioration here and there, above all for the 'deserving poor'; it would enable the more ardent spirits of the C.O.S.[3] to call themselves socialists. But I know no country in the world where this kind of propaganda does more than prick men and women of conscience into that attitude of mind out of which, after painful intellectual effort, a real comprehension of socialism can be born. It ignores all that is implied in the urgent reality of class antagonisms. It refuses to confront the grave problem of the State. It has no sense of the historic movement of the economic process. At bottom, in fact, it is an emotional plea for socialism addressed to comfortable people. On the evidence, when the facts make them feel uncomfortable, charity seems to act as a sufficient anodyne. They rarely go further. Men live too differently to think similarly by being asked to embrace abstractions. If the socialist

[1] The Hammonds were social historians.
[2] Joseph Arch (1826–1919), English labor leader and MP, founder of the National Agricultural Labourers Union in 1872.
[3] Charity Organisation Society.

movement made this method its main reliance, not even the Greek Kalends would see its fulfilment.

But Mr Orwell's argument ought, I think, to be considered by members of the Left Book Club for another reason. *Mutatis mutandis*,[1] it is very like the Labour Party's passion for the British system as democratic, and like the panegyrics many of its leaders address to democracy. Our system is not a democracy pure and simple; it is a capitalist democracy, which is a very different thing. And the problem that capitalist democracy raises as a central issue in all our lives is the possibility of preserving the democracy when the ends it seeks involve the basic alteration of its capitalist character. Many socialists in the Labour Party speak and write as though the political side of our society can be divorced from the economic. The one, they argue, can be kept static while the other is dynamic. Spain, Austria, Germany, ought to convince us that this is not the case. Our democracy is an expression of an economic system the logic of which is now in growing contradiction with its own central principle. I do not think an abstract appeal however eloquent, on behalf of democracy as such will keep British capitalists democratic if the price of their remaining so was all that is involved in the transformation of capitalist into socialist democracy. I do not think so because I look at Franco, Hitler, Mussolini, and see that capitalists enabled them to resist exactly this kind of appeal. I think it is possible that they will accept a democratic victory if we make it clear that the forces behind our conception of democracy are clearly irresistible. But we shall not make them so unless our plea for democracy is built upon a reasoned analysis of the historic process in which we are involved. Mr Baldwin and Mr Attlee are both democrats; but the things for which they are democrats are not really compatible. At bottom, I am not sure that Mr Orwell's kind of socialist would be prepared to pay the price of socialism. And I think he would not pay it because the appeal to be a socialist to which he responded did not in fact make him a socialist at all.

---

[1] The necessary changes having been made.

# 31. Douglas Goldring, *Fortnightly*

April 1937, pp. 505–6

Douglas Goldring (1887–1960), English novelist, critic and editor.

The first half of this thought-provoking book describes what the author saw in the coal areas of Lancashire and Yorkshire. For some months he lived entirely in coal miners' houses. 'I ate my meals with the family,' he writes, 'I washed at the kitchen sink, I shared bedrooms with miners, drank beer with them, played darts with them, talked with them by the hour together.' He went down a mine and spent an hour of agony, crawling to the coal face. He got to know exact details of average working-class budgets, and witnessed the result of mass un-employment at its worst and the cruel effect of the Means Test in breaking up families. He examined, and gives a minute description of, every kind of working-class dwelling, from the horrifying and dis-graceful caravan settlements, at Wigan and elsewhere, to the 'Council' houses which are, all too slowly, being erected to replace them. This section is illustrated with thirty-two photographs of slums, which are calculated to shock even the most complacent.

The second half is partly autobiographical. In it the author explains his attitude on the 'terribly difficult issue of class' and his views on Socialism and Socialists. He was born in the 'lower-upper-middle-class,' educated, with the help of a scholarship, at an expensive public school and afterwards spent five years as a police officer in Burma. When he came home on leave in 1927, he decided he could not go back to be part of that 'evil despotism.' He wanted to submerge himself, 'to get right among the oppressed, to be one of them and on their side against their tyrants.' But he soon discovered that class barriers cannot be broken down in a hurry, and that if you advance too eagerly to embrace your proletarian brother he may not like it. The impoverished 'gentleman' and the working man, under present conditions, are as far apart in their habits and ways of thinking as if they belonged to different races. But that is no reason, since their economic interests are identical, why they should not co-operate for political ends. 'When the widely separate classes who, necessarily, would form any real Socialist party have fought side by side,' says Mr Orwell, 'they may feel quite differently about one another.' But there is a danger that the 'private schoolmaster, the half-starved free-lance journalist, the Colonel's spinster daughter with £75 a year, the jobless Cambridge graduate' and all the rest of the sinking middle class, may be so repelled by Socialism, in the form in which it is now presented, that they will accept the Fascist alternative. 'The ordinary decent man, who is in sympathy with the *essential* aims of Socialism,' the author observes, 'is given the impression that there is no room for his kind in any Socialist party that means business.' It is certainly as true as it is unfortunate that the words 'Socialism' and 'Communism' seem to 'draw towards them with magnetic force every fruit-juice-drinker, nudist, sandal-wearer, sex maniac, Quaker, "nature-cure" quack, pacifist and feminist in England. . . . These people come flocking towards the smell of "progress" like blue bottles to a dead cat.' Mr Orwell also delivers a well-aimed thwack at 'the astute young social-literary climbers who are Communists now, as they will be Fascists five years hence, because it is all the go.'

This brilliant, disturbing book should be read and pondered over by every jobless wearer of an old school tie. Socialists who are puzzled to understand why their party has been steadily losing ground during the past ten years, should read it also.

## 32. Hamish Miles, *New Statesman and Nation*

1 May 1937, pp. 724, 726

Hamish Miles (1894–1937), English translator of George Sand and André Maurois.

Mr Orwell has written a Black Guide to England, explained his own conflict with English caste-consciousness, sketched the intangible but very real battle-front of North and South, peered with fascinated horror into the homes (if that is the word) of the totally submerged poor and into the minds (if that, etc.) of the vaguely well-to-do, rubbed some gritty rock-salt into the sore places of conventional Socialism, and got in some resounding thwacks at Anglo-Communism, tinned food, *Punch*, the highbrows of 'the snootier magazines,' the 'leisure' Utopians, and much else. All in one book. And as Mr Orwell can do a first-rate job of descriptive reporting, can hit hard at cant wherever it seems to him to show its head, can instinctively pack plenty of disputatious matter into one paragraph, it is a living and lively book from start to finish. The honest Tory must face what he tells and implies, and the honest Socialist must face him, too. It may be hard for Mr Orwell to accept such praise from such a notoriously snooty quarter as Great Turnstile:[1] it is fairly clear that the *New Statesman and Nation* is as a pink rag to his bull-wrath. But he must take it.

His exploration of the English scene opens with a stay in a slum lodging-house in the North: four beds to the room, and a tripe and pigs' trotters shop downstairs. Mr Orwell has a positively Gissingesque genius for finding the dingiest house in the most sunless street, and he sketches the horribly self-contained, sub-human universe of his landlord and fellow-lodgers with a precision which, at one point or another, pricks each of one's senses in turn into revolt.

The meals at the Brookers' house were uniformly disgusting. For breakfast you got two rashers of bacon and a pale fried egg, and bread-and-butter

[1] The address of the *New Statesman* in London.

which had often been cut overnight and always had thumb-marks on it. . . . I could never induce Mr Brooker to let me cut my own bread-and-butter; he *would* hand it to me slice by slice, each slice gripped firmly under that broad, black thumb. . . . Several bottles of Worcester Sauce and a half-full jar of marmalade lived permanently on the table. It was usual to souse everything, even a piece of cheese, with Worcester sauce, but I never saw anyone brave the marmalade jar, which was an unspeakable mass of stickiness and dust. Mrs Brooker . . . had a habit of constantly wiping her mouth on one of her blankets. Towards the end of my stay she took to tearing strips of newspaper for this purpose, and in the morning the floor was often littered with crumpled-up balls of slimy paper which lay there for hours. The smell of the kitchen was dreadful, but, as with that of the bedroom, you ceased to notice it after a while.

And that is a comparatively mild passage. I am no anthropologist, but I doubt whether the most rudimentary peoples of the New Hebrides or Papua could produce anything to match the incident (p. 17) which decided Mr Orwell to leave, and of which he only mildly remarks— 'the place was beginning to depress me.'

This is followed by a picture on a bigger scale. A good many people have described the toil of the coal-miner underground, and tried to convey some sense, not so much of its danger, but of the day-in, day-out demands which the work makes on the bodily endurance of the miner, boy and man, through year after year. Glimpses of that continuous muscular and nervous war with darkness, stifling heat, bodily constriction, disease, may be caught now and then in the chill air of some official inquiry into a colliery explosion. Mr Orwell offers a full, coherent description of the travail, more clear and more telling than any that has happened to come my way. To the expert or the experienced it may (and I suspect does) present loopholes for criticism; but to a great majority of people, who merely take it for granted that their household scuttles simply cost thirty-two-and-sixpence a ton to fill, such a description of human cost is, to say the very least of it, salutary. The hardships and squalor of modern warfare have been elaborated often; so far as such things are commensurable, work at the coal-face is an equivalent, going on all the time; the miners are in many ways the 'poor bloody infantry' behind whose line we others live our lives. The point about coal-mining, which Mr Orwell does not say enough about, is the extraordinarily powerful community sense of its workers: the hereditary zeal for the pits and the work of the pits, the vocational pride in the relentless demands that coal-winning makes on one generation after another. It persists, as he is aware, through even the harshest trials of unemployment, in coalfields where the prospects of a renewal of activity seem almost totally obliterated—a kind of racial ardour. And yet, how anomalous the interests of the race can be! One day last winter I crouched in a scooped-out hole on the side of a slag heap in one of the stricken Welsh valleys. There were three miners there, scrabbling for fragments of coal in the tip; three or four hours of probing would, with luck, fill three-quarters of a sack; none of them had had anything like full-time work for seven or eight years; there was a stabbing cold wind. But what did they chiefly talk about? The valley beneath was solidly 'Red.' But the talk ran on football, on a whippet belonging to one of them, which sat there comfortably in a trim, warm, tautly strapped jacket beside the sack, and on the evening's rehearsal of a cantata, in which two of them would be taking part, entitled *The Celestial City*. A digression: but, to the foreigner, an odd sidelight.

The second half of Mr Orwell's book, divided from the first by a clever set of photographic 'documentaries,' turns to an informal survey of political implications. It is personal, unorthodox, refreshing, pungent, and nicely calculated to vex those who are Socialists in their heads rather than by blood. From an unusually varied experience of life (of which his earlier books have given some account), Mr Orwell has extracted some lessons which cannot be readily ignored. He is not primarily concerned with 'the Party' or the Marxian dialectic or plans for the next *x* years. But he is very much concerned with the general psychological attitude of the educated middle class of this country (to which he belongs—and knows it) towards the economic-political problem raised by what he has seen of life in England and elsewhere. He is acutely aware that class-consciousness is not to be exorcised by good will or by verbal argument:

. . . it is not so much like a stone wall as the plate-glass pane of an aquarium; it is so easy to pretend that it is not there, and so impossible to get through it. Unfortunately, it is nowadays the fashion to pretend that the glass is penetrable. . . . Not only the *croyant et pratiquant* Socialist, but every 'intellectual' takes it as a matter of course that *he* at least is outside the class-racket; *he*, unlike his neighbours, can see through the absurdity of wealth, ranks, titles, etc., etc. 'I'm not a snob' is nowadays a kind of universal *credo*. Who is there who has not jeered at the House of Lords, the military caste, the Royal Family, the public schools, the huntin' and shootin' people, the old ladies in Cheltenham boarding-houses, the horrors of 'county' society and the social hierarchy generally? To do so has become an automatic gesture.

This trend, in its wider aspects, he regards as not merely futile, but as in general tending 'to intensify class-prejudice.' And it certainly can lead to a senseless confusion of issues.

If you are a bourgeois 'intellectual' you too readily imagine that you have somehow become un-bourgeois because you find it easy to laugh at patriotism and the C. of E. and the Old School Tie and Colonel Blimp and all the rest of it. But from the point of view of the proletarian 'intellectual,' who at least by origin is genuinely outside the bourgeois culture, your resemblances to Colonel Blimp may be more important than your differences. Very likely he looks upon you and Colonel Blimp as practically equivalent persons; and in a way he is right. . . .

These are not the most important of Mr Orwell's arguments in his examination of the class dilemma in political groupings to-day. But they have considerable force, and should be read and pondered both by those who too readily imagine themselves emancipated from the illogical structure of an unsatisfactory society, and by those who, in his words, find themselves challenged in their secret beliefs and 'driven back to a frightened conservatism.' And there are plenty of both.

# 33. Robert Hatch, *Nation*

30 August 1958, pp. 97–8

Robert Hatch, American film critic and literary editor of the *Nation*.

Orwell's *The Road to Wigan Pier* came out in England in 1937, a few years after he had returned from Burma and just before he went off to Spain. There is no obvious reason for publishing it here twenty years later—when most of its facts and many of its opinions are out of date—and I had supposed that it was another of those exhumations that publishers sponsor in the hope of getting one more play out of a famous name. Maybe so—but it is a wonderfully alive body.

The circumstances surrounding the first appearance of the book are entertaining. Those were the days when the Left Book Club, under the guidance of Harold Laski, John Strachey and Victor Gollancz, was riding the wave of Socialist optimism. The club commissioned Orwell, who had recently shown in *Down and Out in Paris and London* a gift for cruising inconspicuously in the lowest economic strata, to move into the industrial north of England and report on conditions among the miners and related groups of the chronically unemployed. This was a brilliant assignment: Orwell wrote a report that entirely transcends its economic data and becomes an elegy on the spirit of poverty. He traveled down into the mines and looked with wonder on the prodigious labors of the small, malformed miners; he visited in their homes, taking notes on seeping walls, infested cupboards, backed-up drains; he explained with almost weeping anger the psychology of permanent unemployment and why the poor will always—indeed, must always—spend their inadequate shillings on tawdry luxury. It is the writing of an artist with his blood up and it can stand with Hogarth and Dickens.

Having written this much to fulfill his obligation to Gollancz and Co., Orwell started right over again on a companion tract to fulfill an obligation to himself. The second half of the manuscript he turned in to the Left Book Club is a sweeping attack on professional Socialists and theoretical socialism. Those were the days of leagues against war *and* fascism, of starry-eyed reports on the Russian experiment, of reliance on the planned society for the cure of misery. Orwell thought it was cant and ignorance, self-righteousness and shortsightedness and he laid about him with the flat of his hand. Much of what he said was too angry to be just, but he had an instinct for soft spots and he hit them all. Enough of them are still soft to make this good, if bitter, reading today.

Orwell's unsolicited biting of the hand that was then feeding him naturally troubled Laski, Strachey and Gollancz. They didn't agree, and yet their principles would not let them eliminate Part Two of *Wigan Pier* as not being in the contract. So they published the whole work, only adding an explanatory and mollifying note by Gollancz. This brief statement gives the book a final historical glamor—it shunts you back all at once into a period when men still thought of themselves as individually responsible and potent in social affairs. Socialism could be understood in terms of what Mr Laski said to Mr Strachey, what both of them agreed Mr Gollancz should say to the public about Mr Orwell. These men operated on the assumption that they grasped the issues of their day. It may have been an illusion—indeed, you could cite events to show that it was certainly an illusion—but it may be one that we cannot do without. No one today feels as relevant to the welfare of the future as Mr Gollancz felt himself to be in 1937; humility now becomes us as a shroud.

# 34. Philip Toynbee, *Encounter*

August 1959, pp. 81–2

Philip Toynbee (b. 1916), English novelist and journalist.

In the July issue of *Encounter* T. R. Fyvel pointed out that it is the current fashion to make fun of Orwell. One reason for this, surely, is the reason which led that irritated Athenian to vote for the ostracism of Aristides; he was sick of hearing him called 'the Just'. And it is perhaps true that Orwell was prematurely canonised. Because he acted what he believed and because he saw through many of the left-wing follies of his time he became, in the years after his death, something a little bit more than human. Yet the fact remains that though he was human to his would-be calloused finger-tips, Orwell *was* a much better man than most of us. We are reminded of this when we re-read his books, just as we are also reminded of the fact that he was a man of damaging and often irritating limitations.

*The Road to Wigan Pier* was first published in 1937 and was received, as I remember, with obloquy by communists and fellow-travellers, but with enthusiasm by many. The first part, which is a documentary description of his stay in various working-class homes in the north of England, has inevitably dated in some respects. The lists of prices and wages have little meaning now. But we are reminded not only that Orwell was a very good reporter indeed—perhaps the best of his generation—but also that the agonies and heroisms which he describes are a living part of the present day working-class tradition. When we read so many protests about 'unreasonable' strikes, restrictive practices and demarcational disputes, it is well to remember that any working man of over thirty can vividly remember the insecurities and plain miseries of life in the Thirties.

What is most interesting about the tone of Orwell's investigation is that it reads like a report brought back by some humane anthropologist who has just returned from studying the conditions of an oppressed tribe in Borneo. Orwell's constant assumption is that his readers will be amazed and horrified to find out how the English working-classes are living. It must be said that this is partly due to a habit of mind in the author himself. He writes—it is the least pleasant side of him— about 'nancy poets' and 'verminous little lions,' and he sees himself too consciously as the tough and honest man who has really found out the truth instead of simply dealing in high-minded abstractions. There is much in this, of course; but it may be a little misleading to a younger generation. When I was at Oxford, from 1935 to 1938, at least a quarter of my Communist friends were of working-class origin; working-class literature was *de rigueur* (most of it sadly inadequate stuff, but as *factual* as could be) and I was not extraordinary in spending parts of my vacation in the Rhondda Valley.

Yet it is true that Orwell's tone is largely justified by the circumstances of the time. To most middle-class people the industrial working-classes were as remote as the pygmies, and the unemployment figures meant nothing at all in human terms. Today the situation has changed at least in this—that there is no longer any excuse for ignorance.

Orwell's relations with the working-classes were like some long and pleasurably agonising love-affair. He could never be one with them, and he knew it, but nor could he ever leave them alone. He talked about them continuously, sometimes as if they represented some un-attainable perfection, sometimes as if he found them almost un-bearably offensive. The contradictions, even in this one book, are colossal. At one moment he praises the working-class attitude to education:

... there is not one working-class boy in a thousand who does not pine for the day when he will leave school. He wants to be doing real work, not wasting his time on ridiculous rubbish like history and geography. To the working-class the notion of staying at school till you are nearly grown-up seems merely contemptible and unmanly. . . .

And because the beloved adopts this attitude then Orwell himself will jolly well adopt it too—and thereby become the unwitting ally of all those alarmed reactionaries who want to keep the working classes in their places. It is a piece of idiocy which would ruin a book of lesser passion. And it is in the same foolish vein that he denounces middle-class and left-wing intellectuals for not adopting the table manners of the working classes. 'Why should a man who thinks all virtue resides in the proletariat still take such pains to drink his soup silently? It can only be because in his heart he feels that proletarian manners are disgusting.'

Orwell should have spoken for himself: at more enlightened moments he realised that he *was* speaking for himself. There were many radicals then, just as there are many today, who neither believe that all virtue resides in the proletariat nor that the proletarian manners are disgusting. It was Orwell who believed both.

But what is so striking and impressive about this book is not the ill-tempered and extremely conventional attacks on the intelligentsia —who as a group are no better and no worse than the proletariat—but the degree to which Orwell understood the real nature of the English social problem and his own strange role in it. This is particularly true of the second half, which is mainly an autobiographical study of this very subject. To a sensitive, affectionate and enquiring man the barriers of class *are* intolerable, as Orwell found them. In essentials we know that *they* are people like ourselves; and what is more they are not drastically removed from us in space. Except in specialised social areas each class is constantly in the physical presence of other classes—in trains and buses, in the streets and at the cinema, in crowds and in villages. Why then should we be kept apart by inessentials?

And the answer is, of course, that the inessentials are not so inessential as all that, for the most important of them are concerned with the tremendous factor of communication. Usage is trivial; table manners are absurd; the question of whether people smell or not never had the obsessive importance which Orwell gave to it, and has almost none today. But the real separation is precisely one of education and con-sequently of dominant concern. And it is this which makes all the sillier Orwell's deliberately philistine attitude to this vital subject. I am prohibited from real intimacy with an uneducated man—except in moments of extreme common emotion—because all our terms of reference are different. And the real gulf, for a man who has made use of his education, is here and not in any of those external differences of which Orwell made so much.

It is significant that Orwell wrote with particular loathing about working-class intellectuals. They had, in a sense, betrayed him by coming too close, like an adored mistress who suddenly comes down from her pedestal and agrees to go to bed with her lover. His description of this 'type'—as if there were only one type—is incredibly vicious and incredibly conventional: he comes close here to joining hands with those who talk of 'counter-jumpers' and 'little squirts who get too big for their boots.' Of course it is true that in those days there was a certain self-consciousness about many working-class intellectuals: in the intellectual world they were still just rare enough to be thought interesting for their origins as much as for their own persons. But this is much less true today—in spite of the pioneering clamour raised by a few among the new army of scholarship boys. In a few more years intellectual England will be a classless society, in so far as its origins are concerned.

Orwell failed to solve the social problem, both in general terms and in the particulars of his own life. But he was more passionately aware of it than any of his contemporaries. And he was aware of it with his heart as well as with his mind. If we ever succeed in breaking down all artificial barriers between us by means of education (a multitude of natural divisions will happily remain) then Orwell's early passion will certainly have played its part in that achievement.

# HOMAGE TO CATALONIA

1938 (1st American edition 1952)

## 35. Unsigned notice, *Times Literary Supplement*

30 April 1938, p. 286

Mr Orwell arrived in Catalonia in December, 1936, six months after the outbreak of the civil war, with the vague intention of doing some journalism; but instead he enlisted in the militia, took part in the trench warfare around Huesca, was wounded, and after some disheartening experiences in the internal rising in Barcelona in May, 1937, was compelled to flee the country.

The special interest of Mr Orwell's book derives from the fact that he did not enlist in an International Brigade but joined the militia organized by the P.O.U.M. (Workers Party of Marxist Unity), a small Catalan political party, commonly though not entirely accurately described as Trotskyist, and loosely linked with the Anarcho-Syndicalists. Although the war was well under way when the author went to the front, the fighting was of a decidedly amateurish kind. Discipline did not exist in the militia; 'if a man disliked an order he would step out of the ranks and argue fiercely with the officer.' The training given to the youthful recruits from the back streets of Barcelona consisted of old-fashioned parade-ground drill. There were no machine guns available for the purposes of demonstration and scarcely any rifles. In his five months at the front the author, although promoted to be a corporal, saw little active fighting. The grenades were unreliable, the rifles antique, bayonets at first non-existent, the trenches and water filthy, the front stagnant and the direction of operations, to say the least, uncoordinated.

When Mr Orwell returned to Barcelona from this unfruitful piece of trench life in April, 1937, he was surprised to discover that the revolutionary atmosphere of the town, which he had noticed on his arrival in Spain, had disappeared and its aspect become more middle class. This change he attributes mainly to the growing influence of the Communists, who, he maintains, were a right-wing if not a reactionary influence in the Republican Government. It is of course generally agreed that the Communists and Socialists in Spain at that time placed first emphasis on winning the war, whereas the Anarchists and P.O.U.M. first wanted a revolution in favour of full workers' control. This long-drawn-out party squabble is pathetic and has contributed sensibly to General Franco's success. It is difficult to see how any revolutionary triumphs were possible so long as the chaotic military conditions which are described in this book were unchanged. The Communist view of the May rising was that some such clash was inevitable if Catalonia was to be induced to contribute its share to winning the war.

In spite of the many evil memories which he carried away Mr Orwell regretted being forced to leave the scene of the struggle because of his more or less accidental incursion into Catalan party politics; and curiously, in view of his own efforts, he concludes by recording his hope that all the foreigners will be driven out of Spain.

# 36. Geoffrey Gorer, *Time and Tide*

30 April 1938, pp. 599–600

Geoffrey Gorer (b. 1905), friend of Orwell; English social anthropologist; author of *Africa Dances* (1935) and *Himalayan Village* (1938).

George Orwell occupies a unique position among the younger English prose writers, a position which so far has prevented him getting his due recognition. In a period of literary groups he has remained fiercely individualist, in a period of literary affectations he has developed a prose style so simple that its excellencies pass unperceived, in a period of lip service to collective ideas and ideals he has maintained passionately his own integrity and independence. Born a member of the ruling class, the consistent attitude of his novels and autobiographical works—*Down and Out in Paris and London, The Road to Wigan Pier*, and now *Homage to Catalonia*—has been an indignant repudiation of the warped and miserable lives that his class has forced on the majority of the people it dominates. This repudiation has been emotional and not rational; he has cried his disgust in his novels so forcibly that they are almost unbearable, he has set himself against the majority, because he has felt the horrors of oppression and exploitation, not (at any rate primarily) because he has reasoned about them. His political ideas have been, to a certain extent still are, naïve; he has repudiated Authority in any form, Marxist, Fabian or Conservative, relying on what he himself has seen and thought and felt; and because today the general reaction to any political situation is identification with an existing outlook, this personal and political protestant integrity is, if only as a corrective, of extraordinary value.

*Homage to Catalonia* is that phœnix, a book which is at the same time a work of first-class literature and a political document of the greatest importance. In December, 1936, George Orwell went to Barcelona, primarily with a view to writing articles. He did not go with the intention of fighting—for like the rest of us he knew little of the existing situation, and with his distrust of authority would not believe what he was told on any side—and consequently went out under I.L.P. and not Communist protection. In Barcelona the atmosphere of a city under workers' control (and it still was then) showed him something which it was worth risking his life to preserve, and he immediately joined the militia. His I.L.P. protection, his complete ignorance of the Spanish Party groupings, and, one is tempted to say, his destiny, caused him to enrol in the militia of the P.O.U.M., a small dissident Marxist party, Trotskyist in so far as it was anti-Stalinist and believed in world revolution. After the sketchiest of trainings, and with incredibly inadequate equipment he spent four months on the Zaragoza front, in great physical discomfort but with very little fighting. At the end of April he returned on leave to Barcelona, identifying so little with the P.O.U.M. that he wanted to transfer to the International Brigade, when, a few days after his return, the street fighting in Barcelona started. It would seem as though the starting point of the fighting was the attempt of the reinstated gendarmerie, the Civil guards (whether working under Government orders or not) to take the telephone building from the Anarchists who were working it, and the first fighting was the common Barcelona phenomenon of the workers against the police; but over the week during which the fighting took place it developed into a struggle between the Government and the Communists on the one hand against the Left revolutionary Parties, the Anarchists and the other smaller groups, the P.O.U.M., the friends of Durruti[1] and so on. The Communists won, but not really conclusively, and they could not attack their chief opponents, the Anarchists; instead all the blame was put on the numerically completely insignificant P.O.U.M., who were accused the world over as spies and Fascists, planning rebellion and fomenting disorder. His loyalty to his front-line comrades forced George Orwell to take his rôle, as a sentry, during the street fighting, the riot; when it was over he returned as a lieutenant to his militia, regretting that the soldiers at the front had not a tithe of the arms of the police at the rear. Had such arms been available, had political intrigue allowed the militia to be reasonably equipped, perhaps Huesca would have been taken, the course of the war very different. Back at the front, away from the evil intrigues of the city, Orwell was shot by a sniper through the neck, escaping death by a miracle; he returned, barely convalescent, to Barcelona, to dis-

[1] Buenaventura Durruti (1896–1936), leader of the Spanish Anarchists in the Civil War; killed in defense of Madrid.

cover that the P.O.U.M. had been dissolved and its members were being hunted down; he could not return to his wife, for she, too, was under suspicion—her room had been searched and all her papers taken in the middle of the night—and had to spend five nights in hiding, the victim of a senseless witch-hunt. Eventually, he, his wife, and a friend just managed to escape out of the country he had so nearly given his life for.

This bare outline can give little indication of the problems raised and illuminated in his book. The central and essential problem is the present rôle of the Communists. Communist policy (owing chiefly to the international situation of the U.S.S.R.) is now and has been for ten years anti-revolutionary, and outside Russia Communists are more interested in gaining allies for the Soviets in the case of war than in pursuing a working-class policy in their various countries. In Government Spain (heart-breaking though it is to write such things in her agony) it would seem that they suppressed the truly revolutionary situation which existed in the first six months partly for the sake of efficiency, but chiefly to appease and calm the France of the Franco-Soviet pact. The insistence of all Communist organs that there is not, and never has been, anything revolutionary in Government Spain might, in less poignant circumstances, seem comic. It is arguable that thereby they have lost a great deal of working-class help without gaining the protection of those they wished to conciliate. And the 'Left wing' Socialist Parties have been persecuted with a malignancy and sullen spite, with a cruelty and stupidity which is little better (though nevertheless still better) than Fascism. The potential danger to working-class movements the world over is obvious.

I have dwelt at such length on the political implications of *Homage to Catalonia* because of their intrinsic importance and because I think it probable that they will either be distorted or ignored in the greater part of the press. I have no space to dwell on the magnificent literary qualities of the book, its brilliant descriptions of Catalan landscape, of the emotional atmosphere of a revolutionary militia, of Barcelona in different phases, the vividness of the accounts of fighting in the trenches and in the streets, the account of being wounded almost to death, of being hunted like a criminal. Emphatically, this is a book to read; politically and as literature it is a work of first-class importance. It will probably be abused both by Conservatives and Communists; anyone interested in the political situation (whatever their own views) or in literature would be foolish to neglect it.

# 37. John McNair, *New Leader* (London)

6 May 1938, p. 7

John McNair (1887–1968), Independent Labour Party representative in Barcelona 1936–7, General Secretary of the ILP 1939–55, biographer of ILP leader James Maxton. The *New Leader* was the organ of the ILP.

We have waited long for such a book as George Orwell's *Homage to Catalonia*. There have been many books written on the Spanish Civil War, but none containing so many living, first-hand experiences as this.

The writer is not a propagandist. So far as I know, he is a member of no political party. Probably because of this he has demonstrated the age-old truth that art does not need artifice, and that a writer's job is to express in honesty and sincerity the realities of a situation as he sees and experiences them.

In the first fifty pages he tells us all about the discomfort and the comradeship of the P.O.U.M. Workers' Militia. He discovered the discomfort first and the comradeship later. Indeed, this is not surprising as the average Briton takes many things for granted which the Spanish workers and peasants have never known. The fact which stands out clearly is the inherent decency and simplicity of the Spanish worker:—

A Spaniard's generosity, in the ordinary sense of the word, is at times almost embarrassing. If you ask him for a cigarette he will force the whole packet on you. And beyond this, there is generosity in a deeper sense, a real largeness of spirit, which I have met with again and again in the most unpromising circumstances.

This was the raw material out of which sprang the Workers' Militia, which saved Spain from Fascism in the early days, which defended Madrid with unparalleled heroism, and which was laying the foundations of the Workers' State. The value of the Workers' Militia as a revolutionary fighting force was not realised by George

Orwell at first, and it was only afterwards that he saw the virtue of revolutionary self-discipline, which he places higher than the machine-discipline of Capitalist armies.

Behind the apparent confusion and disorganisation, the workers were bending to their task of defeating Fascism at the front and building Socialism at the rear. Many, particularly outside of Spain, have shut their eyes to this fact. The air has been obscured by foolish cries of 'Democracy' and 'Republicanism,' but these slogans left the Spanish workers cold. They had felt the breath of another air; another vision was dimly rising. This is what the author says about it:—

In theory, it was perfect equality, and even in practice it was not far from it. There is a sense in which it would be true to say that one was experiencing a foretaste of Socialism, by which I mean the prevailing mental atmosphere was that of Socialism. Many of the normal motives of civilised life—snobbishness, money-grubbing, fear of the bogs, etc.—had simply ceased to exist. The ordinary class-division of society had disappeared to an extent that is almost unthinkable in the money-tainted air of England; there was no one there except the peasants and ourselves, and no one owned anyone else as his master.

Of course, such a state of affairs could not last. It was simply a temporary and local phase in an enormous game that is being played over the whole surface of the earth. But it lasted long enough to have its effect on anyone who experienced it. However much one cursed at the time, one realised afterwards that one had been in contact with something strange and valuable. One had been in a community where hope was more normal than apathy or cynicism, where the word 'comrade' stood for comradeship, and not, as in most countries, for humbug. One had breathed the air of equality. . . .

In that community where no one was on the make, where there was a shortage of everything but no privilege and no boot-licking, one got, perhaps, a crude forecast of what the opening stages of Socialism might be like. And, after all, instead of disillusioning me, it deeply attracted me. The effect was to make my desire to see Socialism established much more actual than it had been before.

He is right when he says that such a stage did not last. It probably would have lasted if the International Working Class had rallied to the Spanish workers in the same way that International Capitalism rallied to Spanish Fascism, and if anti-Fascist unity had not been weakened by what George Orwell subsequently describes.

George Orwell deals at length, and with conspicuous fairness, with the internal political situation in Spain. The chapters in which he describes the bitter and unscrupulous attacks made on the P.O.U.M. amount to the slow unfolding of an unanswerable case, beside which the slanders and abuse which were used sink to their real level of lying propaganda:—

This, then, was what they were saying about us: we were Trotskyists, Fascists, traitors, murderers, cowards, spies, and so forth. I admit it was not pleasant, especially when one thought of some of the people who were responsible for it. It is not a nice thing to see a Spanish boy of fifteen carried down the line on a stretcher, with a dazed, white face looking out from among the blankets, and to think of the sleek persons in London and Paris who are writing pamphlets to prove that this boy is a Fascist in disguise.

The psychological phenomenon of all this abuse coming from the valiant non-combatants is no new thing. We had a lot of it during the Great War. But it is comforting to know that at the front the P.S.U.C. militiamen and the Communists of the International Brigade never used this sort of language; they left it to the journalists at the rear.

The episode of the Spanish Civil War which has been the most grotesquely distorted is the Barcelona street fighting during the first week in May a year ago. The Communist press of the world has described it as a 'Trotskyist putsch' engineered by the P.O.U.M. in league with Franco. This version has been proved to be a tissue of lies and has no longer any credence among the workers generally.

The chapters in which the author, who was an eye-witness, describes this event are probably the best in the book, and it is here that his impartiality is so precious. His final summing-up appears to be absolutely in accordance with all the known facts—namely, that the street-fighting was caused by aggressions on the part of the Civil and Assault guards against the mass of the Spanish workers, who tried to defend the conquests of the revolution.

He disproves once and for all that any member of the I.L.P. contingent took part in any aggressive action, and that the workers of the P.O.U.M., the C.N.T. and the Left Socialists who manned the barricades were obeying their deepest instincts as workers and defending themselves against the counter-revolutionary forces embodied in the police and the guards.

I would like to say more of this book. It brings back the days and nights which are for ever graven on our memory, but it brings back more than all else the spirit of comradeship which existed then and the hope we had.

Our hope is still unquenchable. The march of the workers is irresistible. The Spanish workers have shown the world that Fascism is vulnerable, and slowly this knowledge is strengthening the workers everywhere.

It is not too late to save Spain even at this late hour. The British and French Labour Movements are at a decisive moment in history. Let them act now. The saving of Spain will be the death-knell of Fascism and the liberation of that mighty movement which will bring in the Socialist State of which George Orwell had a foretaste in Spain and which one day will be.

# 38. P. M. (Philip Mairet),
## New English Weekly

26 May 1938, pp. 129–30

Philip Mairet (b. 1886), editor of the New English Weekly, author of books on Alfred Adler (1928–30) and A. R. Orage (1936).

Mr George Orwell's book on his experiences in Spain hardly needs recommendation to readers of this paper; many of them will probably have hastened to read it as eagerly as did the present reviewer. Knowing already something of this writer's vigour of mind and honesty of purpose, and remembering the illuminating article he contributed to these columns just after returning wounded from the Spanish front, readers will look to his Homage to Catalonia for something new and revealing. Nor will they be disappointed. The book is likely to stand as one of the best contemporary documents of the struggle. Its frank individuality of outlook, combined with a certain political naïveté, gives internal evidence of its freedom from political obscurantism, for what bias it has is naked and wholly unashamed. Its literary quality, which is of a high order, is of the kind that springs from a well-extraverted attention and spontaneous reaction, so that the observations are reliable and convincingly communicated.

Mr Orwell went to Spain for the best of reasons. He believes that Fascism is the greatest danger of modern times, and he thought that in Spain there was a chance that the rising tide of Fascism might yet be turned. He says he went intending to serve the cause with pen rather than hand-grenade, but no one who knows him would expect, when there was a scrap in progress in what he conceived the best of all possible causes, that he could long keep out of it: one doubts if he really expected to himself.

Mr Orwell fought in the front line for some months, then returned to Barcelona and became involved in the street fighting there, following the Valencia Government's seizure of the Telephone Exchange from the worker-group in charge of it. He was afterwards sent to the Aragon front and after ten days' fighting was shot through the neck, escaping death by a centimetre or so: and after recovering from this wound he fled the country, in danger of imprisonment or worse from the Government he had fought for.

During all these adventures he tried, as a highly conscious and interested observer, to understand the military and political situation: but this he found very difficult, the atmosphere being dense with rumours, lying propaganda and local feuds. The press was of little assistance, most of it, local and foreign, being as wholly consecrated to mendacity as it is in any matter connected with the present ideological war. Mr Orwell's claims for his conclusions are modest. He has only tried to report his own part in the Spanish drama and to account as well as he can for the circumstances that directly affected it. In doing this, he has rendered a specific service, besides having produced a brilliant piece of writing.

To a notable extent, this eye-witness's account corrects and even contradicts the account we have received from the leftward press in this country as to what is happening in Spain: especially upon the following points:—

(a) There *was* a 'red' Revolution in Spain. The Parliamentary Government, crumbling in face of Franco's insurrection, was supplanted in effective power by the Socialist, Anarchist and Communist groups controlled by the workmen's committees. It was never a fight for 'constitutional government.'

(b) The Government, increasingly controlled by the Communists under Moscow influence or methods, proceeded to crush out the power of the more indigenous (*e.g.*, Anarchist and Socialist) groups, turning the Revolution into a fight for the *status quo ante bellum* against Franco, which is the solution favoured by Russian foreign policy—and by French and English, on the whole.

(c) With the above aim, the workmen's own committees were proceeded against by methods as arbitrary and tyrannical as those of an Ogpu or Gestapo, and the whole process has been accompanied by a disastrous loss of the original revolutionary ardour.

Against this, of course, a typical Government sympathiser might urge military necessity and say that the Communists (who are now such good democrats) had of course to make all the various groups fighting against Franco toe the same line, by force if required. They might ascribe Mr Orwell's disgust at this so necessary development to political immaturity, and some will even say, probably, that when he sided with his own section of the militia in the Barcelona riots he was bound to get what was coming to him (though it is hard to see what else he could have done). But I do not think his experience is so simply to be disposed of. After all, if you have a popular movement for political freedom, it is rather absurd to suppose that its ends can be achieved by wiping out its very structure, the personal and functional loyalties that brought it about, and substituting something else. If people thought that was going to happen when they formed groups with revolutionary ideals, they would never revolt. They might even sneak over to Fascism, as certainly less trouble and possibly no worse in the end.

Not so Mr Orwell: he remains convinced that a Franco victory would be a disaster a hundred times worse than a Government victory. But he clearly thinks, and has reason to think, the latter might be pretty bad for revolutionary ideals or even for human life generally in Spain. The effect of this honest, realistic book, upon the cannier sort of readers, will be a further warning of the immense complexity of the factors really underlying the ideological war, so that all moral issues are confused, and no faith is left but for those who can believe a pure negative—that the destruction of one -ism or the other is the only thing that matters.

The more sanguine sort of readers, however, will value this book for its emotional warmth—the 'expectation, tickling skittish spirits' in Barcelona when the Anarchist workers still ruled it, the fine faith and comradeship of those amateur, ill-armed soldiers, the magnificent generosity and humanity of passing contacts between men in the trenches, in the streets, in hospitals, moments of exaltation in all the stench and squalor, reminding one of that famous day of dawn of the French Revolution.

This is a human book: it shows us the heart of innocence that lies in revolution; also the miasma of lying that, far more than the cruelty takes the heart out of it.

# 39. A. W. J., *Manchester Guardian*

## 14 June 1938, p. 8

Mr Orwell fought in the P.O.U.M. militia; he considers Fascism the greatest danger of to-day and sees in the Catholic Church of Spain the working man's enemy. The merit of his book is that he takes this stand without being blind to the faults of those who share his beliefs and writes without rant and ideological malice. His story of the fighting in the Aragon hills, in which he took part, reads excellently well, perhaps because he describes things more often than feelings (thus avoiding the main fault of the novelists of war). There is a fine air of classical detachment about his description of war's horrors: 'If there is one thing I hate more than another it is a rat running over me in the darkness.' There are no false heroics and no needless trafficking in sordidness.

The part about the politics of loyal Spain makes confusion clear and the defence of the Trotskyist P.O.U.M. is convincing. The division in Spanish politics lay between those who felt that before the war could be won a social revolution must take place and those, led by the now highly respectable Communists, who held that the winning of the war was more important than radical social change. The revolutionary workers have been defeated, the Communist view has prevailed, and the Spanish Government has become extremely 'Liberal'; but Mr Orwell makes the case for the factiousness of his own comrades very plain. It is characteristic of the Spanish people that even the advance of the foreign enemy could not bring them to settle their political differences without bloodshed.

# 40. D. W. (Douglas Woodruff), *Tablet*

9 July 1938, p. 48

Douglas Woodruff (b. 1897), British historian, author of *Plato's American Republic* (1926) and *Charlemagne* (1934). The *Tablet* is an English Catholic weekly.

*Homage to Catalonia*, by an English volunteer, who joined the Militia in Barcelona in December, 1936, and spent the next six months on the Aragon front or in Barcelona itself, is a work which must be extremely unpalatable to all those people who like to imagine that the Government side in Spain is fighting for Democracy. Mr Orwell is an impressive witness, a patently honest man who writes clearly, easily, and with a wealth of detail from first-hand experience. He arrived to fight against Franco and Fascism, promising himself that he would kill one Fascist at least. Because he went out from England with I.L.P. associations, he found himself in the P.O.U.M. Militia, and therefore on what was destined to be the weaker and the persecuted side in the conflict between the Anarchists and the Communists. The P.O.U.M. (Partido Obrero de Unificación Marxista) as a minority Communist party agreed with the Anarchists on this point: 'The war and the revolution are inseparable.' The Anarchists were the chief elements in the revolution of July 19th, 1936, and their proletarian revolution was the thing they took seriously. They did not at all want, at any time, to pretend that it had not happened. Not merely did they glory in it, particularly in the anti-religious aspect, but they had a very good case for their contention that it was a great military mistake to pretend, as the Communist strategy demanded, that there had never been any revolution, that the Spanish situation was simply a matter of reactionary Fascists attacking a mild Liberal Democratic regime. The Communists insisted upon this as the right story to tell in France, Britain and America; the Anarchists retorted that, at any rate, it was the wrong story to tell in Spain. They argued that no one in Franco's territory was going to be moved to take risks for a *bourgeois* regime, although people might for a genuine revolution.

But the Communists, efficient, centralizing, soon became more and more the directors of policy from November, 1936, as the up-to-date arms began to arrive from Russia, and to be used in equipping the Communist-directed forces, the International Brigade, and then the People's Army.

The Communists, recognizing with their wider experience the necessity for doing things in stages, knew that the real revolution must be postponed until after the war was won, and Mr Orwell and his friends of the P.O.U.M. soon found themselves denounced as Trotsky-ist Fascists, and returned from extreme hardships in the front line to find themselves arrested and thrown into prison.

The author escaped, largely through the presence of mind of his wife, but many of his companions disappeared into Stalinist prisons. Mr Orwell is a singularly equable man, but he writes with some pardonable warmth about the people in England who have accepted all the false-hoods put out by the dominant faction. 'According to the *Daily Worker* (August 6th, 1936),' writes Mr Orwell, 'those who said that the Spanish people were fighting for social revolution or for anything other than *bourgeois* Democracy were downright lying scoundrels.' He contrasts this with the declaration of Juan Lopez, a member of the Valencia Government in February, 1937, 'that the Spanish people are shedding their blood, not for the Democratic Republic and its paper constitution, but for a revolution.' He adds, 'Some of the foreign anti-Fascist papers even descended to the pitiful lie of pretending the churches were only attacked when they were used as Fascist fortresses. Actually, churches were pillaged everywhere and as a matter of course, because it was perfectly well understood that the Spanish Church was part of the capitalist racket.' But 'it was the Communist thesis that revolution at this stage would be fatal, and that what was to be aimed at in Spain was not workers' control but *bourgeois* Democracy.'

Mr Orwell was at the centre of the Barcelona street fighting in May of last year, and shows what a small matter it was, the result of increasing friction between the two great groups, but it led to the proscription and the hounding down of the P.O.U.M., and the pub-lishing of the Communist version all over the world. He very early reached the conclusion that the one thing at stake in Spain is certainly not Democracy, but a choice of dictatorships. In his anger at Com-munist tactics of taking the war first and the revolution afterwards, in his justifiable contempt for the crudeness of a policy which, for long years, taught that Democracy is a term for Capitalism and then suddenly made 'fight for Democracy' into a slogan, he denies the Stalinists their just credit of working for a revolution as complete in Spain as in Russia.

When he concludes: 'It is impossible to read through the reports in the Communist Press without realizing that they are consciously aimed at a public ignorant of the facts, and have no other purpose than to work up prejudice,' he joins hands with people at the other extreme of political thought from his own.

Physically he never found himself very near the Spanish Nationalists, his part of the Front was one where for both sides, the defence had all the advantages, where the weapons were bad, and the hilly countryside very easy to hold; and mentally, he had neither the occasion nor, apparently, the inclination to find out much about the ideas behind the Nationalist movement. 'The Popular Front might be a swindle, but Franco was an anachronism.' It is curious that a man who tells us that for a year or two past the international prestige of Fascism had been haunting him like a nightmare, should not display more intellectual curiosity. He experienced at first hand the utter distortion spread round the world by the dominant revolutionary faction in his part of Spain, and that might have made him rather suspicious of accepting *in toto* their version of the Fascist enemy. 'Only millionaires or romantics,' he writes, 'could want Franco to win.' Yet Mr Orwell himself is a romantic and the best pages of a good book bear witness again and again how very little men, especially when they are Spaniards, are really preoccupied with material ends and standards of living. He knows that men live in their ideals and dreams; he can recognize the greatness in the Spanish soul; he would be rewarded if in that spirit of adventure which made him explore beyond the front line, he would seek to understand the aspirations which inspire the men against whom he went to fight.

# 41. Stephen Spender, *World Review*

June 1950, pp. 51-4

Stephen Spender (b. 1909), English poet and critic, Professor of English at University College, London, author of *The Destructive Element* (1934) and his autobiography *World Within World* (1951).

George Orwell was not a saint—although he was one of the most virtuous men of his day—and he was not a hero—although he was a man of outstanding courage. He was an Innocent, a kind of English Candide of the twentieth century. The Innocent is ordinary because he accepts the values of ordinary human decency; he is not a mystic, nor a poet. Ordinary, and yet extraordinary, because his faith in qualities of truth and decency drives like a drill through the façade of his generation. He is a drill made of steel driving through ordinary things. He happens to believe that two and two make four; and that what happens, happens. The consequences of *really* believing this are shattering. Christ was brought up as a carpenter in a carpenter's shop.

Orwell was *really* what hundreds of others only pretend to be. He was really classless, really a Socialist, really truthful. The rule of his authenticity is made clear perhaps by the exceptional thing which might make him appear to be an upper-class moral adventurer who had neurotically strayed into the camp of the opposing class: the fact that he was an Etonian. For his Eton background was utterly irrelevant. He was what he was simply out of good faith and honesty, not out of neurosis or ecstasy or a sense of mystery. He was perhaps the least Etonian character who has ever come from Eton. He was a tall, lean, scraggy man, a Public House character, with a special gleam in his eye, and a home-made way of arguing from simple premises, which could sometimes lead him to radiant common sense, sometimes to crankiness.

The Spanish Civil War was a situation which seemed almost designed for this instrument to act upon. And bore into it he did, cutting a hole clean through it (it also cut a bullet-hole through his

134

neck), and emerging at the other side. *Homage to Catalonia* contains the neat pile of shavings and sawdust below the operation. It is a better book than *1984*—which it strongly foreshadows—because the Spanish Republic provided a perfect situation for Orwell, whereas in *1984* his powers of political invention are rather strained. The horror of *Homage to Catalonia* is even greater than that of *1984*: but in the earlier book no one can accuse him of having invented tortures; for he is writing of what he has seen. The prophetic insight into the consequences of a state of affairs when human lives and facts are swept aside because they seem to contradict the thesis of 'political necessity' in the form in which it happens to be stated by the ruling party in the Police State, is the same. Orwell's faith in human decency, which goes beyond his terrifying insights into human weakness and malignity, is more impressive in the face of Communist methods in Spain than in a situation which seems fabricated. He never wrote anything more impressive than the last pages of this book: 'This war, in which I played so ineffectual a part, has left me with memories which are mostly evil, and yet I do not wish that I had missed it. When you have had a glimpse of such a disaster as this—and however it ends, the Spanish War will turn out to have been an appalling disaster, quite apart from the slaughter and physical suffering—the result is not necessarily dis-illusionment and cynicism. Curiously enough, the whole experience has left me with not less but more belief in the decency of human beings.'

The disaster which Orwell describes was the liquidation of his fellow militia-men on the Catalan Front, not by the Fascists, but by the Republicans under the domination of the Communists. It seems almost inevitable that when he enlisted in Spain, Orwell should have found himself with the militia of the POUM—the party which was after-wards banned for being Trotskyist. In fact, though, he only went to the Catalan Front and not into the International Brigade by chance. He happened to have references from the ILP which recommended him to the POUM. When he went to the front, he still regarded the Spanish War as a struggle of the united Republic against the Francoist rebellion. The political struggle within the Republican side seemed to him irrelevant. Gradually, however, he discovered that a struggle was going on between those who thought that the revolution should con-tinue throughout the Civil War and those who thought it should be halted until the war was won. As far as Orwell had sympathies, these were with those who wished to concentrate above all on winning the war rather than with those who wished to hurry on the Revolution. On the Catalan Front he witnessed the hopeless inefficiency of the POUM militia, and he regarded their revolutionary and anarchist aspirations as rather dangerous idealism.

It was not until he had returned to Barcelona on leave in 1937 that the sharp conflict between the Communist-dominated central government and the POUM was forced on to him. In May of that year he found himself in street fighting between the police of the Republican Civil Guard and the Syndicalists and members of the POUM. His immediate reaction to this situation is typical of his strength and his weakness: 'The issue was clear enough. On one side the CNT, on the other side the police. I have no particular love for the idealised "worker" as he appears in the bourgeois Communist's mind, but when I see an actual flesh-and-blood worker in conflict with his natural enemy, the policeman, I do not have to ask myself which side I am on.' This clarification may not seem so convincing to the reader as it did to Orwell. After all, 'the police' in this instance were the police of the Republic and the fact of their being in conflict with a section of 'workers' does not automatically put them in the wrong. But Orwell's strength is the insight with which he sees the truth of a situation beyond a position which may at first appear wrong-headed. It was perhaps wrong-headed to go to the Catalan Front at all: but the result of this mistake was that he saw the Spanish fighting in a light far from the propaganda of the Republican side. He may be wrong-headed in his account of the political issues of the conflict between the POUM and the Communists (the evidence is so conflicting that it may be impossible ever to judge of this). But there can be no doubt that his condemnation of the methods used to suppress the POUM is one of the most serious indictments of Communism which has been written. It is possible to argue that the political leaders of the POUM were to some degree responsible for the fighting in Barcelona. But it is not possible to defend the betrayal of the militia on the Catalan Front whose members, when they returned on leave, were arrested in order that they should not tell the soldiers at the front 'that behind their backs their party was being suppressed, their leaders accused of treachery, and their friends and relatives thrown into prison.'

*Homage to Catalonia* makes me reflect on the meaning of the phrase 'the living truth'. This has all too often in history been exploited in order to trample on human freedoms for the sake of some authoritarian teaching which is supposed to bring happiness in this world or the next. Orwell was extremely sceptical of the claim of any cause to represent 'the living truth'. But he himself in his own life was an example of 'the lived truth', which is perhaps the most valuable truth any one can offer to humanity. He made of his own life an acid test of the claims of anti-Fascism in Spain. In political terms a good many of his results are controversial; but as a test of the results of the Spanish War on people's lives, his position is absolutely irrefutable. He leaves us thinking that it will take more than an ideology to save our time. And no idea will result in anything but the kind of disaster he witnessed in Spain unless it is accompanied by a scrupulous regard for the sacredness of the truth of an individual life. Politically, the liquidation of the POUM was not an event of great importance; humanly speaking, it was a greater failure for the Republic even than the defeat.

# 42. T. R. Fyvel, *New Leader* (New York)

16 June 1952, pp. 22–3

T. R. Fyvel (b. 1907 in Switzerland), friend of Orwell, co-editor of Searchlight Books, writer, journalist and broadcaster.

Turning the pages of the new edition of George Orwell's *Homage to Catalonia*, in which he tells of his personal experience during the Spanish Civil War, I felt strangely carried back into a past which has already become part of a dusty history. *Homage to Catalonia* is one of the most moving and truest accounts of that unhappy conflict. Yet, owing to Communist machinations—for Orwell did not, of course, accept the party-line myth of the war—the book sold poorly when first published in London in 1938 and had not appeared in the United States until this year. The present reissue is doubly useful—first, because it shows how Orwell's Spanish experiences helped to shape his political ideals, and second, because it throws sharp light on the way in which a whole generation of intellectuals allowed themselves to be bemused by the myths of the Spanish struggle.

In his introduction to the present edition, Lionel Trilling suggests that Orwell was not so much an artist as a supremely good and honest reporter. I would qualify this judgment. If *Homage to Catalonia* lacks those touches of melancholy insight which give Orwell's later works their literary value, it is because in this early book he was writing with deliberate restraint, keeping his savage indignation in check, because he was still clarifying his own political view.

When Orwell set out in December 1936 to fight for the Spanish Republican forces, he had as yet mingled little with London intellectuals and was new to European politics. But on arriving in Barcelona, he says, he felt with a thrill that he was in the midst of a revolutionary atmosphere, where every establishment had been collectivized, all motor cars commandeered, militia marched through the streets to the sound of music, and even waiters and bootblacks looked you square in the face. 'All this was queer and moving. There was much in it I did not understand, in some ways I did not even like it, but I recognized it immediately as a state of affairs worth fighting for.'

Orwell's experiences in fighting for this state of affairs resembled those of the heroes of his own novels. Through accident, he did not, like most British volunteers, join the Communist-controlled International Brigade; but instead, with some friends from the English Independent Labor party, he joined the militia of the POUM, a small revolutionary left-wing group concentrated mainly in Barcelona. As a member of a hopelessly underequipped and undertrained POUM militia unit, he fought for three months amid the cold and dirt of the Aragon front. In May 1937, he returned on leave to Barcelona to find that, under new Communist control, the zest had gone out of the revolution, the Anarchist trade unions and the POUM were losing ground, and class distinctions were again springing up fast, as was a flourishing black market.

For several days in May 1937, he was involved in confused street fighting which ended when the Anarchist 'Worker's Militia' was put down and Barcelona was taken over by the Communist Assault Guards, men uniformed and armed, Orwell says, with a lavishness he had never seen at the front. He was also disturbed by Communist posters which virulently denounced the POUM as 'counter-revolutionary.' But back he went to his POUM unit on the Huesca front. In renewed fighting, he was badly wounded in the throat, and survived rather miraculously. Discharged from the hospital, he returned to Barcelona to find that the new Communist rulers had just officially proscribed the POUM as 'pro-Fascist' and were arresting its members right and left. After a few chaotic days of hiding in the city, he and his wife and a Scottish friend succeeded in getting across the Spanish frontier—to the safety of capitalist France.

As he reveals himself in this account, Orwell cuts a romantic, typically English figure, as when he is half amused, half shocked by the slatternly inefficiency of the Spanish militia, deeply moved by the 'essential decency' of the Catalan workers, anxious to do his share in the fighting, yet slightly aware of the futility of it all, especially of the street fighting he watched from a Barcelona roof. It is characteristic that he already saw in 1937, when Communist propaganda was still strong, that no good for the Spanish people, least of all a 'democratic solution,' could emerge from this inefficient and sanguinary war between two Spanish armies, one led by Catholic reactionaries, the other by Communists, and both largely composed of conscripts.

Though previously unschooled as to Communist methods, Orwell quickly grasped the nature of the life-and-death struggle going on *inside* the Republican camp. At the outset, he had taken the typical English left-wing view that the war was some sort of 'defence of civilisation against a maniacal outbreak by an army of Spanish Colonel Blimps in the pay of Hitler.' But in Barcelona in the early days of the war, when the Anarchists were still in the saddle, he soon saw that a genuine working-class revolution was at stake. He also saw, at first with surprise, then with clear understanding, that this working-class revolution was exactly what the Communists did *not* want—hence they were systematically crushing it as they took over power.

The international background was clear. Fearful of Hitler, Moscow was angling for a 'popular front' against Fascism, in which the first ally was to be capitalist France, the second, perhaps, capitalist Britain. And in order not to disturb these potential allies, there was to be no workers' revolution in Spain. Hence, even while Moscow supplied the Republicans with arms, its Communist agents were putting down any working-class revolutionary urge with their usual ruthlessness.

*Homage to Catalonia* shows how hard Orwell tried at first to discover some logic in the Communist cause. Perhaps there *were* overriding international necessities. Perhaps any reformist government, he says in his English way, would have found the left-wing extremism of the POUM 'a nuisance.'

But what opened his eyes and aroused his deep anger was the Communist disregard for law and for truth. In Barcelona, he saw men who had risked their lives for the Republican cause flung into prison by the hundreds without charge. He saw thousands of ill-armed POUM militiamen suddenly described by Communist propaganda as 'Trotskyists, Fascists, traitors, murderers, cowards, spies and so forth.' During the confused street fighting in Barcelona in May, there had been no more than 80 rifles at the POUM buildings in the city—he himself held one —and the greatest care was taken they should not be used. Yet, to prop up Communist police control, the story that the POUM had launched an armed revolt in favor of Franco was spread by Communist propaganda all over Spain and, as he saw, repeated in the Communist and pro-Communist press all over the world:

It is not a nice thing to see a Spanish boy of fifteen carried down the line on a stretcher, and to think of the sleek persons in London and Paris who are writing pamphlets to prove that this boy is a Fascist. . . . One of the dreariest effects of this war has been to teach me that the left-wing press is every bit as spurious and dishonest as that of the right.

When Orwell left Spain, the military issue of the war was still undecided. The Spanish Republican forces fought on for another twenty months against Franco; their struggle enabled the Comintern to create the widely-accepted left-wing myth of the Spanish war—the myth that the Soviet Union stood for freedom.

As for Orwell, who saw through this myth, he could only wish the Spanish people well and hope that 'they would win their war and drive out all the foreigners, Russians, Germans and Italians alike.' He had seen enough to realize that the idea of good coming out of a struggle between leftist and rightist oppression was 'eyewash.' The real issue of our time, as he now saw it, was between amoral propaganda and respect for truth, between 'gangster-politics,' whether Nazi or Communist, and the respect for law and decency which, he knew, still prevailed in England.

*Homage to Catalonia* is interesting in showing how Orwell's Spanish experience at the front and rear helped to shape the political ideas of *Animal Farm*, *1984* and his essays. But it also remains one of the few books on the Spanish Civil War which can be read today without qualification.

# 43. George Mayberry, *New Republic*

23 June 1952, pp. 21–2

George Mayberry, American critic and editor.

> *They clung like burrs to the long expresses that lurch*
> *Through the unjust lands, through the night, through the Alpine tunnel;*
> *They floated over the oceans;*
> *They walked the passes: they came to present their lives.*
> *On that arid square, that fragment nipped off from hot*
> *Africa, soldered so crudely to inventive Europe,*
> *On that table land scored by rivers . . .*
>
> SPAIN, 1937—W. H. Auden

Some, like Auden, Stephen Spender, Christopher Caudwell, Ralph Bates, clung to the 'long expresses' to reach 'that tableland.' Others came from all ends of the world, but it was mostly the English whose long affinity for Spain dates back to their superb translations of Cervantes, to George Borrow's semi-comic attempt to retail the Bible in Spain, the already classic historical books of J. B. Trend, Gerald Brenan and Sir Samuel Hoare's gentlemanly admission of error.

Among those who clung to that long express was a lean, spare Englishman, born in India, a civil servant in Burma and in the title of one of his most fascinating books, down and out in Paris and London. This was, of course, the late George Orwell, who had already taken the road to Wigan Pier—the dead-end of humanity.

Before discussing the political aspects of the book, it is necessary to say that for sheer narrative and descriptive power, *Homage to Catalonia* contains passages comparable to the best writing of our time. Its unrelenting descriptions of trench warfare with an almost unbearable emphasis on General Sherman's trademark, and the tortured but uncomplaining account of Orwell's escape from Spain after he became suspect by the Government for which he had fought so ably are remarkable. These passages achieve their effect not only from their realism but from the author's identification with the revolutionary workers and intellectuals, both Spanish and English, with whom he fought.

The weakness of the book, and this is a purely personal observation, is its politics. I believe this to be true of his work as a whole. His best books are the above mentioned *Road to Wigan Pier, Down and Out in Paris and London, Keep the Aspidistra Flying*, and his essays on popular culture. The books that made his fame, *Animal Farm* and *1984* suffer apart from the nature of the forms employed by an abstractness as well as the spleen which seldom appears in his early work.

Orwell went to Spain as a journalist and, caught with the spirit of the people of Barcelona, enlisted with the militia in a unit of the POUM, a small Marxist party. He joined, not for political reasons, but, as in all his subsequent acts, from an innate feeling that it was the only thing he could do. At the front, he was too busy keeping alive and picking the lice off his person to know or care what was going on on the political scene. On his return to Barcelona, he was shocked to find that the non-party enthusiasm of what André Malraux called 'the days of the Apocalypse' were over. The Republican Government, with the collaboration of the Communists, and, according to Orwell, the middle classes, were firmly in control. The POUM and other left wing groups had not been fighting to preserve a republic but to create an equalitarian society and, feeling themselves being saddled with just one more bourgeois democracy, revolted, or resisted the state police, according to which view you accept.

If this sounds confusing, it is. As anyone who has read Gerald Brenan's *The Spanish Labyrinth*, Franz Borkenau's *The Spanish Cockpit*, (whose analysis of the political situation Orwell heavily relies on), or Frank Manuel's *The Politics of Modern Spain*, knows, if not from personal observation, Spain, particularly Catalonia, has been the most politics-ridden country since the French Revolution. Orwell argues, for the most part with fairness and good temper, that the needs of Soviet foreign policy dictated that the necessary line be the one 'the war must come first and then we'll see about the revolution.' To accomplish this meant the suppression of the revolutionary forces, courting the middle class and pious talk about how respectable and democratic the Republic was.

To accept this view one would have to appraise such men as Alvarez del Vayo, Juan Negrín, Dr Walter B. Cannon—the list could be expanded forever—as either fools or knaves. To an idealistic socialist the course of the Spanish Civil War was inevitably disillusioning, but it is at least a moot point that the policy of 'winning the war by whatever means possible'—including dirty pool—was as justified as turning a civil war into a revolutionary war which, after the full-scale intervention of Mussolini and Hitler, had no chance of success. In fairness to Orwell, and to recorded history, the Government's policy led to disaster, but only because of the active intervention of the Fascist nations and, of equal importance, the active non-intervention of the Western democracies. But to say that the liberals and socialists in accepting Communist aid from within and from without Spain was a betrayal is to ignore the rudiments of politics in times of crisis.

It is regrettable to spend so much time on such a fine book by a fine writer in hashing over old scores. But Orwell's enthusiastic vision of an equalitarian socialism might have been paired with a recognition of the fact that 'the road to socialism is paved with bedbugs.' Possibly then he might not have fallen into the sloughs of despond of his last books. To repeat, my political reservations are intended as no reflection on his integrity, humanity, and his love for and mastery of the English language.

# 44. Herbert Matthews, *Nation*

27 December 1952, pp. 597–9

Herbert Matthews (b. 1900), foreign correspondent for the *New York Times*, author of *Eyewitness in Abyssinia* (1937), *The Education of a Correspondent* (1946) and *The Yoke and the Arrows* (1956), on the Spanish Civil War.

The resurrection of buried literary works is not without its dangers. Anything George Orwell wrote is worth reprinting, and we can all give two cheers for the American edition of *Homage to Catalonia*, which was first published in England in 1938. The danger in this case is that Orwell was writing in a white heat about a confused, unimportant, and obscure incident in the Spanish Civil War. There are fewer people in the United States today who know about it than can work out Einstein's theory of relativity. Proof of this can be found in Lionel Trilling's introduction to the book.

Orwell has become a minor classic, and his experience in Catalonia was a turning point in his life. Without it, we would not have had *Animal Farm* and *1984*. Moreover, the Spanish Civil War, whatever one's sympathies, holds a major place in our hectic century. It was the rehearsal for World War II, and because of the role played by Russia and the Communists, the Spanish Civil War has been twisted into a monstrous caricature of fascism versus communism.

Trilling's error—and other critics have fallen into it, too—was to take Orwell literally and uncritically; to assume that because Orwell was in one corner of Spain for a small part of the war he must have known everything about it, and that his story of the betrayal of the social revolution by the Communists must have been true. Orwell's book is being used today as a club to beat those who had other ideas about the war and those who did their best to describe it while it was taking place.

This is a pity, for *Homage to Catalonia* is an honest, vivid, personal account of one man's bitter experience in the Spanish Civil War. If people read it for its literary value, they will have a rewarding experience. If they read it as history, they will be either misled or confused. Orwell went to Spain thoroughly ignorant of politics; he came away still ignorant, but with one priceless piece of wisdom—that communism is a counter-revolutionary movement. Unfortunately for today's readers, he reached this valid conclusion from false premises.

Orwell was a volunteer with a Loyalist militia outfit from December, 1936, to May, 1937. He spent all his time either on the Aragon front or in Barcelona; so he was restricted to a small group of men in a small part of Spain during five months of a war that lasted thirty-two months. In the end he was severely wounded, pursued by the police, and barely succeeded in fleeing to France. At all times he was wonderfully brave, and as patient, decent, honest, and fair-minded as a human being could be.

What happened is that Orwell got caught up in the partisan politics of Loyalist Spain. 'When I came to Spain,' he wrote, 'and for some time afterwards, I was not only uninterested in the political situation but unaware of it. I knew there was a war on, but I had no notion what kind of war. . . . I knew that I was serving in something called the

P.O.U.M. (I had only joined the P.O.U.M. militia rather than any other because I happened to arrive in Barcelona with I.L.P. papers), but I did not realize that there were serious differences between the political parties.'

The result was tragic for Orwell. He was a passionate rebel at heart who was convinced victory could be attained only by a working-class revolution against feudalism, reaction, and conservatism. In fact, it was a civil war with profound and explosive international ramifications; he wanted to fight it as an internal class struggle. From the beginning Orwell was doomed, and anyone who knew what was at stake and what problems were involved could have told him so the day he appeared in Barcelona.

The Partido Obrero de Unificación Marxista (P.O.U.M.) was more complicated than Orwell realized. It was originally a dissident Communist outfit, but it was also dissident, fractional purist-Socialist, mixed up with dissident Anarchists, with Trotskyists and dissident Trotskyists, with ex-Communists and an agglomeration of non-affiliates, men who sought revolution or adventure or merely a haven at a time when it was dangerous not to belong to some leftist or trade-union political movement. The other parties were all very choosy about members; the P.O.U.M. was not, which was why it attracted many foreigners—Germans, Belgians, and English—who were in Catalonia when the war began or who came in later. The P.O.U.M. was also, paradoxically, the most pedantically Marxist of all the Spanish revolutionary parties.

Orwell did not realize it, but the P.O.U.M. was already on the downhill path when he joined the militia, and the disintegration had gone very far by the time of the May, 1937, uprising in Barcelona. It had relatively few members, little trade-union influence, and no more than 7,000 or 8,000 men at the front. The real struggle in Catalonia was between the two great left movements—the Communist-dominated Partido Socialista Unificado de Catalunya (P.S.U.C.) and the Anarchist Confederación Nacional de Trabajadores (C.N.T.). The P.O.U.M. was caught in the struggle and smashed. A few weeks before Orwell arrived in Barcelona the P.O.U.M. had been ejected from the government (December 19, 1936). At that time its leaders baldly stated: 'You cannot govern without the P.O.U.M. and you cannot govern against the P.O.U.M.' Then they set out to try to prove it.

Orwell put the P.O.U.M. program into one sentence—and thereby inadvertently condemned it: 'The war and the revolution are inseparable.' The fact was that the war—that is victory in the war—and the revolution were incompatible. The Loyalists were losing the war because of the revolution. The great popular uprisings of the early months—the militias, the volunteers, the seizure and partition of big landholdings, the occupation of factories, the camaraderie, the heroism —all these things had saved the republic. However, by the time Orwell reached Barcelona the vital need was for unity, discipline, and efficiency. Franco was winning, partly because of German and Italian help, but also because the Rebels, as they were called then, had a unified command. The Loyalists were faced with the necessity of organizing a centralized administration and command or losing the war quickly.

Meanwhile, in September and October, 1936, Stalin began to send arms to Spain. This immediately put the Spanish Communist Party in the ascendancy. The Russians naturally channeled their aid through the Communists, who used their advantage to strengthen their own movement. To Orwell this was a tragedy, because they were Communists and because they were out for themselves. To Spain it happened to be an advantage, because the Communists were the best soldiers, the best administrators, and—this was a paramount consideration— because they were out to win the war first and worry about the revolution afterward, if at all. There was no use saying then, or now, that they were wrong because their motives were crooked and their final aims were evil. 'The thing for which the Communists were working,' Orwell wrote, 'was not to postpone the Spanish revolution till a more suitable time but to make sure that it never happened.' Which did not alter the fact that Communist tactics were probably right during the war.

Orwell felt the power of the Communists but never grasped the fact that the government was not run or controlled by Communists. He learned that after he wrote this book. If he had stayed in Spain long enough to see Stalin pulling up his stakes and slacking off on his aid, he would have noted the weakening of the Spanish Communist Party and the strengthening of the Republicans and Socialists. It was my opinion —and many observers shared it—that Spain never would have gone Communist if the Loyalists had won the war. There was sound basis for this belief, which is another reason why it is important to recognize the episodic character of Orwell's book.

The blow was struck in the uprising of May 5–7, 1937, in Barcelona. Here, again, the complications were extraordinary. The Valencia government had to get control of Catalonia and bring the Anarchists into line. The P.O.U.M. was numerically small and ideologically insignificant and it was not Anarchist, but it was revolutionary and was believed by the government to contain traitorous elements working for Franco and even for Germany and Italy. The fighting began as a quarrel arising from a misunderstanding between the central authorities and the Anarchists. The powerful Communist P.S.U.C. immediately jumped to the government side, and the puny P.O.U.M. got itself involved on the Anarchist side. Within three days at least four hundred and perhaps twice that many people were killed, which made it one of the most sanguinary cases of street fighting in history. It ended when the government sent in detachments of soldiers to restore and maintain order.

Nobody—and this goes for George Orwell—ever knew in detail what happened or why it happened. Orwell spent the whole time on the roof of P.O.U.M. headquarters in the Hotel Falcón waiting to be attacked; he never fired a shot in earnest, nor was he shot at. He got his information on what happened later from his P.O.U.M. friends and—being as always painfully honest—from whatever other sources he could. But the book adds nothing to what was known. The account furnished by the government side was just as detailed and more authoritative and plausible. The suppression of the P.O.U.M. afterward was not a pure Communist plot, as Orwell supposed. It had the support of the U.G.T.—the major Socialist labor organization of Spain—as well as of the government authorities, who were not under Communist domination. In fact, the P.O.U.M. found no friends in its agony—which was significant.

There is no better explanation of the outcome than Orwell's own statement after it was over: 'The Barcelona fighting had given the Valencia government the long-wanted excuse to assume fuller control of Catalonia.' For the first time in five months Orwell saw the Spanish Republican flag!

Orwell had recognized from the beginning that, although he did not understand or like everything he saw, it was 'a state of affairs worth fighting for.' And he never regretted having fought for it, in spite of what happened to him. Spain worked its magic on Orwell, as it did on all of us. He caught the greatness of that time and he has imprisoned it in these pages. Yet the introducer and most of the critics missed it, missed the forest for some grubby trees that came at the end of the journey. Spain did not live up to the hopes, the desires, the ideals, the (alas!) illusions that all, Orwell included, harbored.

F

147

There is no denying that he, personally, had the greatest possible provocation. Horrible injustices were committed, and Orwell and a number of the people he knew suffered from them. That is why this book is one of the most damning to have been written and printed about the Loyalists. It is also a reason for its value as a historical document, and it therefore becomes especially necessary to balance it truly, place it where it belongs. Yet, at the very end, Orwell could write from outside:

It sounds like lunacy, but the thing that both of us wanted [his wife was with him] was to be back in Spain. . . . Curiously enough, the whole experience has left me with not less but more belief in the decency of human beings. And I hope the account I have given is not too misleading. . . . In case I have not said this somewhere earlier in the book I will say it now: beware of my partisanship, my mistakes of fact and the distortion inevitably caused by my having seen only one corner of events. And beware of exactly the same things when you read any other book on this period of the Spanish war.

One must add a postscript to all this, for I have not seen any evidence that Professor Trilling or the critics knew that Orwell became acquainted with some of the Spanish Republican exiles in London in the early years of World War II. After finishing this article, I wrote to Dr Juan Negrín,[1] the last Premier of Republican Spain, asking him to tell me what he remembered about Orwell. I give here the pertinent extracts from Dr Negrín's reply, which he is kindly letting me quote.

As far as I recollect, I first met Orwell some time after August or September, 1940. He was presented to me as an editorialist of the *Observer*, and I was told that he had been in Spain during our war. I did not catch that he had been there, not as a reporter or writer, but as a volunteer in a fighting unit, and I believe I was not aware of that circumstance till I read his book on Catalonia, months after his death.

After we got acquainted, we met several times, and I venture to say that a reciprocal current of esteem, sympathy, and even friendship was established. . . .

Spain was often a matter of conversation, generally in connection with the daily developments of the World War, and occasionally recalling bygone episodes of our civil strife. I remember now that when this point was touched, he was very eager to inquire about the policy, internal and external, of the government I headed, the changes in the line of conduct of the war which I introduced, our problems and difficulties, the many mistakes I later realized to have committed, which I frankly confessed to him, though some of them were unavoidable and would have had to be repeated, once more, even after

---

[1] Juan Negrín (1891–1956), Prime Minister of the Spanish Republic from May 1937 until February 1939, when he went into exile.

the previous experiences; our way of handling the motley conglomerate of incompatible parties, labor unions, and dissident groups and also the frequently self-appointed, largely unconstitutional, local and regional 'governments' with which we had to deal; our foreign policy, especially our relations with Russia, having to take into account that the U. S. S. R. was the only great power supporting us internationally and prepared to provide us, on the basis of cash payment—we never asked it gratuitously of anyone—with the necessary weapons; the causes of our defeat. . . .

I have the impression that Orwell was satisfied with my explanations, given to him without reserve, with all latitude, but strictly confidentially. Unfortunately, at the time his book was unknown to me; otherwise I would have been doing the questioning. . . .

After reading his book, I did not change my opinion about Orwell—a decent and righteous gentleman, biased by a too rigid, puritanical frame, gifted with a candor bordering on naivete, highly critical but blindly credulous, morbidly individualistic (an Englishman!) but submitting lazily and without discernment to the atmosphere of the gregarious community in which he voluntarily and instinctively anchors himself, and so supremely honest and self-denying that he would not hesitate to change his mind once he perceived himself to be wrong. . . .

He came to the chaotic front of Aragon under the tutelage of a group *possibly* infiltrated by German agents (reread what he says about Germans moving freely from one side to the other and what the Nazis officially stated after the war about their activities on our side) but *certainly* controlled by elements very allergic, not only to Stalinism (this was more often than not a pure pretext) but to anything that meant a united and supreme direction of the struggle under a common discipline.

Putting all this together, one gets more than enough to justify the distorted image in Orwell's mind of the happenings of 1937 in Barcelona.

# 45. Hugh Thomas, *New Statesman*

## 20 April 1962, p. 568

Hugh Thomas (b. 1931), Professor of History at the University of Reading, author of *The Spanish Civil War* (1961) and *Cuba* (1971).

Hemingway, Ilya Ehrenburg, Claud Cockburn and I drove up to the front in a taxi painted in anarchist colours. The olive trees stood motionless like sentries against the grey of the sierra. We gave the password—*dignidad*—to a bronzed and smiling militiaman, and were shown to Major Mártinez' command post. Mártinez, peasant son of a long line of peasants, was of the stuff of Goya, Pizarro, Lope de Vega, Cortes. Pointing overhead to where Mussolini's Capronis were beginning once more to circle in a blue sky reminiscent of the background of Velázquez' portraits, Mártinez remarked: 'we are, I fancy, the only European nation who have committed suicide at the hands of others.'

No one actually wrote these words, but there are about 3,000 books or pamphlets about the Spanish Civil War made up of paragraphs in the genre, and many thousand newspaper articles. Nearly all are so repetitious and ephemeral, however, that a single-minded researcher can get through them at the rate of about 40 a day and, by listing all of them in his bibliography, can gain a swift reputation for great learning. About half a dozen of these books are worth reading carefully for their own sake even now, and the best of these is *Homage to Catalonia*. It is written with great lucidity and sincerity. It is very perceptive about war. Nevertheless it is very misleading about the Spanish Civil War.

Orwell went out to Barcelona in December 1936 and joined a column organized by the POUM, an amalgamated group of semi-Trotskyist left-wing parties. After a brief training he went to the front, where he stayed—always with the POUM column—until April 1937. Then he went on leave in Barcelona. His leave coincided with the outbreak of open fighting between the Catalan government, the central Republican government and the communists on the one hand and the more extreme Barcelona anarchists and the POUM on the other. After these May riots, he went back to the front, was wounded

and eventually—and with difficulty since by then his connection with
the POUM made him anathema to the communists—returned to
England in July. The book is simply an account of Orwell's experiences,
written almost in diary form and with the minimum of general information. Since he got on very well with the POUM at the front, he
assumed that the POUM's policy behind the lines was correct. This
was a misjudgment. If the Republicans were to have a hope of winning
the civil war, the only policy was to centralize war production, delay
the revolutionary process (to avoid antagonizing the peasants), establish a regular army in place of the militias and—as long as England and
France continued with Non-Intervention—make certain of a regular
supply of Russian arms. It was communist support for all these policies
that led to their dominance of the Republican cause. The anarchists and
the POUM, through greater idealism, were unable to swallow such
realistic stuff and their stars declined as inevitably as that of the communists rose.

# COMING UP FOR AIR

### 1939 (1st American edition 1950)

## 46. Unsigned notice,
## *Times Literary Supplement*

### 17 June 1939, p. 355

'And yet I've enough sense to see that the old life we're used to is being
sawn off at the roots. I can feel it happening. I can see the war that's
coming and I can see the after-war, the food-queues and the secret
police and the loud-speakers telling you what to think. . . . There are
millions of others like me. . . . They can feel things cracking and
collapsing under their feet.' Thus Fatty (George) Bowling, aged forty-
five, an insurance salesman with a wife and two children. He earns
between five and ten pounds a week, he lives—sleeps, that is —in one of
two hundred identical semi-detached villas in a dormitory suburb
of London, he eats at a Lyons' tea-shop. He is the average sensual man,
it seems, in an English world where the primordial reality is 'an ever-
lasting, frantic struggle to sell things.'

Mr Orwell writes with hard, honest clarity and unswerving precision of feeling. This new novel of his, which is the history of Fatty
Bowling as set down by himself, is controlled in passion, remorseless
and entirely without frills. In its conversational and slangy way it makes
the easiest sort of reading though there is as much direct comment on
the state of the world as there is indirect story-telling. Is it quite a novel?
Perhaps the answer is that, in Mr Orwell's view, the novel we are
used to is also being sawn off at the roots. No more dope or lollipops,
no more wild-goose chases or saving of souls; all that has gone the
way of the lost cities of Peru. For novelist or novel-reader what remains is the chance to get one's nerve back before the bad times begin.

It is an essential point of the book that George Bowling is in no way
an exceptional person. He says of himself that he fits in with his

environment. 'So long as anywhere in the world things are being sold
on commission and livings are picked up by sheer brass and lack of
finer feelings, chaps like me will be doing it.' He is as streamlined as the
rest. But there is something else inside him that is a hangover, as he puts
it, from the past, and during most of a day that he takes off from work,
mainly in order to get a new set of false teeth, the past comes back by a
freakish association of thought. It is the pre-War pattern of life in the
small market town of Lower Binfield, in Oxfordshire, where his
father kept a corn and seed merchant's shop, that he sets out to capture,
and capture it he does with an unsentimental artistry in which tact and
tenderness are beautifully combined. Sunday morning in church, the
smell of sainfoin in the stone passage between kitchen and shop, the
horse trough in the market-place, sugar mice at eight a penny, his
mother rolling pastry, Uncle Ezekiel and his Boer War arguments,
the dame-school and the grammar school—all these are composed into
a picture of an extraordinarily vivid and suggestive kind. It is the boy's
passion for fishing, in cow-ponds and in back-waters of the Thames,
with the minimum of home-made tackle and an astonishing variety
of bait, that is evoked most triumphantly: these pages could not be
bettered. With the decline in the shop's fortunes George becomes a
grocer's errand boy, then a grocer's assistant. There is Elsie, then the
War; then the wilderness that was peace, the Salamander Assurance
Company, marriage with Hilda and Ellesmere Road.

Well, what of it all? For George Bowling at forty-five, twenty
years after the end of the War, almost thirty years after he last held a
rod in his hand, the fishing is, in some sort, an epitome of the world
before 1914. It is typical of a civilization that he feels is at its last kick.
Not that life was softer then than now. Actually it was harder. But
people 'didn't think of the future as something to be terrified of.'
Their dreams were not bounded by barbed wire and slogans. There was
a sense of continuity. It is the ghost of that sense that takes George
back for a few days to a Lower Binfield that is all munition factories
and housing estates and as alien as the moon—and on which, before he
departs, a bombing plane drops a quarter of a ton of explosives by
accident. A defeatist story? In one sense, yes; possibly, despite its air of
calm, a little overwrought, too. In another sense it is the most heartfelt
of cautionary tales, with neither display nor self-righteousness in the
telling, only an impassioned and ruthless honesty of imagination.

# 47. Margery Allingham, *Time and Tide*

24 June 1939, p. 839

Margery Allingham (1904–66), author of detective novels. Dorothea Canfield's novel, *Seasoned Timber*, was also reviewed.

*Coming up for Air* is another careful study of a single character, but George Bowling, Mr Orwell's insurance inspector, is a very different person from Miss Canfield's schoolmaster. They are both defeated men who realize the fact and do not see what there is to do about it, but Bowling is not sorry for himself, and if his author pities him he has the kindliness to hide it.

George is not a hero. He is fat, red faced, middle class and honestly vulgar; not so much the salt of the earth as the bread and cheese and beer of it. His wife is a misery, and his children irritate him when they do not stir up in him a primitive affection and wonderment which embarrasses as well as satisfies him. The book opens with George wondering what it would be best to do with a windfall of seventeen pounds, the existence of which he has not confessed to anyone. It goes on to describe how he ultimately spends it on a sentimental pilgrimage to the home of his boyhood and shows the disillusion which awaited him there. However, that is not all. George's entire life is presented in this short space. We see how and why he became what he is and we receive a pretty good hint of what he will become. This is a fine book, fair comment on one aspect of life today and a sincere picture of the younger ex-Service man dubiously looking into a future which seems even less promising than the past. My only regret is that the story was written in the first person. This device, although it has the important virtue of making the narrative clear and easy to read, tends to falsify the character slightly since George's uncanny perception where his own failings are concerned makes him a little less of the ordinary mortal which his behaviour would show him to be.

# 48. Winifred Horrabin, *Tribune*

21 July 1939, p. 11

Winifred Horrabin, English author of *Working-Class Education* (1924).

If there is one thing future generations will never be able to say, it is that they do not know how we lived, or what we thought about—provided of course, that the Fascist reaction does not destroy all written records.

In a hundred novels the life and thought of our time is being expressed and, as in George Orwell's latest and in many ways best work, as finely expressed as in an accurate photograph.

George (Fatty) Bowling, whose life the book describes, is just an ordinary fellow, a man with everything which should make life interesting, a wife, children, a home, a settled job.

But something has happened to his outer world and he is disgruntled and unhappy. His world has become a kind of dustbin—'the dustbin that we're in reaches up to the stratosphere'—and there seems no escape, he can't even come up for air!

He does, therefore, what we all do, take refuge in fantasy, and his particular fantasy is a belief that his earlier life in the village where he was born, before the war, was all sunshine, loveliness and excitement. So he goes back there on a visit, secretly, away from his nagging wife and his strange unfriendly children, to see if he can re-capture that lost rapture.

Needless to say he finds that his little paradise has just become part of the general dustbin which stretches backward into the past as well as forward into the future.

# 49. John Cogley, *Commonweal*

3 February 1950, pp. 466–7

John Cogley (b. 1916), American editor and author of *Religion in a Secular Age* (1968).

This novel was written about ten years ago but is being published in the United States for the first time. The author's *Nineteen Eighty-Four* and *Animal Farm* were so successful it was apparently decided the reading public is now ready for all the Orwell it can get.

*Nineteen Eighty-Four* was a frightful and frightening look ahead. *Coming Up for Air* in the main is a mellow backward glance. Orwell writes, with a kind of desperate nostalgia, of the easy-going days before the first World War. The first war, he thinks, marked the passing of more than an era. It was the end of a civilization, and of a comparatively beneficent way of life. Ever since, our world has been going through a transitional stage. The violent events of recent history have been little more than a prolonged and bloody birth. A monster like *Nineteen Eighty-Four*, Orwell reminds us, is not brought into the world easily.

George Orwell, a hard man, is frankly sentimental about the world he knew as a boy. 'Christ! What's the use of saying that one oughtn't to be sentimental about "before the war"? I *am* sentimental about it. So are you if you remember it. It's quite true that if you look back on any special period of time you tend to remember its pleasant bits. That's true even of the war. But it is also true that people then had something that we haven't got now.'

What they had was a basic security. Even though physically life was harsher and the cushions of the dedicated Welfare State were unknown, people were more basically secure than now. They had a sense of continuity. 'All of them knew they'd got to die, and I suppose a few of them knew they were going to go bankrupt, but what they didn't know was that the order of things could change. Whatever might happen to themselves, things would go on as they'd known them.'

*Coming Up for Air* is really a novel-ized presentation of this theme. George Bowling, a middle-aged, middle-class suburbanite, tells about a few days in his own life, on the eve of the second World War. George is fat, forty-five, the father of two whining kids and the husband of an unloved and unloving woman. He is an insurance adjuster. An average man. 'At my best moments, I might pass for a bookie or a publican, and when things are very bad I might be touting vacuum cleaners, but at ordinary times you'd place me correctly. "Five to ten quid a week," you'd say as you saw me. Economically and socially I'm about the average level of Ellesmere Road.'

As the book opens, George is a little ahead of himself. He won on the horses and has seventeen quid to spend as he sees fit. He debates between a weekend with a woman and dribbling it away on cigars and double whiskeys. The debate leads him to think about himself. Where is he going? Where has he been? Where is the world going ? Where has it been? Finally George decides to go back to the little place where he grew up. He finds it changed. He finds the woman he loved when she was a slim, lovely girl now listless, ugly and overweight.

Everything has changed. People don't even go fishing any more. 'The very idea of sitting all day under a willow tree beside a quiet pool—and being able to find a quiet pool to sit beside—belongs to the time before the war, before the radio, before aeroplanes, before Hitler.' Even the names of fish sound out of date. 'Roach, rudd, dace, bleak, barbel, bream, gudgeon, pike, chub, carp, tench. They're solid kind of names. The people who made them up hadn't heard of machine-guns, they didn't live in terror of the sack or spend their time eating aspirins, going to the pictures and wondering how to keep out of a concentration camp.'

Orwell is a novelist, and he never forgets it for a minute. In *Coming Up for Air*, he is, of course, making a point. But primarily, he is writing a novel. A less skilful writer undertaking a job like this might have found himself on the lecturer's podium without realizing it, again and again. Orwell never abandons his story. Throughout, he is loyal to his novel and to his characters. What he has to say about the good old days really fits in with the story he is telling. And he is as sentimental about poor old George Bowling as he is about the days before 1914. Poor George! The world today is too much for his kind. 'He's dead, but he won't lie down.' Even when he realizes he is on his way to 1984, he's not quite sure what to do about it.

# 50. Irving Howe, *Nation*

4 February 1950, pp. 110–11

Irving Howe (b. 1920), Professor of English at the City University of New York, author of *Sherwood Anderson* (1951), *William Faulkner* (1952) and *Politics and the Novel* (1957).

In at least one sense George Orwell works within a major strand of English literary tradition. Like Defoe or Dickens before him, he assumes in his writing that there exists a social world external to and decisively impinging on our consciousness. Consequently he examines carefully social relations and status, for once he succeeds in showing 'what happens' to his characters within the social world, the reader may be able to surmise what is also happening inside the characters. It need hardly be added that the dominant strategy of modern writing, whether for ontological or internal literary considerations, is quite different from the one Orwell employs.

I make these unoriginal observations merely to indicate why Orwell's three republished novels, *Down and Out in Paris and London*[1], *Burmese Days*, and *Coming Up for Air*, are not likely to receive the kind of reception they should in this country. The general public will not find in them the titillations of his recent political allegories, and serious readers may pass them by as 'mere journalism' which does not satisfy the current taste for psychology, myth, or that hazy marsh known as 'morality.' Yet I wish to suggest that *Down and Out* and *Burmese Days* are Orwell's best works of fiction and deserve a larger readership than his more sensational books.

In his attitude Orwell is primarily a journalist, a term which in America is taken as a kind of depreciation, perhaps because we have so few good journalists. But Orwell is a first-rate journalist: he has a large gift for the observation of significant details, he is genuinely curious about people, and he is capable of making those limited generalizations of insight which, while not social theory, often tell us

*Down and Out in Paris and London* is *not* a novel.

more about a given moment of experience than a theory can. His literary journalism is consequently acute in its exploration of the social crevices in which our mass culture festers, and his fictional journalism, such as *Down and Out*, is both informative and informed with insight.

*Down and Out* is a modest piece of reportage, obviously autobiographical and a novel only by courtesy, which recounts Orwell's experience as a young intellectual, destitute in Paris and London. His approach to poverty is exactly right: he is serious enough to know it as an evil not to be expunged by chatter about 'values,' and yet he recalls his semi-starvation with wry skimming humor. Precisely because he takes poverty itself so seriously he avoids solemnity about his own suffering.

The Parisian part of *Down and Out* is written in a racy and supple prose which reminds one a bit of the breathless humor of Henry Miller's *Cosmodemonic Rigolade*. (When hired as a *plongeur*—dishwasher —in a Parisian hotel, he is told, 'We will give you a permanent job. . . . The head waiter says he would enjoy calling an Englishman names.') Orwell has a rich sense of anecdote: he delights in the waiter who is a Communist while sober and a patriot while drunk, in the thirty-nine times he was cursed as a *maquereau*[1] during one tour of hotel duty, in the parabolic Saturday-night excitement of his favorite Parisian bistro. With a charming kind of donnish precision, he notes the exact social gradations of hotel life, the utter uselessness of the luxury which forces the *plongeur* to be a slave, the instinctive way women have of drawing back from a badly dressed man 'with a quite frank movement of disgust, as though he were a dead cat.'

The second half of the book, a very careful analysis of English flophouse life, is more somber but if anything more interesting, since we know so much less about the English *Lumpenproletariat*. The particular virtues of this part of the book are the nicety with which it distinguishes the kinds of humiliation to which the indigent are subjected and the sustained and apparently effortless way in which Orwell avoids the slightest condescension in writing about them. Perhaps the best bit in the book is Orwell's description of Bozo, a 'screever' (sidewalk cartoonist) with a vivid mind, a gift for rich speech, and a taste for the classics.

*Down and Out* is superior to anything of its kind written in America, and should be read by at least those people who think poverty a more significant problem than, say, original sin.

[1] Pimp.

Written in a blunt, rather dulled prose, *Burmese Days* tends to be simplistic about human character and to whine about the 'stifling, stultifying world' of heat, prejudice, and deadly stupid women which is British colonialism. But it does create that world with an authenticity and sureness of detail which is possible only to someone who like Orwell, has seen it from the inside. During his younger days Orwell worked in the Burmese police force for a few years, and seems to have reached the conclusion not merely that British imperialism was evil, as E. M. Forster discovered in his visit to India, but that its representatives were mercilessly stupid.

Stupidity and cant, however, are more difficult materials for a novel than social evil. *Burmese Days* is relentlessly honest in its portraits of the vicious whites, the cringing Indian doctor who wishes only to humiliate himself before the whites, the English girl of bohemian background who discovers a natural gift for playing 'burra memsahib,' and the one decent white man who loves the natives but is too weak to break from his fellows. Yet the book never approaches the moral and imaginative grandeur of *A Passage to India*, for Orwell is incapable of the romantic intoxication with the East which gives *A Passage to India* so much of its loveliness, nor has he found any characters as dramatically elevated and representative as Mrs. Moore and Aziz. The mere fact, however, that one thinks to compare Orwell's novel with Forster's masterpiece is evidence that it is a compelling book, one of the few novels arising from the political ferment of the 1930's that are likely to survive their milieu.

*Coming Up for Air*, written just before the war, I find rather trivial. It is the story of an English insurance agent who, with the winnings of a bet, leaves his ugly London suburb and ugly middle-class family to visit the town of his youth. The result is completely predictable: Lower Binfield is now as mechanized as London, all the landmarks of his youth have been violated, etc., etc. The book has a few neat vignettes of middle-class life, but nothing that a good many contemporary English novelists have not done better.

In America Orwell seems to be valued most as a political bogyman pointing to the terrors of the future. But his allegories are thoroughly static, a mere conjured vision of evil in which no serious attempt is made to seek underlying causes. Orwell is not really a political prophet or even a very acute political thinker: he banks too heavily on British common sense, which after a point comes to seem mere self-indulgence. Nor does he have the creativity of the true novelist.

To my taste, the best of Orwell is in the splendid essays on mass culture and the finely sensitive reporting of *Homage to Catalonia* and *Down and Out.*

## 51. Edmund Fuller,
## *Saturday Review of Literature*

18 February 1950, pp. 18–19

Edmund Fuller (b. 1914), American critic, biographer and historian.

It was an irony that George Orwell died just at the time his publishers were issuing three novels antedating the two best sellers upon which his reputation in this country had been built. Any such group review tends toward the 'span-of-career' tone and now his untimely death makes this inevitable.

The first of these reissued volumes, *Down and Out in Paris and London* appeared here in 1933—briefly—and all things considered, there is scant reason for it to be heard from again. This is not to say that it is without interest. For one thing, there must be in this chronicle of abject poverty autobiographical elements bearing upon the tuberculosis that cut short his career. Moreover, some of the writing is splendid and vivid, with fascinating details of the life of the *plongeur* in Paris (a combination of bus-boy and dishwasher) and of the British tramp. (Interesting to compare him with the American hobo.) Bozo, the screever, is an especially notable type of his species.

The book's thesis concerning the eccentrics of this pauper's world is that 'poverty frees them from ordinary standards of behavior.' It is graphic, at times horrific, in its depiction of the extremes of privation. We feel it is all true and that he was there. Curiously, however, in the case of the narrator, there is an effect of a compulsive psychologic drive into this depth of abasement, for I never find myself convinced that he is forced inescapably into this state, without recourse or option.

To call this recital a novel stretches the definition to its limit. It is a set of variations on the theme of poverty and in its repetitiousness yields diminishing returns. But the gravest charge against it, which outweighs its specialized merits, is that there runs throughout a vein of the grossest, most flagrant anti-Semitism that I have seen in years.

*Burmese Days*, published only a year later, is quite another story, a novel of much excellence which evidently did not receive the attention it merited. Unlike the other two which we are discussing, it is a third-person story. Though he is adroit and fluent at first-person narrative, he is better disciplined in the more objective form.

Its story of an up-country jungle town in Burma; of isolated British colonials and corrupt, intriguing native officials is fascinating and well sustained. It is grim and bitter, unrelieved to the final page. But its narrative skill, characterization, and evocation of place are of a high order. It was worth reissuing and might possibly be Orwell's finest piece of literary art, for his two best sellers, excellent as they are of their kind, are specialized and one-dimensional satiric forms. *Burmese Days*, though a work of less breadth and subtlety, can take an honorable place beside *A Passage to India* (which it suggests inevitably) for anyone wishing a complete study of a waning British colonial era.

*Coming Up for Air*, written and published in England about 1938, is issued in this country for the first time and is more interesting now as part of a literary output that has been concluded than for its intrinsic qualities.

George (Tubby) Bowling, forty-five, is 'a fat man who is thin inside.' He is submerged in dreary family life, a dreary social position, and a dreary job with an insurance company. These compound drears have hanging over them the growing threat of war, which conditions, to some extent, everyone's frame of mind and state of nerves. So when George, who tells his own story, bites into the fish-filled frankfurter, it gives him 'the feeling that I'd bitten into the modern world and discovered what it was really made of.'

He is a British Babbitt, a confessed bounder, a little repellent, a little pathetic, thoroughly human. He and his kind do not hold the keys to the kingdom in the world as Mr Orwell more recently saw it shaping up.

The scorn poured out upon our civilization of gadgets and synthetics, regimentation, standardization, and mechanization, and the brief, sharp sketch of bickering left-wing factions and splinter groups fore-shadow the more focussed attack in the later novels.

'There's a chap who thinks he is going to escape! There's a chap who say he won't be streamlined! . . . After him! Stop him!' That was how George felt when he tried to come up for air and his account of it, sometimes very funny, makes a pleasant dish with a sour aftertaste.

Orwell's mood about what was to come with the impending war was gloomy, for he saw George as archetypal. And though the details of his fears were not fulfilled as he thought they might be, the evidence of *Animal Farm* and *Nineteen Eighty-Four* shows that his essential pessimism deepened rather than otherwise.

What of this pessimism then—can anyone deny grounds for it? Not lightly. Then how far can Orwell be considered the prophet and dark oracle of his times? Let us concede his literary skill and his corrosive biting humor at once. *Animal Farm* and *Nineteen Eighty-Four* are excellent tours de force, though owing some of their vogue to timing. Both are limited in their scope by the political reference, which is narrowed so explicitly to anti-Soviet satire as to lose some of its power as broader criticism of human behavior.

But taken with the three earlier novels, which are the chief subject of this review, they supply fairly complete evidence that Orwell did not just dislike the human race; he downright despised it. This was his weakness, early and late, but when he struck the formula of the last two novels, it was his special strength.

He has been likened to Swift by James Hilton, and aptly. But this analogy leads to a clarification. Jacques Barzun said of Swift that he possessed and projected 'ideals which coexist in our world with the corruption he depicts. And not only coexist but exert influence.' Here is Orwell's disadvantage. I find no evidence of such ideals in any of these works, or evidence that Orwell believed they might exist. Like many others who have seen 'what the modern world is made of' with discerning eyes—like Arthur Koestler to some extent—Orwell knew clearly what he was against, but had given up or forgotten what he was for.

# 52. James Stern, *New Republic*

20 February 1950, pp. 18–20

---

James Stern (b. 1904), Irish author of *The Heartless Land* (1932) and *The Hidden Damage* (1947), translator of Kafka and Hofmannsthal.

---

'Of course, you realize . . . that whoever wins this war, we shall emerge a second-rate nation.' . . . 'You know, there's only one remedy for all diseases—I mean Death.'

These remarks were addressed, not during World War II by one adult to another, but in 1915 to Cyril Connolly by his twelve-year-old friend George Orwell, who died last month of tuberculosis.

Orwell's passing has deprived the world of a man whom critics still unborn may well describe as the most important English writer to have lived his whole life during the first half of the twentieth century. Today, without fear of contradiction, we can say that England never produced a novelist more honest, more courageous, more concerned with the common man—and with common sense. Whether in fiction, autobiography, satire, pamphlets or criticism, Orwell never looked back with regret; he wrote constantly of the most urgent contemporary problems, always with the warning voice of the prophet. To literature, to the young and confused, his loss is incalculable.

In a penetrating analysis of T. S. Eliot's *A Choice of Kipling's Verse* (*Horizon*, February, 1942), Orwell observed that 'Much in [Kipling's] development is traceable to his having been born in India and having left school early. With a slightly different background he might have been a good novelist. . . .' Had Orwell himself in mind? Though this is doubtful—for less vain, less subjective a writer never lived—it's a fact that Orwell was born in India and that at the age when Kipling was sub-editing the Lahore *Civil and Military Gazette*, Orwell was still at Eton, being beaten by his contemporaries for turning up late for prayers. Thirteen years later (five of them spent in the Indian Imperial Police), Orwell produced his one strictly orthodox as well as his best novel—a far more balanced picture of Anglo-Indian life than anything

164

written by Kipling. Had the Eton 'background' helped to create *Burmese Days*, that tragic anti-imperialist satire about a corrupt native politician's efforts to get himself elected to the white men's club and the helplessness of a colonial caught between his loyalty to a Burmese doctor and the pukka-sahibism of his colleagues?

One is temped to cry 'Not bloody likely,' but it is not improbable. What is probable is that without the 'background' Orwell—though he would always have been 'a good novelist'—could not have acquired that rare sense of compassion, of justice, that runs through all his work. His great fortune, enhanced of course by the integrity of his character, was that while still in his twenties he had absorbed, had saturated himself in some of the extreme forms of human living in three totally different countries. What other Old Etonian has been a cop in the colonies, literally *Down and Out in Paris and London*, served at table, washed dishes and peeled potatoes sixteen hours a day in both smart and stinking French restaurants? What son of a blimp has tramped in lice-infested rags the streets of English cities, starved, slept with thieves and beggars, and yet—neither thieving nor begging—retained his soul, his sense of humor, and written an entertaining, illuminating social document of men damned by society through no fault of their own?

Where did this ex-King's Scholar, ex-member of the Imperial Police, ex-tramp and ex-scullion go from the flophouses of London? He went to the sprawling slums of Newcastle and Sheffield, to the unemployed mining districts of South Wales,[1] then sat down and hammered out *The Road to Wigan Pier* (1937). A choice of the Left Book Club, *The Road* was Orwell's first popular success. Because he never ceased to shock the middle classes, it was also his last—until the publication of *Animal Farm*, probably of all his works the weakest. Fearful though *The Road* is as an indictment of poverty and oppression, its author does not lose his sense of fair play. In an attack, not on D. H. Lawrence whom he greatly admired, but on the inverted snobbery of the proletarian intelligentsia who 'sneer automatically at the Old School Tie,' Orwell can say: 'Lawrence tells me that because I have been to a public school I am a eunuch.' Stating that he can 'produce medical evidence to the contrary,' he adds, with typical objectivity: 'If you want to make an enemy of a man, tell him that his ills are incurable.'

Unlike Lawrence (who, incidentally, died of the same illness at the same age), Orwell, however angry, seldom sneered at what he abomin-

1 Orwell did *not* visit South Wales before writing *The Road to Wigan Pier*.

ated, did not touch what he did not know. (To those well acquainted with huntin'-and-shootin' England, whole sections of *Lady Chatterley* are utterly absurd.) Again, unlike that genius, Orwell did not travel the world in search of health and a home: he spent the best years of his life, thereby shortening it, on English soil in a ceaseless battle for Socialism—the only ism 'compatible with common decency.' A man of action, he wrote out of the sheer physical experiences he had shared with the men in the mine, the slum, the suburb. A few such experiences would have caused many tougher men to lose heart. He didn't. Only near the end, in the superstate nightmare of *Nineteen Eighty-Four*, did Orwell, already mortally ill, cast aside his humor.

His most humorous book, in fact, a work as steeped in middle-class English life as any early novel by Wells (by whom he was obviously influenced), was written during those awful months leading up to 'Munich,' after Orwell had been seriously wounded fighting Fascism in Spain. *Coming Up for Air* (now published in the US for the first time) is a masterpiece of characterization, an astonishing *tour de force*. 'Do you know the active, hearty kind of fat man,' asks George Bowling, the narrator, 'that's nicknamed Fatty or Tubby and is always the life and soul of the party? I'm that type. . . . A chap like me is incapable of looking like a gentleman.' Now how is it possible for a middle-aged suburban insurance agent thus to describe himself? How, moreover, could such a man write a book about his life, his innermost thoughts, and get away with it? It is possible only because Bowling of Lower Binfield had Orwell's honesty, because the India-born Old Etonian had the Bowlings of Britain nearest his heart, every nuance of their speech on the tip of his tongue. Though deadly serious—a novel that, on the eve of World War II, expressed the almost inexpressible fears of every Englishman, warning them in frightening detail of the coming catastrophe—*Coming Up* has a guffaw on every page. It is probably the only book in which Orwell returned to the past. By so doing, he painted a picture of middle-class England from 1893 to 1938. Through this one man's memories and a return to the scenes of his childhood, Orwell shows how the Bowlings of the villages near London were sucked inexorably into the city, how the country was swallowed up by factories, how the pubs gave way to fancy tea shoppes, the dignified hotels to pewter and chromium, and the deep pond in which young George used to fish for carp to a vast dump for cans.

Disgusted, the middle-aged Bowling turns his back on the ruined land:

I'll tell you [he says] what my stay in Lower Binfield taught me. . . . *It's all going to happen.* All the things you've got at the back of your mind, the things you're terrified of . . . the bombs, the food queues, the rubber truncheons, the barbed wire, the coloured shirts, slogans, the enormous faces, the machine–guns squirting out of bed-room windows. It's all going to happen.

Well, we know what happened. We know that the boy who predicted that Britain would 'emerge a second-rate nation' from World War I was one of the millions who helped prevent those guns from squirting out of English windows in World War II. Does this make him, as some critics have inferred, a false prophet, a man who, because he was born in India and educated at Eton, didn't know that those incapable of looking like gentlemen are as capable as any gent of behaving like heroes? It is more likely that Orwell, just because he knew and loved the Bowlings so well, loathed and feared 'the stream-lined men' so much, felt no cry of warning could be uttered too loud.

# 53.  Charles Rolo, *Atlantic Monthly*

March 1950, pp. 78–80

Charles Rolo (b. 1916), American editor of *Psychiatry in American Life* (1963) and *The Anatomy of Wall Street* (1968).

Shortly before his recent death George Orwell, author of *Animal Farm* and *Nineteen Eighty-Four*, received the first Partisan Review Award 'for a significant contribution to literature,' given not for a single book but 'for a distinguished body of work.' Orwell's writing, the *Partisan Review* observed, 'has been marked by a singular directness and honesty, a scrupulous fidelity to experience that has placed him in that valuable class of the writer who is a witness to his time.' This tribute tidily sums up the essential quality of the three pre-war novels by

Orwell, all of them very different in subject matter, which have just been published by Harcourt, Brace. Two are reissues: *Down and Out in Paris and London* and *Burmese Days*. One is new to American readers: *Coming Up for Air*.

The striking thing about Orwell as 'a witness' is that, while he experienced fully the sordid realities of his time, he remained miraculously uncontaminated. He was one of the few men who traveled to the far Left without an unconditional surrender to dogma; one of the few who traveled away from it sadder and wiser but free of the guilt-complex that has led so many ex-revolutionaries into new extremes, new rigidities of thought. Orwell retained a rebellious clarity of vision which penetrated to the nastiness that is hidden, hushed up, camouflaged by convention. He was profoundly repelled by the cynicism and ruthlessness of the times; the corruption of language by the 'double-think' of politics, bureaucracy, and business; the pervasive sadism embedded in popular commercial culture (he wrote brilliantly about it in *Dickens, Dali and Others*). He was repelled, in every fiber, by hate and brutality.

Incapable of fanaticism, Orwell was an original kind of rebel, a dryly witty debunker of every sort of hypocrisy and cant. His outlook attests to an unshakable conviction that there is something infinitely important called 'decency' which requires no analysis. One finds, in fact, in Orwell a curiously successful fusion of divergent elements: a brilliantly intelligent journalist, with a remarkable documentary talent; a rather tired, saddened, but unobtrusively active moralist; and just a vestige of what was best in Colonel Blimp.

Orwell was born in India, educated at Eton, and then served for five years in the Imperial Police in Burma. His *Burmese Days* is a damning picture of pukka sahibs and imperial justice, and a wonderfully sharp documentary of colonial life. Orwell presents the Burmese to us with equal sharpness—he is far too honest and intelligent to idealize the underdog. The main threads in the story are the abominable maneuvers of a rascally Burmese politician, and a decaying Englishman's desperate courtship of a conventionally-minded young girl just arrived from home. Artistically the novel is Orwell's best, a really distinguished work that seems to me the finest thing in its field since *A Passage to India*.

*Down and Out in Paris and London*, though labeled a novel, sounds like a record of Orwell's lean years after he left Burma. 'Here is the world that awaits you if you are ever penniless,' says the narrator, and he takes the reader on a picaresque journey which yields an intimate acquaintance with the slavery of a dishwasher in Paris and the subhuman existence of a tramp in and around London. The book is a very graphic piece of reportage and wryly amusing in spite of the grimness of the material.

In *Coming Up for Air*, written just before the war, Orwell turns portraitist of the lower middle class. The 'I' is 'a fat middle-aged bloke with false teeth and a red face'; with a nagging wife and a dreary home in one of the hundreds of indistinguishable streets that fester all over the cheap suburbs of London. Exhilarated by a new denture, he decides to take a secret holiday from his family and spend the seventeen pounds he has won at the races on a visit to the little village where he was born. This starts him reminiscing about his childhood, and the novel shapes into a lively personal history which sets in counterpoint the quality of life in England before the First World War and on the eve of the Second. The rich, amusing self-characterization of the narrator—vulgar, clear-sighted, and sympathetic—is a masterly achievement.

The general remarks made earlier about Orwell's writing can be taken as applying with full force to this very able novel. All three books mentioned have strengthened my admiration for Orwell's gifts and my warm liking for his literary personality.

# 54. Isaac Rosenfeld, *Partisan Review*

May 1950, pp. 514–18

In an article on Arthur Koestler, written in 1944, George Orwell complained that no Englishman had as yet published a worth-while novel on the theme of totalitarian politics—nothing to equal *Darkness At Noon*—'Because there is almost no English writer to whom it has happened to see totalitarianism from the inside.' Five years later, with the publication of *1984*, he had become the one exception. He had not in the interval gained any more intimate an acquaintance with the subject; the year he spent fighting with the POUM in the Spanish Civil War was his closest approach to it. The success of *1984* must therefore be attributed to his imagination. But this is precisely the quality in which all his previous work had been weakest.

Orwell was fair, honest, unassuming and reliable in everything he wrote. These qualities, though desirable in every writer, are specifically the virtues of journalism; and Orwell, it seems to me, had always been at his best, not in the novels or political articles, but in casual pieces of the kind he wrote for the *London Tribune* in his column, 'As I Please.' He was a writer in a small way—a different matter from the minor writer, to whose virtuosity and finesse he never aspired. This lack of literary manner enabled him to give himself directly, if sometimes feebly, to the reader; he held back his feelings (even in his account of the Stalinists' responsibility for the Barcelona street fighting in *Homage to Catalonia*, his anger does not rise above the note of 'You don't do such things!') but only in the manner of restraint, and there was nothing hypocritical or false about him. He had all the traditional English virtues, of which he made the traditional compression into one: decency. When he died, I felt as many of his readers who never knew him must have done, that this was a friend gone.

*Down and Out in Paris and London*, one of his earlier books, is the steady Orwell who underwent no apparent development. Recorded here are some of the worst days of his life when he was unemployed, broke and starving. But the tone is substantially the same as that of the article on boys' weeklies in *Dickens, Dali & Others*. The Eton graduate and former Burma policeman accepts dish-washers and tramps as his fellow men without condescension and with only a little squeamishness at the filth of his surroundings. He makes no effort to bend his prose to the sounding of lower depths, and he was to feel no need to make a special adjustment to the language and problems of political journalism when he returned to England to gain some recognition as a writer. Detached yet close observation, dryness, a stamping out of whatever may once have been the snob in him (yet never at the expense of the Englishman) and the correlated stubborn attachment to common sense, to which he sometimes sacrificed his insight—this made up his basic journalistic style, unchanged through the years.

In *Burmese Days*, first published a year later in 1934, there is considerable bitterness as Orwell expresses his disgust with the Indian Civil Service. This is hardly the same man writing. For once he is full of contempt, especially toward his hero, John Flory, though the latter happens to be the only 'decent' character in the novel—he is not bigoted as the rest of the whites, he does not have the Imperial attitude, he is humane toward the natives. Yet he is a weakling, he gives way to alcoholism and the unrelieved colonial ennui, and he is incapable of withstanding the corrupt moral pressure of his colleagues; Orwell cannot forgive him this. His attitude toward this character—in whom there must have been a good deal of himself—is neither completely personal nor detached, and here Orwell betrays a fault which, until 1984, was to remain his greatest as a novelist, a fault of imagination, in not knowing what to do with a character, once the main traits and the setting have been provided. (The Burmese jungle, the character of the natives, their attitude toward the swinish pukka sahibs, the dances and festivals, the pidgin and official English were all excellently reported.) Flory, for all the significance a socialist writer might have given such a characterization, falls into the useless, unimaginative category of the weak liberal—anybody's whipping boy. The only interesting thing in his treatment of him is that it is so thoroughly bad-mannered; the mild Orwell makes not the slightest effort to spare his contempt for the man and ends by having him commit suicide, and the masochistic suggestion which this carries links Flory, however vaguely, with the ultimate characterization of the political hero (Winston Smith) as he who undergoes infinite degradation. Otherwise one is still unprepared for 1984.

Coming Up for Air, written in 1938, reverts to the journalistic style of ease and understatement, the disquietude of Burmese Days worked out of it. But this does not do the novel much good, as it fails to catch the anxiety of the pre-war days. The hero, George Bowling, running out on his job and family for a breather before the war which he knows is coming, refers to himself as a typical middle-aged suburban bloke, and Orwell, for the greater part of the book, is satisfied to treat him at this level. But his concern with politics had apparently been getting ahead of his style. Where Orwell's sense of politics in Burmese Days was of little more than incidental value, in Coming Up for Air it has become the source of the whole book. This, together with the continuing weakness of the novelist's imagination, accounts for such passages as the one in which Bowling, inspecting the shot motor of his car, compares it to the Austro-Hungarian Empire. Moreover, Orwell's politics suddenly appears to be out of joint. (A pity that it had not been more so. It is sometimes an advantage for a political writer to lose his grasp of politics, for the unreality of his observations brings him so much nearer to experience. But this, too, had to wait till *1984*.) Bowling's holiday consists in a return to his boyhood village, which he finds unrecognizably overgrown with factories and ugly housing developments. The values of his youth, Bowling realizes, have vanished for good. But this feeling is presented in such strength, it subverts the politics to a conservative tone. The decency which Orwell had linked, at one level, with the Socialist movement, in which he saw its only chance of surviving, now seems to belong entirely to the laissez-faire days preceding the first World War with their unshaken social traditions, the slower pace, the less highly developed technology. This again may be merely a failure of imagination, Orwell at as great a loss to know what to do with a theme as with a character; but it also suggests that the failure came of a division deep in him. He was a radical in politics and a conservative in feeling.

Though he continued to write his political articles and casual pieces in the same informal and disarming style, as though nothing were happening, his feelings were getting the better of him. This, though I have no evidence for it, I must suppose to be the case on the strength of the fact that he was for many years a sick, and during the writing of *1984*, a dying, man. His style, the character of the man, did not allow conflicts to appear at the surface, which had to remain undisturbed. He kept on writing in the easy manner that disarmed the reader of any suspicion of conflict, remaining empirical and optimistic all the time that he was turning over a metaphysics of evil.

A dying man, one may expect, will find consistency his last concern. Death exempts him from his own habits as much as it does from responsibility to others. Life being what it is in our world, the onset of death is often the first taste a man gets of freedom. At last the imagination can come into its own, and as a man yields to it his emotions take on a surprising depth and intensity. The extreme situation in which Orwell found himself as the rapid downhill course of tuberculosis approached, enabled him for the first time to go from one extreme to the other: from his own sickness to the world's. His imagination, set free, was able to confirm the identity of the two extremes, turning sickness into art.

The torture scenes in *1984* have been compared with The Legend of the Grand Inquisitor.[1] The comparison seems to me forced; a better one, it applies to the novel as a whole, is with Ippolit's 'Essential Explanation' in *The Idiot*. The torturer O'Brien's words to Winston

[1] A central chapter in Dostoyevsky's *The Brothers Karamazov* (1880).

Smith as he is re-educating him, 'The objective of power is power,' are the equivalent, in what they reveal to Smith of a politics stripped bare of morality, of Ippolit's nightmare of the monstrous insect, representing the world of nature without God. That the objective of power is power may long have been obvious to some men, but for the restrained writer who had muffled the terror and disgust politics produced in him, who had held on to a socialist rationale and let out his anti-pathies in an exaggerated idyll of the conservative past—for him such words had a deeper meaning. They mark the end of decency. Decency, meaning precisely the reserve of Orwell's own character, the con-stitutional intolerance of the extreme course, has failed him. Now he is dying. What good has this withholding done? He turns, like Ippolit, against himself, with the cry, not of glad tears of release, but of the jealousy of life, 'I have been cheated!' And now the decent man, Winston Smith, is unremittingly punished for the loss. He is given neither an opportunity for redemption nor even the small com-fort of dying with his inner life intact. His end must be beyond the last extreme, a species of pure diabolism: it is to the embrace of Big Brother that Orwell steers him, one of the most hideous moments of revenge in literature.

It is beside the point to argue that this revenge is the Party's, which will not allow its victims to die unrepentant, or that Orwell was merely following the 'confessions' of the Stalinist trials. These argu-ments are true, but it is also true that Winston (named, if uncon-sciously, to honor his conservative principle) was too close to Orwell for his torturer to be an entire stranger. So close a vengeance is always taken on oneself.

The significant point is that Winston yields. The force to which he is subjected is overwhelming, any man would crack. Yet in novels all actions are willed; the force that seems to break the will is in reality the rationalization of its action. Winston's breakdown covers a multiple suicide. There is first of all Orwell's own suicide, committed, according to the reports one hears, in the course of writing the novel and in the year that followed, when he neglected his health and remained active, though with two best-sellers he must have had the means for a change of climate and complete rest. Winston's yielding is reminiscent also of Ippolit's suicide, which the consumptive bungled only that his death might occur as so much the greater an indignity. There is defiance in this indignity, deliberately sought. Both Winston and Ippolit rebel against a world in which everything is possible, in which 2 + 2 no longer equal 4—by yielding. The defiance is marked by the extent of the yielding. Though Winston hasn't even a squeak of defiance left, so much the more defiant is it, as though he were to say, 'Take away my last shred of decency, will you? Then here—take everything. Here's lungs and liver, mind and heart and soul!' Everything goes, nothing is saved. 'He loved Big Brother.'

This is Orwell finally yielding up the life-long image, the character and style and habits of reason and restraint. I cannot conceive of a greater despair, and if it falls short of the magnificent it is only because Orwell was not a genius. But the mild journalist had at last attained art, expressing the totalitarian agony out of his own, as no English writer had done. He encompassed the world's sickness in his own: in this way, too, it may happen to a man to see totalitarianism 'from inside.' Whether Orwell's vision was true or false, consistent or not, or even adequate to reality, is a separate question, and not, it seems to me, very important in his case. All that matters is the force of the passion with which the man, who began as a writer in a small way, at last came through. The force with which he ended is the one with which greatness begins. This force, it will be observed, was enough to kill a man.

# INSIDE THE WHALE

## 1940

## 55. Arthur Calder-Marshall, *Time and Tide*

### 9 March 1940, pp. 257–8

A reviewer spends his allotted space, saying in so many, so many too many, words 'Read or do not read this book'. When he has finished, there is room for his signature and that's all. In this case, please assume that I have said already, 'Must read. Three essays, Dickens, Boys' Weeklies, Henry Miller. Brilliant writer. Superb'.

Most important is the Dickens essay. My only criticism is that when Orwell talks about 'Dickens's horror of revolutionary hysteria', he means his hysteria about revolution, a hysteria finding outlet in sentimentality even more often than in the fear of mob-violence in *Tale of Two Cities* and *Barnaby Rudge*.

*Inside the Whale*, name essay, deals with Henry Miller, Paris novelist, unpublished in England, and incidentally describes the literary movements of the last thirty years. It is the most trivial of the three essays; but I shall criticize it in what detail space allows, because it is going to prove a centre for literary controversy.

The Spanish Civil War brought many bourgeois writers into contact with politics. Bad Liberals turned bad Socialists overnight. For a brief season, socialist realism appeared to be a literary goal. Then Hitler, Franco and Mussolini won, and there was darkness over Bloomsbury. Why?

Orwell analyses the type writer as public school, university, Bloomsbury, continental tourist and condemns him as soft. He does not know solitude, poverty or the grind of manual labour. He has developed the substitutes for the religion he has lost, his god Stalin, devil Hitler, his paradise Moscow, hell Berlin. His castle in Spain is the Alcazar.[1] So far, so true of most.

[1] The fortress in Toledo and site of the famous victory of the Fascists, who withstood a Loyalist siege and were finally rescued.

I go further than Orwell, say most Marxists of that time were arm-chair revolutionaries, wrote of Communism without joining the Party, had no experience of revolutionary practice to save their Left-bookish-ness from sterility. Some of our poets, like Lucretius, married poetry happily to philosophy, but the novelists, unable to actualize theory, drivelled like latter-day Shavians. Before September 3rd[1] they felt uneasily that they could no longer repeat that duty novel about the intellectual who came to know Marx, yet didn't know where to go from there.

War was declared and Connolly announced the glad tidings that writers could forget their political consciences. One way or other, the issue was now decided. Uninhibited, our writers could dive from the top political board and bathe in the past.

This was good news, because Chamberlain's Government had been given powers to make things hot for writers who said things his Party didn't like. The shadow of Dachau was moving nearer home. Connolly again illumined our darkness.

Our standards are aesthetic, and our politics are in abeyance. This will not always be the case, because as events take shape the policy of artists and intellec-tuals will become clearer, the policy which leads them to economic security, to the atmosphere in which they can create, and to the audience by whom they will be appreciated. At the moment civilization is on the operating table and we sit in the waiting-room. *Horizon*, No. 1.

While capitalist democracy, in its fashionable dress of civilization, is on the operating table, the writers remain strategically in the waiting-room. If the patient recovers even as a Fascist, they can be the first to congratulate. If it dies, they tiptoe out softly humming the Red Flag and when they reach the street, burst into full voice. Socialism's O.K., but Hell, boys, economic security comes first!

Pocket-logic wins every time. But writers have their integrity; they demand a higher motivation for doing what others would do from economic necessity. *Inside the Whale* provides the rationale for sitting on the fence. This is the idea.

You're not in the waiting-room. You're Jonah inside the whale and the whale has glass sides. You look out and see everything, but you aren't touched because you're inside. You're passive, you accept. You don't make judgments. You don't even point to cause and effect, because that might imply judgment. You accept.

. . . What is he (Henry Miller) accepting? . . . the ancient boneheap of Europe,

[1] 3 September 1939 was the beginning of the Second World War.

where every grain of soil has passed through innumerable human bodies . . . an epoch of fear, tyranny and regimentation. To say, 'I accept', in an age like our own is to say that you accept concentration camps, rubber truncheons, Hitler, Stalin, bombs, aeroplanes, tinned food, machine guns, putsches, purges, slogans, Bedaux belts, gas-masks, submarines, spies provocateurs, press-censorship, secret prisons, aspirins, Hollywood films and political murders. . . .

I have not read Mr Miller. But I take Orwell's word that he succeeds, working in this way. Yet I wonder if the nature of one man can provide an aesthetic formula for others. It might release the imaginations of numerous young men, constricted by political conscience, yet without the talent for thinking in terms of groups as well as individuals. It sounds a swell idea, while you are surrounded with transparent blubber. But I suspect that if the view through those glass walls became too wide, the abstracted artist might find himself dragged from the whale to the concentration camp. Does he then accept the rubber truncheon with quietism? Or is the idea that if you keep quiet enough, Sir John Anderson[1] won't notice you?

I have recommended everybody to read *Inside the Whale*. Afterwards, I recommend a book written some time ago by M. Julien Benda, called *Le Trahison des Clercs*.[2]

# 56. P. M. (Philip Mairet), *New English Weekly*

14 March 1940, pp. 307–8

There is no English writer of today whose words came better off the page and into the mind than those of George Orwell; which is a way of saying that he is a good writer, one who knows his business according to the African negro's definition of literature, that it is 'speaking paper.' A book of Orwell's is a book that talks. It is worth asking why

[1] Sir John Anderson (1882–1958) was Home Secretary during 1939–40.
[2] Benda's *The Great Betrayal* (1927) attacked committed literature and proposed that the intellectual should remain above mere emotional and practical concerns.

his books are so much more directly and healthily communicative than the works of most of his contemporaries of similar mental calibre, some of them with more subtle and disciplined minds and not less earnest. Mainly, I think, it is because he is too sincere to write except when he is interested and too active in temperament to be interested in anything without doing something more than write about it.

Men of his critical and cultural level have, for instance, written books about the lives of the poor, but George Orwell did so after working for months as a dish-washer in the cellar of a second-rate Paris café, and an equally squalid spell of experience in London. Later, when the intellectual atmosphere around him was electric with hatred of Fascism and Franco, not a few intellectuals were deeply enough moved to go to Spain, but not, I think, writers of Orwell's reflective powers. He went to kill tyrants, not to collect facts about the situation, but incidentally he got the facts, to his great disillusionment and enlightenment. I believe he did not, before that experience, write anything of the Fascist-Communist convulsion, and only just enough, not too much after it. *O si sic omnes!*[1]

He is thus a full, well-documented writer, upon almost anything he writes about. Take the essay on 'Boys' Weeklies' in his latest volume, an essay which was published elsewhere, and has already received comment in these columns. Why do not more of our young writers get similarly interested in something that is happening just under our noses, such as this vast stream of juvenile literature, and bring it to our notice? Many hours of intelligent curiosity and alert social interest must have been spent by Orwell upon these superficially insignificant publications, and many remembered since his school days: and now his effort to extract their human and social meaning amounts almost to a thrilling journey through some darkest Africa of the world of letters, of which he is the only Livingstone!

The long essay on Dickens which fills nearly half of this volume shows the same spirit of thoroughness in a more familiar field. It is not just an essay by Orwell upon Orwell's opinions, illustrated with examples from Dickens; it is a genuine 'study,' a consistent and careful enquiry into the relations between that phenomenal novelist's works and English society, revealing an exhaustive reading of Dickens' works and of his contemporaries'. This quality of objectivity is still better shown in the essay upon Henry Miller. The peculiar significance of Miller, as Orwell sees him, the thing that makes him well worth

1 'Oh, if all were like that!'

writing about, would hardly have been expressed without a contrasting background; and the background is perhaps the best thing in the book. Miller is presented against a décor of all the best writers of the 'twenties and of the 'thirties, which is not only a bold, independent and spirited piece of writing but should be a durable contribution to English literary history.

Orwell is very English in his ability to form judgements of complex human material that are often arrestingly right, though the conscious philosophy behind the judgments seems to be sketchy or non-existent. He is really a sociological writer, but the only traces of sociological theory that his work exhibits are remains of a Marxism which he has almost outgrown and which it is doubtful if he ever more than half accepted. He is rather like a Pilgrim *from* the Left, to reverse the title of the late S. G. Hobson's autobiography—not that he is likely ever to 'go Right.' It seems to me that he uses a fragment of Marxist ideology now and then, as a substitute for some deeper and more valid criterion which he feels but cannot yet formulate. For example, after finding that current boys' literature is a pretty exact reflection of the class structure and class values of the country, his conclusions suggest that the obscurantism of these periodicals is designed by the publishers, an idea which does not follow of itself, and one doubts if investigation would substantiate it.

In the Dickens essay, in some discussion of servants and masters, Mr Orwell observes that Dickens had a very human conception of their relationship, typified in the case of Pickwick and Sam Weller, among others. Remarking how very different is this relation from the degraded conception of personal service in modern society, and how very much better, he puts it aside as merely a feudal survival, and with apparent regret that Dickens could not imagine a society without any servants at all. This may seem a small matter, and what Orwell says about it is justified in the context, but I feel that it is not really in his nature to have swallowed whole that hashish vision of continual progress in machine civilization abolishing personal mutual service between human beings. What if such relations have also a psychological basis, which a technical revolution as such could only pervert? Orwell is on the brink of recognising that the relation between Pickwick and Weller is of human equality, all the more so because of a specific and limited inequality, and that the modern Equality racket is another huge swindle, when he unfortunately saves himself by clutching at a straw of his Marxist memories. Later he uses the monstrous Marxian phrase that 'all art is propaganda' while giving it a quite different and better content of his own. Such fragments of a Marxian chrysalis still cumber the wings of his thought and still, I think, a little impede its flight.

Orwell is one of the contemporary writers best worth having: he lives to learn, he knows something about the society he lives in, he has courage and, as this book shows, a progressive faculty for criticism. The value of such writers is comparable to that of certain brain-cells to the body; society needs them to keep its consciousness. Also to keep an intelligence free—in his own words—from 'all the smelly little orthodoxies which are now contending for our souls.'[1]

# 57. Unsigned notice,
## *Times Literary Supplement*

20 April 1940, p. 192

Mr Orwell's latest volume consists of three essays, one on Dickens, another on popular boys' weeklies in this country and the third, ostensibly an appreciation of a Paris-American novelist named Henry Miller, a survey of the English literary consciousness since the beginning of the century. The unity of these three essays is not a matter of style alone, though the honesty of thought and the strength of plain statement which run through all of them help to give the book a pattern. Within this pattern, however, Mr Orwell seems to be specially concerned with tracing his own emancipation from various intellectual prepossessions about literature and the present purpose of literature.

On Dickens he starts in alarming fashion. Here, he says, is a nineteenth-century radical, who nevertheless takes up only a 'negative, rather unhelpful political attitude.' There is no condemnation of the 'system' in Dickens, no conception of 'historic necessity.' Dickens believes in kindness, in common decency; he stands for 'a change of spirit rather than of structure.' All this Mr Orwell sets down in tones

[1] This is the conclusion of Orwell's essay on Dickens.

of acute disappointment. He seems, indeed, to be arguing that, incomprehensibly, Dickens is not a revolutionary, not a Marxist; it pains him to confess that Dickens did not envisage the proletarian dawn. Only after he has got these conventional irrelevances of materialist criticism off his chest, in fact, does Mr Orwell proceed to say true and illuminating things about Dickens. Why he feels or felt that Dickens *ought* to have been a Marxist, ought to have had a revolutionary message, only he can tell; but it is plain that, like more rabid critics of this type, he has only an uncertain sense of English history before the Industrial Revolution and no very intimate knowledge of the nature of nineteenth-century English radicalism.

It is a relief to turn to his sagacious and pointed pages of literary appreciation of Dickens and to the concluding portrait of a 'generously angry' spirit—'a type hated with equal hatred by all the smelly little orthodoxies which are now contending for our souls.' Two statements in this essay, by the way, call for particular comment. First, 'he [Dickens] does not write about the proletariat.' And what, pray, are the Plornishes, the Toodles, the Vecks, Jo the crossing sweeper, Betty Higden and Hexam and Riderhood in *Our Mutual Friend*, Codlin and Short and the Nubbles, the pauper and criminal underworld in *Oliver Twist*? Next, in a comparison of Dickens with Tolstoy, 'Dickens is scarcely intelligible outside the English-speaking culture.' But the Russians, it so happens, have scarcely lagged behind the English in taking Dickens to their hearts.

The essay on boys' weeklies of the type of *The Gem* and *The Magnet* makes amusing and instructive reading, though Mr Orwell's analysis ignores the element of pure mental play in such reading and is of much too serious a nature. It may be doubted whether their effect upon the majority of the English male population between the ages of twelve and eighteen is to persuade them to-day that 'the major problems of our time do not exist, that there is nothing wrong with *laissez-faire* capitalism, that foreigners are unimportant comics and that the British Empire is a sort of charity-concern which will last for ever.' An excess of seriousness is likewise apparent in the conclusions drawn from Henry Miller's *Tropic of Cancer*, though here again one is impressed by Mr Orwell's effort to come clean and maintain a blunt and tenacious honesty of mind.

# 58. Max Plowman, *Adelphi*

April 1940, pp. 316–17

---

Max Plowman (1883–1941), friend of Orwell, editor of *Adelphi*
1938–41, author of *A Subaltern on the Somme* (1928).

---

Mr Orwell's title is deceptive, or at least not very explicit. Ostensibly
his new book consists of three first-class literary essays: on Charles
Dickens, on Boys' Weeklies and on the writing of Henry Miller
(author of *Tropic of Cancer*, &c.). But George Orwell has a unitary
purpose in selecting these very differing subjects. He wants to examine
the nature of the world we live in, and he does it by contrast—by
examining peculiar people in order to show the norm. And in his
imagination he has no doubt about where the ordinary man is residing
to-day:

For the fact is that being inside a whale is a very comfortable, cosy, homelike
thought. The historical Jonah, if he can be so-called, was glad enough to
escape, but in imagination, in day-dream, countless people have envied him.
It is, of course, quite obvious why. The whale's belly is simply a womb big
enough for an adult. There you are, in the dark, cushioned space that exactly
fits you, with yards of blubber between yourself and reality, able to keep up an
attitude of the completest indifference, no matter *what* happens. A storm that
would sink all the battleships in the world would hardly reach you as an echo.
Even the whale's own movements would probably be imperceptible to you.
He might be wallowing among the surface waves or shooting down into the
blackness of the middle seas (a mile deep, according to Herman Melville), but
you would never notice the difference. Short of being dead, it is the final,
unsurpassable stage of irresponsibility.

Dickens was politically unconscious, and therefore socially irresponsible. The purveyors of popular literature for boys are shown to
be sleuth-hounds of irresponsible, die-hard conservatism. Henry
Miller is treated as the representative novelist of his time in that he
frankly declines responsibility for what he can't control: he is seen as
a representative writer because he is a literary anarchist in a world

of social anarchy. So the book develops into an amazingly acute and comprehensive social study from the angle of humane literature.

Dickens seems to have the power of evoking from every generation its best literary criticism: a strange effect if you merely consider how photographically topical a novelist he was, and more particularly if you happen to find him almost unreadable, his style is so saturated with the vulgarity of nineteenth century journalese. But take him for all in all, Dickens was *the* man of his age, and because his age was a great one, he remains the standard-bearer of a set of values in the loss of which we can find a lasting criterion of criticism. For the essential decency of a human being was Dickens's perpetual theme, and common decency as a fixed quantity is what we are losing sight of to-day, indeed actually forfeiting in the general surrender to mass ideologies. Dickens was of course an individualist, and individualism we know had got to go; but now we suffer the painful interim, the green-sickness of an adolescent social state in which it is possible for the strident intellectual to believe that the economic security of the mass will safeguard the value of individuality.

This is the great social lie which the imaginative man has to endure in a totalitarian age. And it is in his intense perception of the lie that George Orwell becomes a great writer. He sees it with unique clarity because his whole attitude, both social and political, is that of a man who knows that common decency is fundamental to any tolerable state of existence, and that without the immediate recognition of it as basic, all chatter about liberty and equality is mere intellectual vapour. That he seems to be unconcerned with the religious philosophy of his own humanism is at once a limitation and an advantage. It makes him sensitive to the immediate scene and prevents him from straying into the philosophy and metaphysics that are apt to be the bane of the good novelist, but it leaves him, in an age such as ours, bare to the wind, a boy on the burning deck, a complete critic but essentially a satirist.

So it is that for clean hitting and straight fighting—for taking the ring and showing you where are the soft spots in his opponents—Orwell beats the band. This book is simply studded with clean punches which put popular but tottering figures over the ropes: things like: 'But all the same it was the despised highbrow who had captured the young. The wind was blowing out of Europe, and long before 1930 it had blown the beer-and-cricket school naked, except for their knighthoods,' and 'The outlook inculcated by all these papers (the Boys' Weeklies) is that of a rather exceptionally stupid member of the

Navy League in the year 1910,' and, speaking of the time of Dickens, 'It was an age of enormous families, pretentious meals and inconvenient houses, when the slavey drudging fourteen hours a day in the basement kitchen was something too normal to be noticed. And given the *fact* of servitude, the feudal relationship is the only tolerable one.'

Nominally there is no place to-day for a writer of such independence: he is completely insufferable to every kind of popular clique or mass-opinion. Yet perhaps the most interesting thing about him at the moment is his assured and rising popularity. Is it because intellectual vigour is so rare in a generation of yes-men that no one can ignore a man who has truly made his mind 'a thoroughfare for all thoughts and not a select party'?[1]

# 59. R. H. (Robert Herring), *Life and Letters Today*

June 1940, pp. 312–15

Robert Herring, editor of *Life and Letters Today* and of works by Goldsmith and Sheridan; poet and film critic.

George Orwell has the historical sense, which puts all in its place, and if he puts poets in their place, those who are honest will not resent it. They will see where they belong, from what tradition comes the trend they have joined or engendered and what tradition that is creating—they will take time out to think, and both the time and the thinking are what so many need.

Orwell does not fall into the trap of trying to say the last word about, in the first instance, Dickens; he adds his own clarifying quota to what has previously been written. Seeing him finally as the 'product of his age' he suggests—forcibly—that for all his attacking of institutions,

[1] From Keats's letter of 17 September 1819.

Dickens, so far from being constructive, 'is not even *de*-structive'. When he has dissected him with his dry yet loving skill, the verdict is 'a nineteenth-century liberal, a free intelligence, a type hated with equal hatred by all the smelly little orthodoxies which are now contending for our souls'. I am sorry, slightly, that Orwell himself is even so orthodox as to use the word 'liberal' in its fashionable sense, but you will see where he stands. And if you don't, I shall be forced to add that, after complaining that all Dickens strives for for his characters 'was a dream of *complete idleness*', and that few of them honestly work, he is honest enough to realize that 'in moral outlook no one could be more "bourgeois" than the English working classes'. Only those who know them, as friends as well as figures of faith, have the working courage to say that.

Later, he says much the same, in 'the Shaw-Wells type, always leaping forward to embrace the ego-projections which they mistake for the future', and more pertinently, 'so much of left-wing thought is a kind of playing with fire by people who don't even know that fire is hot'. No one will like being told that, but they have only to read Stephen Spender's *Journal*, so deep in deer-like surprise, to be forced to admit it.

First, however, Orwell discusses a problem overlaid alike by literary historians, psychologists, and writers of post-psycho-analysis memoirs; puberty reading. I call it that, but he calls it *Boys' Weeklies*, and deals with that scarcely underground growth of magazines on which fastens the adolescent's need to read fantasy. He examines the growth, exposes the underlying class-fostered philosophy, inquires of the results of this *Gem* and *Magnet* series in which the boys, for the last twenty-five years at least, have remained the same age, talked the same slang and supported the same sentiments. Though Orwell is here doing, perhaps, his greatest service, I think it is here, nevertheless that, running away with himself, he trips up. Forgotten is the bourgeoisness of the English working-classes, as defined above in his own words; forgotten also is the adolescent routine of living through several stages of civilization; to read *Gem* and *Magnet* is no more than the traditional pulling of wings off a fly. Orwell's sincerity at this moment, I feel, got the better of his talents, for having gone thus far, he could have traced the whole range of this reading—from the penny papers which precede it, *Puck, Chips*, and the rest, to the Edgar Wallaces and even Sherlock Holmes's, let alone Corellis, Glyns, Barclays, Dells, and Henry Newbolts[1] springing

1 These are all contemporary popular novelists.

from it. *Boys' Weeklies* is brilliantly a well-contained essay, but unlike the other two in this book, is not self-contained.

The last, which gives not only the title but the tone to the book, is on Henry Miller. . . . An editor is at this point at a disadvantage; he presumes that anyone interested in real writing has read Henry Miller. He wonders why it is found so necessary to 'discover' this author and realizes that ordinary readers are not able to read him. He realizes why —what Orwell calls 'unprintable words'. I do not think that 'unprintable' words are of necessity unguessable; indeed, I had imagined that the point of words was to guess or suggest; but as Miller does not think so, he is in much the same position as a composer who finds it necessary to express, onomatopœically, passing wind or making water. Orwell does more than give an introduction (indeed, his is on the arch side), he gives an integration. Miller is 'fiddling while Rome is burning and unlike the enormous majority of people who do this, fiddling with his face towards the flames'.

There the essay should have stopped; we can supply the rest; but Orwell himself has to, and supplies too much—'the only imaginative prose-writer of the slightest value who has appeared among the English-speaking races for some years past'. One is slightly hampered in assessment of that by the vagueness of 'for some years past'. But Orwell admits that it may be an overstatement, and what no one can object to is the comment he gives to the background of Miller, a background too long in the forefront.

It is ironical that Orwell's sharpness and detachment, which is after all merely sanity, should to-day seem brilliant. It is ironical to me that, having read this sympathetic study of Miller, I sent the *New Apocalypse* to Orwell for review, feeling he would 'get it' and found, as later printed, that he demands a prose-meaning (unless he is evading the point) from McCaig's 'cover the ground with the grin of a flying fox'. That means something to me, and something which I not only could not, but would *hate*, to 'extract a prose-meaning' from. But it seems only fair to put the two opinions before readers.

# 60. Q. D. Leavis, *Scrutiny*

September 1940, pp. 173–6

Queenie Leavis, wife of critic F. R. Leavis, author of *Fiction and the Reading Public* (1932).

Mr Orwell unlike Mr Muir belongs by birth and education to 'the right Left people,' the nucleus of the literary world who christian-name each other and are in honour bound to advance each other's literary career; he figures indeed in Connolly's autobiography as a school-fellow. This is probably why he has received indulgent treatment in the literary press. He differs from them in having grown up. He sees them accordingly from outside, having emancipated himself, at any rate in part, by the force of a remarkable character. His varied writings bear an unvarying stamp: they are responsible, adult and decent—compare *The Road to Wigan Pier* with Spender's *Forward from Liberalism*, which is a comparison between the testament of an honest man and a helping of flapdoodle.

Mr Orwell has not hitherto appeared as a literary critic, except incidentally, but as a novelist, a social thinker and a critic-participator in the Spanish War. Now he has published three literary essays which, promisingly, are all quite different. One is an examination of Dickens, another an analysis on not altogether original lines of boys' school stories, and the third a piece of contemporary criticism. From his other books we could deduce that he was potentially a good critic. For instance, he takes his own political line—starting from an inside knowledge of the working-class, painfully acquired, he can see through the Marxist theory, and being innately decent (he displays and approves of bourgeois morality) he is disgusted with the callous theorising inhumanity of the pro-Marxists. His explanation (see pp. 168 to 172 of *Inside the Whale*) of the conversion to Russian Communism of the young writers of the 'thirties is something that needed doing and could hardly have been done better. And he drives home his point with a piece of literary criticism, an analysis of a stanza of Auden's *Spain*.

Again, he has lived an active life among all classes and in several countries, he isn't the usual parlour-Bolshevik seeing literature through political glasses; nor is he a literary gangster, his literary criticism is first-hand. These are exceptional qualifications nowadays. Without having scholarship or an academic background he yet gives the impression of knowing a surprising amount about books and authors— because what he knows is live information, not card-index rubbish, his knowledge functions. A wide field of reference (provided it is not gratuitous), outside as well as inside literature proper, is a sure sign of an alert intelligence. While Mr Orwell's criticism is discursive his pages are not cluttered up with academic 'scholarship' nor disfigured with the rash of the exhibitionistic imposters who displayed in *The Criterion*. His writings are not elegant, mannered or polite, or petty either; his style is refreshing, that of the man whose first aim is to say something which he has quite clear in his head—like the pamphleteering Shaw without the irresponsibility (which produced the paradoxes and the cheap effects). He really knows the stuff he is writing about (for instance, Dickens) and has not got it up in a hurry for the occasion (like Spender on Henry James in *The Destructive Element*).

This is his most encouraging book so far, because while his pre-viously successful books have been *The Road to Wigan Pier* and *Homage to Catalonia*, not only timely but valuable in themselves, they had not seemed to lead anywhere. Mr Orwell must have wasted a lot of energy trying to be a novelist—I think I must have read three or four novels by him, and the only impression those dreary books left on me is that nature didn't intend him to be a novelist. Yet his equivalent works in non-fiction are stimulating. It is the more evident because his novels are drawn from his own experience (*Burmese Days* is based on his five years in the Indian Imperial Police service in Burma, others on his experiences as a down-and-out and so on). Yet these novels not only lack the brutal effectiveness of B. Traven's[1] for instance, they might almost have been written by Mr Alec Brown.[2] You see what I mean. He has even managed to write a dull novel about a literary man, which is a feat—an attempt to do *New Grub Street* up-to-date, but Gissing was an artist and Mr Orwell isn't. What an impressive book Mr Orwell made out of his experiences in the Spanish War (*Homage to Catalonia*), but that isn't a novel; in spite of its patches of spleen and illogicality,

[1] Traven is the author of *The Treasure of Sierra Madre* (1927).
[2] Brown is the author of *The Fate of the Middle Classes*, which was reviewed by Orwell in *Adelphi* (May 1936).

what insight, good feeling and practical thinking are revealed in *The Road to Wigan Pier* (for sponsoring which the Left Book Club earned one of its few good marks), but if it had been a novel one can't believe it would have been as stimulating and convincing. It looks as though if he would give up trying to be a novelist Mr Orwell might find his *métier* in literary criticism, in a special line of it peculiar to himself and which is particularly needed now. He is evidently a live mind working through literature, life and ideas. He knows what he is interested in and has something original to say about it. His criticism is convincing because his local criticisms are sound (always a test), and though his is not primarily a literary approach he is that rare thing, a non-literary writer who is also sensitive to literature. Thus his criticism of Dickens, while a lot of it is beside the point from *Scrutiny*'s point of view, contains nuggets of literary criticism (*e.g.*, p. 81), and you can see his superior literary sensibility on the one hand to the Marxist critics of Dickens (*pro* or *con*) and on the other to the Hugh Kingsmill type. He is not sufficiently disciplined to be a considerable literary critic, he is and probably always will be a critic of literature who, while not a Communist, has nevertheless corresponding preoccupations, but the great thing is, he has a special kind of honesty, he corrects any astygmatic tendency in himself because in literature as in politics he has taken up a stand which gives him freedom. He can say just the right things about Comrade Mirsky's nasty book on *The Intelligentsia of Great Britain*, he can tick off Macneice in a characteristic attitude, expose Upward's puerile theorising, diagnose Auden & Co., and 'place' the school of Catholic-convert apologists. Even his enthusiasms—another test—turn out to be sound criticism. Thus, you may think that the only thing wrong with the title-essay of this book is that he seems to think Henry Miller a great novelist, but it turns out after all that he doesn't. He claims for *Tropic of Cancer* no more than that it is an example of the only kind of tolerably good novel that can be written now ('a completely negative, unconstructive, amoral writer, a passive accepter of evil')—and expects, as you and I do, that Miller will 'descend into unintelligibility, or into charlatanism' next.

Whether he will come to anything as a literary critic will probably depend on whether he can keep clear of the atmosphere of Bloomsbury and the literary racket. And there are other dangers. He reminds one of Mr Robert Graves in his promising period in the 'twenties, and Mr Graves's history since, from the standpoint of literary criticism, has been rather a sad one. Probably the best thing for him and the best thing for us would be to export him to interpret English Literature to the foreign student, instead of the yes-men who generally land the chairs of English abroad. Everyone would benefit; though one doesn't see him accepting such an offer. But one thing above all there is to his credit. If the revolution here were to happen that he wants and prophesies, the advent of real Socialism, he would be the only man of letters we have whom we can imagine surviving the flood undisturbed.

# THE LION AND THE UNICORN

## 1941

## 61. Dwight Macdonald, *Partisan Review*

### March 1942, pp. 166–9

Dwight Macdonald (b. 1906), American editor of *Partisan Review* (1938–43) and *Politics* (1944–9), author of *Memoirs of a Revolutionist* (1957) and *Against the American Grain* (1962).

In its virtues and in its defects, *The Lion and the Unicorn* is typical of English leftwing political writing. Its approach to politics is impressionistic rather than analytic, literary rather than technical, that of the amateur, not the professional. This has its advantages. Orwell's consciousness embraces a good deal that our own Marxists have wrongly excluded from their data (though Marx himself most decidedly didn't): such as that British army officers wear civilian clothes off duty, that the British are a nation of flower-lovers and stamp-collectors, the contrast between the goose-step of the German Army and the 'formalized walk' of the British. There is also a *human* quality to Orwell's political writing; you feel it engages him as a moral and cultural whole, not merely as a specialist. For this reason it has a life, an ease and color which our own Marxist epigones seem to feel is somehow sinful; and its values are rarely *inhuman*, however muddled they seem at times.

But there are also the defects of the amateur: if Orwell's scope is broad, it is none too deep; he describes where he should analyze, and poses questions so impressionistically that his answers get nowhere; he uses terms in a shockingly vague way; he makes sweeping generalizations with the confidence of ignorance; his innocence of scientific criteria is appalling. What can one make of a statement like: 'No real revolutionist has ever been an internationalist'? On page 62 he writes:

'It has become clear in the last few years that "common ownership of the means of production" is not in itself a sufficient definition of socialism. One must also add the following: approximate equality of incomes . . . political democracy, and abolition of all hereditary privilege, especially in education.' Six pages later he speaks of 'Russia, the only definitely socialist country.' Obviously not a single one of Orwell's three necessary additions exist in Russia. Since Orwell's anti-Stalinism is well-known, one can only conclude that he is using the term 'socialist' in very different senses in the two passages.

With most of Orwell's generalizations about the present war, I find myself in agreement. 'What this war has demonstrated is that private capitalism *does not work*.' 'Either we turn this war into a revolutionary war or we lose it, and much more besides. . . . It is quite certain that with our present social structure we cannot win. Our real forces, physical, moral or intellectual cannot be mobilized.' 'We cannot establish anything that a Western nation would regard as socialism without defeating Hitler; on the other hand, we cannot defeat Hitler while we remain economically and socially in the nineteenth century.' Recent events in Libya, Malaya, and the English Channel amply document such propositions. Most of Orwell's program, also, seems in general sensible as a first step: nationalization of land, mines, railways, banks and major industries; democratization of education; equalization of personal incomes; freedom for India.

But most of us on the left, from liberals to Trotskyists, would agree on some such program. The real question is Lenin's What Is To Be Done? Specifically, what classes or social groups can be mobilized to win such a program; what should be their attitude towards the existing political regimes and economic systems in England and America? Although Orwell seems to be politically closest to the left Labor Party of Cripps and Laski, he hardly mentions the workingclass in his book and pins his hopes instead on a new middleclass of technicians, doctors, state employees, etc. which has made 'the old classification of society into capitalists, proletarians and petit-bourgeois almost obsolete.' This tendency exists and has often been noted. Nor is there any novelty in the conception of this new 'classless middleclass' as the heir of the future. But Orwell is as deplorably vague about just *how* this new class will take over (and what specific indications already exist that it will) as all the other prophets of such a future have been. He seems to conceive of it as a gradual, osmotic process proceeding steadily within the old social framework. This classless revolution marches under the banner of nationalism, furthermore. Hence it is clear that Orwell, though, oddly enough, he never explicitly says so in the book, favors critical support of the existing Churchill war government.

As one who thinks that only a socialist government can defeat totalitarianism either within or without, and that the only road to such a state is for the workers to insist on replacing the antiquated capitalism represented by Roosevelt and Churchill with their own government, as such a one I can see in the history of the last three years no evidence for Orwell's easy confidence in this gradualist 'revolution.' He recognizes that before his program can be put into effect, 'there will have to be a complete shift of power away from the old ruling class.' But is any one today, including Orwell, able to see any indication of such a shift in England in the last two years? 'Within a year, perhaps even six months,' writes Orwell, 'if we are still unconquered, we shall see the rise of something that has never existed before, a specifically *English* socialist movement.' This was written at the end of 1940. Over a year has passed, and there are no signs of the English socialist movement Orwell so confidently predicted. Despite an almost unbroken string of humiliating defeats, in Africa, Malaya and now the English Channel itself, the reins of power are still firmly in the hands of Churchill, the former admirer of Hitler and Mussolini, the chief organizer of armed intervention against the infant Russian revolution, the leader of the British ruling class in smashing the 1926 general strike. (Orwell has plenty to say about poor old Chamberlain, but is silent on Churchill.) This great democrat has been able since Dunkirk, furthermore, to turn the government back to the old Tory gang and to emasculate— true enough with their enthusiastic cooperation—the Labor Party leadership. There has been a gradualist revolution, all right, but in reverse.

Perhaps the clue to this odd combination of acuteness as an observer and infantilism as a theorist may be found in Orwell's general intellectual orientation. He reacts so violently against the admittedly great defects of the leftwing intellectual tradition of the last two decades as to deny himself as an intellectual. Like Messers Brooks, Mumford, MacLeish and Chamberlain over here, Orwell is bitterly hostile to both internationalism and intellectualism, preaching the virtues of patriotism and denouncing 'Europeanized intellectuals.' He echoes the Brooks-MacLeish Thesis when he criticizes the intellectuals for being 'negative,' 'carping' and 'irresponsible,' and when he writes, 'If the English people suffered for several years a real weakening of morale, so that Fascist nations judged they were "decadent" and that it was safe to plunge into war, the intellectual sabotage from the Left was partly responsible.' Now it is true that the postwar Marxist tradition was over-schematic and timidly 'orthodox,' that it underestimated psychological and cultural factors and tried to apply a mechanical-materialistic yardstick to everything, and that it was purist to the point of sterility. But a reaction to the opposite pole is not the solution, either. A retreat to the kind of common-sense Philistinism which Orwell embraces in matters of theory seems to me even less calculated to preserve the values we both want to preserve than the sectarian Marxism it rejects. There are, of course, as I tried to show in my article on Van Wyck Brooks, deep historical reasons for the rise of this attitude today. There is a dangerous tendency, shown in several of the comments on the issue printed in the last number, to assume that it is mostly a matter of the personal stupidity of Brooks and Co. I would be the last to deny Mr Brooks' mental incompetence, but the roots of the matter unfortunately go much deeper, as we can see when a man of the intelligence and goodwill of Orwell joins the parade.

I'd like to add a few words, finally, on the format of Orwell's book. Why are British books so much more physically attractive than our own? And why do short, cheap books—really long pamphlets—apparently 'go' so much better in England than here? First published in February 1941, this is the first of the 'Searchlight Books,' a series of inexpensive little pocket books on war issues. It is printed on the pleasantly lightweight book paper the English use, has a light binding of unbleached cloth, fits easily into a suit pocket, and altogether is a sensible and unpretentiously attractive little volume. If it were published over here, it would weigh twice as much, would be just too big to fit into the pocket, and would therefore be three times as expensive and half as good-looking. But it probably wouldn't be published here anyway because American publishers seem to think the public won't buy short, cheap original editions. Whatever the former merits of the argument, the war may well have changed things. The 150–200 page book is the ideal medium for political pamphleteering, more topical and pointed than a full-length book and yet offering enough space to go deeper than a magazine article. The time would seem overripe for a 'Searchlight Series' of our own.

# ANIMAL FARM

## 1945

## 62. Graham Greene, *Evening Standard*

### 10 August 1945, p. 6

Graham Greene (b. 1904), English novelist, author of *Brighton
Rock* (1938), *The Power and the Glory* (1940) and *The Heart of the
Matter* (1948).

Whatever you may say about writers—their private lives, their feeding
habits or their taste in shirts—you have to admit, I think, that there has
never been such a thing as a literature of appeasement.

Writers may pass, like everyone else, through the opium dream of
Munich and Yalta, but no literature comes out of that dream.

For literature is concerned above everything else with the accurate
expression of a personal vision, while appeasement is a matter of
compromise.

Nevertheless, in wartime there has to be a measure of appeasement,
and it is as well for the writer to keep quiet. He must not give way to
despondency or dismay, he must not offend a valuable ally, he must not
even make fun . . .

It is a welcome sign of peace that Mr George Orwell is able to
publish his 'fairy story' *Animal Farm*, a satire upon the totalitarian state
and one state in particular. I have heard a rumour that the manuscript
was at one time submitted to the Ministry of Information, that huge
cenotaph of appeasement, and an official there took a poor view of it.
'Couldn't you make them some other animal,' he is reported as saying
in reference to the dictator and his colleagues, 'and not pigs?'

For this is the story of a political experiment on a farm where the
animals, under the advice of a patriarchal porker, get organised and
eventually drive out Mr Jones, the human owner.

The porker does not live to see the success of his revolution, but two other pigs, Snowball and Napoleon, soon impose their leadership on the farm animals. Never had the farm animals worked with such élan for Mr Jones as they now work, so they believe, for themselves. They have a song, 'Beasts of England'; they have the inspiring seven commandments of Animalism, taught them by the old porker, painted on the barn for all to see.

1. Whoever goes upon two legs is an enemy.
2. Whatever goes upon four legs, or has wings, is a friend.
3. No animal shall wear clothes.
4. No animal shall sleep in a bed.
5. No animal shall drink alcohol.
6. No animal shall kill any other animal.
7. All animals are equal.

They have a banner which blows over the farmhouse garden, a hoof and horn in white painted on an old green tablecloth.

It is a sad fable, and it is an indication of Mr Orwell's fine talent that it is really sad—not a mere echo of human failings at one remove. We do become involved in the fate of Molly the Cow, old Benjamin the Donkey, and Boxer the poor devil of a hard-working, easily deceived Horse. Snowball is driven out by Napoleon, who imposes his solitary leadership with the help of a gang of savage dogs, and slowly the Seven Commandments become altered or erased, until at last on the barn door appears only one sentence. 'All animals are equal, but some animals are more equal than others.'

If Mr Walt Disney is looking for a real subject, here it is: it has all the necessary humour, and it has, too, the subdued lyrical quality he can sometimes express so well. But is it perhaps a little too real for him? There is no appeasement here.

As for the others, their life, so far as they knew, was as it had always been. They were generally hungry, they slept on straw, they drank from the pool, they laboured in the fields; in winter they were troubled by the cold, and in summer by the flies. Sometimes the older ones among them racked their dim memories and tried to determine whether in the early days of the Rebellion, when Jones's expulsion was still recent, things had been better or worse than now. They could not remember. . . . Only old Benjamin professed to remember every detail of his long life and to know that things never had been, nor ever could be much better or much worse—hunger, hardship, and disappointment being, so he said, the unalterable law of life.

## 63. Kingsley Martin, *New Statesman and Nation*

8 September 1945, pp. 165–6

---

Kingsley Martin (1897–1969), editor of the *New Statesman* (1930–60), author of *Father Figures* (1966) and *Editor* (1968).

---

In a world choked everywhere with suffering, cruelty and exploitation, the disillusioned idealist may be embarrassed by the rich choice of objects for denunciation. He runs the risk of twisting himself into knots, as he discovers enemies, first to the Right, then to the Left and, most invigorating, at home amongst his friends. He may try to solve his dilemma by deciding on some particular Power-figure as the embodiment of Evil, concentrating upon it all his wealth of frustration and righteous indignation. If he remains only a critic and fails to turn his talent to the search for a practical remedy for a specific evil, he is likely, in time, to decide that all the world is evil and that human nature is itself incorrigible. The alternatives then—we see many contemporary instances—are cynicism or religion and mysticism.

Mr Orwell's Devils have been numerous and, since he is a man of integrity, he chooses real evils to attack. His latest satire, beautifully written, amusing and, if you don't take it too seriously, a fair corrective of much silly worship of the Soviet Union, suggests to me that he is reaching the exhaustion of idealism and approaching the bathos of cynicism. He began as a civil servant, honestly indignant with the misdeeds of the British Empire as he saw it in the Far East. During the Spanish war, a sincere anti-Fascist, he found, like many others of his temperament, that of all the warring groups the most idealistic and least smirched were the anarchists. The fact that they would infallibly have lost the war while the Republican coalition might, in slightly more favourable circumstances, have won it, did not affect his onslaught. At the outset of the World War he repented his past. Realising that Nazi Germany was now an even worse enemy than the British Empire or the Negrin Government, he wrote denouncing the Left, scarcely noticing that it was his own back he was lashing, and that his blows often fell short of others who had not made the mistakes with which he charged them. Now that Germany is defeated, it seems almost accidental that his righteous indignation is turned not, say, against the Americans for their treatment of Negroes, but against the Soviet Union. In Stalin he finds the latest incarnation of Evil.

There is plenty in the U.S.S.R. to satirise, and Mr Orwell does it well. How deftly the fairy story of the animals who, in anticipation of freedom and plenty, revolt against the tyrannical farmer, turns into a rollicking caricature of the Russian Revolution! His shafts strike home. We all know of the sheep, who drown discussion by the bleating of slogans; we have all noticed, with a wry smile, the gradual change of Soviet doctrine under the pretence that it is no change and then that the original doctrine was an anti-Marxist error. (The best thing in Mr Orwell's story is the picture of the puzzled animals examining the Original Principles of the Revolution, and finding them altered: 'All animals are equal,' said the slogan; to which is added, 'but some are more equal than others.') The falsehoods about Trotsky, whose part in the revolutionary period, only secondary to Lenin's, has been gradually erased from the Soviet history books, is another fair count against Stalinite methods. The story of the loyal horse who worked until his lungs burst and was finally sent off to the knackers' yard is told with a genuine pathos; it represents a true and hateful aspect of every revolutionary struggle. Best of all is the character of the donkey who says little, but is always sure that the more things change the more they will be the same, that men will always be oppressed and exploited whether they have revolutions and high ideals or not.

The logic of Mr Orwell's satire is surely the ultimate cynicism of Ben, the donkey. That, if I read Mr Orwell's mind correctly, is where his idealism and disillusion has really landed him. But he has not quite the courage to see that he has lost faith, not in Russia but in mankind. So the surface moral of his story is that all would have gone well with the revolution if the wicked Stalin had not driven the brave and good Trotsky out of Eden. Here Mr Orwell ruins what should have been a very perfect piece of satire on human life. For by putting the Stalin-Trotsky struggle in the centre he invites every kind of historical and factual objection. We are brought from the general to the particular; to the question why Stalin decided to attempt the terrific feat of creating an independent Socialist country rather than risk plunging Russia unprepared into a war of intervention by stirring up revolution in ncighbouring countries. Mr Orwell may say it would have been better if this policy had prevailed, but a moment's thought will evoke in him the brilliant satire he would have written about the betrayal of the revolution, if Trotsky, who was as ruthless a revolutionary as Stalin, had won the day and lost the revolution by another route. This same error compels the reader to ask whether in fact it is true that the Commissar to-day is indistinguishable in ideals and privilege from the Tzarist bureaucrat and the answer is that though many traditional Russian characteristics survive in Russia, the new ruling class is really very different indeed from anything that Russia has known before. In short, if we read the satire as a gibe at the failings of the U.S.S.R. and realise that it is historically false and neglectful of the complex truth about Russia, we shall enjoy it and be grateful for our laugh. But which will Mr Orwell do next? Having fired his bolt against Stalin, he could return to the attack on British or American Capitalism as seen through the eyes say, of an Indian peasant; the picture would be about as true or as false. Alternatively, there is the Church of Rome, Yogi, or at a pinch, the more tedious effort to help find the solution of any of the problems that actually face Stalin, Mr Attlee, Mr Orwell and the rest of us.

# 64. C. C. (Cyril Connolly), *Horizon*

September 1945, pp. 215–16

Mr Orwell is a revolutionary who is in love with 1910. This ambivalence constitutes his strength and his weakness. Never before has a progressive political thinker been so handicapped by nostalgia for the Edwardian shabby-genteel or the under-dog. It is this political sentimentality which from the literary point of view is his most valid emotion. *Animal Farm* proves it, for it truly is a fairy story told by a great lover of liberty and a great lover of animals. The farm is real, the animals are moving. At the same time it is a devastating attack on

Stalin and his 'betrayal' of the Russian revolution, as seen by another revolutionary. The allegory between the animals and the fate of their revolution (they drive out the human beings and plan a Utopia entrusted to the leadership of the pigs—Napoleon-Stalin, Snowball-Trotsky—with the dogs as police, the sheep as yes-men, the two cart-horses, Boxer and Clover, as the noble hard-working proletariat), and the Russian experiment is beautifully worked out, perhaps the most felicitous moment being when the animal 'saboteurs' are executed for some of the very crimes of the Russian trials, such as the sheep who confessed to having 'urinated in the drinking pool' or the goose which kept back six ears of corn and ate them in the night. The fairy tale ends with the complete victory of Napoleon and the pigs, who rule Animal Farm with a worse tyranny and a far greater efficiency than its late human owner, the dissolute Mr Jones.

' Politically one might make to Mr Orwell the same objections as to Mr Koestler for his essay on Russia in *The Yogi and the Commissar*—both allow their personal bitterness about the betrayed revolution to prejudice their attitude to the facts. But it is arguable that every revolution is 'betrayed' because the violence necessary to achieve it is bound to generate an admiration for violence which leads to the abuse of power.' A revolution is the forcible removal of an obsolete and in-efficient ruling-class by a vigorous and efficient one which replaces it for as long as its vitality will allow. The commandments of the Animal Revolution, such as 'no animal shall kill any other animal' or 'all animals are equal' can perhaps never be achieved by a revolutionary seizure of power but only by the spiritual operation of reason or moral philosophy in the animal heart. If we look at Russia without the particular bitterness of the disappointed revolutionary we see that it is an immensely powerful managerial despotism—far more powerful than its Czarist predecessor—where, on the whole, despite a police system which we should find intolerable, the masses are happy, and where great strides in material progress have been made (i.e. inde-pendence of women, equality of sexes, autonomy of racial and cul-tural minorities, utilization of science to improve the standard of living, religious toleration, etc.). If Stalin and his regime were not loved as well as feared the Animal Farm which comprises the greatest land-mass of the world would not have united to roll back the most efficient invading army which the world has ever known—and if in truth Stalin is loved then he and his regime cannot be quite what they appear to Mr Orwell (indeed Napoleon's final brutality to Boxer—if

Boxer symbolises the proletariat, is not paralleled by any incident in Stalin's career—unless the Scorched Earth policy is indicated). But it is unfair to harp on these considerations. *Animal Farm* is one of the most enjoyable books since the war, it is deliciously written, with something of the feeling, the penetration and the verbal economy of Orwell's master, Swift. It deserves a wide sale and a lengthy discussion. Apart from the pleasure it has given me to read, I welcome it for three reasons, because it breaks down some of the artificial reserve with which Russia is written about, or not written about (a reserve which we do not extend to America—nor they to us), because it restores the allegorical pamphlet to its rightful place as a literary force, and lastly because it proves that Mr Orwell has not been entirely seduced away by the opinion-airing attractions of weekly journalism from his true vocation, which is to write books.

# 65. Isaac Rosenfeld, *Nation*

7 September 1946, pp. 273–4

George Orwell, to judge by his writing, is a man, not without imagination, who is never swept away by his imagination. His work as a literary critic and analyst of politics and popular culture runs along a well laid out middle course, kept true to it by an even keel; it is always very satisfying, except when he ventures out into certain waters, as in his reflections on art and poetry in his 'Dickens, Dali, and Others,' where a deep keel has the advantage over an even one. Even when he is wrong, as he was many times during the war in his political comments and predictions, he is wrong in a sensible way. He stands for a common sense and a reasonableness which are rare today, especially when these virtues are removed from the commonplace, as they are in Orwell's case, though not absolutely.

*Animal Farm*, a brief barnyard history of the Russian Revolution from October to just beyond the Stalin-Hitler pact, is the characteristic product of such a mind, both with credit and discredit to its qualities. It puts an imaginative surface on the facts, but does not go far beneath the surface and shows little in excess of the minimum of invention necessary to make the transposition into an animal perspective. The facts are straight, and all the wieldy ones are there; the interpretation, within these limits, is plain and true. The implicit moral attitude toward the real historical events is one of an indignation that goes-without-saying, opposed to the nonsense and chicanery of Party dialectics, and to what has come to be recognized, to a large extent through Orwell's writing, as the well-intentioned, peculiarly liberal act of submission to the tyrant's myth. At least by implication, Orwell again makes clear in this book his allegiance to an older and more honorable liberalism that still holds as its dearest thing the right to liberty of judgment. Nevertheless, this is a disappointing piece of work; its best effort is exerted somewhere on middle ground, between the chuckle-headed monstrosity of orthodox Stalinism and the sated anti-Stalinist intelligence of long standing which already knows all this and a good deal more besides.

In brief, old Major, the pig, shortly before his death, delivers himself of the lessons of his life for the benefit of the animals of Mr Jones's Manor Farm, pointing out to them how they have been exploited by Man (capitalism) and urging the revolutionary establishment of a better society (The Communist Manifesto). The animals drive Mr Jones off the farm and hold it against his attempts to regain possession (Revolution and defeat of the Counter-revolution). Led by two pigs, Napoleon (Stalin), more or less in the background, and Snowball (Trotsky, with a soupçon of Lenin—for simplicity's sake, Vladimir Ilyitch is left out of the picture, entering it only as a *dybbuk*[1] who shares with Marx old Major's identity, and with Trotsky, Snowball's) the animals institute a regime free of Man, based on collective owner-ship, socialized production, equality, etc. The pigs, who are the most in-telligent animals, form a bureaucracy which does not at first enjoy many privileges, this development being held over until the factional dispute over the rate of industrialization and the strategy of World Revolution begins, Snowball-Trotsky is exiled, and Napoleon-Stalin comes to power. Then we have, in their animal equivalent, the important episodes of hardship and famine, growth of nationalism, suspension of workers' rights and privileges, frame-ups, Moscow Trials, fake confessions, purges, philosophical revisions—'All animals are equal'

[1] Yiddish for an evil spirit.

becoming, 'All animals are equal, but some animals are more equal than others'—the Stalin–Hitler pact, etc.—all of which is more interesting as an exercise in identification than as a story in its own right.

What I found most troublesome was the question that attended my reading—what is the point of *Animal Farm*? Is it that the pigs, with the most piggish pig supreme, will always disinherit the sheep and the horses? If so, why bother with a debunking fable; why not, *à la* James Burnham, give assent to the alleged historical necessity? But it is not so—for which we have Orwell's own word in a recent article in *Polemic* attacking Burnham.[1] And if we are not to draw the moldy moral of the pig, what then?

Though Orwell, I am sure, would not seriously advance the bad-man theory of history, it appears that he has, nevertheless, drawn on it for the purpose of writing *Animal Farm*. There are only two motives operating in the parable (which is already an oversimplification to the point of falsity, if we take the parable as intended); one of them, a good one, Snowball's, is defeated, and the only other, the bad one, Napoleon's, succeeds, presumably because history belongs to the most unscrupulous. I do not take this to be Orwell's own position, for his work has shown that he knows it to be false and a waste of time in historical analysis; it is, however, the position of his imagination, as divorced from what he knows—a convenient ground, itself a fable, to set his fable on. (If Marxism has really failed, the most ironic thing about its failure is that it should be attributed to the piggishness of human nature.) It is at this point that a failure of imagination—failure to expand the parable, to incorporate into it something of the complexity of the real event—becomes identical with a failure in politics. The story, which is inadequate as a way into the reality, also falls short as a way out; and while no one has a right to demand of *Animal Farm* that it provide a solution to the Russian problem—something it never set out to do—it is nevertheless true that its political relevance is more apparent than real. It will offer a kind of enlightenment to those who still need it, say, the members of the Book of the Month Club, but beyond this it has no politics at all.

Another way of making this point is to compare *Animal Farm* with Koestler's *Darkness at Noon*. Rubashov, also faced with the triumph of

---

[1] James Burnham is the author of *The Managerial Revolution* (1942), which influenced *1984*. Orwell's article is 'Second Thoughts on James Burnham,' *Polemic*, III (May 1946), pp. 13–33.

ORWELL

the pig, at least asks *why* the pig is so attractive, *why* he wins out over the good. This is a question that can no longer be answered by stating *that* the pig wins out. It is a more sophisticated question, for it realizes that the fact of the triumph is already known, and a more important one, for it leads to an examination of the pig's supremacy along two divergent lines, by way of a specific Marxist analysis of history, or a criticism of Marxism in general, both engaging the imagination at a crucial point. But Orwell's method, of taking a well worn fact that we know and converting it, for lack of better inspiration, into an imaginative symbol, actually falsifies the fact; thus over-extended, the fact of Stalinist 'human nature,' the power-drive of the bureaucracy, ceases to explain anything, and even makes one forget what it is to which it does apply. An indication that a middle of the way imagination, working with ideas that have only a half-way scope, cannot seriously deal with events that are themselves extreme. There is, however, some value in the method of *Animal Farm*, provided it is timely, in the sense, not of newspapers, but of history, in advance of the news. But this is to say that *Animal Farm* should have been written years ago; coming as it does, in the wake of the event, it can only be called a backward work.

# 66. Edmund Wilson, *New Yorker*

7 September 1946, p. 89

Edmund Wilson (1895–1972), American critic and intellectual historian, author of *Axel's Castle* (1931), *To the Finland Station* (1940) and *The Wound and the Bow* (1941).

*Animal Farm*, by George Orwell, is a satirical animal fable about the progress—or backsliding—of the Russian Revolution. If you are told that the story deals with a group of cows, horses, pigs, sheep, and poultry which decide to expel their master and run his farm for themselves but eventually turn into something almost indistinguishable from human beings, with the pigs as a superior caste exploiting the other animals very much as the farmer did, and if you hear that Stalin figures as a pig named Napoleon and Trotsky as a pig named Snowball, you may not think it sounds particularly promising. But the truth is that it is absolutely first-rate. As a rule, I have difficulty in swallowing these modern animal fables; I can't bear Kipling's stories about the horses that resist trade-unionism and the beehive that is ruined by Socialism[1], nor have I ever been able to come under the spell of *The Wind in the Willows*. But Mr Orwell has worked out his theme with a simplicity, a wit, and a dryness that are closer to La Fontaine and Gay, and has written in a prose so plain and spare, so admirably proportioned to his purpose, that *Animal Farm* even seems very creditable if we compare it with Voltaire and Swift.

Mr Orwell, before the war, was not widely known in America or even, I think, in England. He is one of several English writers who were only just beginning to be recognized in those years of confusion and tension and whose good work was obscured and impeded while the war was going on. But I think that he is now likely to emerge as one of the ablest and most interesting writers that the English have produced in this period, and, since he is now getting a reputation in this country, I should like to recommend to publishers that they look up his early novels and memoirs. There is a novel of his called *Burmese Days*, a title deceptively suggestive of reminiscences by a retired official, which is certainly one of the few first-hand and really excellent pieces of fiction that have been written about India since Kipling. Orwell's book is not the set piece and tour de force that E. M. Forster's *A Passage to India* was; but the author, who was born in Bengal and served in the Burmese police, is 'saturated' with his subject, where Forster had to get his up. This book (which, I understand, was allowed to appear in England only in a text that had been modified under pressure of the India Office) attracted, so far as I remember, no attention whatever when it came out over here, but it ought certainly to be republished, with a more striking and appropriate title. It is illuminating as a picture of Burma and distinguished as a work of literature.

[1] 'A Walking Delegate' and 'The Mother Hive.'

# 67. Northrop Frye, *Canadian Forum*

December 1946, pp. 211–12

---

Northrop Frye (b. 1912), Canadian critic, Professor of English at the University of Toronto, author of *Fearful Symmetry* (1947) and *The Anatomy of Criticism* (1957).

---

George Orwell's satire on Russian Communism, *Animal Farm*, has just appeared in America, but its fame has preceded it, and surely by now everyone has heard of the fable of the animals who revolted and set up a republic on a farm, how the pigs seized control and how, led by a dictatorial boar named Napoleon, they finally became human beings walking on two legs and carrying whips just as the old Farmer Jones had done. At each stage of this receding revolution one of the seven principles of the original rebellion becomes corrupted, so that 'no animal shall kill any other animal' has added to it the words 'without cause' when there is a great slaughter of the so-called sympathizers of an exiled pig named Snowball, and 'no animal shall sleep in a bed' takes on 'with sheets' when the pigs move into the human farmhouse and monopolize its luxuries. Eventually there is only one principle left, modified to 'all animals are equal, but some are more equal than others,' as Animal Farm, its name changed back to Manor Farm, is welcomed into the community of human farms again after its neighbors have realized that it makes its 'lower' animals work harder on less food than any other farm, so that the model worker's republic becomes a model of exploited labor.

The story is very well-written, especially the Snowball episode, which suggests that the Communist 'Trotskyite' is a conception on much the same mental plane as the Nazi 'Jew,' and the vicious irony of the end of Boxer the work horse is perhaps really great satire. On the other hand, the satire on the episode corresponding to the German invasion seems to me both silly and heartless, and the final metamorphosis of pigs into humans at the end is a fantastic disruption of the sober logic of the tale. The reason for the change in method was to conclude the story by showing the end of Communism under Stalin as a replica of its beginning under the Czar. Such an alignment is, of course, complete nonsense, and as Mr Orwell must know it to be nonsense, his motive for adopting it was presumably that he did not know how otherwise to get his allegory rounded off with a neat epigrammatic finish.

*Animal Farm* adopts one of the classical formulas of satire, the corruption of principle by expediency, of which Swift's *Tale of a Tub* is the greatest example. It is an account of the bogging down of Utopian aspirations in the quicksand of human nature which could have been written by a contemporary of Artemus Ward[1] about one of the co-operative communities attempted in America during the last century. But for the same reason it completely misses the point as a satire on the Russian development of Marxism, and as expressing the disillusionment which many men of goodwill feel about Russia. The reason for that disillusionment would be much better expressed as the corruption of expediency by principle. For the whole point about Marxism was surely that it was the first revolutionary movement in history which attempted to start with a concrete historical situation instead of vast *a priori* generalizations of the 'all men are equal' type, and which aimed at scientific rather than Utopian objectives. Marx and Engels worked out a revolutionary technique based on an analysis of history known as dialectic materialism, which appeared in the nineteenth century at a time when metaphysical materialism was a fashionable creed, but which Marx and Engels always insisted was a quite different thing from metaphysical materialism.

Today, in the Western democracies, the Marxist approach to historical and economic problems is, whether he realizes it or not, an inseparable part of the modern educated man's consciousness, no less than electrons or dinosaurs, while metaphysical materialism is as dead as the dodo, or would be if it were not for one thing. For a number of reasons, chief among them the comprehensiveness of the demands made on a revolutionary by a revolutionary philosophy, the distinction just made failed utterly to establish itself in practice as it did in theory. Official Marxism today announces on page one that dialectic material-ism is to be carefully distinguished from metaphysical materialism, and then insists from page two to the end that Marxism is nevertheless a complete materialist metaphysic of experience, with materialist answers to such questions as the existence of God, the origin of know-

[1] Artemus Ward, pseudonym of Charles Browne (1834–67), an American humorist.

ledge and the meaning of culture. Thus instead of including itself in the body of modern thought and giving a revolutionary dynamic to that body, Marxism has become a self-contained dogmatic system, and one so exclusive in its approach to the remainder of modern thought as to appear increasingly antiquated and sectarian. Yet this metaphysical materialism has no other basis than that of its original dialectic, its program of revolutionary action. The result is an absolutizing of expediency which makes expediency a principle in itself. From this springs the reckless intellectual dishonesty which it is so hard not to find in modern Communism, and which is naturally capable of rationalizing any form of action, however ruthless.

A really searching satire on Russian Communism, then, would be more deeply concerned with the underlying reasons for its transformation from a proletarian dictatorship into a kind of parody of the Catholic Church. Mr Orwell does not bother with motivation: he makes his Napoleon inscrutably ambitious, and lets it go at that, and as far as he is concerned some old reactionary bromide like 'you can't change human nature' is as good a moral as any other for his fable. But he, like Koestler, is an example of a large number of writers in the Western democracies who during the last fifteen years have done their level best to adopt the Russian interpretation of Marxism as their own world-outlook and have failed. The last fifteen years have witnessed a startling decline in the prestige of Communist ideology in the arts, and some of the contemporary changes in taste which have resulted will be examined in future contributions to this column.

# CRITICAL ESSAYS (US title: DICKENS, DALI AND OTHERS)

## 1946

---

## 68. Stuart Hampshire, *Spectator*

### 8 March 1946, pp. 250, 252

---

Stuart Hampshire (b. 1914), English critic and philosopher, Warden of Wadham College, Oxford.

---

Mr Orwell is a moralist-critic and not an aesthete; he is interested in attitudes to Life rather than in Beauty. His own writing is forthright and vigorous, but never noticeably fine or elaborated; and in the prose literature which he criticises he distinguishes diseases of the mind and political attitudes rather than differences of style. The strength and brilliance of his criticism come from his confidence in his own sanity; he never fails to dig out and expose the perversions and affectations of others, applying a test of enlightened good sense. This robust self-confidence might make a blunt and philistine critic; in fact, it does not, because Mr Orwell's writing always seems to reflect new and entirely independent thinking. His writing follows his thought, which is untrammelled by fashion or prejudice. He seems to live by himself intellectually and to come out to spray poison on 'the smelly little orthodoxies' which he finds growing like weeds around him.

The most brilliant and typical of the ten essays in this book is that on Rudyard Kipling, the longest and most satisfying on Charles Dickens. Mr Orwell exults in savage over-statements of the unpopular view; and he is never happier in his writing than when he is affronting the genteel illusions of what he calls 'the pansy-left'. He is carried away by his pleasure in belabouring the soft lump of civilised prejudice which he finds before him, and is betrayed into rough epigrams, some of which are blatantly untrue. His critical attitude seems to have been formed by reaction against the intellectual fashions of his time; and the reactions have been violent, as though from doctrines intimately known and half-accepted and therefore rejected with a greater sense of liberation. It is not true that his judgement is perverted by the individualist's pride in being in a minority; but the sanity and justice of his critical attitude can only be appreciated against the particular background of Mr Orwell's dislikes. Someone who did not know this background—a French reader, for instance—would not understand why the familiar principles of educated liberalism should be stated with such an accompaniment of aggressive exaggeration. 'A humanitarian is always a hypocrite'; 'No one, in our time, believes in any sanction greater than military power'—the fact that neither of these statements is literally true does not invalidate the extremely subtle and original argument about Kipling in which they occur. But such ferocious over-statements are puzzling unless they are understood in the context of a particular intellectual history and predicament; and this history and predicament are peculiar to intellectuals of the last two decades.

The predicament, which provokes these over-statements and sometimes contradictions, is roughly this: Suppose that one has been convinced by experience that imperialism is evil, and that Marx's analysis of capitalist society was generally correct; suppose also that one hates tyranny and suppression of the truth in any form; then who are one's friends? After 1939—and all these essays were written in or after 1939 —it has not been an easy question. Charles Dickens perhaps, with very many qualifications, which are most carefully and ingeniously elaborated. H. G. Wells, who did not understand violence, is shown to have been no help since 1920. Yeats is a magnificent enemy; Koestler a confused and uncertain friend; Kipling an honest enemy.

'All art is propaganda,' says Mr Orwell, and one cannot discuss his criticism without discussing his politics. Three of the essays deal with the political and social implications of popular art—boys' weeklies, comic postcards and thrillers. There is also an entirely convincing defence of the harmlessness and genuine inanity of P. G. Wodehouse, and a rational appraisal of Salvador Dali. Nowhere in any of these essays is one conscious of any tension between Mr Orwell's penetration and integrity as a critic and the framework of his political beliefs and preferences. He seems to have absorbed the doctrines on which the 'little orthodoxies' are founded, and particularly Marx and Freud, but to have remained open-minded and empirical; he has so placed himself in an assured position above and beyond the warring of the sects, and is in consequence potentially the most authoritative and interesting of English critics. Unfortunately, literary mass-observation—the boys' weeklies, thrillers, post-cards—seem to have deflected him from writing anything which is comparable to the work of Mr Edmund Wilson, the distinguished American critic who has similar if greater authority for the same reasons. The literary mass-observation is amusing and useful, but is easily forgotten, because the conclusions are obvious and already known and only the particular instances are new. They cannot be re-read in this re-printing with the same pleasure as the essays on Dickens, Kipling and Wells.

Mr Orwell's thought and method are so consistent that one could not have guessed, if it had not been stated, that this book represents the products of journalism in the last six years. Almost everybody who reads it will enjoy it and be stimulated by it; it is easily and forcefully written, and, in addition to its intellectual brilliance, has all the qualifications for great popularity—including a barely concealed impatience with highbrows and a suggestion of insularity. Nevertheless, highbrows will enjoy it most.

# 69. Evelyn Waugh, *Tablet*

6 April 1946, p. 176

Evelyn Waugh (1903–66), English novelist, author of *Decline and Fall* (1928), *Brideshead Revisited* (1945), and *The Loved One* (1948). At the end of his life, Orwell planned to write an essay on Waugh.

The *Critical Essays* of Mr George Orwell comprise ten papers of varying length, written between 1939 and 1945, which together form a work of absorbing interest. They represent at its best the new humanism of the common man, of which Mass Observation is the lowest expression. It is a habit of mind rather than a school. Mr

Edmund Wilson in the United States is an exponent and perhaps it is significant that two of Mr Orwell's ten subjects have been treated at length by him. The essential difference between this and previous critical habits is the abandonment of the hierarchic principle. It has hitherto been assumed that works of art exist in an order of precedence with the great masters, Virgil, Dante and their fellows, at the top and the popular novel of the season at the bottom. The critics' task has been primarily to preserve and adjust this classification. Their recreation has been to 'discover' recondite work and compete in securing honours each for his own protegé. This, I believe, is still the critic's essential task, but the work has fallen into decay lately through exorbitance. Critics of this popularly-dubbed 'Mandarin' school[1] must be kept under discipline by a civilized society whose servants they should be. For the past thirty years they have run wild and countenanced the cults of Picasso and Stein, and the new critics, of whom Mr Orwell is outstandingly the wisest, arrive opportunely to correct them. They begin their inquiry into a work of art by asking: 'What kind of man wrote or painted this? What were his motives, conscious or unconscious? What sort of people like his work? Why?' With the class-distinctions the great colour-bar also disappears; that hitherto impassable gulf between what was 'Literature' and what was not. Vast territories are open for exploitation. Indeed the weakness of the new criticism lies there; that, whereas the 'Mandarins' failed by presumptuously attempting to insert cranks and charlatans into the ranks of the immortals, the new humanists tend to concentrate entirely on the base and ephemeral. Mr Orwell's three most delightful essays deal respectively with comic post-cards, 'penny-dreadfuls' and Mr James Hadley Chase. He treats only once of a subject that is at all recondite, W. B. Yeats's philosophic system, and then, I think, not happily.

The longest essay is on Charles Dickens and is chiefly devoted to refuting the opinions of Chesterton and Mr T. A. Jackson.[2] (In this connexion Mr Orwell should note, what is often forgotten, that Chesterton became a Catholic late in life. Most of his best-known work was written while he was still groping for his faith, and though it bears the promise of future realization, contains opinions which cannot be blithely labelled 'Catholic'.) He is entirely successful in his refutation and he fills his argument with brilliantly-chosen illustrations many of which are entirely new, at any rate to me. I had never before

[1] 'Mandarin' is Cyril Connolly's term for elaborate prose stylists.
[2] T. A. Jackson, Marxist critic, author of *Charles Dickens: The Progress of a Radical* (1937).

reflected on the profound fatuity of the future life of the characters implied in their 'happy ending.'

There follows an ingenious analysis of the *Gem* and *Magnet* magazines and their successors. At my private school these stories were contraband and I read them regularly with all the zeal of law-breaking. (The prohibition was on social, not moral grounds. *Chums*, *The Captain* and the *B.O.P.* were permitted. These again were recognized as 'inferior' to *Bevis*, *Treasure Island* and such books, which my father read aloud to me. Thus was the hierarchic system early inculcated.) I think Mr Orwell talks nonsense when he suggests that the antiquated, conservative tone of these stories is deliberately maintained by capitalist newspaper proprietors in the interest of the class structure of society. A study of these noblemen's more important papers reveals a reckless disregard of any such obligation. Here, and elsewhere, Mr Orwell betrays the unreasoned animosity of a class-war in which he has not achieved neutrality.

*The Art of Donald McGill* is, perhaps, the masterpiece of the book, an analysis of the social assumptions of the vulgar post-card. This and *Raffles and Miss Blandish* exemplify the method in which the new school is supreme. Every essay in the book provokes and deserves comment as long as itself. Lack of space forbids anything more than notes. I think Mr Orwell has missed something in his *Defence of P. G. Wodehouse*. It is, of course, insane to speak of Mr Wodehouse as a 'fascist,' and Mr Orwell finely exposes the motives and methods of the Bracken-sponsored[1] abuse of this simple artist, but I do find in his work a notable strain of pacifism. It was in the dark spring of 1918 that Jeeves first 'shimmered in with the Bohea.' Of all Mr Wodehouse's characters Archie Moffam alone saw war service. Of the traditional aspects of English life the profession of arms alone is unmentioned; parsons, schoolmasters, doctors, merchants, squires abound, particularly parsons. Serving soldiers alone are absent, and this is the more remarkable since, so far as the members of the Drones Club correspond to anything in London life, they are officers of the Brigade of Guards. Moreover, it is not enough to say that Mr Wodehouse has not outgrown the loyalties of his old school. When Mr Orwell and I were at school, patriotism, the duties of an imperial caste, etc., were already slightly discredited; this was not so in Mr Wodehouse's schooldays, and I suggest that Mr Wodehouse did definitely reject this part of his upbringing.

[1] Brendan Bracken (1901–58) was Minister of Information during 1941–5.

The belief that Kipling 'sold out to the upper classes' which Mr Orwell shares with Mr Edmund Wilson, is not, I think, sound. What I know of Kipling's private life suggests that he had no social ambitions except so far as in his day the attention of the great was evidence of professional ability. The sinister thing about Kipling was his religion, a peculiar blend of Judaism, Mithraism and Mumbo-jumbo-masonry which Mr Orwell ignores. And here, I think, is found the one serious weakness of all his criticism. He has an unusually high moral sense and respect for justice and truth, but he seems never to have been touched at any point by a conception of religious thought and life. He allows himself, for instance, to use the very silly expression: 'Men are only as good' (morally) 'as their technical development allows them to be.' He frequently brings his argument to the point when having, with great acuteness, seen the falsity and internal contradiction of the humanist view of life, there seems no alternative but the acceptance of a revealed religion, and then stops short. This is particularly true of his criticism of M. Dali, where he presents the problem of a genuine artist genuinely willing to do evil and leaves it unexplained, and in his essay on Mr Koestler, where he reaches the brink of pessimism. I suspect he has never heard of Mgr. Knox's God and the Atom, which begins where he ends and in an exquisitely balanced work of art offers what seems to me the only answer to the problem that vexes him. He says with unseemly jauntiness: 'Few thinking people now believe in life after death.' I can only answer that *all* the entirely sane, learned and logical men of my acquaintance, and more than half those of keen intelligence, do in fact sincerely and profoundly believe in it.

Mr Orwell seems as unaware of the existence of his Christian neighbours as is, say, Sir Max Beerbohm of the urban proletariat. He assumes that all his readers took Mr H. G. Wells as their guide in youth, and he repeatedly imputes to them prejudices and temptations of which we are innocent. It is this ignorance of Catholic life far more than his ignorance of the classic Catholic writers which renders Mr Orwell's criticism partial whenever he approaches the root of his matter.

It remains to say that Mr Orwell's writing is as readable as his thought is lucid. His style is conversational. Sometimes it lapses into the barrack-room slang of the class-war, as when he uses the word 'intellectual' to distinguish, merely, the man of general culture from the manual labourer instead of, as is more accurate, to distinguish the analytic, logical habit of mind from the romantic and æsthetic. It is a pity, I think, to desert the *lingua franca* of polite letters for the jargon of a coterie.

Perhaps in a journal largely read by the religious, it should be mentioned that one of the essays, 'Some Notes on Salvador Dali,' was suppressed in a previous publication on grounds of obscenity. There and elsewhere Mr Orwell, when his theme requires it, does not shirk the use of coarse language. There is nothing in his writing that is inconsistent with high moral principles.

# 70. Harry Levin, *New Republic*

6 May 1946, pp. 665–7

Harry Levin (b. 1912), Professor of English at Harvard, author of *James Joyce* (1941), *The Overreacher* (1952) and *The Gates of Horn* (1963).

English critics, by circumscribing their definition of culture, have missed a great deal. Inheriting their criteria from Walter Pater, an Oxford don, or Matthew Arnold, a school inspector, they have confined themselves to the higher manifestations of art. They have dealt more effectually with the elegiac past than with the distracting present. Until quite recently they have hesitated to acknowledge that heaven and earth contain more things than fall within the academic curriculum. They have never quite outgrown the peculiar tutelage of an educational system which bases itself on the coalition between intellectual superiority and social snobbery. Thus T. S. Eliot can impose his opinions with a schoolmaster's authority, while William Empson exerts his perceptions with a schoolboy's precocity. Even Cyril Connolly, though morbidly conscious of the obsolescent institutions behind him, cannot say goodbye to all that; he can merely shore up personal fragments for some historical museum; with Connolly the critical faculty seems to have turned inside out. It opens up and ranges afield, however, with his Eton classmate and fellow-travelling free-lance, George Orwell. In this, the first book of Orwell's criticism to be published here—as in his political writing, his Burmese novel and his column for *Tribune* (London)—the critic seems to have rolled up his shirt-sleeves, discarded the old school tie and shouldered the difficult task that confronts English writers today.

The range and direction of these ten essays are succinctly implied by the title, since Dickens comes so very close to the center of every Englishman's consciousness, where Dali is about as peripheral as any international eccentric could be. The most pictorial of novelists and the most literary of painters, they are caricaturists both; but where Dickens' exaggerated shading elicits our sympathies, Dali's slick surfaces lure us in order to shock us. Where Dickens redeems the grotesque with a common touch, Dali seasons the commonplace with more than a touch of perversity. Somewhere perhaps in Mrs Jarley's waxworks or Mr Krook's junkshop or Noddy Boffin's dustheap there may be glimmerings of the surrealist iconography: the tiny crutches that prop up weary eyelids, the bureau drawers that emerge from feminine torsos, the putrescent donkeys that lie in state on grand pianos. But Orwell is less interested in comparisons than in contrasts. His review of Dali's autobiography contrasts refreshingly with the pretentious hedging of its American reviewers, equally afraid to be taken in or left out. Orwell, without hesitating or indulging in higher criticism, puts his finger on the *mot juste:* 'It is a book that stinks.' From this clear-cut response, once it has been registered, there can be no appeal. Indeed it should gratify the coprophagic imagination of the autobiographer.

But the relationship between art and morality is still so confused that this very essay, an explicit attempt to hold the artist up to moral standards, was suppressed by its original publishers. The English have their Lord Eltons and Alfred Noyeses, even as we have our cultured philistines, ever willing to confound a book with its subject and to condemn them both indiscriminately. Special pleas for esthetic discrimination, at the other extreme, appeal to what Orwell calls 'Benefit of Clergy'—a doctrine which absolves painters like Dali, or poets like Pound, from responsibility for the things they say. Responsible critics like Orwell, while recognizing Dali's masterly draftsmanship, cannot overlook his childish exhibitionism: 'He is as anti-social as a flea.' He is, we must admit, an impudent parasite. It is historically significant, in view of the perennial friction between the bohemian and the bourgeois, that his scurrilous gestures should be so extravagantly rewarded. 'Dali's fantasies cast light on the decay of capitalist civilization,' as Orwell is able to show in phosphorescent detail. But he never forgets that 'the artist is also a citizen.' Orwell's canon is always 'the bedrock decency of a human being.' And when these norms are flouted, he is neither cynically amused nor bitterly indignant, but—as he himself says of Dickens—'generously angry.'

The central essay is more genially affirmative, for the great contribution of Dickens was 'to express in a comic, simplified and therefore memorable form the native decency of the common man.' There is melodramatic villainy in this world simply because men do not heed his message, 'Behave decently.' He is anxious to change not institutions but hearts: hence his feeling for childhood, his zeal for education. Yet his characters never grow, or struggle internally, as Orwell observes in comparing him with Tolstoy. If they appear to be static, frequently monstrous, is it not because of the molds in which they are cast? And is it not institutional reform, rather than moral regeneration, that Dickens inspires in us? Even the simplest code of decency bristles with class angles and ideological implications, though these may be more evident to us than to Dickens' countrymen. Orwell shrewdly notices how seldom workmen are described at their work, how often lower-class spokesmen turn out to be family retainers; but he also concedes that humor is finally subversive, that it stages a wholesome revolt against all authority. His interpretation is well balanced if inconclusive, oscillating between the revolutionist who asks, 'How can you improve human nature until you have changed the system?' and the moralist who replies, 'What is the use of changing the system before you have changed human nature?'

But few of us, happily, must be yogis or commissars; most of us may be something in between; and Orwell is much too English, too pragmatic, to be stalemated by Arthur Koestler's rhetorical dilemmas. When Koestler offers facile pessimism as a consolation for the lost optimism of the Left, Orwell reminds us that life involves a continuous choice of evils; that the world can still be bettered albeit never perfected, by socialism. Looking back across two wars toward the early aspirations of the century, he revaluates two mentors of his generation, the utopian Wells and the atavistic Kipling. Though Wells' prophecies cannot be said to have weathered Hitler's fulfilments, time has corroborated some of Kipling's half-civilized insights—this realization that 'men can only be civilized while other men, inevitably less civilized, are there to guard and feed them.' Eliot's recent discovery of Kipling is, for Orwell, 'a sign of the emotional overlap between the intellectual and the ordinary man.' Most of his own attention is directed to those overlapping regions where highbrows can move incognito among lowbrows. It is hard to traverse that middle ground without leaning over backwards: defending P. G. Wodehouse, for example, while accusing Yeats of fascism. The pioneering strength of these studies, however, lies in their comprehensive grasp and trenchant analysis of the patterns of popular culture.

Orwell's characteristic method is not so much to sharpen distinctions as to mediate between extremes, to include those elements which are excluded from sharper and more one-sided formulations. The greatest literature derives its wholeness, he knows, not only from the intransigent intellectuality of Don Quixote but from the easy-going vulgarity of Sancho Panza. Tense modernity has banished the latter to the subterranean realm of the comic postcard, and thither Orwell enterprisingly pursues it. Further explorations draw him to such popularly appreciated and critically neglected *genres* as the crime story and the boys' magazine. There he finds that the code of 'cricket' has been undermined by the recent infiltration of 'Yank Mags.' The Anglo-Saxon conception of playing the game against odds, however naïve and snobbish, is morally superior to the leader-principle, the cult of brute power, the worship of such culture heroes as Tarzan and Superman and the G-man. Against these he balances the more traditional figures of Robin Hood, Mickey Mouse and Jack the Giant-Killer. The parable of the triumphant underdog, the winning of the all-but-lost cause, sets the pattern for Dickens' happy endings; it also provides the impetus for the socialistic myth, as Orwell points out; and it has given Churchill some of his most magnificent occasions.

But our immediate world seems to bear a closer resemblance to the Daliesque landscape than to the Dickensian Christmas story. Robin Hood cannot hold out against the G-man, Mickey Mouse is no match for Tarzan, and Jack the Giant-Killer—pitted against Superman—experiences a failure of nerve. The odds that overwhelm the artist today are truly gigantic, as James T. Farrell shows in his timely pamphlet, 'The Fate of Writing in America.' It is heartening to be reminded that critical intelligence, though dwarfed by the combined forces of philistinism, commercialism and reaction, is still functioning; that it is determined to face them squarely, without either descending to their own abysmal levels or being abstracted into transcendental spheres.

# 71. Eric Bentley,
## *Saturday Review of Literature*

### 11 May 1946, p. 11

Eric Bentley (b. 1916), drama critic and former Professor of English at Columbia University; author of *The Playwright as Thinker* (1946) and *Bernard Shaw* (1947).

This book introduces to the American public a very talented English critic. Talented and symptomatic, George Orwell's career seems to have been a brave attempt to live down his Anglo-Indian and Etonian background (the Etonian part of which was all too vividly described in Cyril Connolly's *Enemies of Promise*). As policeman, school-teacher, bum, Spanish Loyalist, Home Guardsman, radical editor, and foreign correspondent for a Conservative paper he has kept himself on the go and, like another Koestler, has sought experiences which would bring him close to the central events of our time.

How has he come through? With flying colors, some will say, as a champion of liberty and of everything that is of good report. Personally I find the outcome more complex and more ambiguous.

The theme of *Dickens, Dali and Others* I take to be that in the past forty years—the span of Mr Orwell's lifetime—a vast revolution has taken place in Western life, that Mr Orwell is painfully aware of all its characteristics and complications, and that he is very angry because many people are so little aware of the revolution that they can go on living—culturally at least—in a nineteenth-century world that has no 'objective' existence. Mr Orwell's anger is all the greater because he too prefers nineteenth-century values and wishes we could really get back to them.

In protest against his background Mr Orwell is a radical, but as the product of his background he is embarrassed by radicalism. To some extent this embarrassment is a good thing, since it makes Mr Orwell acutely aware of silliness and eccentricity on the left. And it has driven him to adopt a splendid forthrightness of manner; his style is a model for all who would write simply and forcefully. But behind the fine front of plainness is a malaise as marked as Mr Connolly's. As with Koestler, the subjective element in the radicalism is far too large. The pressure of an almost personal resentment too often makes itself felt. A too evident *anxiety* prevents Mr Orwell's satire on Russia—*Animal Farm*—from being more than an outburst. The result is bigotry. If one section of the left has as its motto 'Stalin can do no wrong' the other, to which Mr Orwell belongs, is just as obsessively concerned to show that Stalin can do no right.

In our world, where can a revolted Etonian turn? Mr Orwell looks around him and sees our popular culture—the boys' magazines, the 'naughty' postcards, the detective stories, nearly all of them refusing to acknowledge that anything has happened since 1910. (But 'I for one should be sorry to see them vanish,' says Mr Orwell of the 'naughty postcards.') He looks at a 'modernistic' artist—Dali—and finds him false. What an age to live in! 'Freud and Machiavelli have reached the outer suburbs.' How much nicer it must have been when Freud and Machiavelli had got no further than Bloomsbury! So Mr Orwell turns to some of our older contemporaries. Unfortunately Shaw and Laski are looking at Europe through the wrong end of the telescope. Wells is still living in the world of his youth. Kipling? Worth feeling wistful about, worth envying, but 'a Conservative, a thing that does not exist nowadays.' The study of Yeats brings Mr Orwell to the woebegone conclusion: 'By and large the best writers of our time have been reactionary in tendency.' The only essay in Mr Orwell's book that is full of enthusiasm is equally full of nostalgia. It is an essay on Charles Dickens, who is portrayed as an Orwell before the flood—'a nine-teenth-century liberal, a free intelligence, a type hated with equal hatred by all the smelly little orthodoxies which are now contending for our souls.' *Dickens, Dali and Others* might be read as a dirge for nineteenth-century liberalism. But if Orwell is a bit of a Zola, it is a pity that the best Dreyfus he can find is P. G. Wodehouse.

The most impressive feature of the book is not its unwitting revela-tion of its author but its keen analysis of popular culture. If Mr Orwell has the worries, the tics, and the yearnings of the old-fashioned liberal doomed to live in this utterly illiberal century, he has also the old liberal's best qualities: straightforwardness, generous intelligence, and a serious devotion to culture. In America the critic who most closely resembles him is Edmund Wilson. Both men practise an admirable style that is close to good reporting and good debate—the heritage of the liberal's free press and free discussion. They have the same political attitude (anti-Russian leftism) and similar literary interests (Dickens, Kipling, Yeats). They are both at their best in territory where sociology and literature overlap.

Mr Orwell at least—I will not say Mr Wilson—is distinctly shaky in purely political and purely literary criticism—in *Animal Farm* and in his study of Henry Miller (*Inside the Whale*). Avoiding these two poles *Dickens, Dali and Others* is Orwell at his best. Which is saying a great deal. Few people have ever said better things about the culture of the masses. I would specify as little masterpieces the following essays: 'Boys' Weeklies,' 'The Art of Donald McGill,' and 'Raffles and Miss Blandish.' I hope they stimulate American critics to analyze the comic-strips and the pulps. The brilliance of Mr Orwell's pioneer effort should put them on their mettle.

# 72. Wylie Sypher, *Nation*

## 25 May 1946, p. 630

Wylie Sypher (b. 1905), American critic and art historian, Professor of English at Simmons College in Boston, author of *Four Stages in Renaissance Style* (1955) and *Rococo to Cubism in Art and Literature* (1960).

George Orwell, a liberal critic with an international background—birth in India, education in England, life in Burma and Paris, fighting in the Spanish war, and service with London newspapers (and *Partisan Review*) as correspondent—is better introduced to American readers by *Dickens, Dali and Others* than by his recent labored satire on Stalinism, *Animal Farm*. The present collection of essays—social interpretations of Dickens, Kipling, Yeats, Dali, Koestler, and subliterary matter such as boys' weeklies and penny postcards with 'funny' illustrations of fat women, smacked bottoms, mothers-in-law, etc.—shows how Orwell moves in the ill-defined area of 'popular culture' between rigid Marxist and aesthetic values, between the academy and the press. He is not doctrinaire; he undoubtedly feels that he is, as he said earlier, a liberal writer at a moment when liberalism is coming to an end.

Orwell judges literature by its social bearings, but his socialism is not a *mystique*. With Dickens, he belongs in a nineteenth-century tradition of 'free intelligence,' not much liked by what he calls 'the smelly little orthodoxies' of the left. His fighting in the Spanish war—where he discovered that inter-party politics is a cesspool—and his conviction during the London blitz that 'bourgeois democracy is not enough, but it is very much better than fascism' have not dulled his sense that the fruits of the war must be revolutionary or else the war has been lost. Though he does not approve of Koestler's defection and pessimism, he has come to realize, with Koestler, that revolutions are betrayed by violence and abuse of power, and that 'to make life livable is a much bigger problem than it recently seemed.' As in the case of nineteenth-century liberals like J. S. Mill, the logic of Orwell may at any moment terminate only in a sense of the difficulties involved. All this will not satisfy the little orthodoxies. Yet a good many liberals will go along with Orwell's inconclusive tolerance.

This tolerance appears in his literary judgments. He will not condemn Dickens as a pseudo-revolutionary; he defends the platitudes of Kipling because of their survival value ('since we live in a world of platitudes, much of what he said sticks'); he attempts to distinguish between the artistic and social significance of Dali; he finds that Wodehouse is no quisling or traitor—especially compared with the Conservatives who practiced appeasement—but only an anachronism, like H. G. Wells; he regards the 'Donald McGill' funny postcards as a saturnalia for the man-in-the-street—and thus significantly extends Enid Welsford's appraisal of the social value of the Fool.[1] But he is frankly worried about the sadism and power-worship of the 'Yank Mags' and detective stories that have replaced the more 'sporting' genteel thriller like 'Raffles'—because 'snobbishness, like hypocrisy, is a check upon behavior whose value from a social point of view has been underrated'! The analysis of the cultural lag in the 1910 ideals of the boys' weeklies has direct bearing on the distinctly American problem of the soap opera and comics.

The essay on Dickens—arguing that Dickens is neither a bourgeois

[1] See Enid Welsford, *The Fool: His Social and Literary History* (1935).

sentimentalist nor 'proletarian' nor 'almost' Catholic, but a moralist—shows how easily Orwell holds his social interpretation in suspense above the literary fiction while he relishes Dickens's grotesquerie, picturesqueness, and gusto. One wishes here, as elsewhere, that Orwell would increase the dimensions of his observation and relate the profusion of irrelevancy in Dickens, say, to that in Browning, the Dickensian attitude toward work to that in Carlyle, or the moralizing of Dickens to that of Mrs Gaskell.

His issue with Dali is frankly art and morality. Orwell's answer seems equivocal: that Dali is competent as a draftsman but disgusting as a human being. The fact is that Dali, as painter, is a fraud because he is an exhibitionist. The composition in 'Mannequin Rotting in a Taxicab' doesn't much matter so long as the subject itself is, in our society, disgusting, just as counter-Reformation representations of disembowelings are likely to be. Orwell puts the right question: *Why* is Dali like that? But he makes no effort to answer it. His comment on Yeats is also inconclusive. Without being doctrinaire, Orwell might have demonstrated that the vagueness of texture which he cannot explain in the poetry of Yeats is a mark of that social alienation that similarly expresses itself in Swinburne, Tennyson, and the prose of Ruskin.

The abiding disillusionment of Orwell with the left-wingers who have wished 'to be anti-fascist without being anti-totalitarian' has at least emancipated him from a line. This flexibility is well attested by his appreciation of Henry Miller's resigned, narcissistic pacifism. The essay on Miller's unsocial quietism, appropriately called 'Inside the Whale,' properly belongs with the others here reprinted from English editions. One misses it—as well as Orwell's customary unself-conscious use of four-letter words.

# 73. Edmund Wilson, *New Yorker*

25 May 1946, pp. 82–4

I have heard it said in England of George Orwell that he was 'a combination of Leftism and Blimpism.' This is perfectly true, and, with his talent as essayist, journalist, and novelist, it has made him a unique figure among the radical intellectuals of the turbid thirties and forties. It has also made him sometimes slightly ridiculous, but his not fearing to appear ridiculous is one of the good things about him. He does not belong to the literary world of liberal and radical opinion which has mastered all the right sets of answers and slips easily into all the right attitudes. His thought is often inconsistent; his confident predictions often turn out untrue; a student of international socialism, he is at the same time irreducibly British and even not free from a certain provincialism; and one frequently finds him quite unintelligent about matters that are better understood by less interesting and able critics. But, with all this, he has the good English qualities that, in the literary field at any rate, are beginning to seem old-fashioned: readiness to think for himself, courage to speak his mind, the tendency to deal with concrete realities rather than theoretical positions, and a prose style that is both downright and disciplined. If it is true that he has never succeeded in satisfactorily formulating a position, it is true, also, that his impulses (though they sometimes conflict), in pointing to what he does and he does not want, what he does and does not like, make, in their own way, a fairly reliable guide, for they suggest an ideal of the man of good will (to use an overworked and wistful phrase) still alive in a benumbed and corrupted world.

George Orwell's new book of essays—*Dickens, Dali & Others*—contains some curious examples of his Blimpism and insularity. 'What,' he was asking in 1941, 'has kept England on its feet during the past year? In part, no doubt, some vague idea about a better future, but chiefly the atavistic emotion of patriotism, the ingrained feeling of the English-speaking peoples that they are superior to foreigners. For the last twenty years the main object of English left-wing intellectuals has been to break this feeling down, and if they had succeeded, we might be watching the S.S. men patrolling the London streets at this moment.' (But isn't it a part of the business of the socialists of whatever country to try to induce their compatriots to take an international point of view?) And later in the same essay: 'The early Bolsheviks may have been angels or demons, according as one chooses to regard them, but at any rate they were not sensible men'—as if the political logic of the buckling social system in Russia, with no habit of democratic government and no powerful middle class, could give results that would commend themselves as 'sensible' to a British civil servant of the class from which Orwell comes! In Orwell's essay on Dali, the code of the public school comes to the surface in an unexpected connection. In writing about the painter's autobiography, he calls attention to certain incidents which Dali says he remembers from his childhood: his pushing another boy off a bridge, his kicking his three-year-old sister in the head, and his biting a dying bat which was already covered with ants. These actions, Orwell suggests, which set the tone for Dali's whole career, are not precisely cricket. 'In his outlook, in his character,' Orwell writes, 'the bedrock decency of a human being does not exist.' Yet 'if you say that Dali, though a brilliant draughtsman, is a dirty little scoundrel, you are looked upon as a savage.' One's first impulse is to laugh at this, and to regret that the buffooneries of Dali, a professional creator of scandal, have succeeded in getting a rise out of Orwell, who has often shown himself so shrewd. The trouble is with Dali that his outrages are infantile and superficial. He hasn't the depth to be really shocking. But, on reflection, one comes to the conclusion that this instinct on Orwell's part that is revolted by the pushing of the boy off the bridge and the biting of the dying bat is the same one that gagged at the Moscow trials, and that there is really some connection between the little and the big monstrosities. Both are symptoms of the moral disease that has invaded the contemporary world.

The progress of this disease Orwell shows in a remarkable paper, in which he is to be seen at his best, called 'Raffles and Miss Blandish,' a study of the change in the attitude toward crime between 1900 and 1939, as exemplified by two popular novelists. The gentleman burglar Raffles was, as Orwell points out, a cricketer, and, in his way, a man of honor; the characters in *No Orchids for Miss Blandish*, a pseudo-American shocker which was prodigiously popular in England, have no honor of any kind and make an appeal merely sadistic and sexual. Orwell's essays on popular literature from a sociological point of view—'Boys' Weeklies,' 'The Art of Donald McGill' (a producer of comic picture postcards), and 'In Defense of P. G. Wodehouse'—are always of special interest. This is a kind of thing that is rarely attempted, of which Orwell is, in fact, I believe, the only contemporary master. And when he deals with such more serious writers as Dickens, Kipling, Yeats, and Arthur Koestler, it is mainly from this semi-political, semi-sociological point of view. His essays on Dickens and Kipling to some extent suffer from a tendency to generalize about the first-rate writer, the whole work of a man's career, without following his development as an artist (as one can do about a serial in a boy's magazine, which, for decades, can remain the same), and from a habit of taking complex personalities too much at their face value, of not getting inside them enough. Orwell does not see, for example, that Dickens was more attracted than repelled by horror and violence. The novelist may seem to shudder at the revolutionary-mob scenes in *Barnaby Rudge* and *A Tale of Two Cities*, but it is he, after all, who has let them loose, and it is plain that he is fascinated by them. And does Dickens not incorporate himself in, does he not really love and admire, the perverse and ogreish Quilp as he cannot do with Little Nell? Orwell does not, in this Dickens essay, seem to have gone over his ground quite thoroughly, for he makes points about Dickens' limitations which can easily be refuted by reference to obvious books. It is not, for example, true that Dickens has 'no friendly pictures . . . of naval men.' In *Edwin Drood*, one of the most admirable characters is precisely a naval man, Mr Tartar. Nor is it true that 'in his attitude toward servants Dickens is not ahead of his age' and created only comic servants. With his own family background of ladies' maids and butlers, he was able to see particularly clearly the breaking down of the feudal relationship between masters and servants in England, as he had presented it in Mr Pickwick and Sam Weller; and, in *Bleak House*, he dramatized the graduation of the servant class into an independent middle class in the career of Mr Rouncewell, the housekeeper's son, who becomes a successful manufacturer, compels Sir Leicester Dedlock to receive him as a gentleman, and runs against him in a Parliamentary election.

But all these essays are original and interesting. I read most of them when they first came out in magazines, and I have reread them here with pleasure. There will be more to say about George Orwell when his satire, *Animal Farm*, which is now having a great success in England, is published over here in the autumn.

# 74. John Middleton Murry, *Adelphi*

## July 1946, pp. 165–8

John Middleton Murry (1889–1957), husband of Katherine Mansfield, friend of D. H. Lawrence, founder of *Adelphi* (1931), author of books on Keats (1925), Blake (1933) and Swift (1954). This is a composite review on Orwell and Connolly.

---

From Mr Cyril Connolly's autobiography published in 1938 I learned that George Orwell and he were contemporaries in College at Eton. The blurb of Mr Orwell's *Critical Essays* tells me that he was born in 1903; the preface to *The Condemned Playground* that Connolly's essay on Sterne, his impressive début as a critic, was written in 1927, when he was 23. So he appears to be a year junior to Orwell. Orwell left Eton in 1921 to go into the Burma Police; Connolly in 1922 to go to Oxford. All these dates may not be exact. It does not greatly matter. Their purpose here is merely to suggest that it is profitable to compare the two.

They are probably the two most gifted critics of their generation: by my historical scale a well-marked generation—the first that escaped any direct scathing by the war of 1914–18. That scuppered me, though I took no direct part in it, but worked in the security of the War Office: and, rightly or wrongly, I have always felt that there was a gulf between those who experienced the last war and those who didn't. That experience gave my thinking the bias of a religious quest, turned me from a fairly promising literary critic into 'primarily a moralist.' T. S. Eliot once described me thus to myself. I was surprised, and rather chagrined at the moment; but on rumination found the label apt—and therefore helpful. That was in the days of the brief revival of *The Athenæum* (1919–1921) over which I presided—really as a fish out of water. I well remember the shock of astonishment when, a year or two later, I read Mr Raymond Mortimer's death sentence upon me. Writing in the *New Statesman* he said that many had regarded me as the coming leader of the intelligentsia; 'but waking no such matter.' I had been unconscious of the role for which I had been cast, and when I slipped out of it, in order to become what I was, I was as relieved as everybody else must have been.

That perfunctory reminiscence is to place myself in regard to Orwell and Connolly. Between me and both of them there is a gulf: a gulf created by my experience of the war of 1914–18. But there is also a gulf between them: and that sets me much nearer to Orwell than to Connolly. To me Connolly's values seem wrong, Orwell's right. The difference between me and Orwell lies in the fact that I have a religion, or a religious philosophy. It is no merit, or fault of mine that I have one. I started out naked as a new-born babe in this regard; but I just had to grow one in order to make continued existence possible. 'One cannot *live* in rebellion,' said Ivan Karamazov. I found it true: and with the help of a whole galaxy of heroes—Rousseau, Keats, Shakespeare, Jesus, Spinoza and Goethe, in particular—and some private experience of my own, I learned a kind of fundamental acceptance, on the whole joyful rather than resigned, which became second nature to me. If I had not had this, my values (I think) would have been very much what Orwell's are. I agree with them: particularly with his conviction that a certain basic human decency is the most precious thing in the world. How to define it I do not know—it might be called plain goodness, or kindliness. It is warm; and it has a horror of cruelty of any kind towards a human being—above all, of the atrocities that are committed in the name of love, of one kind or another: from the parent who warps the children and the wife who makes life a burden to her husband to the modern monster of the Leader who destroys millions for the sake of Utopia.

All this I share with Orwell; but I wear my rue with a difference: very perceptible at the moment when the Spanish Civil War turned him into a combatant on the side of the Anarchists, and me into a pacifist. Pacifism, I suspect, rather worries Orwell. He is, on the whole, singularly just and generous; but I have known him come nearer to downright misrepresentation of his opponent in this matter of pacifism than in any other. I conclude therefore that he is rather afraid of it—even to the point of not reading what pacifists write. Thus he declares that pacifism is 'a product of the British Navy' (which is true) as though that disposed of it: whereas it is merely the *pons asinorum*[1] of honest pacifism. Not enough pacifists have got across it. But that's another matter.

[1] Bridge of asses.

The lack of imagination, indeed the moral blindness of much British pacifism is, in itself, a minor affair; but it is also a manifestation of a peculiar British dishonesty which excites Orwell's just anger and indignation. It appears, more dangerously because on a larger scale, in the toadying to Soviet Russia by British social democrats. That is possible only because those who practise it have no actual experience of totalitarianism and are incapable of an imaginative one: they are insulated from the formative experience of continental Europe. Orwell begins his essay on Koestler by pointing out that all English books on totalitarianism are worthless compared to Silone, Malraux, Salvemini,[1] Borkenau,[2] Victor Serge[3] and Koestler himself.

There is almost no English writer to whom it has happened to see totalitarianism from the inside. In Europe, during the past decade and more, things have been happening to middle-class people which in England do not happen even to the working class. Most of the European writers I have mentioned above, and scores of others like them, have been obliged to break the law to indulge in politics at all; some of them have thrown bombs and fought in street battles, many have been in prison or the concentration camp, or fled across frontiers with false names and forged passports. One cannot imagine, say, Professor Laski indulging in activities of that kind.

Elsewhere, Orwell describes Laski (and Bernard Shaw) as looking at such things as purges and deportations 'through the wrong end of the telescope.' This recalls to me Lawrence's final judgment on Shaw: 'Our leaders have not loved men: they have loved ideas, and been willing to sacrifice passionate men on the altars of the blood-drinking, ever ash-thirsty ideal.'

Lawrence wrote that in 1919: and ever since that time lack of love for men and the willingness to sacrifice them to the ideal have grown apace. Communism and Fascism have corrupted the morals of Europe. Men's minds are prostrate before naked power. And everything is contaminated. Catholicism, the visible alternative to Communism at the religious level, was the accomplice of Mussolini and the instigator of Franco. Democracy, the visible alternative to it, at the political level, is being undermined by Communism: important British Trade Unions are in favour of the affiliation of the Communist to the Labour

[1] Gaetano Salvemini (1873–1957) was an Italian anti-Fascist historian.
[2] Franz Borkenau wrote *The Spanish Cockpit* (1937), which Orwell praised very highly. See I, pp. 267–8.
[3] Serge's most famous book is *Memoirs of a Revolutionary* (1951).

Party, apparently in utter ignorance of the absolute contradiction of principles between them.

It is hard to say exactly where Orwell stands in the moral chaos. He objects to what he thinks is Koestler's conclusion:

There is nothing for it except to be a short-term pessimist, i.e., to keep out of politics, make a sort of oasis in which you and your friends can remain sane, and hope that somehow things will be better in a hundred years. At the basis of this lies his hedonism which leads him to think of the Earthly Paradise as desirable. Perhaps, however, whether desirable or not, it isn't possible. Perhaps some degree of suffering is ineradicable from human life, perhaps the choice before man is always a choice of evils, perhaps even the aim of Socialism is not to make the world perfect, but to make it better. All revolutions are failures, but they are not all the same failure. It is his unwillingness to admit this that has led Koestler's mind temporarily into a blind alley, and that makes *Arrival and Departure* seem shallow compared to his earlier books.

I also think that *Arrival and Departure* seems shallow compared to the earlier books: but I do not believe that Orwell has discovered why. Not that I have done so. Orwell gives two reasons: one, the basic hedonism of Koestler which leads him to believe that the Earthly Paradise is desirable. It depends on what you mean by the Earthly Paradise. A society a little more just than Britain, and much more tolerant than Russia would be an Earthly Paradise to millions of Europeans at this moment. It may be impossible. But it cannot fairly be called a hedonist Utopia. And it is impossible to prove that it is impossible. The second reason is Koestler's unwillingness to admit that 'though all revolutions are failures, they are not all the same failure.' That has a specious neatness. Either it is a truism—for no two revolutions are alike either in their success or their failure; or it is the assertion that some revolutions achieve more of their ideal aims than others, and that we have to judge between them and support those in which there is a preponderance of good. That is a difficult judgment: above all today. There is a general desire to believe that Communist revolutions are better than Fascist revolutions: that the former are, on the whole, good, the latter, on the whole, bad. But the second proposition is a great deal more convincing than the former.

In fact, there is more to be said for the proposition that all revolutions are bad, than for the proposition that some are, on the whole, good. The present condition of Europe is the product of a whole catena of revolutions. Yet,

Since about 1930 (says Orwell) the world has given no reason for optimism whatever. Nothing is in sight except a welter of lies, hatred, cruelty, and ignorance, and beyond our present troubles loom vaster ones which are only now entering into the European consciousness. It is quite probable that man's major problems will *never* be solved. But it is also unthinkable!

Surely, not unthinkable. The doctrine of the eternal recurrence is one way of thinking it, orthodox Christianity another, even if (as Orwell says) it is based on a belief in life after death, which few thinking people now hold. But it is hard to think it and retain a sense of purposeful living without adopting a religious attitude. 'The real problem (says Orwell) is how to restore the religious attitude while accepting death as final.'

But what is meant by saying death is 'final'? Presumably that it is 'total annihilation.' But there are many possible beliefs between that and believing in a life after death in which the human personality is perpetuated. On the other hand, I wonder whether 'a religious attitude' is possible to anyone who really believes in total annihilation at death. For though the fact of conscience—or the moral imperative—remains, it is difficult to avoid making deductions from the fact of conscience which seriously affect the belief in annihilation. If the moral imperative is experienced as an imperative, the fact must have metaphysical implications.

After all, what is 'a religious attitude'? Basically, I suppose, the conviction that man's allegiance to what is revealed to him as the Good is in harmony with the inscrutable purpose of human existence. That is manifestly incompatible with a conviction of *total* annihilation at death, even if the immortality be no more than that of a posthumous influence. The problem then is to restore man's allegiance to the Good, in a climate of opinion in which the old belief in an immortality which simply consists in the prolongation of personal existence appears to be impossible.

I cannot help believing that man's allegiance to the Good will reassert itself in time. But it may be a long time, and a very bitter one. The modern worship of power will have to work itself out: and one can hardly imagine it will work itself otherwise than by catastrophe. For it is ubiquitous today. As Orwell says,

People worship power in the form in which they are able to understand it. A twelve-year-old boy worships Jack Dempsey. An adolescent in a Glasgow slum worships Al Capone. An aspiring pupil at a business college worships Lord Nuffield. A *New Statesman* reader worships Stalin. There is a difference in intellectual maturity, but none in moral outlook.

That is the crucial matter for Orwell: to hang on, somehow, to morality—to the moral law. He maintains it vigorously against the two major influences working today to undermine it: the belief that all things are lawful in pursuit of a political ideal, and the belief that æsthetic excellence compensates for moral obliquity. These two beliefs have corrupted the British intelligentsia. They are conspicuous in its chief organ, the *New Statesman*.

# 75. Newton Arvin, *Partisan Review*

September 1946, pp. 500–4

Newton Arvin (b. 1900), former Professor of English at Smith College, author of books on Hawthorne (1929), Whitman (1938) and Melville (1950).

George Orwell is a good, swingeing critic in a familiar British tradition, the tradition of John Dennis[1] and Dr Johnson, of William Gifford,[2] of Macaulay and G. K. Chesterton. It is the tradition of 'commonsensical' criticism, of the critical broadsword and even the battle-axe of downrightness and plain dealing and no nonsense, of 'all theory is for it and all experience against it.' We have had very few, if any, such critics in this country, for Poe, in spite of his neurotic harshness, was essentially of a different kidney, and I suppose no one would maintain that Mr Bernard De Voto really qualifies. George Orwell himself is hardly a Johnson or a Macaulay, but he has a generous supply of the intellectual robustness (which must, one feels, have a physical basis), the freedom from mere abstractness, the impatience with

---

[1] John Dennis (1657–1734) was the author of *The Grounds of Criticism in Poetry* (1704) and *The Genius and Writings of Shakespeare* (1712).
[2] William Gifford (1756–1826) was notorious for his ferocious attacks on Keats and Hazlitt in the *Quarterly Review*.

'nonsense,' the capacity for realistic perception, and the general bluntness that we associate with those names.

All this makes him an excellent writer on certain sorts of subjects. He is, for example, not only vigorous but really acute on the 'popular culture' of his sub-title. The essays in this volume on 'Boys' Weeklies,' on the sub-literary or proto-literary fiction he deals with in 'Raffles and Miss Blandish,' and on the comic postcards of one Donald McGill —these essays not only furnish us with the richest information about the music-hall level of British culture to-day but throw a straight, direct, unblinking light on its frightening significance, for the 'American' violence which the newer French writers so much admire has had its influence, or at least its parallels, on a low stratum of English popular literature. Orwell is admirable on this whole question, and his particular gifts make it possible for him to write sensibly and spiritedly about figures like Dickens, Kipling, and Wells; indeed, his long essay on Dickens brings out most of his best qualities. I don't know that anyone has shown quite so fully or so knowingly just what effect Dickens's urban-middle-class derivation had on his mentality, his imagination, and his sense of values. The claim that Dickens was a 'revolutionary' writer in any well-defined, positive, or intellectually instructed sense is pretty well exploded in this piece.

One would look in it in vain, however, for the kind of insights one finds in Edmund Wilson's essay; and, in general, Orwell's talents are for the heftier jobs of criticism—jobs which need to be done—rather than for its more painful, prolonged, and patient tasks of discrimination. The old English impatience with 'putting too fine a point upon it,' the old English distrust of half-tones, of ambiguities, of personal and intellectual deviations, these are very strong in Orwell, and they not only incapacitate him for writing very well about a person like Yeats, but they inject an unpleasant note of anti-intellectualism and even philistinism into his better pieces.

There are uncomfortably too many jibes here at ' "enlightened" people,' at what Orwell not very urbanely calls 'pansy-left circles,' at whipping-boy Marxists and liberals. There are too many dicta such as this: 'The nineteenth-century Anglo-Indians, to name the least sympathetic of his [Kipling's] idols, were at any rate people who did things'—as they could not have been if their outlook had resembled E. M. Forster's. Or this: 'It is a great thing in his [Kipling's] favour that he is not witty, not "daring," has no wish to *épater le bourgeois*. . . . Even his worst follies seem less shallow and less irritating than the "enlightened" utterances of the same period, such as Wilde's epigrams or the collection of cracker-mottoes at the end of *Man and Superman*.' Well, here is one reviewer who prefers Oscar Wilde's epigrams, if it comes to that, to the 'very beautiful lines' from Kipling which Orwell quotes admiringly:

> *Oh, hark to the big drum calling,*
> *Follow me—follow me home!*

Heaven knows what sort of epithet one may draw down on one's head for saying this, but Orwell might well remember, for example, Dr. Johnson's famous and unfortunate remark (in 1776): 'Nothing odd will do long. *Tristram Shandy* did not last.' Commonsensical criticism can be curiously senseless.

We have by no means had a surfeit of it recently, however, on the level on which Orwell writes; and in the cultural situation that confronts us today—with so much pedantry, constipation, and pretense on the one hand and so much machine-tooled savagery on the other—Orwell's critical work is too humane at its core and too salutary in its main effects not to elicit a sense of gratitude.

# 76. George Woodcock, 'George Orwell, 19th century Liberal'

*Politics*, December 1946, pp. 384-8

George Woodcock (b. 1912), friend of Orwell, Canadian author of *The Crystal Spirit* (1966), *Gandhi* (1971) and *Aldous Huxley* (1972).

The English writers of the 1930's have worn badly in an ensuing decade, with perhaps three important exceptions—George Orwell, Herbert Read and Graham Greene. It is difficult not to connect this fact with their political records, for these three were the only writers of real significance who did not at one time or another become deeply involved with the Communist Party and suffer a subsequent disillusionment which drove them back to an unrealistic social isolation. For nearly five years in the middle of the 1930's, the Communist Party kept an effective hold on most of the best English writers. When events in Spain and the manifest dishonesties of Stalinist policy caused them to leave the Communist entourage, these writers tended to retire into a false and somewhat guilty detachment. Their attitude was quite different from the conscious, and in some respects valid, detachment of a writer like Henry Miller, who saw the evils of the world as part of an inevitable process of destruction, and felt he could do little more than become right within himself. The English ex-Communist writers, on the other hand, still felt something should be done, but nevertheless decided to eschew social activity. This equivocal attitude undoubtedly played its part in causing their failure to realise the promise they had shown during the formative years of the 1930's.

Of the three writers whom I have indicated as exceptions to this tendency, all had been aware throughout the 1930's of the faults of both capitalist society and also of the ascendant Stalinism. Herbert Read was an anarchist, Graham Greene a Catholic of that socially conscious type which reached its best development in Eric Gill, and George Orwell an independent socialist with libertarian tendencies, whose peculiar experiences, particularly in Spain, led him early to a distrust for the Communists which has become his best-known single characteristic. Ask any Stalinist today what English writer is the greatest danger to the Communist cause, and he is likely to answer 'Orwell.' Ask the ordinary reader what is the most familiar of Orwell's books, and he is likely to answer *Animal Farm*. Inquire in any circle of anarchists or independent socialists who regard opposition to totalitarian communism as an important task of the militant left, and you will find Orwell's name respected as a writer who, when the Communist cause was most popular in this country, did not hesitate to denounce the falsehood and disregard for elementary human liberties which are essential to Communist methods of political action. Indeed, it is perhaps because this anti-Communist side of Orwell's writing has been stressed so much both by his critics and by his friends that it is necessary to give a wider picture of his literary achievement and of the character of his writing.

Orwell is a writer whose work is essentially autobiographical and personal. Several of his books are devoted to the direct description of his own experiences; in his novels can be seen clearly the influence of incidents which have occurred during his life, and in his political essays there is always a strong upsurge of personal likes and dislikes, of scraps of experience which have made some recent and powerful effect on his imagination. Indeed, the connection between Orwell's work and even the minor events of his life is so close that, for those who are friendly with him, it is an interesting pastime to trace recent conversations reproduced with considerable faithfulness in his articles in periodicals. I have met few writers whose work was so closely integrated with their daily action and observations.

For this reason, it is perhaps best to begin a closer study of Orwell's work with a biographical sketch which will help to show why he evolved differently from his English contemporaries.

I

Orwell was born into the impoverished upper-middle class, a particularly unhappy section of English society where a small income is strained to the utmost in the desperate struggle to keep up appearances, and where, for the very fact that social position is almost all these people possess, snobbery is more highly developed and class distinction more closely observed than anywhere else in the complicated hierarchy of English society. 'I was very young,' he tells us, 'not much more than six, when I first became aware of class distinctions,' and in *The Road to Wigan Pier* he gives a clear description of the whole attitude of this poor-genteel class, 'the shock-absorbers of the bourgeoisie' as he calls them, towards the working class.

Later, Orwell was sent to Eton. He went there with a scholarship, and, as he tells us, 'On the one hand, it made me cling tighter than ever to my gentility; on the other hand it filled me with resentment against the boys whose parents were richer than mine and who took care to let me know it . . . The correct and elegant thing, I felt, was to be of gentle birth but to have no money. This is part of the *credo* of the lower-upper-middle class. It has a romantic, Jacobite-in-exile feeling about it which is very comforting.' It was the feeling of resentment that first made him think in revolutionary terms. He read the works of Shaw and Wells, the latter of whom was to become a great influence, and began to describe himself as a Socialist. 'But I had no grasp of what Socialism meant, and no notion that the working class were human beings.'

Up to this stage, Orwell's progress had much in common with that of his contemporary writers of the 1930's—the genteel middle-class home, the upper-class school, the continual struggle in youth between an ingrained snobbery and a sentimental revolutionism. But the difference lay in subsequent experiences. While most of the other public-school writers, who formed the backbone of the Communist support during the 1930's, went on to the universities, became schoolmasters, and gained a purely academic knowledge of social problems, perhaps ending by going to Spain as journalists or broadcasters, Orwell's life gave him the opportunity of seeing imperialism in action at close quarters, and of observing the troubles of the workers from among them, as well as experiencing the Spanish civil war in a more direct manner than most English writers.

At a little under twenty, he joined the Indian Imperial Police in Burma, then still administered as part of India. He worked in this force for five years, during which he witnessed imperialism at its worst, saw hangings, floggings and filthy prisons, and was forced to assert a superiority over the Burmese which he never really felt. All this is portrayed with great vividness in his first novel, *Burmese Days,* and in one or two short sketches, such as 'Shooting an Elephant' and 'A Hanging', an early essay which described the really brutal side of British rule. At the end of his five years in this service, Orwell went home. He decided not merely to eschew the service of an imperialism which he had come to hate, but also to try and do something to expiate his guilt by identifying himself, if not with the Burmese natives, at least with the oppressed lower classes of his own country. I quote at length the passage from *The Road to Wigan Pier* in which he describes his conversion:

I was not going back to be a part of that evil despotism. But I wanted much more than merely to escape from my job. For five years I had been part of an oppressive system, and it had left me with a bad conscience. Innumerable remembered faces—faces of prisoners in the dock, of men waiting in the condemned cells, of subordinates I had bullied and aged peasants I had snubbed, of servants and coolies I had hit with my fist in moments of rage (nearly everyone does these things in the East, at any rate occasionally: orientals can be very provoking), haunted me intolerably. I was conscious of an immense weight of guilt that I had got to expiate. I suppose that sounds exaggerated; but if you do for five years a job that you thoroughly disapprove of, you will probably feel the same. I had reduced everything to the simple theory that the oppressed are always right and the oppressors always wrong: a mistaken theory, but the natural result of being one of the oppressors yourself. I felt that I had got to escape not merely from imperialism but from every form of man's dominion over man. I wanted to submerge myself—to get down among the oppressed, to be one of them and on their side against their tyrants. And, chiefly because I had had to think everything out in solitude, I had carried my hatred of oppression to extraordinary lengths. At that time failure seemed to me to be the only virtue. Every suspicion of self-advancement, even to 'succeed' in life to the extent of making a few hundreds a year, seemed to me spiritually ugly, a species of bullying.

It will be seen that Orwell's conversion came from a far deeper experience—emotionally as well as intellectually and physically—than that which made the Spenders and Audens in their college rooms and parental country rectories declare a mental adherence to communism. Orwell's socialism has never been so intellectually elaborated as that of the orthodox leftist writers. It has always been a kind of generalised conception in which the greatest tenet is human brotherhood, and Orwell has shared with most English working-class—as distinct from middle-class—socialists a profound distrust for the subtler shades of

Marxist discussion. Indeed, like William Morris, he has never identified himself as a Marxist. On the other hand, his natural caution has always kept him away from the kind of silliness which made the English poets of the time create heroes out of party bureaucrats and, like Day Lewis, write inane verse about feeling small when they saw a Communist! (However, Orwell's attitude had its own failings, which we will discuss later.)

Out of the feeling of the need for expiation arose a desire for participation in sufferings of the poorest. Following this impulse, Orwell went among the tramps and outcasts of London, the really destitute people who fill the dosshouses and the casual wards, who sleep on the Thames embankment and spend their lives tramping the roads from one end of England to the other, who live by begging and a whole variety of occupations, none of which is much more than a cover for mendicancy. For long periods, at times from choice, at other times from necessity as well, he lived among these people on the very periphery of society, the people who had been brought so low that they were pushed right outside the fabric of normal class society and reached a kind of brotherhood where a common misfortune neutralised all differences of origin under its impartial weight.

During the next ten years Orwell took a variety of jobs which all kept him near the poverty line. He worked as a dishwasher in Paris hotels and restaurants, as a private schoolteacher, as a bookshop assistant, as a petty grocer in his own account. It was all grist for the literary mill.

A second turning point in his career came in 1936, when he went to fight as a militiaman in Spain. He admits that at the time his ideas of the issues in the war were extremely vague. He saw, like most English leftists at the time, a simple conflict between the Spanish people and their Fascist enemies. It was only the accident of his being sent to Spain under the auspices of the I.L.P. and thus finding himself in the Marxist opposition group of the POUM that led him to realise with a peculiar intensity the true nature of the situation within the government, by which the Communists and the right-wing elements were seeking to gain all power to themselves by the suppression of the genuinely revolutionary elements, such as the anarchists and the POUM. Orwell fought on the Aragon and Huesca fronts, was wounded and returned to Barcelona, to be involved, almost immediately, in the fighting of the May days of 1937, when the Communists sought to deprive the anarchists and the POUM of their positions of advantage within the city. Later, when the great proscriptions began, he had to escape from Spain with the Stalinist police on his heels. In *Homage to Catalonia* he combines a very capable description of conditions on the Spanish fronts and in Barcelona with one of the few clear and honest accounts of the actual events in Barcelona in May, 1937, and also an effective exposure of the propaganda lies which were used in the left-wing press to whitewash the Communists.

After leaving Spain, he lived in England and in French Morocco, and when the war began he became an official of the BBC in their Indian service. In a discussion which I had with him at the time he defended his activities by contending that the right kind of man could at least make propaganda a little cleaner than it would otherwise have been, and I know that he managed to introduce one or two astonishing items into his broadcasts. But he soon found there was in fact little he could do, and he left the BBC in disgust to become literary editor of the *Tribune*, at the period when that paper was at its best level during Bevan's campaign against Churchill. In the past four years Orwell has become a successful journalist, and the recent success of *Animal Farm* has brought him into the ranks of best-selling novelists. But he remains an important influence among the more revolutionary of the younger English writers, a rallying point for what intelligent anti-Stalinism exists outside the right-wing on one hand and the Trotskyists on the other, and an honest exposer of things he considers evil.

2

Orwell's work falls into two main divisions. On the one side there are the four novels, and the books of reportage, like *Down and Out In Paris and London*, in which social ideas, although present, cannot be regarded as dominant. And, on the other side, there are a number of books, written mostly since 1936, in which the social motive is more important, but where the aesthetic element enters strongly into the writing and structure, or becomes dominant in long descriptive passages, as in *Homage to Catalonia* or *The Road to Wigan Pier*. To this class belong, beside the books already mentioned, *The Lion and the Unicorn*, a heretical survey of the relationship of Socialism to the English mind, *Critical Essays* and *Inside the Whale*, two volumes of literary-political essays, *Animal Farm*, and a number of uncollected but important essays on various social themes.

In assessing Orwell's work, it might be well to take as a starting point a confession which he made in a recent issue of *Gangrel*, an English little magazine.

What I have wanted to do throughout the past ten years is to make political writing into an art. My starting point is always a feeling of partisanship, a sense of injustice. When I sit down to write a book, I do not say to myself, 'I am going to produce a work of art.' I write it because there is some lie that I want to expose, some fact to which I want to draw attention, and my initial concern is to get a hearing. But I could not do the work of writing a book, or even a long magazine article, if it were not also an aesthetic experience. Anyone who cares to examine my work will see that even when it is downright propaganda it contains much that a full-time politician would consider irrelevant. I am not able, and I do not want, completely to abandon the world-view that I acquired in childhood. So long as I remain alive and well I shall continue to feel strongly about prose style, to love the surface of the earth, and to take a pleasure in solid objects and scraps of useless information. It is no use trying to suppress that side of myself. The job is to reconcile my ingrained likes and dislikes with the essentially public, non-individual activities that this age forces on us.

This passage of self-analysis is useful because it does give us fairly accurate clues to the nature of Orwell's writing. It indicates the honesty and indignation that inspire it, the concern for certain humanist values, the perception of fraud and the shrewd eye for pretence; it also shows, perhaps less clearly, the essentially *superficial* nature of Orwell's work, the failure to penetrate deeply into the rooted causes of the injustices and lies against which he fights, and the lack of any really constructive vision for the future of man. To these considerations I shall return. But for the present I will discuss the literary merits of Orwell's work, which, in my opinion, are much more consistent and impressive than the political qualities.

Firstly, Orwell's writing is fluent and very readable. There is probably no writer in England today who has gained such a colloquial ease of expression, at the same time without diminishing the quality of style. Even his journalistic fragments, unimportant as they may be from any other point of view, are distinguished from the work of other journalists by their excellent style. In his novels and books of reportage, Orwell has an intense power of description. If one compares *Burmese Days* with, say, Forster's *Passage to India*, the sharper vividness with which the surface aspects of Oriental life are conveyed in Orwell's book is quite impressive. Yet this faculty of description is combined with, and perhaps balanced by, a great economy of effect and wording which gives a clean and almost athletic effect to Orwell's writing. There is no unnecessary emotion, no trappings of verbiage and superfluous imagery, no place—even in the more purple passages— where one can feel that a paragraph is unnecessary or that the book would have been as good if it had been omitted. *Animal Farm* is, of course, the best example of this virtue; no-one else could have given the whole bitter history of the Russian failure in so condensed and yet so adequate an allegory.

But these virtues of economy, clarity, fluency, descriptive vividness, are all *superficial* virtues. They do not make up for a lack of deeper understanding which is evident in Orwell's work. His description of the Eastern landscape and of the attitude of Europeans towards Orientals may be the best of its kind; nevertheless, one fails to find understanding of the mentality and peculiar problems of Oriental people. Unlike Lafcadio Hearn, Orwell has never tried to think like an Oriental. And, indeed, his work is characterised throughout by a failure to think in other than Orwellian terms, or to create situations out of the imagination. All his novels are more or less autobiographical, in that they deal with the kind of people he has met, or the kind of experiences he has had. Of course, this is not a failing in itself—but in Orwell it is part of an inability to perceive or imagine deeply, and this is perhaps the cause of the failure of the people in his novels to be anything more than caricatures, except when, like Flory in *Burmese Days*, they are true Orwellians, or, like the insurance agent Bowling in *Coming Up for Air*, they have a kind of schizoid nature, and Orwellise in their thoughts in a way which hardly fits their external, worldly natures. This failure to create three-dimensional characters, with profoundly observed inner lives like the people in Dostoevsky or even Henry James, is a common fault among the liberally-minded type of novelist who is concerned to illustrate some social theme in his work. It is to be found in all the great English radical novelists—Godwin, Dickens, Wells—and Orwell is truly in the tradition of these writers.

There is, for instance, something quite Dickensian in the unlikely straggle of events forming a novel like *The Clergyman's Daughter*, which is even endowed with that perennial obsession of English radical novelists, the fraudulent private school, and which contains a selection of peripheral characters who, for all Orwell's direct experience of this borderland life, have the simplicity and oddness of true Dickens characters. And the influence of Wells is equally clear, particularly in

*Animal Farm*, which contains several echoes of *The Island of Dr. Moreau*.\*
It is an interesting point that Orwell should have written good critical
essays on the novelists whose work resembles his own, while he fails
almost completely to appreciate the virtues of more complex writers
like Henry Miller or W. B. Yeats, who are little more to him than examples of the odd perversity of intellectuals who do not subscribe to
the radical cause in Orwell's own simple way.

3

Orwell's political writing is rarely satisfying. Occasional articles, on
the borderline of politics and literature, such as the essays on boys'
weeklies, crime fiction and political language, are small masterpieces in
a limited field. But beyond such bounded fragments of observation,
Orwell's social writings rarely justify completely our expectations.
They concern 'the surface of the earth,' they generalise issues in a way
which demonstrates a simplicity of thought that is part of his character
and unlikely to change, they never penetrate into the deeper levels of
social existence or human experience.

Orwell's role is the detection of pretences and injustices in political
life, and the application to social matters of a very rough-and-ready
philosophy of brotherhood and fair play. He plays, somewhat self-
consciously, the part of the 'plain man,' and in this fulfills a necessary
function. A hundred Orwells would indeed have a salutary effect on
the ethics of social life. But the 'plain man' always has limitations, and
the greatest is his failure to penetrate below the surface of events and
see the true causes of social evils, the massive disorders in the very
structure of society, of which individual evils are merely symptoms. I
have never, for instance, seen or heard Orwell give any sound analysis
of the political trends in England today, and on such important
subjects as money, property and the State he seems to have little idea
except the usual vague slogans which have inspired the Labour Party
for many generations.

\* The main points of contact are actually direct reversals. The rule of *Animal Farm*
is 'Whatever goes upon two legs is an enemy,' the law of *The Island of Dr. Moreau* is
'Not to go on all fours.' *Animal Farm* ends with the pigs turning to men, *The Island of
Dr. Moreau* with the manufactured men reverting to animals. There is also the scene
in the latter book where Prendick sees the pig-men going on all fours and then upright,
which may have entered unconsciously into the plot of *Animal Farm*.

His attitude towards the State is typical. In a recent symposium in *Horizon* on the economic condition of the writer, he said, 'If we are to have full Socialism, then clearly the writer must be State-supported, and ought to be placed among the better-paid groups. But so long as we have an economy like the present one, in which there is a great deal of State enterprise but also large areas of private capitalism, then the less truck a writer has with the State, or any other organized body, the better for him and his work. There are invariably strings tied to any kind of official patronage.' The inconsistencies are obvious. If, when the State is only partially in control, it is a bad thing to be patronised by it, it must be worse when it is wholly in control. And if 'there are invariably strings tied to any kind of official patronage,' then the artist will certainly be well and truly strangled when he accepts the patronage of the total state, Socialist or otherwise. Incidentally, this passage is a good example of the obscurity into which Orwell sometimes falls when talking of political ideas. From the first clause one would imagine him an advocate of a total State, whether we call it Socialist or otherwise, but in reality he advocates no such thing. From conversations with him, I gather that he conceives, again very vaguely, something more like a syndicalist federation than a real State in the traditional socialist model.

There are times when the general superficiality of Orwell's attitude leads him to sincere but unjust condemnation of people or groups, because he has not been able to understand their real motives. His attack on pacifists because they enjoyed the unasked protection of the British Navy, and his 'demolition' of Henry Miller for leaving Greece when the fighting started are examples of this kind of injustice. Orwell has never really understood *why* pacifists act as they do. To him passive resistance during the war was at best 'objective support' of Fascism, at worst inverted worship of brutality; he fails to see the general quality of resistance in the pacifist's attitude, the resistance to violence as a social principle rather than to any specific enemy.

Indeed, it is one of Orwell's main faults that he does not seem to recognise general principles of social conduct. He has ideas of fair play and honesty; concentration camps, propaganda lies and so forth are to be condemned. But in a more general sense his attitude is essentially opportunist. For instance, he contends seriously that we must have conscription during the war, but that once the war has ended we must resist it as an infringement of civil liberties. During the war we must jail 'fascists,' but afterwards we must let them carry on their propa-

ganda at will. In other words, we can have freedom when it is convenient, but at moments of crisis freedom is to be stored away for the
return of better days.

A similarly opportunist attitude impelled him, in *The Lion and the
Unicorn*, to point out the power of patriotism over the English mind,
and to claim that socialists should use this element in popular mytho-
logy as a means of gaining popular support. He failed to understand
the fundamentally evil nature of patriotism as a producer of war and a
bulwark of authority, and also overlooked that patriotism is not far
from nationalism and that the union of nationalism with socialism is
worse in its effects than plain reactionary nationalism, as has been seen
in Germany and Russia.

Orwell is essentially the iconoclast. The fact that his blows sometimes hit wide of the mark is not important. The great thing about
Orwell is that when he exposes a lie he is usually *substantially* right,
and that he will always pursue his attacks without fear or favour. His
exposures of the myth of Socialist Russia, culminating in *Animal Farm*,
were a work of political stable-cleansing which contributed vastly to
the cause of true social understanding, and it is for such achievements
that we can be grateful to Orwell, and readily forgive the inconsistencies
and occasional injustices that accompany them.

If iconoclasm is Orwell's role in political writing, then we can
hardly expect the opposite virtue; and, indeed, we find that he has
little to say on *how* society can be changed and what it should become.
On these points he has largely accepted the Labour Party line, with a
few deviations to the left, but he seems to have no clear conception of a
socialist society, beyond a rather vague idea that brotherhood is the
essential basis of socialism. This is, indeed, an important fact which
many socialists seem to have forgotten, but it belongs less to an era of
state socialism than to the liberalism of the past or the anarchism of the
future. And, indeed, while Orwell is by no means an anarchist—
although he often joins them in attacking specific injustices—he is very
much nearer to the old-style liberal than to the corporate-state socialists
who at present lead the Labour party. This distinguishes him from most
of his contemporaries, for the liberal is a rare survivor in the atomic
age, and a liberal like Orwell who has developed the necessary vigour
of attack is even less common. His old-fashioned pragmatism, his
nineteenth-century radical honesty and frankness, his respect for such
excellent bourgeois mottoes as 'Fair Play' and 'Don't kick a man when
he's down,' which have been too much vitiated by the sneers of

Marxist amoralism, his consideration for the freedom of speech and writing, are all essentially liberal virtues.

In one of his essays there is a portrait of Dickens which might not inappropriately be applied to Orwell himself. 'He is laughing, with a touch of anger in his laughter, but no triumph, no malignity. It is the face of a man who is always fighting against something, but who fights in the open and is not frightened, the face of a man who is *generously angry*—in other words, of a nineteenth-century liberal, a free intelligence—a type hated with equal hatred by all the smelly little orthodoxies which are now contending for our soul.' The open fighting, the generous anger, the freedom of intelligence, are all characteristics of Orwell's own writing. And that very failure to penetrate to the fundamental causes of social evils, to present a consistent moral and social criticism of the society in which they lived, which characterised the nineteenth century liberals, has become Orwell's own main limitation.

# 1984

1949

## 77. Fredric Warburg, Publisher's Report

### 1948

'In *All Authors are Equal* (London: Hutchinson, 1973), pp. 103–4. Fredric Warburg (b. 1898), founder of Secker & Warburg, served in the Home Guard under Orwell; author of *An Occupation for Gentlemen* (1959).

This is amongst the most terrifying books I have ever read. The savagery of Swift has passed to a successor who looks upon life and finds it becoming ever more intolerable. Orwell must acknowledge a debt to Jack London's *Iron Heel*, but in verisimilitude and horror he surpasses this not inconsiderable author. Orwell has no hope, or at least he allows his reader no tiny flickering candlelight of hope. Here is a study in pessimism unrelieved, except perhaps by the thought that, if a man can conceive *1984*, he can also will to avoid it. It is a fact that, so far as I can see, there is only one weak link in Orwell's construction; *he nowhere indicates the way in which man, English man, becomes bereft of his humanity.*

*1984* is *Animal Farm* writ large and in purely anthropomorphic terms. One hopes (against hope?) that its successor will supply the other side of the picture. For what is *1984* but a picture of man unmanned, of humanity without a heart, of a people without tolerance or civilization, of a government whose *sole* object is the maintenance of its absolute totalitarian power by every contrivance of cruelty. Here is the Soviet Union to the nth degree, a Stalin who never dies, a secret police with every device of modern technology.

*Part One sets the scene.* It puts Orwell's hero, Winston Smith, on the stage. It gives a detailed and terrifying picture of the community in which he lives. It introduces the handful of characters who serve the plot, including Julia with whom Winston falls in love. Here we are given the telescreen, installed in every living-room, through which the secret police *perpetually* supervise the words, gestures, expressions and thoughts of all members of the Party; newspeak, the language devised by the Party to prevent thought; the big brother (B.B.) whose face a metre wide is to be seen everywhere on placards, etc.; double-think, the formula for 100% political hypocrisy; the copiously flowing synthetic gin, which alone lubricates the misery of the inhabitants; the Ministry of Truth, with its three slogans—War is Peace, Freedom is Slavery, Ignorance is Strength—and its methods of obliterating past events in the interests of the Party.

The political system which prevails is Ingsoc = English Socialism. This I take to be a deliberate and sadistic attack on socialism and socialist parties generally. It seems to indicate a final breach between Orwell and Socialism, not the socialism of equality and human brotherhood which clearly Orwell no longer expects from socialist parties, but the socialism of marxism and the managerial revolution. *1984* is among other things an attack on Burnham's managerialism; and it is worth a cool million votes to the conservative party;* it is imaginable that it might have a preface by Winston Churchill after whom its hero is named. *1984 should be published as soon as possible, in June 1949.*

*Part Two contains the plot*, a very simple one. Winston falls in love with a black-haired girl, Julia. This in itself is to be considered heretical and illegal. See Part I, sec. 6 for a discussion of sex and love, but in any case 'the sexual act, successfully performed, was rebellion. Desire was thoughtcrime. . . .' A description of their lovemaking follows, and these few passages alone contain a lyrical sensuous quality utterly lacking elsewhere in the book. These passages have the effect of intensifying the horrors which follow.

Julia and Winston, already rebels, start to plot; contact O'Brien, a fellow rebel as they think; are given 'the book' of Emmanuel Goldstein, the Trotsky of this community; and Winston reads it. It is a typical Orwellism that Julia falls asleep while Winston reads part of the book to her. (Women aren't intelligent, in Orwell's world.) Goldstein's book as we may call it (though it turns out later to

*This judgment has nothing to do with my political sympathies at that time. By then was almost certainly a floating voter.

have been written by the secret police) is called 'The Principles of Oligarchical Collectivism' and we are given many pages of quotations from it. It outlines in a logical and coherent form the world situation as Orwell expects it to develop in the next generation. (Or does it?) It would take a long essay to discuss the implications of the astounding political philosophy embodied in this imagined work, which attempts to show that the class system, which was inevitable until circa 1930, is now in process of being fastened *irrevocably* on the whole world at the very moment when an approach to equality and liberty is for the first time possible. The book is quoted in Part 2, sec. 9, which can almost be read as an independent work.

Before passing to Part 3, I wish to call attention to the use made by Orwell of the old nursery rhyme, Oranges and Lemons, said the bells of St Clements. This rhyme plays a largish part in the plot and is worth study. It ends, it will be remembered, with the words 'And here comes the chopper to chop off your head.' This use of a simple rhyme to achieve in due course an effect of extreme horror is a brilliant and typical Orwellism which places him as a craftsman in the front rank of terror novelists.

*1984* by the way might well be described as a horror novel, and would make a horror film which, if licensed, might secure all countries threatened by communism for 1000 years to come.

*Part Three contains the torture, breakdown, and re-education of Winston Smith*, following immediately upon his arrest in bed with Julia by the secret police. In form it reminds one of Arthur Koestler's *Darkness at Noon*, but is to my mind more brutal, completely English, and overwhelming in its picture of a thorough extermination of all human feeling in a human being. In this part Orwell gives full rein to his sadism and its attendant masochism, rising (or falling) to the limits of expression in the scene where Winston, threatened by hungry rats which will eat into his face, implores his torturer to throw Julia to the rats in his place. This final betrayal of all that is noble in man leaves Winston broken and ready for re-education as a willing adherent of Ingsoc, the necessary prelude in this society to being shot for his 'thoughtcrime', for in Ingsoc there are no martyrs but only broken men wishing to die for the good of their country.

'We shall meet in the place where there's no darkness.' This phrase, which recurs through the book, turns out to be in the end the brilliantly lit passage and torture chambers of the Ministry of Love. Light, for Orwell, symbolizes (I think) a horrible logical clarity which leads to death and destruction. Darkness, as in the womb and perhaps beside a woman in the night, stands for the vital processes of sex and physical strength, the virtues of the proles, that 80% of the population of Ingsoc who do the work and do not think, the 'Boxers' of *Animal Farm*, the pawns, the raw material without which the Party could not function.

In Part III Orwell is concerned to obliterate hope; there will be no rebellion, there cannot be any liberation. Man cannot stand against Pain, and the Party commands Pain. It is almost intolerable to read Part III which, more even than the rest of the book, smells of death, decay, dirt, diabolism and despair. Here Orwell goes down to the depths in a way which reminds me of Dostoievsky. O'Brien is his Grand Inquisitor, and he leaves Winston, and the reader, without hope. I cannot but think that this book could have been written only by a man who himself, however temporarily, had lost hope, and for physical reasons which are sufficiently apparent.

These comments, lengthy as they are, give little idea of the giant movement of thought which Orwell has set in motion in *1984*. It is a great book, but I pray I may be spared from reading another like it for years to come.

# 78. Julian Symons, *Times Literary Supplement*

## 10 June 1949, p. 380

Julian Symons (b. 1912), friend of Orwell, English critic and author of detective novels. Six days after Symons' review had appeared Orwell wrote to him:

I think it was you who reviewed *1984* in the *TLS*. I must thank you for such a brilliant as well as generous review. I don't think you could have brought out the sense of the book better in so short a space. You are of course right about the vulgarity of the 'Room 101' business. I was aware of this while writing it, but I didn't know another way of getting somewhere near the effect I wanted. (IV, p. 502–3.)

It is possible to make a useful distinction between novelists who are interested primarily in the emotional relationships of their characters and novelists for whom characters are interesting chiefly as a means of conveying ideas about life and society. It has been fashionable for nearly half a century to shake a grave head over writers who approach reality by means of external analysis rather than internal symbolism; it has even been suggested that the name of novelist should be altogether denied to them. Yet it is a modern convention that the novel must be rather visceral than cerebral. The novel in which reality is approached through the hard colours of outward appearance (which is also, generally, the novel of ideas) has a respectable lineage, and distinctive and distinguished modern representatives. Among the most notable of them is Mr George Orwell; and a comparison of *Nineteen Eighty-Four*, his new story of a grim Utopia, with his first novel *Burmese Days* (published originally fifteen years ago and recently reissued) shows a curious and interesting journey of the mind. It is a queer route that Mr Orwell has taken from Burma to the Oceania of *Nineteen Eighty-Four*, by way of Catalonia and Wigan Pier.

*Burmese Days* tells the story of Flory, a slightly intellectual timber merchant, marooned among a group of typical Anglo-Indians in a small Burmese town. Bored by his surroundings and disgusted by his

251

companions, Flory becomes friendly with an Indian doctor; but he is for a long time too timid to risk offending the opinion of the white men he despises by proposing the doctor as a member of the European Club. This problem in social relationships is one of the narrative's two poles of interest: the other is Flory's unhappy, self-deceiving love for Elizabeth, niece of one of the Anglo-Indians. Elizabeth is a thoroughly commonplace girl, perfectly at home in the European Club, but Flory invests her with qualities that exist only in his tormented imagination. When he has been robbed of all illusion about Elizabeth, and thus about his own possible future, Flory shoots himself; Elizabeth marries the Deputy Commissioner of the district; the Indian doctor, robbed of Flory's support, is the victim of a plot to disgrace him made by U-Po-Kyin, a rascally Burman, who—a last ironical stroke—obtains membership of the European Club.

What is particularly noticeable about *Burmese Days* is that the two poles of its narrative are very unequal in strength. The passages dealing with conflicts between whites and natives, and with the administrative problems facing the British, are written with subtlety; and Mr Orwell's attitude is remarkable, both in its avoidance of false idealism about the British and of false sentimentality about the Burmese. The part of the book that explores Flory's relationship with Elizabeth is in comparison crude and naive; and this is because Mr Orwell is already a novelist interested in ideas, rather than in personal relationships. When he is forced to deal with them, here and in later books, he does so often in terms of a boys' adventure story. When Flory first meets Elizabeth, for example, she likes him because he drives away some harmless water-buffaloes, of which she is terrified. Friendship ripens when they go out shooting, and he is successful in killing a leopard. Her final rejection of him is symbolized by the fact that he is thrown from a pony when about to show off in front of her, by spearing a tent peg. It is true that other motives influence Elizabeth's conscious rejection of Flory; but it is obvious that this very simple underlying symbolism is important for Mr Orwell himself. He shows great insight into the political and ethical motives of his characters; he seldom puts a word wrong when he looks at very varied facets of external reality; but his view of man as an emotional animal is often not far away from that of the boys' weeklies about which he has written with such penetration. It is such a mingling of subtlety and simplicity that makes *Animal Farm* a perfect book in its kind: in that fairy-story with an unhappy ending there are no human relationships to disturb the fairy-tale pattern and the political allegory that lies behind it.

It is natural that such a writer as Mr Orwell should regard increasingly the subject rather than the form of his fictional work. *Burmese Days* is cast fairly conventionally in the form of the contemporary novel; this form had almost ceased to interest Mr Orwell in 1939, when, in *Coming Up For Air*, the form of the novel was quite transparently a device for comparing the England of that time with the world we lived in before the First World War. In *Coming Up For Air*, also, characterization was reduced to a minimum: now, in *Nineteen Eighty-Four*, it has been as nearly as possible eliminated. We are no longer dealing with characters, but with society.

The picture of society in *Nineteen Eighty-Four* has an awful plausibility which is not present in other modern projections of our future. In some ways life does not differ very much from the life we live to-day. The pannikin of pinkish-grey stew, the hunk of bread and cube of cheese, the mug of milkless Victory coffee with its accompanying saccharine tablet—that is the kind of meal we very well remember; and the pleasures of recognition are roused, too, by the description of Victory gin (reserved for the privileged—the 'proles' drink beer), which has 'a sickly oily smell, as of Chinese rice-spirit' and gives to those who drink it 'the sensation of being hit on the back of the head with a rubber club.' We can generally view projections of the future with detachment because they seem to refer to people altogether unlike ourselves. By creating a world in which the 'proles' still have their sentimental songs and their beer, and the privileged consume their Victory gin, Mr Orwell involves us most skilfully and uncomfortably in his story, and obtains more readily our belief in the fantasy of thought-domination that occupies the foreground of his book.

In *Nineteen Eighty-Four* Britain has become Airstrip One, part of Oceania, which is one of the three great world-States. The other two are Eurasia and Eastasia, and with one or the other of these States Oceania is always at war. When the enemy is changed from Eurasia to Eastasia, the past is wiped out. The enemy, then, has always been Eastasia, and Eurasia has always been an ally. This elimination of the past is practised in the smallest details of administration; and incorrect predictions are simply rectified retrospectively to make them correct. When, for instance, the Ministry of Plenty issues a 'categorical pledge' that there will be no reduction of the chocolate ration, and then makes a reduction from thirty grammes to twenty, rectification is simple. 'All that was needed was to substitute for the original promise a warning that it would probably be necessary to reduce the ration at some time in April.' The appropriate correction is made in *The Times*, the original copy is destroyed, and the corrected copy placed on the files. A vast organization tracks down and collects all copies of books, newspapers and documents which have been superseded. 'Day by day and almost minute by minute the past was brought up to date.'

To achieve complete thought-control, to cancel the past utterly from minds as well as records, is the objective of the State. To this end a telescreen, which receives and transmits simultaneously, is fitted into every room of every member of the Party. The telescreen can be dimmed but not turned off, so that there is no way of telling when the Thought Police have plugged in on any individual wire. To this end also a new language has been invented, called 'Newspeak,' which is slowly displacing 'Oldspeak'—or, as we call it, English. The chief function of Newspeak is to make 'a heretical thought—that is, a thought diverging from the principles of Ingsoc (English Socialism in Oldspeak)—literally unthinkable.' The word 'free,' for example, is still used in Newspeak, but not in the sense of 'politically free' or 'intellectually free,' since such conceptions no longer exist. The object of Newspeak is to restrict, and essentially to order, the range of thought. The end-objective of the members of the Inner Party who control Oceania is expressed in the Newspeak word 'doublethink,' which means:

To know and not to know, to be conscious of complete truthfulness while telling carefully-constructed lies, to hold simultaneously two opinions which cancelled out, knowing them to be contradictory and believing in both of them: to use logic against logic, to repudiate morality while laying claim to it, to believe that democracy was impossible and that the Party was the guardian of democracy; to forget whatever it was necessary to forget, then to draw it back into memory again at the moment when it was needed, and then promptly to forget it again: and, above all, to apply the same process to the process itself.

The central figure of *Nineteen Eighty-Four* is a member of the Outer Party and worker in the records department of the Ministry of Truth, named Winston Smith. Winston is at heart an enemy of the Party; he has not been able to eliminate the past. When, at the Two Minutes' Hate sessions the face of Emmanuel Goldstein, classic renegade and backslider, appears on the telescreen mouthing phrases about party dictatorship and crying that the revolution has been betrayed, Winston feels a hatred which is not—as it should be—directed entirely against Goldstein, but spills over into heretical hatred of the Thought Police, of the Party, and of the Party's all-wise and all-protecting figurehead, Big Brother.

Winston's heresy appears in his purchase of a beautiful keepsake album which he uses as a diary—an activity likely to be punished by twenty-five years' confinement in a forced labour camp—and in his visits to the 'proles'' areas, where he tries unsuccessfully to discover what life was like in the thirties and forties. He goes to the junk shop where he found the album and buys a glass paperweight; and he is queerly moved by the old proprietor's quotation of a fragment of a forgotten nursery rhyme: 'Oranges and lemons, say the bells of St. Clement's.' Sexual desire has been so far as possible removed from the lives of Party members; and so Winston sins grievously and joyously with Julia, a member of the Junior Anti-Sex League.

The downfall of Winston and Julia is brought about through O'Brien, a friendly member of the Inner Party, who reveals that he, too, is a heretic. They are admitted to membership of Goldstein's secret organization 'the Brotherhood,' which is committed to the overthrow of the Party. But O'Brien is not in fact a member of 'the Brotherhood'—if indeed that organization is not simply an invention of the Inner Party—and the benevolent-seeming proprietor of the junk shop belongs to the Thought Police. Winston is arrested and subjected by O'Brien to physical and mental coercion; its effect is to eradicate what O'Brien calls his defective memory. The past, O'Brien tells him, has no real existence. Where does it exist? In records and in memories. And since the Party controls all records and all memories, it controls the past. At last Winston is converted to this view—or rather, his defective memory is corrected. Our last sight of Winston shows him sitting in the Chestnut Tree café, haunt of painters and musicians. A splendid victory has been announced, and Winston hears of it not with scepticism but with utter belief. He looks up at the great poster of Big Brother.

Two gin-scented tears trickled down the sides of his nose. But it was all right, everything was all right, the struggle was finished. He had won the victory over himself. He loved Big Brother.

The corrosion of the will through which human freedom is worn away has always fascinated Mr Orwell; *Nineteen Eighty-Four* elaborates a theme which was touched on in *Burmese Days*. Flory's criticism of

Burma might be Winston Smith's view of Oceania: 'It is a stifling, stultifying world in which to live. It is a world in which every word and every thought is censored. . . . Free speech is unthinkable.' And Flory's bitter words: 'Be as degenerate as you can. It all postpones Utopia,' is a prevision of Winston saying to Julia in his revolt against Party asceticism: 'I hate purity, I hate goodness! I don't want any virtue to exist anywhere.' But in *Nineteen Eighty-Four* the case for the Party is put with a high degree of sophistical skill in argument. O'Brien is able easily to dispose of Winston in their discussions, on the basis that power is the reality of life. The arrests, the tortures, the executions, he says, will never cease. The heresies of Goldstein will live for ever, because they are necessary to the Party. The Party is immortal, and it lives on the endless intoxication of power. 'If you want a picture of the future, imagine a boot stamping on a human face—for ever.'

Mr Orwell's book is less an examination of any kind of Utopia than an argument, carried on at a very high intellectual level, about power and corruption. And here again we are offered the doubtful pleasure of recognition. Goldstein resembles Trotsky in appearance, and even uses Trotsky's phrase, 'the revolution betrayed'; and the censorship of Oceania does not greatly exceed that which has been practised in the Soviet Union, by the suppression of Trotsky's works and the creation of 'Trotskyism' as an evil principle. 'Doublethink,' also, has been a familiar feature of political and social life in more than one country for a quarter of a century.

The sobriety and subtlety of Mr Orwell's argument, however, is marred by a schoolboyish sensationalism of approach. Considered as a story, *Nineteen Eighty-Four* has other faults (some thirty pages are occupied by extracts from Goldstein's book, *The Theory and Practice of Oligarchical Collectivism*): but none so damaging as this inveterate schoolboyishness. The melodramatic idea of the Brotherhood is one example of it; the use of a nursery rhyme to symbolize the unattainable and desirable past is another; but the most serious of these errors in taste is the nature of the torture which breaks the last fragments of Winston's resistance. He is taken, as many others have been taken before him, to 'Room 101.' In Room 101, O'Brien tells him, is 'the worst thing in the world.' The worst thing in the world varies in every case; but for Winston, we learn, it is rats. The rats are brought into the room in a wire cage, and under threat of attack by them Winston abandons the love for Julia which is his last link with ordinary humanity. This kind of crudity (we may say with Lord Jeffrey) will never do;

however great the pains expended upon it, the idea of Room 101 and the rats will always remain comic rather than horrific.

But the last word about this book must be one of thanks, rather than of criticism: thanks for a writer who deals with the problems of the world rather than the ingrowing pains of individuals, and who is able to speak seriously and with originality of the nature of reality and the terrors of power.

# 79. Harold Nicolson, *Observer*

12 June 1949, p. 7

Sir Harold Nicolson (1886–1968), diplomat, diarist, historian and biographer of King George V (1952).

Mr George Orwell's latest book, *Nineteen Eighty-Four*, can be approached either as a novel embodying a political argument or as an indictment of materialism cast in fictional form. As a novel, it is straightforward. The hero, Winston Smith, is a civil servant verging upon middle age who is unable to adjust himself to the totalitarian system under which he works. He falls in love with a clerk in his office, is arrested for holding subversive views, and after much physical and mental suffering repudiates both his opinions and his girl. Winston Smith himself is portrayed with convincing detail; the girl, Julia, is not intended to be much more than a lay figure; and the remaining characters loom as gigantic thunder-clouds of terror or drift past the narrative, whimpering in trails of mist. The Inferno atmosphere of the story is cunningly created and well maintained.

Mr Orwell's purpose, however, was not to compose a romance with an unhappy ending. He set out to write a cautionary tale, by which to convince us of the terrible results which will follow if through inattention we allow our humanistic heritage to be submerged in a flood of materialism.

ORWELL

The world against which Mr Orwell warns us is the world which
emerged after the atomic war of 1950 and after the ten years of conflict,
revolution, and counter-revolution which then ensued. Russia by then
had absorbed the whole of Europe and created the super-State Eurasia;
the United States had welded the Americas and the British Empire
into the super-State Oceania; a third super-State had arisen later under
the name of Eastasia: Great Britain had been reduced to the function
and title of 'Airstrip One.' Each of these three world-masses had been
subjected to a totalitarian system, known respectively as 'Neo-
Bolshevism,' 'Ingsoc,' and 'Death-Worship'; their political philoso-
phies were indistinguishable, yet each regarded the other with fanatical
hatred; they were in a constant state of war.

The doctrines and structure of Ingsoc (the system governing
Oceania in general and Airstrip One in particular) are described in
detail. At the summit of the pyramid stood Big Brother, the mystical
personification of State power, whose identity, and even whose
existence were in doubt. Below him came the Inner Party, the brains
of the whole organism, who controlled the Outer Party or functional
class. The remaining eighty-five per cent. of the population were
known as the 'proles,' enjoyed no political or social rights, and were
relegated to the status of animals.

The aim of the Inner Party was to seek power entirely for its own
sake: 'not wealth or luxury or long life or happiness: only power,
pure power.' For this purpose it was necessary for them to eradicate all
individual thoughts or feelings. The Thought Police, or 'Thinkpol,'
were aided by a dreadful device, known as the 'telescreen,' by which
they were able to watch the movements, listen to the conversations,
and even note the expressions of every individual citizen. A momentary
flicker of doubt upon the features of an individual would be noted as a
'facecrime'; the perpetrator of such an outrage would be 'vapourised'
and his existence expunged from the records; he would become an
'Unperson.' The whole of past and current history was distorted and
falsified; the very language was obliterated in order to eliminate the
expression of all non-mechanical thought; sex was discouraged, the
family disrupted, the children taught to spy and hate. By such methods
the individual was constrained to abandon his personality, a dark
uniformity was created, a listless apathy infused, a condition of dingy
boredom enforced. Mr Orwell has well succeeded in impressing upon
us this awful twilight of the mind.

The book is impressive: it is not convincing. It does not possess either the high imaginative force of Aldous Huxley's *Brave New World*, or the self-contained logic of Mr Orwell's own *Animal Farm*. The reader of the latter book, once he had accepted the initial premises, found no difficulty in accepting the deductions. The reader of *Nineteen Eighty-Four* is unable to surrender to a similar suspension of disbelief. People who were twenty-five in 1960 (when Ingsoc was established) would only have been forty-nine in 1984: they would not have lost all memory of the past. It would have been physically impossible for the staff of Thinkpol to be so assiduous as to observe all the movements of the Outer Party members all the time. Such inconsistencies of detail prevent our surrendering ourselves wholly to Mr Orwell's thesis: but it is an excellent thesis none the less.

# 80. Diana Trilling, *Nation*

25 June 1949, pp. 716–17

Diana Trilling (b. 1905), wife of Lionel Trilling; American literary critic and editor of D. H. Lawrence.

Although George Orwell's *Nineteen Eighty-Four* is a brilliant and fascinating novel, the nature of its fantasy is so absolutely final and relentless that I can recommend it only with a certain reservation. This is Mr Orwell's picture of the way the world ends: actually it does not end at all, physically—one would even welcome some well-placed atom bombs—but continues in a perpetual nightmare of living death. Thirty-five years from now, according to Mr Orwell's grim calculation, there will be three great powers on this planet, any two of which will be constantly at war with the third, not for ascendancy but in order to maintain the political and economic status quo—'War is peace,' as the party slogan has it. For the rulers of the future state it is enough that people are allowed to exist; their welfare—in any sense in which we understand the word—does not have to be taken into account. The dehumanization of man has reached its ultimate development. Love, art, pleasure, comfort, the sexual emotions, have all been recognized as the consumer products of a society based upon the freedom of the individual, and they have been liquidated. Life—if it can be called life—goes on only so that power may go on.

Mr Orwell's description of how this dictatorship operates is ingenious in the extreme. The population is divided into Inner Party, Outer Party, and 'proles.' The economy of the state is always a war economy. The head of the government is Big Brother, he of the ubiquitous face, whose all-seeing eye follows one wherever there is light. The strong arm of power is the Thought Police; the greatest sin against the state, Crimethink. To help the police detect subversion every public or private room is equipped with a telescreen which records each move and utterance of the individual citizen. There is a Ministry of Truth whose function it is to eradicate whatever may have been said yesterday which is no longer policy today, and a Ministry of Love where dissidence is educated into orthodoxy before it is exterminated. There is a state language, Newspeak, consisting only of such words as make freedom of thought impossible.

Here is Mr Orwell's vision of the future. The fact that the scene of *Nineteen Eighty-Four* is London and that the political theory on which Mr Orwell's dictatorship is based is called Ingsoc, which is Newspeak for English socialism, indicates that Mr Orwell is fantasying the fate not only of an already established dictatorship like that of Russia but also that of Labor England; and indeed he states very clearly that 'by the fourth decade of the twentieth century all the main currents of political thought were authoritarian. . . . Every new political theory, by whatever name it called itself, led back to hierarchy and regimentation.' This assimilation of the English Labor government to Soviet communism is surely from any immediate political point of view, unfortunate. On the other hand, whatever our partisanship for the present English revolution as against the present situation in Russia, we must recognize that the generalization in the lesson Mr Orwell is teaching is a proper one. Even where, as in his last novel, *Animal Farm*, Mr Orwell seemed to be concerned only with unmasking the Soviet Union for its dreamy admirers, he was urged on by something larger than sectarianism. What he was telling us is that along the path the Russian revolution has followed to the destruction of all the decent human values there have stood the best ideals of modern social enlightenment. It is this idealism he has wished to jolt into self-awareness. In the name of a higher loyalty, treacheries beyond imagination have been committed; in the name of Socialist equality, privilege has ruled unbridled; in the name of democracy and freedom, the individual has lived without public voice or private peace—if this is true of the Soviet Union, why should it not eventually be equally true of the English experiment? In other words, we are being warned against the extremes to which the contemporary totalitarian spirit can carry us, not only so that we will be warned against Russia but also so that we will understand the ultimate dangers involved wherever power moves under the guise of order and rationality.

With this refusal to concentrate his attack upon Soviet totalitarianism alone Mr Orwell reasserts the ability, so rare among intellectuals of the left, to place his own brand of idealism above the uses of political partisanship. It is very difficult to pin a political label on the author of *Nineteen Eighty-Four*: if one has heard that Mr Orwell is now an anarchist, one can of course read his new novel as the work of an anarchist—but one can just as easily read it as the work of an un-fashionable, highly imaginative democrat or of an old-fashioned libertarian. Yet one cannot help being thrown off, I think, by something in the book's temper, a fierceness of intention, which seems to violate the very principles Mr Orwell would wish to preserve in the world. Whereas *Animal Farm* was too primitive a parable to capture the emotions it wished to persuade, the new book exacerbates the emo-tions almost beyond endurance. Even apart from the cruelty of its imagination—and Mr Orwell has conceived the inconceivable—one is disturbed by the book's implacable tone and the enormous pressure it exerts upon the reader, in such marked contrast, by the way, to the relaxed, beautifully civilized tone of Mr Orwell's literary and sociolog-ical essays. To make this criticism is not to ask for quietism as the method of combating the passions which are destroying modern life. But it is to wish that there were more of what E. M. Forster calls the 'relaxed will' in at least those of us who, like Mr Orwell, are so acutely aware of the threats of power.

# 81. Daniel Bell, *New Leader* (New York)

25 June 1949, p. 8

Daniel Bell (b. 1919), Professor of Sociology at Harvard, author of *The End of Ideology* (1960) and *The Radical Right* (1963).

When Thomas More in 1516 described an imaginary island, he called it *Utopia*, which in Greek means, literally, 'nowhere.' The frightening aspect of George Orwell's imaginary world is that it is somewhere—in and around us.

*Nineteen Eight-Four* pictures life thirty years hence under *Ingsoc* (English Socialism), a unit of Oceania, one of three super-states in a permanent war for world hegemony. Ingsoc life is dingy, but if drabness were the only constituent element of Orwell's museum of horror, the novel and even Ingsoc life would be bearable. What makes it a shuddering, sickening, gripping spectacle is the remorseless piling on of detail upon detail, like a fingernail drawn ceaselessly across a blackboard, of a human society stripped of the last shreds of community, where even the sexual act is a cold, distasteful, jerky moment of copulation, performed because artificial methods are not yet sufficiently perfect to reproduce the species, and where fear and anxiety are the daily staple of life—not as in the concentration camps a dull and inured fear, but under the corrosive stimuli of hate, a high-tension, twitching exhaustion from which dreams and even sleep offer no escape.

*Nineteen Eighty-Four* is the story of Winston Smith, a member of the outer Party, and his downfall which started at the *moment* doubt first crossed his mind. Smith works in Minitrue, the Ministry of Truth; he corrects past records when the present fails to bear out party predictions, expunges the names of men who have been 'vaporized' and writes articles in Newspeak, the official language of Oceania (which has not displaced the vernacular but is used for all documents).

Smith's tasks are central to the state, for the party slogan is: 'Who controls the past, controls the future, and who controls the present, controls the past.'

Ingsoc's *Newspeak* is designed to express the life of Oceania in its most fitting way and to make all other modes of thought impossible. It does so through words like *artsem* (artificial insemination), *Minitrue* and *Minipax* (the ministry of peace), and in its most subtle form in words like *crime-stop* (halting one's expression just before it becomes dangerous) and the most basic concept of *Newspeak*, *doublethink* (the ability to accept two contradictory expressions at the same time as true).

Only members of the Inner Party are fully capable of *doublethink*; the larger group, in the Outer Party, are not always capable of such nuances and rarely master the full technique. The *proles*, eighty-five percent of the population, are incapable of any thought.

All groups, however, are capable of hate, which is constantly whipped up either by the spectacle of mass hangings in the public square or by the image of Emmanuel Goldstein, the goatee-bearded betrayer of the revolution. The fear created by the threats of Goldstein is overcome only by Big Brother, whose kindly black-mustachioed face appears on the screens to efface the ranting, threatening Goldstein.

The seed of doubt is present in Winston Smith, nevertheless. Whether it is a primal urge of curiosity or an accident of fate is never entirely clear. The seed burgeons when he meets Julia, whose sex urge is strong enough to break the bounds of puritanism ordained by the party. With her simple instincts, Julia understands the party's motivations most clearly:

'When you make love you're using up energy; and afterwards you feel happy and don't give a damn for anything. They can't bear you to feel like that. They want you to be bursting with energy all the time. All this marching up and down and cheering and waving flags is simply sex gone sour.'

Winston's eyes are opened to the techniques of manipulation and the party's purposes by O'Brien, a member of the Inner Party. O'Brien gives Winston a copy of Goldstein's 'book,' which reveals the secret history of the party. This document, presumably the most forthright statement of Orwell's own credo, is a projection of James Burnham's *Managerial Revolution*.

In the end, however, Winston is betrayed by O'Brien, who in reality is one of the heads of *thoughtpol*. In a chapter unmatched in recent literature for its unrelenting description of inquisition and torture, Winston betrays Julia and himself. He not only confesses but finally comes to love the party and Big Brother.

The shrinking gap between imagination and reality is what heightens one's sense of fear in reading Orwell. Apparently there is nothing too extreme (either technically or psychologically) for the mind to contrive out of fantasy, that is not already present today.

The week Orwell's novel was published the *Sunday Times* reported a rival to *newspeak:* 'model English,' a new universal language 'with sentences having one word order and no idioms, with words having one meaning, one pronunciation, one spelling and one form and with letters having one sound and one shape.' A University of Washington sociologist who saw the need for a law-abiding language devised it.

Oceania controls its populace through *telescreen*, which brings voice and video images into a room but also allows those at the station controls to peer into the room at the same time. Yet *Factory Management and Maintenance* recently reported the development of *Vericom*, a television scanning device which allows a plant manager to watch his workroom and see who is shirking and who is working.

In the Litany of despair, however, we still have not reached the point of no return. Winston breaks and submits—and what is the guarantee that we all may not similarly submit when the shadow engulfs us? At first the 'outer man' in Winston submits because he cannot hold out against the ingenious and fiendish pain devices that cause him to 'confess.' The 'inner man,' the secret voice of 'self,' still holds true, but that is not safe either. In a slip of the tongue, in a glance and in a dream it betrays Winston and he is brought face to face with the ultimate of torture—the most dreaded thing in the world and perhaps the secret of all 'confessions.'

What is it? No single device. No general idea. It varies from individual to individual. It is that which a man fears more than any other thing in the world. It may be a way of dying or a form of abasement; it may be a secret shame or a secret longing: exposure to it, however, is what he cannot face and must deny. In the case of Winston Smith, it was a fear of rats. His torturers fitted over his face a cage-like mask in which were two scabrous rats. At a signal the door between cage and face is dropped, leaving the rats free to leap. And out of his primal dread Winston, to save his life, betrays Julia and his 'self.'

One last horror still remains, which is no less frightening for being metaphysical than real; for Orwell, actually, is not writing a tract on politics but a treatise on human nature. The secret of the inner party is that for the first time in human history, it has mastered the usage of pure power.

Once the secret of pure power is learned, Orwell suggests, the human being becomes completely malleable. And in that submission, the small flickering flame of self-consciousness, the ability of detachment which distinguishes men from other animals becomes extinguished.

Ultimately Winston submits because he feels helpless before O'Brien. In that helplessness and out of that fear arises a surging emotion he calls love. Between the executioner and the victim, Camus once wrote, is the most intimate bond. In the end, Winston wants to obey O'Brien, and that is the point of no return.

Is this our world-to-be? Is this Socialism? Many will protest that Orwell has written an effective picture of totalitarianism, but not *democratic* Socialism. But other than our protestations of sincerity and intentions of decency, what concrete dikes are we erecting against the rising flood-tide of horror?

Orwell is writing a morality play which preaches the absolute truth that man is an end in himself. But while we may live always in quest of final judgment, we do exist in the *here and now*. Consequently our need is of some empirical judgments that can state with *some* certainty the consequences of an action. Is, for example, the action of the British Labor government in creating a wage freeze the imposition of controls whose consequence is the acceleration of power concentration and the total state? Or is the creation of a central intelligence agency in the U.S.—voted recently by Congress—with the power to plant agents in every voluntary association in the country, including trade unions, another step toward that end? Are not these irreversible steps, and hence, the danger that we are being warned against?

What are the safeguards and the checks? Tradition? Intelligent citizenship? Democratic awareness? Participation? Are these enough when power is at stake? Professor Harold Lasswell, in his book *Power and Personality*, has proposed a National Personal Assessment Board, a democratic elite of skill, to devise and administer personality tests that would weed out those obsessed with power. And Dr C. S. Bluemel, a psychiatrist, in his *War, Politics and Insanity* would limit the suffrage right to university graduates who had majored in the social sciences and who had been certified as free of personality disorders by the faculty. At this point, sanity itself teeters on the balance, the obsessive fear arises and as the prophet Micah concludes, in Morton Wishengrad's fable of the *Thief and the Hangman*, 'when society plays the hangman, who is the hangman's hangman.'

What then is the answer? Perhaps the first, halting step is the admission that there are no definite answers and a radical suspicion of any such claims. The second, the recognition of an ancient insight, restated in modern times by Tillich, Buber and other religious humanists, that the human condition is limited because the ego is a form of power and that every human relationship, particularly the most intimate, inflicts pain and tension, upon each other. And finally, that any social action has to be tested pragmatically (in Dewey's use of the word) by its minimal infringement on the carefully defined set of values which stakes out man as the measure of *man's* things.

Such a program runs the danger possibly of being colorless and unappealing for those who seek a forthright reproach to the spirits taunting them with foreboding images of their fate. Yet we cannot live the primitive martyrdom demanded by Kierkegaard, or the withdrawal from the times contemplated by Schelling[1] or the nihilistic despair of their twentieth century existentialist successors. One has to live *in* the world, and accept it in all its frightening implications. One has to live consciously and self-consciously, in the involvement and in the alienation, in the loyalty and in the questioning, in the love and in the critical appraisal. Without that persistent double image we are lost. At best we can live in paradox.

[1] Friedrich Schelling (1775–1854) was a German philosopher.

# 82. Philip Rahv, *Partisan Review*

July 1949, pp. 743–9

Philip Rahv (1908–74), Russian-born American critic and editor of *Partisan Review*, was Professor of English at Brandeis University in Boston and author of *Image and Idea* (1957).

George Orwell has been able to maintain an exceptional position among the writers of our time seriously concerned with political problems. His work has grown in importance and relevance through the years, evincing a steadiness of purpose and uncommon qualities of character and integrity that set it quite apart from the typical products of the radical consciousness in this period of rout and retreat. A genuine humanist in his commitments, a friend, that is, not merely of mankind but of man (man as he is, not denatured by ideological abstractions), Orwell has gone through the school of the revolutionary movement without taking over its snappishly doctrinaire attitudes. His attachment to the primary traditions of the British empirical mind has apparently rendered him immune to dogmatism. Nor has the release from certitude lately experienced by the more alert radical intellectuals left him in the disoriented state in which many of his contemporaries now find themselves. Above all endowed with a strong sense of reality, he has neither played the prophet in or out of season nor indulged in that wilful and irresponsible theorizing at present so much in vogue in certain radical quarters where it is mistaken for independent thought. It can be said of Orwell that he is the best kind of witness, the most reliable and scrupulous. All the more appalling, then, is the vision not of the remote but of the very close future evoked in his new novel—a vision entirely composed of images of loss, disaster, and unspeakable degradation.

This is far and away the best of Orwell's books. As a narrative it has tension and actuality to a terrifying degree; still it will not do to judge it primarily as a literary work of art. Like all Utopian literature, from

Sir Thomas More and Campanella[1] to William Morris, Bellamy[2] and Huxley, its inspiration is scarcely such as to be aesthetically productive of ultimate or positive significance; this seems to be true of Utopian writings regardless of the viewpoint from which the author approaches his theme. *Nineteen Eighty-Four* chiefly appeals to us as a work of the political imagination, and the appeal is exercised with gravity and power. It documents the crisis of socialism with greater finality than Koestler's *Darkness at Noon*, to which it will be inevitably compared, since it belongs, on one side of it, to the same genre, the melancholy mid-century genre of lost illusions and Utopia betrayed.

While in Koestler's novel there are still lingering traces of nostalgia for the Soviet Utopia, at least in its early heroic phase, and fleeting tenderness for its protagonists, betrayers and betrayed—some are depicted as Promethean types wholly possessed by the revolutionary dogma and annihilated by the consequences of their own excess, the *hubris* of Bolshevism—in Orwell's narrative the further stage of terror that has been reached no longer permits even the slightest sympathy for the revolutionaries turned totalitarian. Here Utopia is presented, with the fearful simplicity of a trauma, as the abyss into which the future falls. The traditional notion of Utopia as the future good is thus turned inside out, inverted—nullified. It is now sheer mockery to speak of its future. Far more accurate it is to speak of its *unfuture*. (The addition of the negative affix 'un' is a favorite usage of Newspeak, the official language of Ingsoc—English socialism—a language in which persons purged by the Ministry of Love, i.e., the secret police, are invariably described as *unpersons*. The principles of Newspeak are masterfully analyzed by Orwell in the appendix to his book. Newspeak is nothing less than a plot against human consciousness, for its sole aim is so to reduce the range of thought through the destruction of words as to make '*thoughtcrime* literally impossible because there will be no words in which to express it.')

The prospect of the future drawn in this novel can on no account be taken as a phantasy. If it inspires dread above all, that is precisely because its materials are taken from the real world as we know it, from conditions now prevailing in the totalitarian nations, in particular the Communist nations, and potentially among us too. Ingsoc, the system established in Oceania, the totalitarian super-State that unites the English-speaking peoples, is substantially little more than an extension

[1] Tommaso Campanella (1568–1639), Italian author of *The City of the Sun* (1602).
[2] Edward Bellamy (1850–98), American author of *Looking Backward* (1888).

into the near future of the present structure and policy of Stalinism, an extension as ingenious as it is logical, predicated upon conditions of permanent war and the development of the technical means of espionage and surveillance to the point of the complete extinction of private life. Big Brother, the supreme dictator of Oceania, is obviously modeled on Stalin, both in his physical features and in his literary style ('a style at once military and pedantic, and, because of a trick of asking questions and then promptly answering them . . . easy to imitate'). And who is Goldstein, the dissident leader of Ingsoc against whom Two Minute Hate Periods are conducted in all Party offices, if not Trotsky, the grand heresiarch and useful scapegoat, who is even now as indispensable to Stalin as Goldstein is shown to be to Big Brother? The inserted chapters from Goldstein's imaginary book on *The Theory and Practice of Oligarchical Collectivism*, are a wonderfully realised imitation not only of Trotsky's characteristic rhetoric but also of his mode and manner as a Marxist theoretician. Moreover, the established pieties of Communism are at once recognizable in the approved spiritual regimen of the Ingsoc Party faithful: 'A Party member is expected to have no private emotions and no respites from enthusiasm. He is supposed to live in a continuous frenzy of hatred of foreign enemies and internal traitors, triumph over victories, and self-abasement before the power and wisdom of the Party.' One of Orwell's best strokes is his analysis of the technique of 'double-think,' drilled into the Party members, which consists of the willingness to assert that black is white when the Party demands it, and even to believe that black is white, while at the same time knowing very well that nothing of the sort can be true. Now what is 'doublethink,' actually, if not the technique continually practiced by the Communists and their liberal collaborators, dupes, and apologists. Nor is it a technique available exclusively to Soviet citizens. Right here in New York any issue of *The Daily Worker* or of *The Daily Compass* will provide you with illustrations of it as vicious and ludicrous as any you will come upon in Orwell's story. As for 'the control of the past,' of which so much is made in Oceania through the revision of all records and the manipulation of memory through force and fraud, that too is by no means unknown in Russia, where periodically not only political history but also the history of art and literature are revamped in accordance with the latest edicts of the regime. The one feature of Oceanic society that appears to be really new is the proscription of sexual pleasure. The fact is, however, that a tendency in that direction has long been evident in Russia, where a new kind of prudery, disgusting in its unctuousness and hypocrisy, is officially promoted. In Oceania 'the only recognized purpose of marriage was to beget children for the service of the Party.' The new Russian laws regulating sexual relations are manifestly designed with the same purpose in mind. It is plain that any society which imposes a ban on personal experience must sooner or later distort and inhibit the sexual instinct. The totalitarian State cannot tolerate attachments between men and women that fall outside the political sphere and that are in their very nature difficult to control from above.

The diagnosis of the totalitarian perversion of socialism that Orwell makes in this book is far more remarkable than the prognosis it contains. This is not to deny that the book is prophetic; but its importance is mainly in its powerful engagement with the present. Through the invention of a society of which he can be imaginatively in full command, Orwell is enabled all the more effectively to probe the consequences for the human soul of the system of oligarchic collectivism— the system already prevailing in a good part of the world, which millions of people even this side of the Iron Curtain believe to be true-blue socialism and which at this time constitutes the only formidable threat to free institutions. Hence to read this novel simply as a flat prediction of what is to come is to misread it. It is not a writ of fatalism to bind our wills. Orwell makes no attempt to persuade us, for instance, that the English-speaking nations will inevitably lose their freedom in spite of their vigorous democratic temper and libertarian traditions. 'Wave of the future' notions are alien to Orwell. His intention, rather, is to prod the Western world into a more conscious and militant resistance to the totalitarian virus to which it is now exposed.

As in *Darkness at Noon*, so in *Nineteen Eighty-Four* one of the major themes is the psychology of capitulation. Winston Smith, the hero of the novel, is shown arming himself with ideas against the Party and defying it by forming a sexual relationship with Julia; but from the first we know that he will not escape the secret police, and after he is caught we see him undergoing a dreadful metamorphosis which burns out his human essence, leaving him a wreck who can go on living only by becoming one of 'them.' The closing sentences of the story are the most pitiful of all: 'He had won a victory over himself. He loved Big Brother.' The meaning of the horror of the last section of the novel, with its unbearable description of the torture of Smith by O'Brien, the Ingsoc Commissar, lies in its disclosure of a truth that the West still refuses to absorb. Hence the widespread mystifications produced by the Moscow Trials ('Why did they confess?') and, more recently, by the equally spectacular displays of confessional ardor in Russia's satellite states (Cardinal Mindszenty and others). The truth is that the modern totalitarians have devised a methodology of terror that enables them to break human beings by getting inside them. They explode the human character from within, exhibiting the pieces as the irrefutable proof of their own might and virtue. Thus Winston Smith begins with the notion that even if nothing else in the world was his own, still there were a few cubic centimeters inside his skull that belonged to him alone. But O'Brien, with his torture instruments and ruthless dialectic of power, soon teaches him that even these few cubic centimeters can never belong to him, only to the Party. What is so implacable about the despotisms of the twentieth century is that they have abolished martyrdom. If all through history the capacity and willingness to suffer for one's convictions served at once as the test and demonstration of sincerity, valor, and heroic resistance to evil, now even that capacity and willingness have been rendered meaningless. In the prisons of the M.V.D. or the Ministry of Love suffering has been converted into its opposite—into the ineluctable means of surrender. The victim crawls before his torturer, he identifies himself with him and grows to love him. That is the ultimate horror.

The dialectic of power is embodied in the figure of O'Brien, who simultaneously recalls and refutes the ideas of Dostoevsky's Grand Inquisitor. For a long time we thought that the legend of the Grand Inquisitor contained the innermost secrets of the power-mongering human mind. But no, modern experience has taught us that the last word is by no means to be found in Dostoevsky. For even the author of *The Brothers Karamazov*, who wrote that 'man is a despot by nature and loves to be a torturer,' was for all his crucial insights into evil nevertheless incapable of seeing the Grand Inquisitor as he really is. There are elements of the idealistic rationalization of power in the ideology of the Grand Inquisitor that we must overcome if we are to become fully aware of what the politics of totalitarianism come to in the end.

Clearly, that is what Orwell has in mind in the scene when Smith, while yielding more and more to O'Brien, voices the thoughts of the Grand Inquisitor only to suffer further pangs of pain for his persistence in error. Smith thinks that he will please O'Brien by explaining the Party's limitless desire for power along Dostoevskyean lines: 'That the

Party did not seek power for its own ends, but only for the good of the majority. That it sought power because men in the mass were frail, cowardly creatures who could not endure liberty or face the truth, and must be ruled over and systematically deceived by others stronger than themselves. That the choice for mankind lay between freedom and happiness, and that, for the great bulk of mankind, happiness was better. That the Party was the eternal guardian of the weak, a dedicated sect doing evil that good might come, sacrificing its own happiness to that of others.' This is a fair summary of the Grand Inquisitor's ideology. O'Brien, however, has gone beyond even this last and most insidious rationalization of power. He forcibly instructs Smith in the plain truth that 'the Party seeks power for its own sake. We are not interested in the good of others; we are interested solely in power. . . . Power is not a means; it is an end. One does not establish a dictatorship in order to safeguard a revolution; one makes a revolution in order to establish the dictatorship. The object of persecution is persecution. The object of torture is torture. The object of power is power. Now do you begin to understand me?' And how does one human being assert his power over another human being? By making him suffer, of course. For 'obedience is not enough. Unless he is suffering, how can you be sure that he is obeying your will and not his own? Power is in inflicting pain and humiliation. Power is in tearing human minds to pieces and putting them together again in new shapes of your own choosing.' That, precisely, is the lesson the West must learn if it is to comprehend the meaning of Communism. Otherwise we shall go on playing Winston Smith, falling sooner or later into the hands of the O'Briens of the East, who will break our bones until we scream with love for Big Brother.

But there is one aspect of the psychology of power in which Dostoevsky's insight strikes me as being more viable than Orwell's strict realism. It seems to me that Orwell fails to distinguish, in the behavior of O'Brien, between psychological and objective truth. Undoubtedly it is O'Brien, rather than Dostoevsky's Grand Inquisitor, who reveals the real nature of total power; yet that does not settle the question of O'Brien's personal psychology, the question, that is, of his ability to live with this naked truth as his sole support; nor is it conceivable that the party-elite to which he belongs could live with this truth for very long. Evil, far more than good, is in need of the pseudo-religious justifications so readily provided by the ideologies of world-salvation and compulsory happiness, ideologies generated both by the

Left and the Right. Power is its own end, to be sure, but even the Grand Inquisitors are compelled, now as always, to believe in the fiction that their power is a means to some other end, gratifyingly noble and supernal. Though O'Brien's realism is wholly convincing in social and political terms, its motivation in the psychological economy of the novel remains unclear.

Another aspect of Orwell's dreadful Utopia that might be called into question is the role he attributes to the proletariat, a role that puts it outside politics. In Oceania the workers, known as the Proles, are assigned to the task of production, deprived of all political rights, but unlike the Party members, are otherwise left alone and even permitted to lead private lives in accordance with their own choice. That is an idea that appears to me to run contrary to the basic tendencies of totalitarianism. All societies of our epoch, whether authoritarian or democratic in structure, are mass-societies; and an authoritarian state built on the foundations of a mass-society could scarcely afford the luxury of allowing any class or group to evade its demand for complete control. A totalitarian-collectivist state is rigidly organized along hierarchical lines, but that very fact, so damaging to its socialist claims, necessitates the domination of all citizens, of whatever class, in the attempt to 'abolish' the contradiction between its theory and practice by means of boundless demagogy and violence.

These are minor faults, however. This novel is the best antidote to the totalitarian disease that any writer has so far produced. Everyone should read it; and I recommend it particularly to those liberals who still cannot get over the political superstition that while absolute power is bad when exercised by the Right, it is in its very nature good and a boon to humanity once the Left, that is to say 'our own people,' takes hold of it.

# 83. Samuel Sillen, *Masses and Mainstream*

## August 1949, pp. 79–81

Samuel Sillen was the editor of *Masses and Mainstream*, a Communist journal published in America.

Like his previous diatribe against the human race, *Animal Farm*, George Orwell's new book has received an ovation in the capitalist press. The gush of comparisons with Swift and Dostoyevsky has washed away the few remaining pebbles of literary probity. Not even the robots of Orwell's dyspeptic vision of the world in 1984 seem as solidly regimented as the freedom-shouters who chose it for the Book of the Month Club, serialized it in *Reader's Digest*, illustrated it in eight pages of *Life*, and wrote pious homilies on it in *Partisan Review* and the New York *Times*. Indeed the response is far more significant than the book itself; it demonstrates that Orwell's sickness is epidemic.

The premise of the fable is that capitalism has ceased to exist in 1984; and the moral is that if capitalism departs the world will go to pot. The earth is divided into three 'socialist' areas, Oceania, Eurasia and Eastasia, which unlike the good old days of free enterprise are in perpetual warfare. The hero, Winston Smith, lives on Airstrip One (England) and balks at the power-crazed regime. He is nabbed by the Thought Police, tortured with fiendish devices, and finally he wins the privilege of being shot[1] when he learns to love the invisible dictator.

Orwell's nightmare is also inhabited by the 'proles,' who constitute a mere 85 per cent of Oceania and who are described with fear and loathing as ignorant, servile, brutish. A critic of Orwell's earlier novel in the *Saturday Review of Literature* expressed a profound insight when he noted: 'The message of *Animal Farm* seems to be . . . *that people are no damn good.*'

'People are no damn good'—that is precisely the message of this plodding tale as well. For Orwell, life is a dunghill, and after a while the 'animals' look 'from pig to man, and from man to pig, and from pig to man again; but already it was impossible to say which was which.'

---

[1] Winston is *not* shot at the end of *1984*.

As a piece of fiction this is threadbare stuff with a tasteless sex angle which has been rhapsodically interpreted by Mark Schorer in the New York *Times* as a 'new discovery of the beauty of love between man and woman.' This new discovery is well illustrated by the following scene in which Winston Smith makes love to Julia, a fellow-rebel against the dictatorial regime:

'Listen. The more men you've had, the more I love you. Do you understand that?'

'Yes, perfectly.'

'I hate purity, I hate goodness. I don't want any virtue to exist anywhere. I want everyone to be corrupt to the bones.'

'Well, then, I ought to suit you, dear. I'm corrupt to the bones.'

'You like doing this? I don't mean simply me; I mean the thing in itself?'

'I adore it.'

That was above all what he wanted to hear. Not merely the love of one person, but the animal instinct, the simple undifferentiated desire: that was the force that would tear the Party to pieces.

According to *Life* magazine this is 'one of the most furtive and pathetic little love affairs in all literature.'

Or consider this: Orwell's hero, who is supposed to awaken what the reviewers call 'compassion,' is interviewed by a man whom he believes to be the leader of the underground resistance to the tyrannical regime:

'You are prepared to cheat, to forge, to blackmail, to corrupt the minds of children, to distribute habit-forming drugs, to encourage prostitution, to disseminate venereal diseases—to do anything which is likely to cause demoralization and weaken the power of the Party?'

'Yes.'

'If, for example, it would somehow serve our interests to throw sulphuric acid in a child's face—are you prepared to do that?'

'Yes.'

The author of this cynical rot is quite a hero himself. He served for five years in the Indian Imperial Police, an excellent training center for dealing with the 'proles.' He was later associated with the Trotskyites in Spain, serving in the P.O.U.M. and he freely concedes that when this organization of treason to the Spanish Republic was 'accused of profascist activities I defended them to the best of my ability.' During World War II he busied himself with defamation of the Soviet Union.

And now, as Lionel Trilling approvingly notes in *The New Yorker*, Orwell 'marks a turn in thought.' What is the significance of this turn?

The literary mouthpieces of imperialism have discovered that the crude anti-Sovietism of a Kravchenko[1] is not enough; the system of class oppression must be directly upheld and *any* belief in change and progress must be frightened out of people.

Like Trilling, the editorial writers of *Life* have shrewdly seized upon Orwell's generalized attack on the 'welfare state' to attack not only the Soviet Union but [Henry] Wallace and the British Laborites. 'Many readers in England,' says *Life*, 'will find that his book reinforces a growing suspicion that some of the British Laborites revel in austerity and would love to preserve it—just as the more fervent New Dealers in the U.S. often seemed to have the secret hope that the depression mentality of the '30's, source of their power and excuse for their experiments, would never end.'

In short, Orwell's novel coincides perfectly with the propaganda of the National Association of Manufacturers, and it is being greeted for exactly the same reasons that Frederick Hayek's *The Road to Serfdom* was hailed a few years back.

The bourgeoisie, in its younger days, could find spokesmen who painted rosy visions of the future. In its decay, surrounded by burgeoning socialism, it is capable only of hate-filled, dehumanized anti-Utopias. Confidence has given way to the nihilistic literature of the graveyard. Now that Ezra Pound has been given a government award[2] and George Orwell has become a best-seller we would seem to have reached bottom. But there is a hideous ingenuity in the perversions of a dying capitalism, and it will keep probing for new depths of rottenness which the maggots will find 'brilliant and morally invigorating.'

[1] Victor Kravchenko was a Soviet defector who attacked Stalin in *I Chose Freedom* (1946).
[2] Pound, who broadcast pro-Fascist speeches from Italy during the Second World War, was awarded the Bollingen poetry prize in 1949.

# 84. Golo Mann, *Frankfurter Rundschau*

## 5 November 1949, p. 6

Golo Mann (b. 1909), German historian, author of *History of Germany Since 1789* (1968), former Professor of History at Claremont College. Written in Claremont, California; translated by Michael Richter and Jeffrey Meyers.

---

The writer George Orwell, a socialist and fanatical fighter for individual freedom, is an outsider in English literature. He stands completely apart, though not as passionately and consciously as, for example, G. B. Shaw. Orwell's ironical fairy tale, *Animal Farm*, has become known throughout the world. *1984*, his satirical novel about the future, is a warning to the world, a very vivid presentation of the terror that could occur in the near future if all the implications of totalitarian ideas were put into practice and we were all forced to live in a world of fear.

Martin Esslin has adapted Orwell's fascinating book as a BBC radio play. The moving performance directed by Julius Gellner was like a fantastic nightmare, especially for Germans, who perhaps more than any other nation can feel the merciless probability of Orwell's utopia. Listeners were fascinated by the cold passion and inescapable consequences of the story. The intense performance was an emotional warning to those who even today are not free from totalitarian dreams.

Like Orwell's utopian novel, the inevitable result of totalitarian attitudes was the theme of a radio play by Christian Bock, *Fatal Reckoning*. After its first performance by North-West German Radio the author, who thought he had not yet found the best form for his theme, rewrote the play. *Fatal Reckoning* concerns the consequences of the command that after a certain moment four and four will no longer equal eight, but six.[1] This is what Bock's citizen—the clerk Linie—has to come to terms with. Linie is expected to see reason in acts of despotism and to substitute the command of the state for his own conscience and personal judgment. Since Linie is unfortunately an

[1] Bock's $4 + 4 = 6$ is obviously derived from Orwell's $2 + 2 = 5$.

individualist, the state organism—simply called 'the center' by Bock
—destroys him. The performance by South-West Radio under the
direction of Karl Peter Biltz, with the magnificent music of Carl
Sezuka, was excellent. Wolfgang Golisch spoke the part of the clerk
Linie in a passionate and convincing manner.

*1984*, the celebrated new novel by the English author George Orwell
takes place in London in the year of the title. England is no longer
called England but 'Airstrip One,' a province of Oceania which has its
center of gravity in North America. Besides Oceania there are two
other powers on earth: Eurasia—i.e. Europe and Russia—and East
Asia. These three powers are engaged in a permanent war for control
of a densely populated but militarily helpless no-man's land situated
between them in India, Africa and Indonesia. The war is conducted,
however, without a desire to win, for none of the powers is interested
in bringing it to an end. There is even a suspicion that the government
of Oceania occasionally fires rockets on to London in order to remind
the population of the war and keep them in a state of fear and hatred.
By tacit agreement, fatally destructive weapons like the atomic bomb
are not used by any of the powers. War determines the character of the
inner regime of Oceania and—so Orwell makes us believe—of the other
two super powers as well. In fact, the three one-party dictatorships are
as alike as three eggs. This does not prevent the ministry of propaganda
in Oceania—its official name is the Ministry of Truth—from conducting
a merciless campaign against the shocking acts of cruelty committed
by the inferior Eurasians—until the moment when Oceania comes to
an agreement with Eurasia to combine their strength against East
Asia.

These sudden changes of sides are very frequent, and as soon as they
take place, the past is appropriately changed by the Ministry of Truth.
The diabolical enemy of the world now is—and consequently always
has been—East Asia. Those who know better and try to remember
things that no longer exist and therefore have never existed, are re-
educated in the prisons of the Thought Police. They are liquidated,
'vapourized'; and they become 'un-persons' who never existed,
whom no one is allowed to mention and whom no one wants to
mention. Those in power also control the past.

The society of Oceania consists of three classes: the dominant and
knowledgeable elite, called the 'Inner Party'; the closely supervised
and perpetually cheated agents of this power, called the 'Outer Party';
and the 'Proles,' the unaffiliated masses who have to be kept under

control by acts of terror or by entertainment, but who are otherwise unimportant.

The dictator has the title of 'Big Brother,' and his portrait with a bushy moustache looks down threateningly from every wall. He is a man without equal, knowing everything, having invented everything, always correctly predicting everything. It is not quite clear whether he really exists. He seems to be destined to an eternal life, and his acts of heroism reach further back into the past than would normally be possible. But the detestable traitor and rebel against the party, the Jew Emmanuel Goldstein, never existed; he is an invention of the party, pure and simple. Periodically, the hatred of the masses for this non-existent founder of 'Goldsteinism' is systematically aroused, especially during the so-called 'Hate Week' which takes place once a year and reaches its climax in the public execution of thousands of war criminals. The 'Ministry of Peace' is responsible for war. The 'Ministry of Love' concerns itself with all political crimes, especially the so-called 'Thought-crime.' The 'Ministry of Plenty' administers an economy of perpetual war and permanent shortage.

The ugly misery of life in 1984 is perhaps the strongest impression that remains with the reader. Despite constantly victorious 'production battles' and successfully completed five-year plans, there are never enough goods to buy. Everything is state owned, everything is *ersatz* and 'victory'; victory coffee, victory gin, even the apartment block in which the hero of the story lives is called Victory Mansions. There is a smell of cabbage on the staircase, the running water is luke-warm at best, and the lift is out of order. There are no new machines and no fantastic inventions: men live off the old capital. The only technical innovation introduced by Orwell is the telescreen, a television set that simultaneously records the picture of the spectator and that is installed in the flats of all party members, who are under constant surveillance by the Thought Police. Everything else is imaginative, not technical fantasy: the official language of the party, for example, the so-called 'Newspeak', which is designed to make free thought impossible through repulsive abbreviations and simplifications; or the three great slogans of the party: 'Peace is War,' 'Freedom is Slavery,' 'Ignorance is Truth'.

This is a portrait of English society in the year 1984, an essential point of the book. Orwell has been much less successful in portraying human affairs and in transforming the utopia into a narrative. Despite everything, there is a love story. There are also the prisons of the

Thought Police. A clerk of the Ministry of Truth, Winston Smith, is jailed for rebelling against the party and joining the Goldstein opposition, for he does not realize that Goldstein's writings were actually written by the party. At this point everything becomes confused and unbelievable, for Goldstein writes so well and truly, and expresses Orwell's own opinions so clearly, that no super-Goebbels[1] could have written his book. The torture chambers of the Thought Police are equally unconvincing; sadists like Koestler and Malraux,[2] with their experience of civil war, are much more successful in this respect. Orwell had to show, of course, how and why Winston fails in his opposition to the party, and how his spirit and will are broken, but he did not need papier-mâché torture machines to do this.

But what does George Orwell intend? Surely not to show what the earth will inevitably look like in 1984. He is not a fatalist, not a mistaken 'scientific' prophet. Nor is he a malicious individualist who comforts and amuses himself by predicting how sad life will be and how people deserve nothing better. He warns and wants to help. He warns of the dangers that are typical of our age anywhere, not only behind the Iron Curtain. American mass magazines like *Life* and *Reader's Digest* have pounced upon *1984* and given the book the widest possible publicity as an anti-Communist pamphlet. This is good in so far as it makes more people read Orwell. But it is *not* good in so far as it makes him into a political pamphleteer, which he is not; and in so far as it conveys to the American reader a complacent security, which is unfounded. This kind of magazine commentary is, thank God, not possible in our country. Or is it?

Orwell borrowed from present-day Russia more than from any other country for his fictitious description of the future. He also borrowed some things from Fascism and Nazism. And his own English environment is also apparent in the rationed misery, the lack of *joie de vivre*, the drabness and the austerity, for these have not been freely invented by Orwell. But the meaning of the small details and the newspaper articles that provided the material evidence are completely irrelevant. It is much more important that his vigorous intuition, clear vision, sympathy and anger have exposed dangers which are present everywhere, and that he has sharpened our eyes so that we can see them. The author is too deeply and too seriously an enemy of Bolshev-

[1] Joseph Goebbels (1897-45) was the Nazi Minister of Propaganda.
[2] Mann is referring to Koestler's *Darkness at Noon* (1940) and Malraux's *Days of Wrath* (1935).

ism and of any kind of mass tyranny for his book to be merely anti-Russian. Picard has written a book with the title *Hitler Within Ourselves*.[1] Orwell's only theme is the totalitarian danger that lies within ourselves and in all the political systems of our time.

Thus it is not the kind of anti-Russian book of which we already have more than enough, but a conservative book. The main concern of Orwell's novel is the recognition of how closely human freedom is allied to historical veracity, to a faithful accounting of the past. His people live in a rootless, uninformed and frightened present which looks backwards into the mist of the past instead of conquering history by research and keeping it alive by respect. 'Whoever has power dominates the past.' That is to say, absolute power cannot be maintained without depriving human beings of their past, the beauty and value of the past, and without giving them a concoction of lies invented by the Ministry of Truth. Conversely, the hero of the story can free himself from the domination of party ideology only by remembering his earliest childhood impressions, by recalling traditional England as it was before the 'Revolution,' by preparing the way to the historical truth that leads back to the real past. When Winston conspires against the dictatorship with his girl friend they emphasize their fatal decision by drinking real wine, and they cannot find a better thing to drink to than 'To the past'.

[1] Max Picard's *Hitler in uns selbst* was published in Neuchâtel, Switzerland in 1946.

# 85. I. Anisimov, *Pravda*

## 12 May 1950

In *Current Digest of the Soviet Press*, 1 July 1950, pp. 14–15.

In recent times there has been wide dissemination of fantastic novels and stories which contain the most gruesome predictions of what mankind may expect in the near future. The authors of such prognostications confidently anticipate third and even fourth world wars and relish the horror of mass extermination of people with atomic and bacteriological bombs. With evil joy they predict that an end will necessarily be put to culture, art and mankind as a whole.

In inventing their squalid fantasies, these writers, if we may be pardoned for calling them that, describe the monsters which will inhabit the earth after mankind has eliminated itself from its face. These will be monkeys or bats who, it is said, will 'attain a higher spiritual level than human beings.' What misanthropy!

The works of misanthropic fantasy very closely resemble one another. Especially monstrous are two books which are fervently advertised and published every place corrupted by the activity of American imperialism. These books, written by Anglo-American cosmopolitans A. Huxley and G. Orwell, are entitled respectively 'Ape and Essence' and '1984'. . . .

Mr Orwell is in every way similar to Mr Huxley, especially in his contempt for people, in his aim of slandering man. And while the one cries out, 'The voice of the proletariat is the voice of the devil,' the other, slobbering with poisonous spittle, does not lag far behind him. For in describing a most monstrous future in store for man, he imputes every evil to the people. He is obliged to admit that in 1984, when the events in the novel take place, capitalism will cease to exist, but only for opening the way to endless wars and the degradation of mankind, which will be brought down to the level of robots called 'proles.'

It is clear that Orwell's filthy book is in the spirit of such a vital organ of American propaganda as the *Reader's Digest* which published this work, and *Life* which presented it with many illustrations.

Thus, gruesome prognostications, which are being made in our times by a whole army of venal writers on the orders and instigation of Wall Street, are real attacks against the people of the world. . . .

But the people are not frightened by any such fears of the instigators of a new war. The people's conscience is clearer today than ever before. The foul maneuvers of mankind's enemies become more clearly understandable every day to millions of common people.

The living forces of peace are uniting ever more firmly into an organized front in defense of peace, freedom and life. They are the only hope man has for the salvation of culture. Led by the Soviet Union, these forces are mighty and indomitable. They will assure mankind happiness and prosperity despite the monstrous intrigues of the imperialists, the instigators of war.

# 86. Herbert Read, *World Review*

June 1950, pp. 58–9

Sir Herbert Read (1893–1968), poet and art critic; broadcast at BBC with Orwell; author of *Naked Warriors* (1919), *English Prose Style* (1928) and *The Contrary Experience* (1963).

Orwell's last work will undoubtedly rank as his greatest, though I suspect that *Animal Farm* will end by being the most popular, if only because it can be read as a fairy-tale by children. But *1984* has a far greater range of satirical force, and a grimness of power which could perhaps come only from the mind of a sick man. As literature, it has certain limitations. Satire, as Swift realised, becomes monotonous if carried too far in the same vein, and he therefore sent Gulliver to several different countries where human folly took on distinct guises. Though both writers have in common a savagery of indignation, the comparison of their work cannot be carried very far. Fundamental to

Swift is a certain *disgust* of humanity and *despair* of life; fundamental to Orwell is a *love* of humanity and a passionate desire to live in freedom. There is a difference of style, too, for though both practised a direct and unaffected narrative, Swift's is still playfully baroque—or, rather, baroquely playful. A more useful comparison is with Defoe—and this comparison holds good for the whole of Orwell's output. Defoe was the first writer to raise journalism to a literary art; Orwell perhaps the last. One could make direct comparisons between their writings if it would serve any purpose (between, say, *The Road to Wigan Pier* and the *Journal of the Plague Year*), but I prefer an indirect comparison between *1984* and *Robinson Crusoe*. The desert island is a long way from the totalitarian State; nevertheless, there is the same practicality in the construction of both books, and Winston Smith, 'his chin nuzzled into his breast in an effort to escape the vile wind,' slipping 'quickly through the glass doors of Victory Mansions, though not quickly enough to prevent a swirl of gritty dust from entering along with him', is the same Little Man hero who, as Robinson Crusoe, being one day at Hull, 'went on board a ship bound for London . . . without any consideration of circumstances or consequences, and in an ill hour, God knows.' Strictly speaking, *Robinson Crusoe* is neither a satire nor an Utopia, whereas *1984* is an Utopia in reverse—not an *Erewhon*, which is an Utopia upside-down. *Erewhon* is still written after the ameliorative pattern of *Utopia* itself: you may, paradoxically, be punished for being ill, but the ideal is health. In *1984* the pattern is malevolent; everything is for the worst in the worst of all possible worlds. But the pattern begins in the present—in our existing totalitarian States.

On page 157 there is a significant sentence which might be taken as the motif of the book: *By lack of understanding they remained sane.* The crime of Winston Smith, the hero of *1984*, was the use of a critical intelligence, his Socratic inability to stop asking questions. That 'ignorance is bliss' is no new discovery, but it has generally been assumed that understanding, which brings with it a sense of responsibility, an awareness of suffering and a tragic view of life, has compensations of a spiritual nature. It has been the object of modern tyrannies to deny man this sense of responsibility, and gradually to eliminate all feelings. The greatest enemies of the totalitarian State are not ideas (which can be dealt with dialectically) but aesthetic and erotic sensations. In the love of objective beauty, and in the love of an individual of the opposite sex, the most oppressed slave can escape to a free world. Religion is not so dangerous because it tends to be ideological and can be undermined by propaganda. But the sympathy of love, and the empathy of art—these feelings must be eradicated from the human breast if man's allegiance to Caesar (Big Brother) is to be complete. Orwell does not deal with the totalitarian hostility to art, but the dramatic quality which makes his satire so readable is due to his perception of the totalitarian hostility to love. ' "They can't get inside you," she had said. But they could get inside you. "What happens to you here is *for ever*" O'Brien had said. That was a true word. There were things, your own acts, from which you could not recover. Something was killed in your breast: burnt out, cauterised out.'

Orwell was a humanitarian—always moved by sympathy, by human love. The inconsistencies of his political opinions sprang from this fact. Consistently he would have been a pacifist, but he could not resist the Quixotic impulse to spring to arms in defence of the weak or oppressed. It would be difficult to say what positive political ideals were left this side of his overwhelming disillusion with Communism. In his last years he saw only the menace of the totalitarian State, and he knew he had only the force left to warn us. It is the most terrifying warning that a man has ever uttered, and its fascination derives from its veracity. Millions of people have read this book. Why? It has no charm; it makes no concession to sentiment. It is true that there are some traces of eroticism, but surely not enough to make the book, for those who seek that sort of thing, a worthwhile experience. An element of sado-masochism in the public may explain the strange success of this book. In the past the success of a book like Foxe's *Book of Martyrs*[1] was not due to a disinterested love of the truth, or even to a hatred of Catholicism. Foxe himself was a tolerant man, but there is no evidence that his book produced a mood of tolerance in his millions of readers. I would like to think that the reading of *1984* had effectively turned the tide against the authoritarian State, but I see no evidence of it. Of Orwell's readers must it also be said: By lack of understanding they remain sane?

[1] John Foxe's *Book of [Protestant] Martyrs* was published in 1563.

# 87. Czeslaw Milosz, *The Captive Mind*

1953

---

*The Captive Mind*, trans. Jane Zielonko (London: Secker & Warburg, 1953), p. 42.

Czeslaw Milosz (b. 1911 in Lithuania), Polish poet, translator of Shakespeare, broadcaster and diplomat; now lives in France. *The Captive Mind* analyzes the negative impact of Communism on four Polish writers.

---

A great many of them have read Koestler's *Darkness at Noon*. A few have become acquainted with Orwell's *1984*; because it is both difficult to obtain and dangerous to possess, it is known only to certain members of the Inner Party. Orwell fascinates them through his insight into details they know well, and through his use of Swiftian satire. Such a form or writing is forbidden by the New Faith because allegory, by nature manifold in meaning, would trespass beyond the prescriptions of socialist realism and the demands of the censor. Even those who know Orwell only by hearsay are amazed that a writer who never lived in Russia should have so keen a perception into its life. The fact that there are writers in the West who understand the functioning of the unusually constructed machine of which they themselves are a part astounds them and argues against the 'stupidity' of the West.

# 88. James Walsh, *Marxist Quarterly*

January 1956, pp. 25-39

The *Marxist Quarterly* was published in London by Lawrence & Wishart.

*1984* continues the same trend as *Animal Farm*, except that is it more neurotic and that the depressing hatred of everything approaching progress is more evident: it is directed, remember, not against the Soviet Union or even the British Communist Party alone, but against 'English Socialism.'

The same basic lack of knowledge of what Orwell is writing about is as significant as his hatred of it. The book contains long theses on politics and economics and, Lord bless us, the English language, which must be as silly to the informed as they are boring to the ordinary reader. But it is not so much in these, which are after all written by one or other of his characters and possibly intentionally ridiculous, as in the attitudes and philosophical assumptions out of which *1984* is constructed that Orwell reveals his ignorance about people, about the working class and about the Communist Party.

In a recent letter published in the *Manchester Guardian* (5 January 1955) Mr R. Palme Dutt[1] made some interesting points about the philosophical implications in *1984*:

The ideas which Orwell depicts as dominating the world in *1984* reflect the ideas not of communism, of which he knew very little, but of present-day Western monopoly capitalism, whose outward manifestations he experienced with horror and loathing but without understanding either the cause or the cure. This can be very simply demonstrated. The central 'heresy' of his 'rebel' hero, for which he is tortured, is that 'reality is something external, objective, existing in its own right'. This is the standpoint of materialism, of communism. The central axiom of the tyranny which he describes is that 'reality is not external; reality exists in the human mind and nowhere else'. This is the

---

[1] R. Palme Dutt (1896-1974) was a leading British Communist.

characteristic standpoint of all current Western idealist philosophy, favoured by the ruling class.

This is penetrating criticism, and strikes at the basis upon which many of the situations in *1984* are constructed. The cut in the chocolate ration, transformed by propaganda into an increase, the publication of mythical percentage increases in production (which attempt to strike at the very substantial increases of the Soviet Union and People's Democracies), the destruction of historical facts by the Ministry of Truth—all these are the products of a philosophy which holds that all of the people can be fooled for all of the time. Mr Dutt's criticism goes a long way towards accounting for the feature of the book which often puzzles Orwell's admirers: the heavy preoccupation with refinements of inquisition and torture. The fifty pages of inquisition, in which a tremendous amount of trouble is taken by the dictatorship to make Winston Smith believe that two and two make five, are in fact the justification for the book's existence. They are the ultimate end of the trends of thought revealed in *The Road to Wigan Pier* and *Animal Farm*, that ordinary people are stupid enough and weak enough to repudiate their own experience, to disbelieve their own eyes, if forced to do so by the pressure of skilful propaganda. The conclusions of *1984* are foreshadowed in Orwell's description of an 'ideal' fascist state in *The Road to Wigan Pier*.

It would probably be a stable form of society, and the chances are, considering the enormous wealth of the world if scientifically exploited, that the slaves would be well fed and contented. It is usual to speak of the fascist objective as the 'beehive' state, which does a great injustice to the bees. A world of rabbits ruled by stoats would be nearer the mark.

Once again the futility of comparison with Swift comes to mind. Swift's agony was the result of the conflicts in a warm and passionate human personality possessing high standards of human conduct and human relationships with an acute perception of the often inhuman conduct of men in an exploiting society. Does the writer of *1984* have these high standards of conduct and integrity?

True to the principles of doublethink, the Party taught that the Proles were natural inferiors who must be kept in subjection by the application of a few simple rules. In reality very little was known about the proles. It was not necessary to know much. So long as they continued to work and breed, their other activities were without importance. Left to themselves like cattle turned loose upon the plains of Argentina, they had reverted to a style of life that appeared to be natural to them, a sort of ancestral pattern. . . . To keep them in control was not difficult. . . . It was not desirable that the proles should have strong political feelings. . . . And even when they became discontented, as they sometimes did, their discontent led nowhere, because being without general ideas, they could only focus it on petty specific grievances. The larger evils invariably escaped their notice. . . . As the Party slogan put it: 'Proles and animals are free'.

The implications of this passage scarcely need pointing out. The socialist hell which bears so close a resemblance to the fascist hell described above can only be discerned as such by the sensitive middle-class mind of an Orwell: the working class is incapable of deciding whether it is happy or unhappy. The passage and the book are an insult, as the passage in *The Road to Wigan Pier* is an insult, to the countless thousands of people who perceived what the Nazis were about, refused to be bought or tortured into submission, and gave their lives in defence of humanity.

The results of this kind of sensitivity and philosophy in terms of the actual writing are so bad that it is embarrassing to have to talk about them. They are manifest not so much in the coarse use of language so noticeable in *The Road to Wigan Pier*:

In the highbrow world you get on, if you get on at all, not so much by your literary ability as by being the life and soul of cocktail parties and kissing the bums of verminous little lions. . . .

as in the persistent whining tone he finds himself compelled to adopt both in *The Road to Wigan Pier* and in *1984*. They are manifest in the perpetual dreariness of the situations, right from the first page of *1984*:

It was a bright cold day in April, and the clocks were striking thirteen. Winston Smith, his chin nuzzled into his breast in an effort to escape the vile wind, slipped quickly through the glass doors of Victory Mansions, though not quick enough to prevent a swirl of gritty dust from entering along with him.

The hallway smelt of boiled cabbage and old rag mats. At one end of it a coloured poster, too large for indoor display, had been tacked to the wall. It depicted simply an enormous face, more than a metre wide: the face of a man of about forty-five, with a heavy black moustache and ruggedly handsome features. Winston made for the stairs. It was no use trying the lift. Even at the best of times it was seldom working, and at present the electric current was cut off during daylight hours. It was part of the economy drive in preparation for Hate Week.

The not-very-slick tricks hardly need pointing out here, copied as they are from the Graham Greene school. Orwell's neurotic hatreds are revealed: continental socialism which has brought even its decimal system, steel-and-glass industrialism, the smell of the lower classes. This dismal trial of prejudice continues right through the book; this sensitive soul of the middle class Orwell has been bruised by capitalism, which he hates, and by socialism, which he hates more. He joins the socialist movement for a while, long enough to learn a few superficial facts about it, and then runs shrieking into the arms of the capitalist publishers with a couple of horror-comics which bring him fame and fortune, and recognition of his individuality and love of freedom. There is a lack of originality, a dreariness about this career which the Orwell of *The Road to Wigan Pier*, in the sentence quoted at the head of this article, had at least been clever enough to see.

A book recently published by Isaac Deutscher, himself a socialist renegade, throws interesting light on this feature of Orwell's make-up. *Heretics and Renegades* informs us that the idea, plot, chief characters, symbols and indeed the whole climate of *1984* were in fact copied by Orwell from a novel by a petit-bourgeois Russian writer Eugene Zamiatin (1884–1937). Zamiatin was involved with the Social Democratic Party in the revolution of 1905, but left Russia soon after the October revolution of 1917 to live the life of an emigré, publishing *We* in Paris in the early twenties. Orwell knew of this novel and wrote an essay in *Tribune* on 6 January 1946 in which he observed that Huxley's *Brave New World* had been partly derived from it and wondered why this fact had never been pointed out. *We* dealt, wrote Orwell, 'with the rebellion of the primitive spirit against a rationalised, mechanised and painless world.' As described by Orwell, the novel is about a society dominated by an ephemeral character known as The Benefactor who employs a 'thought police' known as the Guardians. All the people wear uniforms, and live in glass houses so that their daily lives may be supervised by the political police. Sex is strictly rationed. The chief character falls in love with a party member and becomes involved in an underground movement; the crime is discovered by the Guardians and ultimately the hero is 'cured' by torture.

The fact that Orwell borrowed so much and so closely is of some importance as evidence of certain inadequacies in his make-up. But ultimately the fact of his borrowing is of less significance than an examination of what he does with his material when he has got it. In the case of Orwell, we find ourselves in the company of a mind which is so limited by the nature of prejudices arising out of his status in capitalist society that he is incapable, despite a certain fluent strength, of producing anything which can be legitimately described as a work of art. We discover, as was suggested at the beginning of this article, that Orwell is little more than a mouthpiece for some of the most deep-seated petit-bourgeois illusions and prejudices. These appear so regularly that they could be listed in tabular fashion.

There is the lack of confidence in working-class organisation noted in *The Road to Wigan Pier*. By *1984* this has become a hatred of it. He draws freely upon his wartime experience with the B.B.C. and the Ministry of Information to build up a picture of the socialist bureaucratic hell. That he uses this kind of ruling class experience against the working class does not say very much for either his artistic integrity or his perception. Nevertheless, in the propaganda game, some of the mud eventually sticks: he manages to strengthen the conditioned response of the middle classes towards working-class political organisation as something dishonest, indecent, against the laws of nature. He strengthens the conviction, which is stated explicitly in *The Road to Wigan Pier* and is implicit in many of the situations in *Animal Farm*, that the ruling classes have all the initiative and all the ideas, although they are sometimes inefficient and sometimes selfish. The pigs on Manor Farm are constantly finding not only that they lack the technical knowledge and experience of man, but also that they can never assimilate it. The animals find it impossible even to manipulate the tools, the instruments of production. And the initial revolution, remember, occurs 'spontaneously', 'almost before the animals realised what had happened', and is directly the result of the selfishness and the inefficiency of the farmer. The failure of the windmill project is inherent in the structure of the whole book: the animals are not really capable of running the farm at all. These books strike at the self-confidence of the working class. More important perhaps, since their effect on working-class thought has been negligible, they strike at the confidence in the working class of its potential allies.

Against the Communist Party itself Orwell uses one of the most effective of the capitalist propaganda weapons developed over the past thirty-five years. He has told you that politics is a dirty game, he has told you that working-class organisation is something almost indecent: through it all runs the constant theme that the Communist Party is hypocritical and dishonest. The comparative success of this theme in the war of ideas is important and will bear some thinking about.

It seizes hold of one of the central features of Communist philosophy and practice which is most opposed to the trends of ruling class thought and is, in a society dominated by ruling class ideas, hardest to understand. Because of the nature of their philosophy, which insists on the essential inter-relatedness of all human activity, and on the inevitability of change, and because of their past revolutionary experience, Communists approach each individual problem with a dual aim in mind. In campaigning for a better drainage system for a street of houses, or for a sixpence an hour rise in a particular trade, Communists have the aim of achieving the immediate result as desirable in itself, but also of taking the struggle for the emancipation of the working class one stage further, of increasing the class-consciousness of those involved in the struggle and deepening their understanding of politics, of strengthening working-class organisation, of winning new members for the Communist Party. These aims—not in fact separable except for the purposes of discussion—are what capitalist propaganda has seized on as the most objectionable, because most dangerous, feature of working-class organisation. The awareness of these aims on the part of those involved reveals that their struggles are not instinctive and blind, but have a clear direction whose aim is the abolition of capitalism itself, and therefore are they very dangerous. Thus Communists 'cannot be trusted', 'have an axe to grind', and so on—the variations are innumerable.

This is the line of Orwell's main attack on the Communist Party, and he throws in everything he has learnt in his longish career as a petty colonial dictator and as a minor official in the main capitalist propaganda agency, together with many unconsidered trifles from the Nazis. He pushes his story to a stage at which all meaning in terms of credible human action is lost—a crippling disadvantage to the novel, but not entirely crippling to the propaganda. The whole paraphernalia of the destruction of facts by the Ministry of Truth, the business of Big Brother, who may or may not exist, of the anti-communist Trotskyite 'Brotherhood', which also may or may not exist, of the wars which may or may not be in progress and which are changed with such bewildering frequency—all this makes difficult reading, but in the present world situation, in the situation of the cold war, some of it inevitably sticks. You don't really believe it, but then you don't have to for the book to do its work. It is enough that some vague impressions of an inhuman nightmare remain and are associated by a number of the tricks of the trade with the word 'communist'. The conditioned response, which can only operate in the hysterical atmosphere of a cold war, has been strengthened. In this respect Isaac Deutscher's conclusions are interesting:

*1984* is in effect not so much a warning as a piercing shriek announcing the advent of a black millenium, the millenium of damnation. The shriek, amplified by all the mass-media of our time, has frightened millions of people. But it has not helped them to see more clearly the issues with which the world is grappling. It has only increased the waves of panic and hate that run through the world and obfuscate innocent minds . . . it has shown them a monster bogey and a monster scapegoat for all the ills that plague mankind. . . .

...h cannot be examined
...984 is merely one weapon
...d against the progressive
...nd before. Its success, its
...r propaganda. It cannot
...er to it. Books like *1984*
...sion of the working class
...f the right-wing Labour

...to Orwell in the sense of
...novel by Ehrenburg[1] or
...d help. *1984* thrives on a
...nly by the rising move-
...l war and its policies, for
...tient and constant work
...ays its indispensable part.
...n personally as human
...and hypocritical intel-
...but are normal people
...already on the way out.
...ltogether.

...journalist, and defender of the

*...eroes of the Empty View* (1954).

# OBITUARIES

## 89. V. S. Pritchett, *New Statesman and Nation*

28 January 1950, p. 96

George Orwell was the wintry conscience of a generation which in the 'thirties had heard the call to the rasher assumptions of political faith. He was a kind of saint and, in that character, more likely in politics to chasten his own side than the enemy. His instinctive choice of spiritual and physical discomfort, his habit of going his own way, looked like the crankishness which has often cropped up in the British character; if this were so, it was vagrant rather than puritan. He prided himself on seeing through the rackets, and on conveying the impression of living without the solace or even the need of a single illusion.

There can hardly have been a more belligerent and yet more pessimistic Socialist; indeed his Socialism became anarchism. In corrupt and ever worsening years, he always woke up one miserable hour earlier than anyone else and, suspecting something fishy in the site, broke camp and advanced alone to some tougher position in a bleaker place; and it had often happened that he had been the first to detect an unpleasant truth or to refuse a tempting hypocrisy. Conscience took the Anglo-Indian out of the Burma police, conscience sent the old Etonian among the down and outs in London and Paris, and the degraded victims of the Means Test or slum incompetence in Wigan; it drove him into the Spanish civil war and, inevitably, into one of its unpopular sects, and there Don Quixote saw the poker face of Communism. His was the guilty conscience of the educated and privileged man, one of that regular supply of brilliant recalcitrants which Eton has given us since the days of Fielding; and this conscience could be allayed only by taking upon itself the pain, the misery, the dinginess and the pathetic but hard vulgarities of a stale and hopeless period.

But all this makes only the severe half of George Orwell's character. There were two George Orwells even in name. I see a tall emaciated man with a face scored by the marks of physical suffering. There is the ironic grin of pain at the ends of kind lips, and an expression in the fine eyes that had something of the exalted and obstructive farsightedness one sees in the blind; an expression that will suddenly become gentle, lazily kind and gleaming with workmanlike humour. He would be jogged into remembering mad, comical and often tender things which his indignation had written off; rather like some military man taking time off from a private struggle with the War Office or society in general.

He was an expert in living on the bare necessities and a keen hand at making them barer. There was a sardonic suggestion that he could do this but you could not. He was a handyman. He liked the idea of a bench. I remember once being advised by him to go in for goat-keeping, partly I think because it was a sure road to trouble and semi-starvation; but as he set out the alluring disadvantages, it seemed to dawn on him that he was arguing for some country Arcadia, some Animal Farm, he had once known; goats began to look like escapism and, turning aside as we walked to buy some shag at a struggling Wellsian small trader's shop, he switched the subject sharply to the dangerous Fascist tendencies of the St John's Wood Home Guard who were marching to imaginary battle under the Old School Tie.

As an Old School Tie himself, Orwell had varied one of its traditions and had 'gone native' in his own country. It is often said that he knew nothing about the working classes, and indeed a certain self-righteousness in the respectable working class obviously repelled his independent mind. So many of his contemporaries had 'gone native' in France; he redressed a balance. But he did know that sour, truculent, worrying, vulgar lower class England of people half 'done down,' commercially exploited, culturally degraded, lazy, feckless, mild and kind who had appeared in the novels of Dickens, were to show their heads again in Wells and now stood in danger of having the long Victorian decency knocked out of them by gangster politics.

By 'the people' he did not mean what the politicians mean; but he saw, at least in his Socialist pamphlets, that it was they who would give English life of the future a raw, muddy but unmistakable and inescapable flavour. His masochism, indeed, extended to culture.

In a way, he deplored this. A classical education had given him a taste for the politician who can quote from Horace; and as was shown in the lovely passages of boyhood reminiscence in *Coming Up for Air*, his imagination was full only in the kind world he had known before 1914. Growing up turned him not exactly into a misanthrope—he was too good-natured and spirited for that—but into one who felt too painfully the ugly pressure of society upon private virtue and happiness. His own literary tastes were fixed—with a discernible trailing of the coat—in that boyish period: Bret Harte, Jules Verne, pioneering stuff, Kipling and boys' books. He wrote the best English appreciation of Dickens of our time. *Animal Farm* has become a favourite book for children. His Burmese novels, though poor in character, turn Kipling upside down. As a reporting pamphleteer, his fast, clear, grey prose carries its hard and sweeping satire perfectly.

He has gone; but in one sense, he always made this impression of the passing traveller who meets one on the station, points out that one is waiting for the wrong train and vanishes. His popularity, after *Animal Farm*, must have disturbed such a lone hand. In *1984*, alas, one can see that deadly pain, which had long been his subject, had seized him completely and obliged him to project a nightmare, as Wells had done in his last days, upon the future.

## 90. Arthur Koestler, *Observer*

29 January 1950, p. 4

Arthur Koestler (b. 1905 in Hungary), friend of Orwell, author of *Darkness at Noon* (1940) and *The Yogi and the Commissar* (1945).

To meet one's favourite author in the flesh is mostly a disillusioning experience. George Orwell was one of the few writers who looked and behaved exactly as the reader of his books expected him to look and behave. This exceptional concordance between the man and his work was a measure of the exceptional unity and integrity of his character.

An English critic recently called him the most honest writer alive; his uncompromising intellectual honesty was such that it made him appear almost inhuman at times. There was an emanation of austere harshness around him which diminished only in proportion to distance, as it were: he was merciless towards himself, severe upon his friends, unresponsive to admirers, but full of understanding sympathy for those on the remote periphery, the 'crowds in the big towns with their knobby faces, their bad teeth and gentle manners; the queues outside the Labour Exchanges, the old maids biking to Holy Communion through the mists of the autumn mornings . . .'

Thus, the greater the distance from intimacy and the wider the radius of the circle, the more warming became the radiations of this lonely man's great power of love. But he was incapable of self-love or self-pity. His ruthlessness towards himself was the key to his personality; it determined his attitude towards the enemy within, the disease which had raged in his chest since his adolescence.

His life was one consistent series of rebellions both against the condition of society in general and his own particular predicament; against humanity's drift towards 1984 and his own drift towards the final breakdown. Intermittent hæmorrhages marked like milestones the rebel's progress as a sergeant in the Burma police, a dishwasher in Paris, a tramp in England, a soldier in Spain. Each should have acted as a warning, and each served as a challenge, answered by works of increasing weight and stature.

The last warning came three years ago. It became obvious that his life-span could only be prolonged by a sheltered existence under constant medical care. He chose to live instead on a lonely island in the Hebrides, with his adopted baby son, without even a charwoman to look after him.

Under these conditions he wrote his savage vision of 1984. Shortly after the book was completed he became bedridden, and never recovered. Yet had he followed the advice of doctors and friends, and lived in the self-indulgent atmosphere of a Swiss sanatorium, his masterpiece could not have been written—nor any of his former books. The greatness and tragedy of Orwell was his total rejection of compromise.

The urge of genius and the promptings of common sense can rarely be reconciled; Orwell's life was a victory of the former over the latter. For now that he is dead, the time has come to recognise that he was the only writer of genius among the *littérateurs* of social revolt between the two wars. Cyril Connolly's remark, referring to their common prep-school days: 'I was a stage rebel, Orwell a true one,' is valid for his whole generation.

When he went to fight in Spain he did not join the sham-fraternity of the International Brigades, but the most wretched of the Spanish Milicia units, the heretics of the P.O.U.M. He was the only one whom his grim integrity kept immune against the spurious *mystique* of the 'Movement,' who never became a fellow-traveller and never believed in Moses the Raven's Sugar-candy Mountain—either in heaven or on earth. Consequently, his seven books of that period, from *Down and Out* to *Coming up for Air* all remain fresh and bursting with life, and will remain so for decades to come, whereas most of the books produced by the 'emotionally shallow Leftism' of that time, which Orwell so despised, are dead and dated to-day.

A similar comparison could be drawn for the period of the war. Among all the pamphlets, tracts and exhortations which the war produced, hardly anything bears re-reading to-day—except, perhaps, E. M. Forster's *What I Believe*, a few passages from Churchill's speeches, and, above all, Orwell's *The Lion and the Unicorn*. Its opening section, 'England Your England,' is one of the most moving and yet incisive portraits of the English character, and a minor classic in itself.

*Animal Farm* and *1984* are Orwell's last works. No parable was written since *Gulliver's Travels* equal in profundity and mordant satire to *Animal Farm*, no fantasy since Kafka's *In the Penal Settlement* equal in logical horror to *1984*. I believe that future historians of literature will regard Orwell as a kind of missing link between Kafka and Swift. For, to quote Connolly again, it may well be true that 'it is closing time in the gardens of the West, and from now on an artist will be judged only by the resonance of his solitude or the quality of his despair'.

The resonance of Orwell's solitude and the quality of his despair can only be compared to Kafka's—but with this difference: that Orwell's despair had a concrete, organised structure, as it were, and was projected from the individual to the social plane. And if 'four legs good, two legs bad,' is pure Swift, there is again this difference: that Orwell never completely lost faith in the knobby-faced yahoos with their bad teeth. Had he proposed an epitaph for himself, my guess is that he would have chosen these lines from Old Major's revolutionary anthem, to be sung to a 'stirring tune, something between "Clementine" and "La Cucuracha" ':

> *Rings shall vanish from our noses,*
> *And the harness from our back . . .*

*For that day we all must labour,*
*Though we die before it break;*
*Cows and horses, geese and turkeys,*
*All must toil for freedom's sake.*

Somehow Orwell really believed in this. It was this quaint belief
which guided the rebel's progress, and made him so very lovable
though he did not know it.

# 91. Bertrand Russell, *World Review*

June 1950, pp. 5–7

Lord Russell (1872–1970), mathematician, philosopher and Nobel
Prize winner; author of *Principia Mathematica* (1910–13) and *An
Outline of Philosophy* (1927).

George Orwell was equally remarkable as a man and as a writer. His
personal life was tragic, partly owing to illness, but still more owing
to a love of humanity and an incapacity for comfortable illusion. In
our time the kind of man who, in Victorian days, would have been a
comfortable Radical, believing in the perfectibility of Man and ordered
evolutionary progress, is compelled to face harsher facts than those
that afforded our grandfathers golden opportunities for successful
polemics. Like every young man of generous sympathies, Orwell was
at first in revolt against the social system of his age and nation, and
inspired with hope by the Russian Revolution. Admiration of Trotsky,
and experience of the treatment meted out to Trotskyists by Stalinists in
the Spanish Civil War, destroyed his hopes of Russia without giving
him any other hopes to put in their place. This, combined with illness,
led to the utter despair of *1984*.

Orwell was not by nature pessimistic or unduly obsessed by politics.
He had wide interests, and would have been genial if he had lived at a

less painful time. In an admirable essay on Dickens, he even allows himself to comment not unsympathetically upon Dickens's belief that all would be well if people would behave well, and that it is not the reform of institutions that is really important. Orwell had too much human sympathy to imprison himself in a creed. He sums up Dickens by describing him as 'laughing, with a touch of anger in his laughter, but no triumph, no malignity. It is the face of a man who is always fighting against something, but who fights in the open and is not frightened, the face of a man who is *generously angry*—in other words, of a nineteenth-century liberal, a free intelligence, a type hated with equal hatred by all the smelly little orthodoxies which are now contending for our souls.'

But our age is dominated by politics, as the fourth century was dominated by theology, and it is by his political writings that Orwell will be remembered—especially by *Animal Farm*.

*Animal Farm* naturally suggests comparison with *Gulliver's Travels*, particularly with the part dealing with the Houyhnhnms. Orwell's animals, it is true, including even the noble horse, are not much like Swift's incarnations of frosty reason. But Orwell, like Swift after Queen Anne's death, belonged to a beaten party, and both men travelled through defeat to despair. Both embodied their despair in biting and masterly satire. But while Swift's satire expresses universal and indiscriminating hate, Orwell's has always an undercurrent of kindliness: he hates the enemies of those whom he loves, whereas Swift could only love (and that faintly) the enemies of those whom he hated. Swift's misanthropy, moreover, sprang mainly from thwarted ambition, while Orwell's sprang from the betrayal of generous ideals by their nominal advocates. In a penetrating essay on *Gulliver*, Orwell set forth justly and convincingly the pettiness of Swift's hopes and the stupidity of his ideals. In neither respect did Orwell share Swift's defeats.

There is a very interesting little essay by Orwell on 'Wells, Hitler and the World State', written in 1941, at the beginning of which year Wells, unwarned by his silliness of 1914, was maintaining that Hitler's offensive power was spent: 'his ebbing and dispersed military resources are now probably not so very much greater than the Italians before they were put to the test in Greece and Africa,' Wells is quoted as announcing. Countering Wells's propaganda for a World State, Orwell retorts: 'What is the use of pointing out that a World State is desirable? All sensible men for decades past have been substantially in agreement with what Mr Wells says; but the sensible men have no power. Hitler is a criminal lunatic, and Hitler has an army of millions of men.' To the end of his days Wells could not face the fact that 'sensible men have no power.'

Orwell faced it, and lived, however bleakly and unhappily, in the actual world. Elderly Radicals, like Wells and myself, find the transition to a world of stark power difficult. I am grateful to men who, like Orwell, decorate Satan with the horns and hooves without which he remains an abstraction.

Our age calls for a greater energy of belief than was needed in the eighteenth and nineteenth centuries. Imagine Goethe, Shelley and Wells confined for years to Buchenwald; how would they emerge? Obviously not as they went in. Goethe would no longer be 'the Olympian', nor Shelley the 'ineffectual angel',[1] and Wells would have lost his belief in the omnipotence of reason. All three would have acquired knowledge as to the actual world, but would they have gained in wisdom? That would depend upon their courage, their capacity to endure, and the strength of their intellectual convictions. Most philosophers have more breadth of outlook when adequately nourished than when driven mad by hunger, and it is by no means a general rule that intense suffering makes men wise.

The men of our day who resemble Goethe, Shelley or Wells in temperament and congenital capacity have mostly gone through, either personally or through imaginative sympathy, experiences more or less resembling imprisonment in Buchenwald. Orwell was one of these men. He preserved an impeccable love of truth, and allowed himself to learn even the most painful lessons. But he lost hope. This prevented him from being a prophet for our time. Perhaps it is impossible, in the world as it is, to combine hope with truth; if so, all prophets must be false prophets. For my part, I lived too long in a happier world to be able to accept so glowing a doctrine. I find in men like Orwell the half, but only the half, of what the world needs; the other half is still to seek.

[1] Matthew Arnold's description of the poet in *Essays in Criticism, Second Series* (1888).

# SHOOTING AN ELEPHANT

1950

---

## 92. E. M. Forster, *Listener*

2 November 1950, p. 471

---

Edward Morgan Forster (1879–1970), English novelist, author of
*Howards End* (1910) and *A Passage to India* (1924).

---

George Orwell's originality has been recognised in this country; his
peculiar blend of gaiety and grimness has been appreciated, but there
is still a tendency to shy away from him. This appeared in our reception
of his most ambitious work, *1984*. America clasped it to her uneasy
heart, but we, less anxious or less prescient, have eluded it for a variety
of reasons. It is too bourgeois, we say, or too much to the left, or it
has taken the wrong left turn, it is neither a novel nor a treatise, and
so negligible, it is negligible because the author was tuberculous, like
Keats; anyhow we can't bear it. This last reason is certainly a respectable one. We all of us have the right to shirk unpleasantness, and
we must sometimes exercise it. It may be our only defence against the
right to nag. And that Orwell was a bit of a nagger cannot be denied.
He found much to discomfort him in his world and desired to transmit
it, and in *1984* he extended discomfort into agony. There is not a
monster in that hateful apocalypse which does not exist in embryo today. Behind the United Nations lurks Oceania, one of his three world-
states. Behind Stalin lurks Big Brother, which seems appropriate, but
Big Brother also lurks behind Churchill, Truman, Gandhi, and any
leader whom propaganda utilises or invents. Behind the North
Koreans, who are so wicked, and the South Koreans, who are such
heroes, lurk the wicked South Koreans and the heroic North Koreans,
into which, at a turn of the kaleidoscope, they may be transformed.

Orwell spent his life in foreseeing transformations and in stamping upon embryos. His strength went that way. *1984* crowned his work, and it is understandably a crown of thorns.

While he stamped he looked around him, and tried to ameliorate a world which is bound to be unhappy. A true liberal, he hoped to help through small things. Programmes mean pogroms. Look to the rose or the toad or, if you think them more significant, look to art or literature. There, in the useless, lies our scrap of salvation.

If a man cannot enjoy the return of spring, why should he be happy in a Labour-saving Utopia? . . By retaining one's childhood love of such things as trees, fishes, butterflies and toads, one makes a peaceful and decent future a little more probable. By preaching the doctrine that nothing is to be admired except steel and concrete, one merely makes it a little surer that human beings will have no outlet for their surplus energy except in hatred and hero worship.

The above is a quotation from *Shooting an Elephant*, this posthumous volume of essays. Here is another quotation from it:

If you wanted to add to the vast fund of ill-will existing in the world at this moment, you could hardly do it better than by a series of football matches between Jews and Arabs, Germans and Czechs, &c., &c. . . . each match to be watched by a mixed audience of 100,000 spectators.

Games are harmless, even when played unfairly, provided they are played privately. It is international sport that helps to kick the world downhill. Started by foolish athletes, who thought it would promote 'understanding', it is supported today by the desire for political prestige and by the interests involved in the gate-moneys. It is completely harmful. And elsewhere he considers the problem of Nationalism generally. British imperialism, bad as he found it in Burma, is better than the newer imperialisms that are ousting it. All nations are odious, but some are less odious than others, and by this stony, unlovely path he reaches patriotism. To some of us, this seems the cleanest way to reach it. We believe in the roses and the toads and the arts, and know that salvation, or a scrap of it, is to be found only in them. In the world of politics we see no salvation, we are not to be diddled; but we prefer the less bad to the more bad, and so become patriots, while keeping our brains and hearts intact.

This is an uneasy solution, and no one can embrace Orwell's works who hopes for ease. Just as one is nestling against them, they prickle. They encourage no slovenly trust in a future where all will come right, dear comrades, though we shall not be there to see. They do not even provide a mystic vision. No wonder that he could not hit it off with H. G. Wells. What he does provide, what does commend him to some temperaments, is his belief in little immediate things and in kindness, good-temper and accuracy. He also believes in 'the people', who, with their beefy arms akimbo and their cabbage-stalk soup, may survive when higher growths are cut down. He does not explain how 'the people' are to make good, and perhaps he is here confusing belief with compassion.

He was passionate over the purity of prose, and in another essay he tears to bits some passages of contemporary writing. It is a dangerous game—the contemporaries can always retort—but it ought to be played, for if prose decays, thought decays and all the finer roads of communication are broken. Liberty, he argues, is connected with prose, and bureaucrats who want to destroy liberty tend to write and speak badly, and to use pompous or woolly or portmanteau phrases in which their true meaning or any meaning disappears. It is the duty of the citizen, and particularly of the practising journalist, to be on the lookout for such phrases or words and to rend them to pieces. This was successfully done a few years ago in the case of 'bottle-neck'. After 'a vicious circle of interdependent bottle-necks' had been smashed in *The Times*, no bottle-neck has dared to lift its head again. Many critics besides Orwell are fighting for the purity of prose and deriding officialese, but they usually do so in a joking off-hand way, and from the aesthetic standpoint. He is unique in being immensely serious, and in connecting good prose with liberty. Like most of us, he does not define liberty, but being a liberal he thinks that there is more of it here than in Stalin's Russia or Franco's Spain, and that we need still more of it, rather than even less, if our national tradition is to continue. If we write and speak clearly, we are likelier to think clearly and to remain comparatively free. He gives six rules for clear writing, and they are not bad ones.

Posthumous sweepings seldom cohere, and *Shooting an Elephant* is really a collection of foot-notes to Orwell's other work. Readers can trace in it affinities with *Animal Farm* or *1984* or *The Road to Wigan Pier* or *Burmese Days*. They can also trace his development. The earlier writing (*e.g.* the title-essay) is forceful but flat. There are no reverberations. In the later work—despite his preoccupation with politics—more imaginative notes are sounded. We part company with a man who has been determined to see what he can of this contradictory and disquieting world and to follow its implications into the unseen—or anyhow to follow them round the corner.

# 93. T. R. Fyvel, *Tribune*

3 November 1950, p. 16

Of how many contemporary English writers can it be said—and I am here not referring to deliberate eccentricity—that each page or paragraph bears the unmistakable imprint of their style? Since George Orwell rigorously avoided mannerism, it is the more remarkable that one can say this about almost anything he wrote. It is especially remarkable in these days, because even cursory reading of the current English literary output suggests strongly that most of the writers have read far too much, whether of each other's writings or of *Times Lit. Supp.* leaders. The result is a type of literary criticism or of social reportage which might be by anybody or appear anywhere, interchangeably in the *Sunday Times* or the *New Statesman*, in *Time and Tide* or (at least on occasions) in *Tribune*.

George Orwell was one of the few who stood out from this literary intermingling. Especially since his death there have been many tributes to his 'honesty'; but this generalised judgment needs breaking down. What distinguished Orwell was first that his political beliefs were genuine. To speak candidly: this quality has become rare enough on the literary Left. There seem to be two chief reasons for its diminution. Since Labour achieved power in 1945, the barren outlook of what Alex Comfort[1] in the last issue of *Tribune* called 'Bevinocracy' has undoubtedly created a growing gap between the Labour movement and those writers who called themselves Left-wing. Equally, however, the test of realities has shown up a good deal of Left-wing literary views as bogus, or as no more than skin-deep and willingly sloughed, together with earlier delusions about Communism. If Orwell, however, had the imaginative courage not to let himself be repelled by the aggressive philistinism of some of the chief Labour leaders, this was no accident. His stand derived from the fact that his own Left-wing views were both genuine and deep-rooted, the result of a long and hard struggle to identify himself with the genuine English Radical tradition that stretches from Tom Paine to the welfare state of today.

[1] Alex Comfort (b. 1920), English poet, novelist and sociologist.

The second aspect of Orwell's honesty was his readiness to remain always aware that today, as he put it, there was 'no such thing as keeping out of politics.' Certain critics have deplored his preoccupation with political polemic. He was conscious of this preoccupation, but he did not indulge in it because he was opposed to art for art's sake, but because he believed—and who should say he was wrong—that the defence of literature and free speech against the threats of their increasingly powerful enemies was today more important than (let's say) escape into simulated enthusiasm about the charms of Victorian lady novelists.

A third aspect of Orwell's honesty as a writer was his uncompromising refusal to adapt his style (or even worse, his outlook) to what an editor might require or thought his readers required. Whether engaged on a novel, a political essay, or a lighter weekly column, he wrote in the same forthright way—a quality rare in journalists' and critics' circles today.

All these qualities are in various ways illustrated in this first posthumous volume of Orwell's collected writings—I believe another volume will soon follow. The present collection contains three early autobiographical sketches, six longer essays dealing variously with the relations of politics, literature and language, and a number of the popular shorter sketches he wrote for *Tribune*. In the well-known piece 'Shooting an Elephant' (which appeared originally in the first *Penguin New Writing*) we have Orwell candidly analysing his own mixed feelings about imperialism at the time when he served as a young police officer in Burma. The mixed feelings were to be expected: more surprising is the gift of sharp visual memory to which he gave less scope in his later writings. The collective will of a Burmese crowd had forced him to shoot an elephant which had killed a man. And he writes:

When I pulled the trigger I did not hear the bang. . . but I heard a devilish shout of glee that went up from the crowd. In that instant, too short a time, one would have thought, even for the bullet to get there, a mysterious, terrible change had come over the elephant. He neither stirred nor fell, but every line of his body had altered. He looked suddenly stricken, shrunken, immensely old, as though the frightful impact of the bullet had paralysed him without knocking him down. At last after what seemed a long time—it might have been five seconds, I dare say—he sagged flabbily to his knees. His mouth slobbered. An enormous senility seemed to have settled upon him. One could have imagined him thousands of years old. I fired again into the same spot. . .

The essay on 'Politics and the English Language' is a diverting exercise in demolishing various current styles. Orwell is here not concerned only with the hack journalism which has turned phrases such as *jackboot, Achilles' heel, hotbed, melting pot, acid test, veritable inferno* or tags like *a consideration which we should all do well to keep in mind* into so much verbal refuse. Singling out the educated fellow-traveller as the most dangerous linguistic debaser of all, Orwell reveals a sardonic gift of mimicry:

A comfortable English professor defending Russian totalitarianism cannot say outright, 'I believe in killing off your opponents when you can get good results by doing so.' Probably, therefore, he will say something like this:

'While freely conceding that the Soviet regime exhibits certain features which the humanitarian may be inclined to deplore, we must, I think, agree that a certain curtailment of the right to political opposition is an unavoidable concomitant of transitional periods, and that the rigours which the Russian people have been called upon to undergo have been amply justified in the sphere of concrete achievement.'

Now, where have we read all that before? (Orwell was, of course, aware that there was a small truth as well as a large untruth in the assertion he puts in the mouth of his professor, but he claims correctly that this does not excuse the mental dishonesty implied in these defensive euphemisms).

The last pieces in this collection, the shorter sketches reprinted from *Tribune*, show Orwell in his 'As I Please' mood, writing ironically, at times deliberately trailing his coat, sometimes a little absurd in his prejudices. He often used these brief asides, I feel, to bridge the gap between the political incorruptibility he preached and his personal life, that of a rather unmethodical, shy and imaginative artist. One of the most satisfying of these short essays is 'Riding Down to Bangor,' a description of American nineteenth century 'good-bad books.' This gives Orwell the chance to reveal his own basic nostalgia—a nostalgia for the safer world of pre-1914 mingled with that of his own childhood. Discussing the impression 'not only of innocence but a sort of native gaiety, a buoyant, carefree feeling' that one receives from nineteenth century American children's books, he puts his finger shrewdly on the cause. With all its own troubles, he says, nineteenth century America was still fortunately outside the main stream of modern history and was free from the nightmares besetting modern man, the nightmares of war, state interference and mass unemployment. Orwell's conviction that the year 1914 was like a historic barrier shutting off modern man from a safer, more innocent past was probably his strongest emotional belief. It was such a year, of course. But I remember often suggesting to him that the children of today, with all their adaptability, could probably play as cheerfully and innocently as those of two generations ago. Intellectually, he saw the point; but emotionally he could never quite bring himself to agree.

# 94. Christopher Sykes, *New Republic*

## 4 December 1950, pp. 30–1

Christopher Sykes (b. 1907), English diplomat and soldier; author of *Four Studies in Loyalty* (1946), biographer of Orde Wingate (1959) and Nancy Astor (1972).

George Orwell's writing and character can be described by a somewhat overworked idea: he was extremely 'Hamletish,' not in the sense that he was a morbid brooder—he was never that—but in the deeper sense of being able to see both sides of many questions with equal and therefore puzzling sympathy. He was an essentially paradoxical man. He was a person who saw through prejudice, but was never rid of his own. He hated the use of un-thought-out political catch-phrases, and yet he could use words such as 'Left' and 'reactionary' as though they contained precise meaning. He ridiculed the pretensions and affectations of people who regarded themselves as advanced thinkers, 'the Pansy-Left' as he sometimes called them, but he never lost an absurd conviction that everyone on the opposite political side was basically mad or wicked. I believe he would rather have been killed than have committed any action in the least treacherous to the rights and liberties of artists, but his understanding of pictures and poetry was negligible. This saintly man regarded sanctity as rubbish.

The present book has nine of his longer essays (not hitherto published in book form) and nine lighter pieces from his contributions to the English Labour weekly, *Tribune*. He was a philosophical writer whose descriptive essays contained almost as much of his thought as did his political work. The first two of these pieces—'Shooting an Elephant' and 'A Hanging'—are examples of his formidable evocative power and also acute studies of the experience of guilt combined with authority. An essay on Tolstoy's hatred of Shakespeare, and another on *Gulliver's Travels*, are as good literary criticism as his great essays on Kipling and Dickens, essays which have had a decisive influence and rescued many from 'Pansy-Left' narrowness; but I think it is a pity that the two essays, 'Politics and the English Language' and 'The Prevention of Literature,' have been included. They contain much admirable sense, but they contain, too, some over-stated views, and some prophecies as doubtful as those of James Burnham which he so rightly mocks in the last of the longer pieces.

All the same, I will make one prophecy myself. George Orwell will be read for a long time to come, but for a reason which might not have much pleased him—namely, that he is such splendid entertainment. His themes are usually distressing, but somehow his valiant treatment of them sends our spirits up. On the few occasions when I met him we talked of melancholy subjects—and he made my day.

## 95. Edmund Wilson, *New Yorker*

### 13 January 1951, p. 76

*Shooting an Elephant and Other Essays*, a posthumous collection of papers by George Orwell, contains miscellaneous pieces relating to various phases of this unconventional writer's life. The first two, 'Shooting an Elephant' and 'A Hanging,' deal, like his novel *Burmese Days*, with Orwell's experience as an officer in the Indian Imperial Police. The first of these tells the story of his reluctantly and probably unwisely killing a runaway work elephant, because he knew that the natives expected it of him and that it was necessary in order to keep up the prestige of the British occupation. It is curious to compare this story with the hunting exploits celebrated by Hemingway. Orwell is interested not in the danger or in the victory over the brute, which he could not bear to watch dying, but in scrutinizing his own motives and deducing their social implications. The third sketch, 'How the Poor Die,' is an episode in the self-imposed pilgrimage, the submergence in the misery of modern life—described in *The Road to Wigan Pier* and *Down and Out in Paris and London*—by which, having resigned from the police, he attempted to expiate his years as an agent of imperial oppression. The rest of the essays deal mostly with the problems of the radical attitude that he was then compelled to develop and with the reflections to which he was led by the assignments of literary journalism by which he had to make a living. Among the most interesting of these are essays on the damaging effects on language and literature of current political pressures, and a long piece called 'Second Thoughts on James Burnham,' which seems to me the best thing of its kind, the best job of destructive criticism, that I have seen in recent years. Orwell suggests that the inner consistency of the not always congruous positions taken up by Burnham in his various books—first as prophet of the Managerial Revolution, then as student of Machiavellianism, and finally as alarmist against the menace of Stalin—is to be found in an unconscious admiration for power in whatever form it may appear.

The death of George Orwell a year ago was something one had half expected but that one had tried to hope would not happen. One gathers that he had ruined his health through the privations of his slumming experiences and the injuries he received in the Spanish War, in which he had fought on the Republican side. He came down with tuberculosis and spent the last years of his life in hospitals. He has recently seemed so much to represent a tradition that had few spokesmen in literature— the middle-class British liberalism that depended on common sense and plain speaking and that believed in the rights of the citizen to earn a decent living, to think and say what he pleased, and to enjoy himself unmolested—that one came apprehensively to feel as if the point of view itself were fading away with Orwell. His fidelity to it had led him, by roads that took him far from the middle class, afield into what looked to him a wilderness, where it was difficult for him to get his bearings. He was a radical who feared and detested the Kremlin; a Marxist who was disgusted by the fashionable socialism of the thirties; a product of the best schools who tried to identify himself with the lower middle class. There was no place for him, and he had to die. It is interesting to go back today to a passage in Cyril Connolly's *Enemies of Promise*, in which he tells of his conversations with Orwell when they went out for walks in their school days. 'Of course, you realize,' Orwell would say, 'that, whoever wins this war [the first one], we shall emerge a second-rate nation.' On one occasion, Connolly writes, Orwell, 'striding beside me,' said 'in his flat ageless voice: "You know, Connolly, there's only one remedy for all diseases." ' Connolly at once thought of sex. 'No.' said Orwell, 'I mean Death!' When he died, thirty years later, he had written, in the nightmare prophecy of *Nineteen Eighty-Four*, the sentence of death that he dreaded for everything he had trusted and loved.

# 96. C. V. Wedgwood, *Time and Tide*

10 February 1951, p. 120

Dame Cicely Veronica Wedgwood (b. 1910), English historian, author of *The Thirty Years War* (1938), *Oliver Cromwell* (1939) and *William the Silent* (1944).

This posthumous volume of hitherto unpublished essays by George Orwell challenges the reviewer to attempt some kind of a summing-up. There is perhaps nothing in the present volume which ranks among the best of his work, but all of it is interesting and the years covered by the essays (the earliest was written in 1931, the latest in 1949) are the significant years of his life and writing.

There are three typical descriptions of actual experience. One concerns the shooting of a runaway elephant, one the hanging of a criminal and the third, and to my mind incomparably the best, describes the inside of a Paris hospital in a poor quarter. Through all three runs that powerful, concealed undercurrent of compassion which gave to Orwell's writing on subjects of this kind its hard, unemotional power. His reporting is sometimes as cold as that winter night in Paris when, as a pneumonia patient, he walked barefoot across two hundred yards of open ground without slippers (they had none large enough for him) to the unwelcoming ward beyond. When he is describing human suffering Orwell's writing seems to be tautened from within by the intensity of the emotion which he deliberately exiles from his words. That is perhaps why he is at his best, as a writer, when he is describing experience. The strength of his feelings and his determination that they shall not intrude make his style spare and economical, while his acute observation and sensibility make its very bleakness the more powerful. In his political and critical writing, where his mind was more concerned than his heart, his sentences, although always serviceable and clear, were often rather carelessly wrought.

The debasement of language, and the consequent deterioration of thought had become by the end of his life of the first importance to Orwell. This is a main theme in *1984*. But his concern was not that of the grammarian or the aesthete. He was not interested in the maintenance of correct grammar as such, still less in the preservation of obsolescent words or the rhythm and shape of sentences. He was interested exclusively in meaning and was profoundly disturbed by the growth of meaningless phrases and by the use of language not to convey but to conceal meaning. He perceived very accurately the effect that this has on politics. His essay on 'Politics and the English Language' sums up the dangers without the least ambiguity. Yet this essay is by no means Orwell's writing at its best and it is conceivable that its uncouthness is deliberate. He was arguing about something far more important than good English.

His conscience and his intellect perpetually drove him to face the hardest problems and to reach the most uncompromising decisions, yet there are in all his books moments of fugitive beauty and grace. Even in the bitter gloom of *1984* there is the copse with the sun aslant between the young trees where Winston and Julia meet. From moments like this it is clear that Orwell felt acutely, perhaps too acutely, the poetry as well as the tragedy of life. If he chose to write, whether prophetically, descriptively or critically, of the tragedy, it was because the times and the psychological exigencies of his character compelled him to do so.

# ENGLAND YOUR ENGLAND (US title: SUCH, SUCH WERE THE JOYS)

1953

## 97. Stephen Spender, *New Republic*

16 March 1953, pp. 18–19

Reading these essays, I could not but visualize a scene in a London pub. A tall lean man with scraggy neck, Adam's apple, bright eyes, and the sort of face I associate with a clay pipe, is holding forth. He is surrounded by a group of working-class people, but he has a wary eye on a bearded figure leaning over the bar some yards away, and even while he himself is talking, he is listening to the Intellectual's conversation. Suddenly he interrupts himself in the middle of a monologue about the British middle-class in order that the whole company may hear the Intellectual say a few words in French. At this, he cannot altogether repress a smile which indicates that among the workers the Intellectual has committed a social gaff; he has spoken in a foreign language correctly.

The workers themselves, I think, do not feel that this strange man who comes to the Pub every night is one of them. Some of the things he says—as when he says that freedom is going shortly to disappear from the face of the earth—they listen to incredulously. Others—as when he talks about the English workers themselves—embarrass them. All the same, they have a vague feeling that he is on their side, and his talk in some way fascinates them. Holding forth, they think, is his hobby. And deep down, they feel sorry for him. What they understand is that he is sick and sad and that he has a vision of terrible realities which they prefer not to think about.

George Orwell is an extremely English writer. He is a man with a grouse. He holds forth about his grievances—the intelligentsia, the rich, the Stalinists, nationalists of every kind. He has simple views about matters which more learned men have not been decided about; for example, he thinks that God and belief in immortality are nonsense. The views of nearly everyone except himself, especially those of writers who are religious, he seems to attribute to a desire to be fashionable, if not to bad faith. All the same, he is real and has a real point of view. The strength of his position as against most of his intellectual opponents is that they have been irresponsible, even if they have not actually betrayed our freedoms; whereas he has practised what he preached. He is a social democrat who has fought for his beliefs and voluntarily lived like a poor man.

More than this he cares simply and passionately for intellectual freedom. His real grievance against his fellow writers is that they have not paid the price of freedom. He does not blame them so much for changing sides as for not sticking consistently to one or two values and being prepared to live and die for them. These values really are *habeas corpus* and the duty to be honest as a writer, even though as a citizen one has to take sides in a political conflict. In a revealing passage, he says that the writer should, in our political age, 'split himself into two compartments,' the artist who recognizes 'objective truth' and the political partisan.

This volume is happily chosen. In the course of it, Orwell states simply and clearly all his main ideas, and the reader is able to see how these have roots in his personal experience. For example, the resemblance of the world of his preparatory school to that of *1984* is striking. Cross-gates was in fact a miniature police state in which Sim, the headmaster, was Big Brother, and there were tortures and confessions. All the same, curious obsessions crop up in Orwell's childhood which it is difficult to explain. For example, one day walking outside the school, he saw a man looking at him, and immediately he concluded that this man must be a spy employed by the headmaster to report on the activities of the boys out of school; he remarks that it would not have seemed extraordinary to him that the headmaster would employ a whole army of spies. Then, after a list of very genuine grievances about the conditions which the sons of the upper-class British endure at public schools, he complains that Eton schoolboys have fried fish for supper, as though this were as bad as all the other things.

The shadow of *1984* lies, indeed, over the whole volume, till the reader begins to realize that Orwell's last work resulted from the accumulated experience of years and was not just a bitter outburst of disillusionment after the Second World War. *1984* had roots in the

First World War, and in the school experiences I have mentioned which go back before then. For *1984* is based simply on the idea of a kind of arithmetic progression of horror; we discover this when, in the essay entitled 'Looking Back on the Spanish Civil War,' written in 1943, Orwell asks who would have imagined in 1925 that twenty years hence slavery would return to Europe. Elsewhere he shows his conviction that the area of freedom is diminishing, that the growth of the police state is inevitable, that the kinds of freedom to which we attach importance will be unthinkable in terms of the ideologies of tomorrow, that the writer in the liberal tradition is a mere survival, and that if there are writers at all in a totalitarian world of tomorrow they will be an entirely different kind of animal, unimaginable to us who are living today. The very illuminating essay 'Inside the Whale,' on Henry Miller's *Tropic of Capricorn*, is a curious foreshadowing of the love affair between Winston Smith and the girl secretary in *1984*. Orwell writes:

From now onwards the all-important fact for the creative writer is going to be that this is not a writer's world. That does not mean that he cannot help bring the new society into being, but he can take no part in the process *as a writer*. . . . It seems likely, therefore, that in the remaining years of free speech any novel worth reading will follow more or less along the lines that Miller has followed.

Then he adds the curious prophecy about Miller himself: 'Sooner or later I should expect him to fall into unintelligibility or charlatanism.'

'Looking Back on the Spanish War' is the central essay in the book: Spain—as for so many others—is the turning point in Orwell's disillusionment. Here again we are in the world of *1984*. The truth about the Spanish War is perhaps already irrecoverable, because it has been hidden under so much untruthful propagandist thinking on both sides. He adds that he is frightened lest 'the very concept of objective truth is fading out of the world.'

Only two things remain for Orwell. One is the hope that the workers are too firmly grounded in the short-term day-to-day solid pre-occupations of their lives to be taken in by what he would have called not 'The Age of Anxiety' but 'The Age of Lies.' The other is a patriotic faith in the power of England somehow to survive. Both these hopes he upholds against the Intelligentsia.

There is a great deal of fun and entertainment to be derived from this book, but very little that is comforting. From his grave, Orwell accuses the intellectuals of cowardice and irresponsibility, and he certainly says enough to give some of us, myself included, bad consciences. He does though show a way of intellectual honesty combined with decent public spiritedness which can be followed, if we are prepared to pay the price of not escaping into easy material conditions and tricky positions. Immediately after reading this book I read the most recent number of a leading literary review and felt extraordinarily depressed.

# 98. Unsigned notice,
## *Times Literary Supplement*

### 4 December 1953, p. 771

The second posthumous collection of George Orwell's critical essays contains seven articles written for 'little magazines' during or after the war, together with extracts from *The Road to Wigan Pier*, *Inside the Whale* and *The Lion and the Unicorn*. The selection thus made has the merit of tracing several threads in Orwell's writing, although it is a pity that such a characteristically perverse and brilliant book as *The Road to Wigan Pier* is apparently to remain out of print.

The various talents revealed here are perhaps not thus blended together in any single one of Orwell's books. First, and most obvious, is his wonderful capacity for descriptive writing, shown particularly in the extracts from *The Road to Wigan Pier*; this was grounded in his almost poetic sensitivity to ugly landscapes:

The canal path was a mixture of cinders and frozen mud, criss-crossed by the imprints of innumerable clogs, and all round, as far as the slag-heaps in the distance, stretched the 'flashes'—pools of stagnant water that has seeped into the hollows caused by the subsidence of ancient pits. It was horribly cold. The 'flashes' were covered with ice the colour of raw umber, the bargemen were muffled to the eyes in sacks, the lock gates wore beards of ice. It seemed a world from which vegetation had been banished; nothing existed except smoke, shale, ice, mud, ashes and foul water.

Then there is his determined intellectual denunciation of fashionable intellectual attitudes, shown here in such essays as 'Writers and Leviathan' and 'Looking Back on the Spanish Civil War'; the plain-man, common-sense social criticism which is seen here at its best in 'Notes on Nationalism,' at its worst in the haphazard observations on 'Anti-Semitism in Britain'; and the insistent need to discover his own nature which led him always to generalize from his particular experience, sometimes wildly but often with insight.

What emerges from the book is a character, rather than a set of ideas: a man with much general sympathy for humanity, who yet had a deeper feeling for landscape and ideas than he had for human beings; a Socialist driven by some complex personal necessity to write as the conscience of other British Socialists. He searched for uncomfortable truths as a matter of principle, and when he found them the people discomfited were almost always his Socialist friends. There were times when it seemed that he had no zest for any struggle but a hopeless one; and had the Labour Party fought an election under his tattered banner the words on it might have read, 'Towards Socialism, and a lower standard of living for all.'

Such was George Orwell. Yet this summation of the man's nature and ideas misses something both of his quality as an artist and of his idealism. His work reached the full artistic stature of which he was capable only in *Animal Farm*; he was one of those rare artists really inspired by political ideas, and in an essay called 'Why I Write' he says that *Animal Farm* 'was the first book in which I tried, with full consciousness of what I was doing, to fuse political purpose and artistic purpose into one whole.' Here he triumphantly succeeded and it is probably true, as he says at the end of the same essay, that 'It is invariably where I lacked a *political* purpose that I wrote lifeless books and was betrayed into purple passages.'

Orwell's idealism also was political and of a kind that could at times cut right through a fog of doubts and contradictions to reach what was for him an enduring truth. He has been regarded by many as a 'man of the Left' whose ideas were limited to a narrow anti-Sovietism: but this book contains many reminders of the positive, and even militant, nature of his Socialism:

Behind all the ballyhoo that is talked about 'godless' Russia and the 'materialism' of the working class lies the simple intention of those with money or privileges to cling to them. . . . How right the working classes are in their 'materialism'! How right they are to realize that the belly comes before the soul, not in the scale of values but in point of time! Understand that, and the long horror that we are enduring becomes at least intelligible. All the considerations that are likely to make one falter . . . fade away and one sees only the struggle of the awakening common people against the lords of property and their hired liars.

Orwell tended always to see human beings as symbolic figures in a social pattern; and he was moved to these remarks by the memory of a P.O.U.M. militiaman in Spain, seen as a symbol of 'the flower of the European working class, harried by the police of all countries.'

# 99. Angus Wilson, *Observer*

## 24 January 1954, p. 8

Angus Wilson (b. 1913), English novelist, Professor of English at the University of East Anglia, author of *Anglo-Saxon Attitudes* (1956) and *The Middle Age of Mrs Eliot* (1958).

The esteem, the affectionate respect in which George Orwell was held grew very rapidly in the few years immediately before and after his death. It has hardly diminished since. The circumstances of his life had made him a *détraqué*[1] English intellectual, at once familiar with the inner sanctum of the intelligentsia and yet not quite on the respectable visiting list; his temperament made him prefer to cock a snook through the windows at the mandarins inside, even after they were prepared to give him the place of honour at dinner. From this vantage point, he saw more clearly and earlier what was happening to the English intellectual world than the most sensitive member of the cosy little family group inside. He saw them threatening Hitler and refusing the arms to make their threats real; he saw them swooning over Spanish heroism and ignoring the terrible reality; he saw them flirting coyly with Stalin and frowning when Siberia was mentioned.

[1] Unconventional.

318

The contrast between these antics and the reality outside bred a nightmare vision in him. This nightmare he made it his life's work to convey and he was able to do so in a clear, smooth-flowing yet structurally solid prose. When the windows of the cosy house blew in and some of the more tasteful pink tiles blew off the roof, it was not surprising that its denizens, now frightened, not to say a little hysterical, began to acclaim him as a prophet. That they did so without resentment was made easier by the fact that there was in Orwell's own work, particularly in *1984*, a note of hysteria that responded to their own. The prophet had not only predicted the dangers of their previous follies, but he seemed to give licence for the more illiberal antics in which they were about to indulge to make up for their past blindness. Perhaps it is the greatest of George Orwell's virtues that he did, in fact, no such thing; he remained consistently Socialist to the end.

The present volume of essays, in particular 'Why I Write' and the brilliant analysis of Henry Miller, 'Inside the Whale,' illustrates admirably this combination of aesthetic devotion and political honesty which made him so powerful a prophet, but it also illustrates certain serious blindnesses which are no less important to all who are not solely concerned to find a prophet on whom to lay their sins. We do not have so many considerable writers that we can afford to see them buried beneath the laurels of their votaries, and it is all too likely that if a more reasoned view of Orwell's work is not established now, a later generation, more aware of its defects, may assign it to unmerited oblivion.

These defects lie largely, I suspect, in exactly the same factors which made him so acute a discerner of the unreality of English 'progressive' thought. If he stood outside the window and saw truly, he also stood outside and failed to see at all. He had all the defects of vision of the typical English public school 'rolling stone,' the chap who returns from the Klondike or the Witwatersrand full of warmth in his heart for the 'old country' and distrust for the 'pen pushers' who have stayed behind and 'got her into the mess she's in.' Yet so much that he loved in the 'old country' had already almost disappeared before 1914. The description of a working-class family in the essay 'North and South,' like the speech of the workers in *1984*, belongs to the music hall of the nineties. Despite his radical sympathies, Orwell remained distrustful, almost ignorant, of the education which was changing the class he sentimentalised. In an essay on Kipling he attacks the intellectuals for refusing the responsibility of authority, yet, like Kipling, the authority

he meant was that of the 'man on the spot,' the District Commissioner
or the local planter; of the great English professional and administrative tradition he remained sublimely oblivious—the liberal tradition
of the best Civil Servants, lawyers or dons.

The truth is that by leaving Eton not for Oxford or Cambridge, but
for 'experience of the world,' he lost more than he gained. He lost
touch with those in all classes whose lives were in fixed patterns, the
*rangés*[1] of the world. In the present volume the essay 'Looking Back
on the Spanish War' wonderfully illustrates his deep understanding of
the lost, the wandering and the submerged, but there is hardly a single
really well-observed 'conventional' character in all his work. To see
Orwell's contribution to English letters in the shadow of these defects
is surely only to appreciate more fully the peculiar intensity of his
vision and the extraordinary brilliance of the craft with which he
expressed it.

## 100. Henry Popkin, *Kenyon Review*

Winter 1954, pp. 139–44

One more posthumous volume of George Orwell's essays is a new
reminder that Orwell was always, equally, a social historian and an
autobiographer. The social history is usually on the surface. It starts
with the 19th Century, a time of poverty, hard work, and faith in the
future. This faith began to be realized early in the 20th Century, but
World War I put an end to progress. The precise moment of change may
be different in different essays; it may be the Boer War or World War I
—1910, 1914, or 1918. The 'I' of *Coming Up for Air* has trouble dis-
tinguishing: 'Before the war, and especially before the Boer War, it
was summer all the year round.' In America, the highwater mark seems
to have been reached just before the Civil War, but the point is always
that things were better 'before the war.' Following the 1920's, 'a period

---

[1] Ordered.

of irresponsibility,' the 'thirties fostered poverty, which had now become meaningless because it was unnecessary; totalitarianism, which is unlike any of the older, gentler, Victorian or Edwardian forms of conservatism; and bully-worship, a product of totalitarianism and of the weak moral fibre of left-wing intellectuals. The future is just as certain a part of the historical pattern as the past, for the worst is yet to come: the spread of world totalitarianism, bringing with it the death of culture and freedom.

Almost every word Orwell ever wrote records one stage or another of this chronicle of incipient chaos. Most of the essays in *Dickens, Dali, and Others* examine such evidence of the early, happy period as the hopeful reformism of Dickens and the Edwardian origins of Wells, Wodehouse, Kipling, and others. In the essays gathered in the posthumous books and in his earlier novels, Orwell pictured our present woes, tempered a little by hope and nostalgia. The terrible future is the subject of the last novel, *1984*.

Social history requires a place as well as time, and Orwell's place is England, the center of his world. The happy life of the first decade of this century is seen as distinctively English, as in *Coming Up for Air*:

The old English order of life couldn't change. For ever and ever decent God-fearing women would cook Yorkshire pudding and apple dumplings on enormous coal ranges, wear woollen underclothes and sleep on feathers, make plum jam in July and pickles in October.

One of the essays in *Such, Such Were the Joys* offers a catalog of the English virtues: patriotism, a simple code of decent conduct, respect for law, belief in liberty, individualism, love of flowers, and lack of artistic talent. This is a handy list because it shows where Orwell the autobiographer is joined to Orwell the social historian. These are precisely Orwell's virtues. In respect to the last and oddest of the virtues, one recalls Lionel Trilling's assertion, 'He was not a genius.' Mr Trilling demonstrates that possession of this quality is entirely in Orwell's favor, just as Orwell himself managed to compliment the English people on their lack of talent. The other virtues are precisely the English traits and ethical rules of thumb that Orwell championed in his writings, in all the years that he complained of the death of patriotism and of 'bedrock decency' or urged his readers to plant trees and love flowers. They are the deadly virtues from which the protagonists of three of Orwell's novels flee and to which they half-gladly, half-resignedly return.

Orwell's social history, like his English loyalty, only partially conceals a substructure of autobiography. He was born in 1903, and his childhood therefore coincided with the Edwardian Era, which, by an effort of will, he sometimes extended to 1914 or 1918. He was particularly revealing about the nature of these loyalties in his essay on Dickens, where he observed that 'nearly everyone feels a sneaking affection for the patriotic poems he learned as a child.' After applying nostalgia as a literary criterion, he accused himself: 'And then the thought arises, when I say I like Dickens, do I simply mean that I like thinking about my childhood?' He found the question unanswerable.

Another key passage occurs in *Coming Up for Air*:

1913! My God! 1913! The stillness, the green water, the rushing of the weir! It'll never come again. I don't mean that 1913 will never come again. I mean the feeling inside you, the feeling of not being in a hurry and not being frightened, the feeling you've either had and don't need to be told about, or haven't had and won't ever have the chance to learn.

As a matter of fact, Orwell *did* mean that 1913 will never come again. The character in the novel was twenty in 1913, but Orwell was ten. Surely the emotions here described belong to the security of childhood: 'the feeling of not being in a hurry and not being frightened.' They are not the exclusive property of the children of 1913; they were possible even to the children of the troubled 'thirties, and they will be shared by the children of the 'fifties, if they are permitted to grow up.

Such passages as these help to explain Orwell's preferences, in literature as in life. He loved everything Edwardian, everything he had first encountered before 1918: good bad poetry and good bad novels, Raffles, the boys' weeklies, Kipling's thin red line of Empire-builders, H. G. Wells's dream of the future, even P. G. Wodehouse's spats-wearing heroes. All of these seemed right, natural, and defensible to Orwell because they were supremely right and natural when he first knew them. It is no great exaggeration to say that Orwell frequently let nostalgia overpower his judgment, but, in listing these private reasons why he felt as he did, we must not forget one additional indispensable reason why he considered World War I the great watershed of our century: apparently it was.

Orwell's Edwardian leanings help to explain the unresolved dilemma of his later years—the conflict between his socialism and the pessimism that found its fullest expression in *1984*. In the essay 'Inside the Whale,' in the present collection, Orwell made some useful observations about another literary exponent of nostalgia—especially useful, that is, when we measure them against Orwell himself. He remarked that D. H. Lawrence was basically pessimistic even though his heart leaped up when he beheld primitive peoples—Indians, Etruscans, and others:

But what he is demanding is a movement away from our mechanized civilisation, which is not going to happen. Therefore his exasperation with the present turns once more into idealism of the past, this time a safely mythical past, the Bronze Age. When Lawrence prefers the Etruscans (*his* Etruscans) to ourselves it is difficult not to agree with him, and yet, after all, it is a species of defeatism, because that is not the direction in which the world is moving.

Orwell was too modern to be nostalgic about the Bronze Age. Instead he idealized the Edwardians—which was almost equally a species of defeatism. I say almost because the Edwardians themselves were not defeatists, and no good sentimental-Edwardian could be pledged entirely to the past. This paradox mirrors the full complexity of Orwell's alternating hopes and fears for the future: hopes because the Edwardians like Shaw and Wells (both of whom Orwell ultimately disowned), looked ahead—and fears because Edwardian hopefulness was booby-trapped in World War I and nothing can get us back to the Edwardian Eden of 1913. It is a genuine dilemma, as impossible to resolve as Orwell's self-questioning about his fondness for Dickens.

What Orwell really wanted was 1913 and not the unlikely socialist Utopia that might lie beyond 1984. We are told that the totalitarians will take over and that perhaps, sometime, somehow, they will be dislodged. Orwell knew Jack London's *The Iron Heel*, a novel that predicts just such a future for the world. Neither London nor Orwell could suggest how the dislodgment of totalitarianism might come to pass. In *1984*, the only note of hope is in the efforts of Emmanuel Goldstein, Big Brother's nemesis. Goldstein, like Orwell, is an old Edwardian, for he writes:

The world of today is a bare, hungry, dilapidated place compared with the world that existed before 1914, and still more so if compared with the imaginary future to which the people of that period looked forward. In the early twentieth century, the vision of a future society unbelievably rich, leisured, orderly and efficient—a glittering antiseptic world of glass and steel and snow-white concrete—was part of the consciousness of nearly every literate person.

This is, of course, Orwell's nostalgia, complete with its Edwardian Utopianism. But Goldstein's reality is brought into question, and his would-be follower, Winston Smith, becomes a devout believer in Big Brother. Orwell evidently resolved his dilemma by concluding that a probably permanent catastrophe for the free world was inevitable.

Why, then, did Orwell go on? Why did he continue to warn and to threaten the left-wing intellectuals who were, he could observe, too stupid to understand him? Because he was an indignant man, because he had discovered at an early age that he had 'a power of facing unpleasant facts' and that he felt the need to record them. Like Keats's Hyperion, he became one of 'those to whom the miseries of the world / Are misery, and will not let them rest.' He was angry even when anger had no logical place in his unhappy *Weltanschauung*.

This bitter, critical strain is visible even when, in the title essay of *Such, Such Were the Joys*, Orwell is recalling his education at a private school. He provides a detailed narrative not only of what happened but also of what he thought and felt—his fear that some 'Mrs Form' (the sixth form) was going to beat him, that he was at fault for revealing that a caning had not hurt him, that he was again at fault when his master broke a riding crop while beating him. Both the past humiliation and the present indignation are startlingly real, although Orwell wrote his account of these events almost forty years after they took place. On the other hand, look at Cyril Connolly's record of the same school days in the same school. He describes the same happenings, the same tyrants, and the same petty tyrannies. Although he must have been equally wretched at St Wulfric's, he is now willing to let bygones be bygones. He understands at last what necessity and what insecurity forced the headmaster and his wife to be so vicious; the welts have healed, and the indignities are forgiven. It was not so with Orwell, who not only harbored but treasured his resentments. His humiliation at school was evil, and, though complaint is now futile, Orwell could no more ignore it than he could ignore the inanities of the left-wing intellectuals' line on world politics and on Spain.

Remembering his school in this way was a real test for Orwell. His school days fell in the period that his nostalgia romanticized. He could sentimentalize about the art of the time—especially the popular art— but his most rigorous standards were always reserved for life and not art. He was primarily a critic of life, and, unlike that softer Edwardian, Connolly, he would not, for the sake of nostalgia, relax his standards of humanity.

The chief target of Orwell's honest anger was the anti-Orwell, a sort of negative photograph of himself: the left-wing intellectual, whose defects corresponded exactly to Orwell's Edwardian, English virtues. The left-wing intellectual underestimates the national spirit, worships foreign bullies, and thinks that smelling flowers dissipates energy that ought to go into the revolution. If this portrait of the intellectual sounds like caricature, Orwell's never does. Actually, Orwell became unconvincing only when, by straying into a sometimes embarrassing praise of the common man, he tried to offer an alternative. (He seems to have been happily unaware of the American cult of the common man.) Since Orwell agreed with Lionel Trilling that there is no conservative intelligentsia, 'Down with the leftist intellectual!' must mean 'Up with the noble worker!' Orwell therefore wrote a poem in honor of a soldier who 'was born knowing what I had learned / Out of books and slowly.' In the essay 'Looking Back on the Spanish War,' he assailed the treachery of the intellectuals and praised the workers who kept up the struggle after the others quit. Finally, this belated Rousseauism makes everything just a little too simple.

Orwell's attacks on the left-wing intellectuals, like his account of his school days, are best appreciated when we have a negative touchstone for comparison; Peter Viereck, with *The Shame and Glory of the Intellectuals*, is conveniently at hand. Both Orwell and Viereck are made uncomfortable by most modern writing, but, whenever the topic came up, Orwell would disclaim any knowledge of literary criteria and get on to something else. He never identified modern, or modernist, literary attitudes with his principal enemy, Stalinism. He left that gaucherie to Mr Viereck, who has created that strange hybrid, Gaylord Babbitt, a 'Stalinoid' (Mr Viereck's word), who quotes the *Partisan Review*! It is a relief to turn to Orwell's honesty and good sense. In the decade when Auden and other poets of his generation were Marxists, it must have been tempting to lump Stalinism and aestheticism together, but Orwell was as honest a debater as he was a reporter. He fought his separate battles separately. There were not many names that he did not call the left-wing intellectual, but he never called him 'aesthete.'

Doubtless Orwell was not a genius, but it is not as easy as it looks to do what Orwell did so very well. If it looks easy to write personal recollections, to attack left-wing intellectuals, or to interpret the popular arts, then consider, respectively, the tepidity of Cyril Connolly, the intemperate rage of Peter Viereck, and the flounderings of Leo Gurko (in the recent *Heroes, Highbrows, and the Popular Mind*). We need these negative touchstones to remind us that Orwell, for all his nostalgia and for all his unresolvable dilemmas, was personally—and it is practically impossible to put this on any other basis—superior to his political and literary commitments, to anything he ever did, even to his skill as an essayist. We praise the honest, angry man revealed in these essays more even than the essays that reveal the man.

# 101. John Wain, *Twentieth Century*

January 1954, pp. 71–8

John Wain (b. 1925), English novelist, critic and Professor of Poetry at Oxford; author of *Hurry On Down* (1953), *The Living World of Shakespeare* (1964) and his autobiography *Sprightly Running* (1962).

Orwell's essays are obviously much better than his novels. As a novelist he was not particularly gifted, but as a controversial critic and pamphleteer he was superb, as good as any in English literature. The novels do not add any new dimension to the ideas already put forward in the essays; they merely start them moving, like clockwork toys, in the hope of catching the attention of passers-by. Thus it comes as a shock to discover, for instance, that *Down and Out In Paris and London* is an earlier work than *The Clergyman's Daughter*; the novel is so inept, so obviously the product of inexperience and a lack of interest in the form it belongs to, the pamphlet so mature, balanced and successful. Finally, of course, Orwell came into his enormous popular success with two books that were not novels at all. *Animal Farm* is not even fiction, since the 'story' was there already in contemporary history, only waiting to be transposed into a fable.

Thus it is not in any provocative or paradoxical spirit that one says, quite simply, that *Critical Essays* is a better book than *1984*, or that the essay on *King Lear* will ultimately have more readers than *Animal Farm*. Orwell was pushed into writing fiction by the appalling imbalance of modern literary taste, which dictates that no book shall have more than a handful of readers unless it is a novel. But when his purely con-temporary vogue has died down, his reputation will be in the hands of bookish and thoughtful people, who do not share the mania for fiction above all else, and then the essays will rise to the top and the novels sink to the bottom. Already it is clear that the best strategy for Orwell's enemies is to concentrate on the novels, and keep quiet, as far as possible, about the fact that he was an essayist. For instance Mr Hopkinson, who with extraordinary astuteness managed to get his bitter attack on Orwell published and advertised by the British Council as one of their series 'Writers and their Work'[1]—a stroke of genius worthy of the Florentine[2]—gives most of his space to picking holes in the novels, and mentions the essays only in grudging asides. The result is as meaningful as a criticism of Eliot which gave most of its attention to the plays, on the grounds that more people have seen Eliot's plays than have read his poems or essays. There is no need for us to make the same false distribution of weight: and therefore it is in order to say at once that a new volume of Orwell's essays is more important than the discovery of an unpublished novel would be.

Of course one must fairly admit that *England Your England* is sub-stantially less interesting than the two volumes of essays already in print. Orwell was a man of comparatively few ideas, which he took every opportunity of putting across, and a collection of his essays which gets anywhere near completeness will obviously contain the same ideas expressed a number of times with rather little variation. The selection from his occasional writings which he made himself (*Critical Essays*, 1946) has very little direct repetition; the first posthumous volume, *Shooting An Elephant*, contains echoes of *Critical Essays* and also internal echoes; while this third volume is, inevitably, a collection of scraps presenting almost nothing that was not said better elsewhere in Orwell's works.

This does not mean, however, that it is superfluous. On the contrary, it is a work of commanding interest, and not only for the obvious reason, that it is by Orwell. For one thing, the selectors have admitted the principle of reprinting passages from his early and unobtainable

[1] See Tom Hopkinson, *George Orwell* (London, 1953).
[2] Niccolò Machiavelli (1469–1527), Italian historian and political thinker, author of *The Prince* (1532).

books; for another, it contains a long essay which Orwell himself rejected, and it is always interesting to ask why an author suppresses work that had seemed good enough to publish not long before. Let me deal with these two points in turn.

The unobtainable books drawn on are *The Road to Wigan Pier* and *The Lion and the Unicorn*. Selecting passages in this way is a thankless task, and obviously the selectors could not hope to please anyone but themselves; but even so I must confess that the golden opportunity seems to me to have been missed. It is clear enough that this will be the last volume of barrel-scrapings from the Orwell stock, so that anything not included here will have small chance of emerging in the future. Hence, no doubt, the excellent decision to include extracts from his books as well as a round-up of scattered articles. The trouble is that this decision was implemented in too feeble a way. *Wigan Pier*, for instance, is often said to be Orwell's worst book; but, even supposing this to be true, an author's best paragraphs or pages, even his best chapter, might occur in his worst book. (This is especially true of an author interested primarily in ideas.) The first part of *Wigan Pier* contains passages that Orwell never again equalled, but one would never think so from the two snippets reprinted here. The first two chapters should have been reproduced entire; they consist of a description of life in the industrial north during the depression, and their purpose is to serve as an introduction, a kind of preliminary barrage, for the political argufying that takes up the body of the book. In other words, these two chapters are a *Down and Out* in miniature, or, if you prefer to look at it another way, an expanded version of the kind of descriptive essay he gave us in 'How The Poor Die'. They contain unforgettable portraits (it is always the *real* people, from the Italian militiaman in *Catalonia* to Paddy and Bozo in *Down and Out*, who are most vivid in Orwell); we ought at least have been given the sketch of Mr and Mrs Brooker, who kept the tripe shop and took in boarders —Mrs Brooker lying in bed all day and wiping her mouth on strips of newspaper, and Mr Brooker 'always moving with incredible slowness from one hated job to another. . . . In the mornings he sat by the kitchen fire with a tub of filthy water, peeling potatoes at the speed of a slow-motion picture.' (I quote from memory, and, being out of England with no access to books, had better apologize here and now for the lack of precise references in what follows.) The Brookers and their lodgers are better examples of Orwell's power of human portraiture than anything in the novels, and the descriptions of various

features of working-class life in England at that period have a sting of
pity and anger so urgent that to find anything comparable one has to
go back to Langland.[1] But one looks in vain for any sample in this
book; *Wigan Pier* has missed its chance, and will now sink, with the
bad passages dragging the good ones down, to the satisfaction, no
doubt, of Mr Hopkinson. Again, the early novels, poor as they are,
contain some set pieces which could have been extracted with no loss
of intelligibility. An obvious choice would have been the chapter in
*The Clergyman's Daughter* where Orwell suddenly breaks into dramatic
form, abandoning the realistic method of the rest of the book, in
order to draw his nightmare picture of a night spent in Trafalgar
Square; and possibly the description of a typical day's hop-picking in
Kent, from the same book, would have interested many readers. All
in all, one cannot but be disappointed that passages like these have been
pushed out to make room for comparatively light-weight essays which
repeat things Orwell had already hammered home.

The second point I mentioned above, that the book contains a long
essay which Orwell himself virtually suppressed, is, happily, a good
mark for the editors. (I put the word in the plural instinctively, because
these things are usually done by a sort of informal committee.) When
Orwell issued his *Critical Essays*, he reprinted two of the three long
pieces which make up *Inside the Whale*; the title essay, which he
dropped, is given here; and, while it is not one of his classic pieces of
criticism, it is interesting to read it with an eye to the reasons for his
having allowed it to go out of print.

To begin with, it is obviously written from the depths of despair, a
despair more convincing than that of *1984*, because it was based on a
straight reading of the omens without the complicating factor of fatal
illness. The essay is chiefly concerned with Henry Miller, and in order
to make out a case for Miller it includes a long retrospect of twentieth-
century literature, from the standpoint of 'tendency'. Orwell considers
in turn the Georgians, the cosmopolitan 'twenties, and the political
'thirties, and in turn he rejects them. The Georgians are the simplest
case, as he takes it for granted that no post-1918 reader can feel anything for them but contempt; Housman 'just jingles', Brooke's
*Grantchester* is 'a sort of accumulated vomit from a stomach stuffed with
place-names', and as for the Squires and Shankses, well, 'The wind
was blowing from Europe, and long before 1930 it had blown the

---

[1] William Langland (*c.* 1331–1400), English poet, author of the satiric and allegorical
*Piers Plowman* (*c.* 1362).

beer-and-cricket school naked, except for their knighthoods.' When he turns to the dominant writers of the 'twenties, Orwell is inclined to take them very seriously; indeed he pays their work the highest compliment he ever did pay to a work of literature; he said it was likely to survive. (It was one of the weaknesses of Orwell's literary criticism that he declared survival 'the only test worth bothering about', thereby side-stepping the really important questions.) But from this point of view, these writers stand convicted of 'a too Olympian attitude, a too great readiness to wash their hands of the immediate problem.' He felt that there was something heartless about the lifelong devotion to an æsthetic ideal (Joyce), the worship of primitivism in a world that was obviously becoming more and more industrial and urbanized (Lawrence), the 'Christian pessimism which implies a certain indifference to human misery' (Eliot).

Passing to the 'thirties, Orwell again found disappointing results. Here, indeed, was 'purpose', but in his view it was too facile, too orthodox, and above all, too soft and unrealistic. The characteristic writers of the period are all 'the kind of person who is always some-where else when the trigger is pulled'. (Surely he was right about this, by the way; witness that characteristic figure of our time, the man who was a left-wing poet in the 'thirties and married a rich wife in the 'fifties.)

The conclusion to which he was driven was therefore one of utter pessimism for the future of literature. If the 'twenties were too loftily standing apart from the dogfight, 'the literary history of the 'thirties seems to justify the opinion that a writer does well to keep out of politics'. Yet on an earlier page he had said, 'a novelist who simply disregards the major public events of his time is generally either a footler or a plain idiot', and there is not much sign of wavering from this position as the essay unfolds itself. *Therefore* Miller is an important writer. He has stepped aside from political 'awareness' without joining 'the huge tribe of Barries and Deepings and Dells who simply don't notice what is happening.'

I should say that he believes in the impending ruin of Western Civilization much more firmly than the majority of 'revolutionary' writers; only he does not feel called upon to do anything about it. He is fiddling while Rome is burning, and, unlike the enormous majority of people who do this, fiddling with his face towards the flames.

This is obviously the product of that despair which quite naturally overtook a man of letters when the bombers began to stream down the runways in 1939. Miller, who under normal conditions can be seen as a writer with about the same allowance of talent as, say, Robert Ross,[1] is suddenly puffed up into a major figure because he provides an 'objective correlative'[2] for Orwell's disgust and disappointment. (The reason he did not feel 'called upon' to do anything about the break-up of Western Civilization was because he belonged to a neutral country and knew perfectly well that there was no reason why he should ever hear a shot fired in anger in his life.) But for Orwell it was different, and when the end of the war found him, to his own surprise, still alive and writing, and even planning new books, the whole thing began, in retrospect, to look silly. But there was a more personal reason for withdrawing the essay. Not merely because it had praised an author who was not, on the whole, worth praise; but because both implicitly, by boosting Miller, and explicitly, in statements like the following, it had denied the possibility of writing books such as the ones Orwell was going to write during the rest of his life.

The passive attitude will come back, and it will be more consciously passive than before. Progress and reaction have both turned out to be swindles. Seemingly there is nothing left but quietism robbing reality of its terrors by simply submitting to it. . . . A novel on more positive, 'constructive' lines, and not emotionally spurious, is at present very difficult to imagine.

Clearly it was impossible for Orwell to continue holding this kind of opinion after the first dazed condition of shock and hopelessness had worn off. It would have left him with nothing to live for. His life was devoted to battling for human justice and decency, and in defence of the underdog; and it may be all very well for Miller, or someone like him, to declare that it doesn't matter if things fall to pieces alto-gether and there are no ideals left. When things fall to pieces it is always the underdog who suffers and the bully, the toady, and the clever liar who come out on top, and Orwell saw this clearly enough. If the imaginative writer abdicates his minimal human responsibility, his duty to put in a word on the right side now and again, his position is ultimately intolerable; however you may choose to re-phrase it, the old idea of 'profit with delight', i.e. moral instruction made palatable, has got to stay.

[1] Robert Ross (1869–1918), friend and literary executor of Oscar Wilde.
[2] Eliot's critical phrase from 'Hamlet and His Problems' (1919), where he writes 'the only way of expressing emotion, in the form of art, is by finding an "objective correlative"; in other words, a set of objects, a situation, a chain of events, which shall be the formula of that poetic emotion.'

It was this realization that made Orwell so concerned, in his later years, with the problems of honesty and truthfulness in the writer. He was born into a world where, on the whole, there was very little censorship of the printed word, and grew up in a worsening atmosphere until, by the time of his death in 1950, it had actually become difficult to speak the truth even in minor matters—difficult because of the psychological pressures on the writer. Hence Orwell's first concern, to which he can be seen anxiously returning on page after page of this volume, is the writer's duty to keep his mind free of fetters. Very briefly his point is this: if you accept anything on trust, if you give up your mental independence and submit to any orthodoxy, you are disqualified as an author. You may be a journalist, an ad. man or a party hack, but an author you cannot be. If there is even one subject on which you cannot be perfectly frank, that means there will be a paralysed corner of your mind, and the paralysis is always likely to spread. Everyone is familiar with Orwell's endless jeering at Russophile writers and politicians who have to change their fundamental beliefs every time the Moscow line is switched, and his love of repeating stories like the one about the 'Comrade' who went out to the lavatory during a meeting, to find that a surprise news bulletin over the radio had caused the 'line' to be changed during his absence. But while all this is admirable, while we accept Orwell eagerly as a great ally in the Cold War, we should not overlook the fact that in his eyes *every* orthodoxy was hateful. He spoke of '*all* the smelly little orthodoxies which are contending for our souls', not just *some* of them. In this connexion it is a pity that the editors did not give us a chance to reconsider the remarkable essay on Eliot's *Four Quartets*, which he published in *Poetry London* during the war. I have not the article by me, of course, but briefly the gist is this. Orwell is casting about for some explanation of what he considers the falling-off in Eliot's poetic powers since the *Waste Land* period, and comes to the conclusion that the poet's conversion to Anglo-Catholicism is at the root of it, since, by embracing the doctrines of the Church, Eliot has found himself committed to believing, or pretending to believe, theories as to the origin of the world, the nature of life, etc., which nobody really holds. A simple Spanish peasant, who believes in Heaven and Hell as literally as he believes in New York, though he has never seen New York, can hold his belief without damage to his imagination; but when a subtly-thinking modern man of letters joins the Church, he does so for a complex of reasons, some of which are social, and henceforth he is to some extent blinkered. His vision becomes less acute because he is not free to look in any direction he chooses. There is, of course, an argument against this; for one thing it is arguable that by preferring *The Waste Land* to the *Quartets* Orwell is falling into a similar trap, allowing his imagination to be headed off by his intellect with its anti-religious bias; but it is a pity that the challenge is not taken up by some critic who is honest enough to consider the issue seriously. Certainly the lady who was put up to 'answer' Orwell in the same issue of the magazine did not make a very satisfactory job of it, and it is disappointing that the editors of this volume ran away from their obligation to bring this essay into the light.

The other major point that Orwell hammered home was again one that would occur to a sceptic more readily than to a believer: namely, the falsification of history. 'Truth will prevail,' said someone, I think Patmore,[1] 'When no one cares if it prevail or not'; but, as Orwell pointed out, when both sides are busy faking the historical records to show that they have been in the right all along, you can easily reach a stage when the facts are simply not available. His major exercise on this theme is, of course, the 'Ministry of Truth' business in *1984*, but it is all there in the piece about the Spanish war in this book. After discussing a specific example—the presence or non-presence of a Russian force in Spain—he says:

The implied objective of this line of thought is a nightmare world in which the Leader, or some ruling clique, controls not only the future but *the past*. If the Leader says of such and such an event, 'It never happened'—well, it never happened. If he says that two and two are five—well, two and two are five. This prospect frightens me much more than bombs.

Christians would retort that Truth has an existence of its own outside our world; but unless they are right, it is certainly true that heroic actions can be performed, saintly lives led, and great thoughts written down, and nobody need ever know anything about it.

And so this carelessly produced book is a major event. It is for us to keep Orwell's example constantly before us. So let us end on a personal note. 'When I was about sixteen,' he tells us in 'Why I Write',

I suddenly discovered the joy of mere words, i.e. the sounds and associations of words. The lines from *Paradise Lost*—
So hee with difficulty and labour hard
Moved on: with difficulty and labour hee,

[1] Coventry Patmore (1823–96), minor English poet.

which do not now seem to me so very wonderful, sent shivers down my back-bone.

I think I can guess why.

## 102. George Elliott, *Hudson Review*

### Spring 1957, pp. 149–54

George Elliott (b. 1918), American novelist, poet and Professor of English at Syracuse University; author of *Parktilden Village* (1958) and *Among the Dangs* (1961). At the author's request I reprint the revised version of this composite review, 'George Orwell,' from *A Piece of Lettuce* (New York: Random House, 1964), pp. 161–70.

Rereading Orwell, I was struck with the frequency and the vigor with which he strained against the rationalistic materialism he usually asserted. He was opposed in principle to Christianity as to all religion, yet he said that in losing Christianity we (i.e. he and his primary audience of Anglo-American liberals) lost incomparable riches. He attacked Swift for being opposed to scientific advance, the enlightenment, and social progress; yet he could also write (*Inside the Whale*): 'Progress and reaction have both turned out to be swindles.' He wrote that the popular loss of belief in personal immortality was the most important social phenomenon of the age. He made a wry and bitter joke that sometimes he could almost believe there was an order of things outside time and space. In *A Clergyman's Daughter* (1935) he wrote a phantasmagorial chapter in the form of a play, which includes, without irony or comedy, the following stage direction to the reader: 'As he (a priest who is reciting the Lord's Prayer backward) reaches the first word of the prayer he tears the consecrated bread across. The blood runs out of it. There is a rolling sound, as of thunder, and the landscape changes . . . Monstrous winged shapes of Demons and Arch-demons are dimly visible, moving to and fro.' Yet, despite the fame of *1984* and the enormous respect in which Orwell is held, I propose that he is a failed prophet.

One should, I think, realize that Gandhi's teachings cannot be squared with the belief that Man is the measure of all things and that our job is to make life worth living on this earth, which is the only earth we have. They make sense only on the assumption that God exists.

('*Reflections on Gandhi*')

Not that Orwell was, or claimed to be, a prophet in the full sense. A prophet is one who speaks poetically from divine inspiration, and Orwell was a prose atheist; furthermore, a prophet is one whose audience (and a prophet must have an audience) *believes* that he speaks from divine inspiration, and almost none of the Anglo-American audience to whom Orwell addressed himself will credit a man with speaking God's word. Orwell strove, at his best, to speak directly from his own conscious experience, and blunt prose is the proper instrument for such speech; a true prophet does not deal chiefly with the sorts of truth that fit into prose.

Of course, no honest person claims that happiness is *now* a normal condition among adult human beings; but perhaps it *could* be made, and it is upon this question that all serious political controversy really turns.

('*Politics vs. Literature*')

Yet he is a sort of prophet—at least he is viewed as one, the secular prophet of socialism. Secularism can have no analogues to saints, for good men, of whom Orwell was surely one, men who are splendidly virtuous, honorable, upright, courageous, honest, and concerned with right behavior, are not necessarily in a special connection with God as saints are; but it has its analogues to prophets, who speak, and are thought of as speaking, the truth, experienced and reasoned-upon moral and political truth, the truth behind the shifting confusion and lies of events, the steady truth. Prophets do not systematize, are no theologians, no philosophers even; Orwell sticks to his experience as faithfully as any Jeremiah to the word of God, and if it leads him into anti-socialistic or self-contradictory statements he is unconcerned, as are his readers. Prophets use satire as one of their scourges, and Orwell is excellent at satire; indeed, had he been more systematizing and inventive, like his admired Swift, he might have composed satires of a high order; but his chief satire, *Animal Farm*, sticks to (is stuck with) the political facts

335

too nearly. Prophets tell the people, especially the mighty and chosen, what they ought to have done and ought to do, and boldly promise actual punishments for their transgressions and dreamlike rewards for their obedience to the right; all this Orwell does. Prophets want you to hear the word, not their delivery of it; in Orwell's plain, public prose, you never detect a murmur of vanity even when his own experiences are his subject. Prophets want to change the way you think and act; and I am sure that politically we, his readers, now think and act as we do in some measure because of what Orwell wrote.

On the whole the literary history of the 'thirties seems to justify the opinion that a writer does well to keep out of politics.

('*Inside the Whale*')

Even as a secular prophet, though he was the best of his age, Orwell failed at last. His profound and enduring message, adumbrated in earlier essays, is finally summed up and given its strongest images in *1984*, which was intended to reveal not only the direction of our political drift but also, prophetically, man's inmost nature. Politically, he says, men are interested in power, and the ideals they profess only whitewash this true motive. The aim of the modern totalitarian state is to 'reduce consciousness,' to obliterate personality and the exercise of the spirit. Now these are the sorts of strictures one needs and wants prophets to make; in them one can recognize aspects of reality; they are true. However, Orwell, like many another provincial from the Enlightenment, was so shocked at discovering that men are not innately perfectible and good that he decided they are more corruptible than they actually are. He goes on: because of technological progress, greater social organization, more effective methods of propaganda (in sum, because of scientific advances and analytical ways of thinking), rulers are now free to exert their power more and more undisguisedly and will finally be able consciously to exert power just for its own sake. But with this distortion he loses his readers; it belongs to an artificiality like that of a horror movie. (*1984* was turned into a very bad horror movie.) This, of all the insights he claims the most profound, is untrue, and its untruth darkens his other insights. I believe that those who get and monstrously abuse great power do it in the name of dialectical materialism, for greater Germany, the Mikado, the poor, God and country, to save the world for . . . In any case, what they think they are doing it for is inextricably involved with their doing it. Those who are conscious of their impulse to power and try to exert power only for their own satisfaction are merely cruel; and cruelty is not so potent a force as love of a cause, however bad, for cruelty has limits and is satiable, but perverted love never has enough. The tormentor's speech in *1984*, setting forth the rationale of the rulers of that society, is a distorting mirror which is intended to show us the very core of ourselves. Because Orwell has previously told us so much about ourselves and our time which we have recognized as true, we approach this revelation with excitement; but the excitement is transformed into a simply nervous excitement, such as one gets from a mad-scientist movie. What do we learn from the tormentor's speech? That George Orwell thought that cruelty, when divorced from love, can become the strongest human impulse. In so particular a distortion it is not so much ourselves we see as a curious pathology. Swift is like a man with cancer who says men are wholly disgusting vessels of disease, and because sometimes we feel so we say yes, we are; but Orwell is like a man with cancer who says everyone else has cancer too, and we say no, only some men have cancer, most are not so sick as that, as for me I have asthma and a slipped disc.

> It is forbidden to dream again;
> We maim our joys or hide them;
> Horses are made of chromium steel
> And little fat men shall ride them.
>
> (from a poem included in '*Why I Write*')

Why his failure as a prophet? For one thing, a great or even a successful prophet must be a forceful artist, preferably a good poet, and Orwell was a slight artist. His poetry is rhyming notions; even his judgments on poetry are of value only when he is treating it as a social symptom; he is far more sensitive to bad prose than to good poetry. His novels have the merit of containing descriptions which might have been incorporated in essays or books of reportage, but as novels they are not very good. His one allegory is accomplished and entertaining, but it does not penetrate far beyond the local politics that occasioned it; still, its satire, while slight, is pure and intense; I would guess that if any fiction of Orwell's is much read a century from now it will be *Animal Farm*. He was a master of the miniature art of the conscious essay, along with Edmund Wilson, Julian Huxley, Aldous Huxley, T. S. Eliot, Yvor Winters, Lionel Trilling, Virginia Woolf . . . ; such writers are sophisticated and intelligent and say something worth saying, and they know how to distribute their information and ideas in such a way as to produce pleasing surprises and a cumulative sense of understanding; but they are not prophetic. Imagine Isaiah chopping his vision up and parceling it into essays. Of the humble art of reporting, too, Orwell is a master, one with few peers. *Homage to Catalonia* is, I think, much the best book Orwell wrote. His gifts as a reporter and social analyst could have found no more suitable material to work with, for he was able to use the microcosm of his own experience in the Spanish Civil War to comprehend the nature of that war—that war which was, in turn, a sort of microcosm of political struggle in this age, right against left and left against itself. Further, the book is an honest account of a soldier's experience in war and revolution, which is its own reward. But imagine Thucydides on the one side or Augustine on the other restricted to their own exterior experiences and to a faithful rendering of the reports of others. Orwell is not an artist of the first rank because he succeeded only in the lesser arts of essay-writing and reporting.

I think I should only feel what one invariably feels in revisiting any scene of childhood: How small everything has grown, and how terrible is the deterioration in myself!

('Such, Such Were the Joys . . .')

Psychologically, the root of Orwell's failure was, no doubt, his extreme sensitivity to cruelty and to the unjust exercise of authority. This native quality was aggravated into a malady by his experiences in his first public school (not so bad, according to Christopher Hollis, who was there, as Orwell makes out), in Eton, and in the British army in Burma.[1] A man who was and who thinks he was, much abused as a child is likely to identify himself unconsciously with all sufferers and to be disposed to hate violently all authorities. The emotional logic of such a man seems to run: suffering is the worst thing in the world; the people most loving and worthy of love have suffered greatly; therefore (!!) let us rid the world of suffering so that people may love one another. 'Privation and brute labor have to be abolished before the real problems of humanity can be tackled' ('Looking Back on the Spanish War'). Socialism provides an excellent program for a man with such logic: let us revolt against authority for the sake of the sufferers (i.e., against capitalists for the sake of the proletariat) and create a world (i.e., a socialist state) where there will be neither exploiters nor ex-

---

[1] Orwell was in the Burmese Police, not the British Army.

ploited. In explaining this about Orwell, I have accounted for only a little; for one thing, he himself was conscious that civilization demands rulers and that the suffering that results from being exploited was as likely to obliterate men as to fill them with love (see his 'Marrakech'); more important, though his sensitivity to cruelty and suffering was part of what drove him to write and to become a socialist, it does not begin to explain his limitations. And his limitations, I think, distorted his views more than his illness did; it was because of his limitations that he could suppose, as Swift did not, that all men suffered from his own malady.

Like everyone who was in Barcelona at the time, I saw only what was happening in my immediate neighborhood, but I saw and heard quite enough to be able to contradict many of the lies that have been circulated. . . . It is a horrible thing to have to enter the details of inter-party polemics; it is like diving into a cesspool. But it is necessary to try and establish the truth, so far as it is possible.

(Homage to Catalonia, Chapter X)

His greatest limitation was his rationalistic view of things, his materialism. Some of his minor limitations, of course, were strengths. His Britishness, for example, was total, but he knew it and some of his best insights derive from this very knowledge; he was struck with the facts of his experience, but from his experience he wrote what must be the best book likely to be written on the Spanish Civil War; he looked mostly for the social function of works of literature, but he served as a sort of corrective to the esoterics who have been over-running literary criticism. But other of his minor limitations enfeebled him. One of the most startling was his fitful historical imagination; though he understood such important recent changes in the West as the loss of popular belief in immortality, yet he displayed an abysmal ignorance of the Middle Ages, about which he often repeated the eighteenth-century clichés. He believed politics and social problems are, at least nowadays, more important than all the rest of life together and pollute all of it, a belief that is possible only to one who denies, among other things, the validity of religious experience. He had a weakness for generalizing; he sometimes wrote as though all civilized men were London-dwelling materialists with an atavistic love of flowers. He took a rather quantitative view of excellence, when he happened not to be thinking of a given man or act; so that he could suggest that poetry, just because its true audience is limited to the speakers of one language, is inferior to prose, which can be translated for all men. But most damaging, he put his trust in conscious reason as the measure of all things, and he wanted to look only at that which can be seen by the plain light of day. Bertrand Russell did as much but with less damage to himself as a writer, for the logic which Russell was good at had, like a natural science, nothing to do with politics and ethics, which were the core of Orwell's concern. Thus limited, he was hostile to, denied, or was indifferently skeptical about matters of the greatest importance, God, the unconscious, sin and evil; he was inadequate to deal with poetry, love, religious emotions and rituals; and he could not consciously believe that human suffering might be more than a matter of endurance, sado-masochism, and willed destruction. The materialist rationalism which has been the binding spirit and philosophy of the age of science has at no time or place been stronger than during Orwell's generation in England; as a prophet he knew it was partial and often false, but as a creature of the age he could not break its bonds.

Among the Europeans opinion was divided. The older men said I was right, the younger men said it was a damn shame to shoot an elephant for killing a coolie, because an elephant was worth more than any damn Coringhee coolie. And afterwards I was very glad that the coolie had been killed; it put me legally in the right and it gave me a sufficient pretext for shooting the elephant. I often wondered whether any of the others grasped that I had done it solely to avoid looking a fool.

('Shooting an Elephant')

When he was not striving against the limits of his philosophy, as he was not when he wrote these words which conclude his most powerful essay, then he sometimes in no way failed. The strength of 'Shooting an Elephant' is more than literary; it is moral too. The essay is in part a confession of the author's weakness and wrong-doing, and the ring of the prose is absolutely true; it is also that high kind of confession in which the writer sees his deed as being at once his own, typical of the class to which he belongs, and human beyond person and class, so that both the low deed and the seeing of it are made the reader's own as well. But finally there is no difference between the literary and the moral in this essay: purged as it is of all self-regard, even of self-abasement, the essay is in itself the act of an upright man and citizen, and its cleanness is his honesty.

## 103. Anthony Powell, *Daily Telegraph*

3 October 1968, p. 22

Anthony Powell (b. 1905), at Eton with Orwell; English novelist
and author of *The Music of Time* series.

George Orwell died in 1950 in his 47th year. His family came originally
from Scotland (his real name was Eric Blair) but had lived in South-
West England for about two centuries. They were soldiers, clergymen,
doctors, with an Indian Civil connection.

Orwell gained an Eton scholarship, served five years in the Burma
police, resigned to take up writing and plumb the depths of social
misery, was wounded serving against Franco in the Spanish Civil
War. His health prevented him from joining the army in the second
world war. In 1945 his satire *Animal Farm* was published, a book that
immediately became a classic.

It was an excellent idea to mingle chronologically letters, essays and
journalism in these volumes so that they form what is roughly a
narrative, and include all his writings except the novels. The editing is
admirable, with just the notes required and a superlative index. To include a fair amount of quite trivial stuff like reviews was also sound,
because Orwell himself set great store by the day-to-day work that
earns a living, and such material adds to the picture of him.

We begin with an immensely characteristic letter he wrote at the
age of 17 while still a schoolboy to (Sir) Steven Runciman, an Eton
contemporary. Orwell had managed to be left behind at an inter-
mediate station on the way back from an O.T.C. camp. He had

enough for his fare home and 7½d over. He could stay the night at the Y.M.C.A. for 6d, but that left only 1½d for food. Orwell bought 12 buns and slept out. Here, we feel, is the germ of the Orwell who later deliberately got drunk in the Mile End Road to see how he was treated when arrested.

This is the first letter, though the reader's curiosity is aroused by a sentence written to Cyril Connolly in 1938: 'What you say about finding old letters of mine makes me apprehensive.' This could hardly refer to the earliest letter to Mr Connolly included here and dated 1936.

Orwell's most effective writing might be said to fall into three main groups, because the early naturalistic novels (which he himself later disparaged) are more interesting for the light they shed on their writer than as novels.

First comes the reportage. This was a genre in which Orwell was particularly skilled. Pieces like 'The Spike' or 'Hop-picking' are written in that deceptive manner that makes you feel you have been brilliantly told exactly what happened, and that the writer has done this without any trouble at all to himself. Secondly, there are the amusing essays like those on Donald McGill comic picture-postcards or the *Gem* and *Magnet* stories about Greyfriars School. These might be said to shade off into Orwell's journalism as a columnist.

As a columnist—or in the London letters to *Partisan Review*—one sometimes feels his innate eccentricity and wilfulness take over, even when the ideas are lively and out of the ordinary. There will be generalisations like 'all writers are lazy' (what about Balzac and Dickens, for that matter, Orwell himself?), or an astonishing supposition that Jews cannot be naval officers.

The fact is that Orwell had so much cut himself off from 'bourgeois' life that he was sometimes out of touch about how it functioned. His love of the past caused one side of him to cling to the idea that nothing ever changed, while his 'clever schoolboy' background did not always keep him entirely free from what might be called the superior sort of historical cliché.

His third group of writings consists of the political fantasies, *Animal Farm* and *1984*. These represent the final stage of Orwell's development, and have a quite peculiar interest in relation to the rest of his life and work.

*Animal Farm* (begun in 1943) has the rare distinction of being at the same time an attractive and popular children's book, and a savage and damaging satire on Communism. One of the most interesting aspects of these four volumes is the way they show how the left-wing press of the 1930s and 1940s was so Communist dominated that Orwell's articles were barred from publication. When it came to *Animal Farm* even quite 'uncommitted' publishers were *afraid* to take the book on.

Orwell's exposure of the ruthless, totalitarian nature of Communism is his greatest political achievement. It happens to be chiefly linked with what is also his most accomplished literary work. The interesting point about the manner in which Orwell finally found his expression in fantasy is that he had always rigorously extirpated anything of the sort from his earlier writing and deprecated it in his criticism. This is well illustrated throughout this miscellaneous collection.

For example, he takes Dickens to task for allowing Magwich, the escaped convict in *Great Expectations*, to threaten Pip with over-picturesque imagery: 'There's a young man hid with me, in comparison with which young man I am an Angel . . . .' One has the feeling that Orwell was always suppressing this side of himself, the childish, imaginative side, which some psychologists say we all need from time to time to allow freedom, and that he did this with some odd results. Oddest of all was that when he released these forces he became a world best-seller.

An instance of a perceptive Orwell comment is that contemporary preoccupation with naturalistic sexual descriptions will seem to later generations like the over-exuberance of the death of Little Nell. These volumes are a mine of enthralling material for those who want to study one of the most notable figures of our time. They prompt the fascinating speculation about what would have happened if—as he at one moment suggested—Orwell had called himself 'H. Lewis Allways.'

## 104. Conor Cruise O'Brien, *Listener*

12 December 1968, pp. 797–8

Conor Cruise O'Brien (b. 1917), Irish historian, critic and statesman; UN representative in Katanga 1961; author of *Parnell and His Party* (1957), *Writers and Politics* (1965) and *Camus* (1969); presently Irish Minister of Posts and Telegraphs.

This collection has some puzzling features. 'These four volumes,' writes Mrs Orwell in her introduction, 'are not the *Complete Journalism and Letters of George Orwell*, but with the novels and books they make up the definitive Collected Works. Ian Angus and I have not set out to make an academic monument because neither his work nor his personality lends itself to such treatment and the period he lived in is too recent for any real history to have been written of it.' It appears, therefore, that the promise of the title is misleading: *Collected Essays, Selected Journalism and Selected Letters* would have been more accurate. And what is the point of claiming that this edition 'with the novels and books' makes 'the definitive Collected Works', while at the same time abjuring any intention to make 'an academic monument'? If the edition were in fact definitive, it could not escape being academic, and being a monument—indeed *the* monument—to George Orwell. It may or may not be the case that neither Orwell's work nor his personality lends itself to such treatment, but if they do not, then they do not lend themselves either to 'definitive Collected Works' or even to four stout miscellanies at a price of £10. As for 'real history', that is an elusive entity, but the period in question is one on which many competent historians have worked, and it is less wrapped in obscurity than most other periods of history. It is hard to resist the conclusion that the editors wish to claim definitive status for their edition without incurring the responsibilities which such a claim should imply.

This is disturbing, and not merely for technical reasons. The collected essays are already easily and widely available—and serve no purpose in the present collection except to bulk it out—but for what is important in the present edition, i.e. the letters and journalism, we are obliged to rely on the editors' powers of selection. The misleading title and the large and amorphous claims made and withdrawn in the introduction do not encourage implicit confidence in the selection made.

If the edition is not what it appears to be—and I think this has been shown—what then is it? It seems to this reviewer that the main significance of its appearance at this time, and in this form, is as a contribution to a cult. This is an Anglo-American edition, and edited with an American public prominently in mind. George Orwell's American public is, I think, significantly different from his public on this side of the Atlantic. For his American admirers, the author of *Animal Farm* and *1984* is above all, the prophet of anti-communism. This note is struck in this edition at the outset. The jacket of Volume One refers to him as 'a dedicated political commentator and journalist'. Mrs Orwell's introduction makes this more explicit: he was 'a committed socialist and a dedicated anti-communist'.

Now it is obvious that Orwell was anti-communist, in the sense that he detested Soviet policy, and especially those who in England were the unavowed spokesmen of that policy, from the mid-Thirties up to his death. But he was not only anti-communist, not even only socialist-but-anti-communist. He was a puritan, with a lively hatred of intellectual dishonesty, and an extremely good nose for it. He liked to apply the 'bastinado'—as he characteristically put it—not only to fellow travellers but to, among others, 'professional Roman Catholics'. The form of intellectual dishonesty most influential during his last years—he died, after a long illness, on 21 January 1950—was a pro-communist form. He hated the communist literary Mafia in England, France and elsewhere. But had he lived to witness, through the Fifties, the rise of another literary Mafia, this time of anti-communists 'dedicated' to the unavowed service of United States policy, and standing in all essentials in the same relation to Washington as the crypto-communists had stood to Moscow, it is clear from the whole tenor of his writing that his disgust would soon have found vent. From the point of view of the 'committed socialists and dedicated anti-communists' who took part in the complex and camouflaged manoeuvres of the Congress for Cultural Freedom,[1] it was rather fortunate that Orwell died when he died. Had he lived, it might not have been so easy to claim him. As it is, it has been possible to claim him as a patron

[1] CIA front which sponsored *Encounter* and other intellectual magazines.

saint, and to exploit his merits, by a sort of parasitic reversibility, in the service of some dubious activities. He would, in a way, have enjoyed the kind of logic which was implicit in the way his name has been used:

Orwell was an honest man.

Orwell was a socialist anti-communist.

A, B and C are socialist anti-communists.

∴A, B and C are honest men.

I am sure that Mrs Orwell—whom I take to be a rather unpolitical person—uses the term 'dedicated anti-communist' with simplicity and sincerity. It remains unfortunately true that this description, used in 1968, commends Orwell to people—apologists for the Vietnam War, for example—whose approval would have horrified him. And this imposing, if rather inflated, edition will be a welcome acquisition for the book-shelves of such people, at a time when anti-communist writers who are both dedicated and respected are not easy to find.

Although these four volumes contain some moderately interesting new material—notably the 'Wartime Diary' in Volume Two, the 'Extracts from a Manuscript Notebook' in Volume Four and a few of the letters—on the whole they do little to change the view of Orwell that one may form from reading his well-known published works. Most of the letters are business-like and not notably revealing, and Orwell's minor journalism, though it wears better than most people's would, is still not very interesting. The only surprise I received from the contents of this collection was contained in Volume One, and concerned Orwell's position in the immediate pre-war period. From the fact of Orwell's service on the Republican side in Spain, and from his whole-hearted support for the British war-effort from the moment war broke out, it was natural to assume that he had taken, from at least 1936 on, a consistently militant anti-fascist position. Some of his own wartime retrospective references to the evil effects of the pacifism of the intellectual Left also suggest this. But in fact, from May 1938 up to the Russo-German Pact, his position was one of determined opposition to the drift to war with Germany, and he characteristically made explicit the most unpalatable consequences of this position. After Munich he thought England was in for 'a period of slow fascisation, a sort of Dollfuss-Schuschnigg Fascism'[1] but that this would be better than having the Left identified as 'the war party'. By January 1939 he was advocating preparation for underground anti-war activity in

1 Dollfuss and Schuschnigg were the Austrian chancellors before Hitler's *Anschluss*.

England during 'the coming war'. The underground campaign would have two sections: 'the dissident left like ourselves and the idealistic Hitler-fascists, in England more or less represented by Mosley'[1] (March 1939). He wrote at the same time of 'this "anti-fascist" racket' and later argued that the British Empire was 'a far greater injustice' than fascism (July 1939). Yet when the war broke out he supported his country, out of plain patriotism, and broadcast on its behalf to the Empire, against fascism. The anti-war position soon became almost incomprehensible to him. 'The intellectuals who are at present pointing out that democracy and fascism are the same thing etc depress me horribly' (January 1940).

Being a socialist, a revolutionary, an anti-imperialist, or following any other political theory, were very much less important in practice than being an Englishman. And Orwell's enduring hatred of the English intellectuals of his day arose mainly, I think, from a feeling that some of them took their intellectual activity more seriously than he did, in the sense that if the logic of their ideas led to un-English conclusions, they would be capable of following that logic, instead of doing 'instinctively'—a word he favoured—the English thing, and dumping the ideas. What he most disliked about communism, I believe, was not its ruthlessness, dishonest propaganda and other obvious defects, but the fact that it was capable of making Englishmen unpatriotic.

Orwell believed in the decency—another favourite word—and honesty of ordinary Englishmen, and he did his best in his own life and writing to live up to his conception of an Englishman. His honesty and decency—with him, real and solid virtues—pulled him in several different directions. Honesty inquired into, and exposed, the abuses, injustices and shams of the society in which he lived; decency demanded drastic action; Orwell became a socialist and claimed to be a revolutionary. But honesty also inquired into, and exposed, the shams etc of contemporary 'socialisms' and socialists; decency was revolted at what revolution actually entailed; so Orwell's socialism and 'revolution' did not in practice go beyond what English people thought was reasonable.

Curiously, this situation was disguised by the very plainness of Orwell's language: a characteristic which linked him to the English of the past rather than to those of his own day. Plain language has a tendency to become extreme—which is why the other kind of

[1] Oswald Mosley (b. 1896), leader of the British Nazi Party.

language is generally preferred—and thus a laudable peculiarity of style made Orwell seem more extreme than in fact he was. Many Englishmen, no doubt, early in 1939, shared Orwell's general political ideas of that time, but only Orwell felt called upon to push the logic of these to the conclusion of imagining himself collaborating with 'idealistic Hitler-fascists'—a conclusion which, once stated with rigour, he completely rejected in practice, or—more likely—simply forgot ever having made.

He was not a great political thinker or a great novelist, but his combination of ordinariness of feeling with unusual control over the resources of plain speech made him a great journalist, pamphleteer and fabulist. He was, both by precept and example, a great cleanser of the English language, and a great teacher of younger writers of English prose. It would be a pity if the present younger generation, which could and should learn from him how to write English, were to remain cut off from him by assurances that he was a dedicated anti-communist, and by the thought of the dedicated anti-communists whom they actually know. There is a gulf in communication here, erected by the fact that the period of his last writings was the period of the beginning of a new orthodoxy, which he never lived to criticise, and which as the result of its own abuses is contemptuously rejected by the educated young today. The word 'dedicated'—which is not the kind of word he liked—both dates him in a particularly damning way and requires of him the kind of superficial consistency which he refused.

Those who wish to protect a reputation for consistency require ambiguities, which provide lines of retreat. Orwell's recklessly plain prose always says what he thinks he means at the time. The present time is so different from 1948–50 that he should no more be presented as fixed at that point than he should remain for ever associated with his position of 1938–39. What should be remembered is the free, candid, often mistaken mind of a man who asserted and defended human decency: a more disconcerting enterprise than he originally reckoned it to be.

# 105. Irving Howe, *Harper's*

January 1969, pp. 97–103

Renoir said he painted with his penis. Had they troubled to think about it, Balzac might have said he wrote with his guts, Conrad with his nerves, Jane Austen with her eyebrows, George Orwell, however, wrote with his bones. To read again his essays, together with previously uncollected journalism and unpublished letters, as they have been brought together in this superb four-volume collection, is to encounter the bone-weariness, and bone-courage, of a writer who lived through every public disaster of his time: the Depression, Hitlerism, Franco's victory in Spain, Stalinism, the collapse of bourgeois England in the Thirties. Even when he wanted to pull back to his novels and even when he lay sick with tuberculosis, Orwell kept summoning those energies of combat and resources of irritation which made him so powerful a fighter against the cant of his age. His bones would not let him rest.

For a whole generation—mine—Orwell was an intellectual hero. He stormed against those English writers who were ready to yield to Hitler; he fought almost single-handed against those who blinded themselves to the evils of Stalin. More than any other English intellectual of our age, he embodied the values of personal independence and a fiercely democratic radicalism. Yet, just because for years I have intensely admired him, I hesitated to return to him. One learns to fear the disappointment of fallen heroes and lapsed enthusiasms.

I was wrong to hesitate. Reading through these four large volumes— the sheer *pleasure* of it can't be overstated—has convinced me that Orwell was an even better writer than I had supposed. He was neither a first-rank literary critic nor a major novelist, and certainly not an original political thinker; but he was, I now believe, the best English essayist since Hazlitt, perhaps since Dr Johnson. He was the greatest moral force in English letters during the last several decades: craggy, fiercely polemical, sometimes mistaken, but an utterly free man. In his readiness to stand alone and take on all comers, he was a model for every writer of our age. And when my students ask, 'Whom shall I read in order to write better?' I answer, 'Orwell, the master of the plain style, that style which seems so easy to copy and is almost impossible to reach.'

If you look through them casually, the earliest of Orwell's essays seem to share that blunt clarity of speech and ruthless determination to see what looms in front of one's nose that everyone admires in his later essays. The first important essay reprinted here came out in 1931, when Orwell was still in his late twenties, and is called 'The Spike.' It describes his experience as an unemployed wanderer on the roads of England, finding shelter in a 'spike,' or hostel, where the poor were given a bed and two or three meals but then required to move along. The piece makes one quiver with anger at the inhumanity of good works, but it is absolutely free of sentimentalism, and almost miraculously untainted by that sticky *luving* condescension of Thirties radicalism.

Any ordinary writer should be willing to give his right arm, or at least two fingers, to have written that piece. Yet a close inspection will show, I think, that it doesn't reach Orwell's highest level as social reporter. There is still an occasional clutter of unabsorbed detail, still a self-consciousness about his role as half-outsider barging in upon and thereby perhaps subtly betraying the lives of the men on the road. The discipline of the plain style—and that fierce control of self which forms its foundation—comes hard.

But for Orwell, it also came quickly. In a piece called 'Hop Picking,' written only a few months later and never before published, Orwell describes some weeks spent as an agricultural worker in the hop fields. The prose is now keener:

Straw is rotten stuff to sleep in (it is much more draughty than hay) and Ginger and I had only a blanket each, so we suffered agonies of cold for the first week. . . .
Dick's Cafe in Billingsgate . . . was one of the very few places where you could get a cup of tea for 1d, and there were fires there, so that anyone who had a penny could warm himself for hours in the early morning. Only this last week the London City Council closed it on the ground that it was unhygienic.

In 'Hop Picking' Orwell had already solved the problem of narrative distance, how to establish a simultaneous relationship with the men whose experience he shares and the readers to whom he makes the experience available. 'Hop Picking' was a small effort in the kind of writing Orwell would undertake on a large scale a few years later, when he produced his classic report on the condition of English miners, *The Road to Wigan Pier*. What Orwell commanded, above all, was a natural respect for the workers. He saw and liked them as they were, not as he or a political party felt they should be. He didn't twist them into Marxist abstractions, nor did he cuddle them in the fashion of New Left populism. He saw the workers neither as potential revolutionists nor savage innocents nor stupid clods. He saw them as ordinary suffering and confused human beings: quite like you and me, yet because of their circumstances radically different from you and me. When one thinks of the falseness that runs through so much current writing of this kind—consider only the 'literary' posturings of Murray Kempton[1]—it becomes clear that Orwell was a master of the art of exposition.

Other sides of Orwell's talent soon begin to unfold. He develops quickly, for in regard to him the idea of *pressure* is decisive. His career can be understood only as a series of moral and intellectual crises, the painful confrontation of a man driven to plunge into every vortex of misery or injustice that he saw, yet a man who had an obvious distaste for the corruption of modern politics.

Even in casual bits of journalism, his voice begins to come through. He seldom had the patience as a literary critic to work his way deeply into a text, though he did have an oblique sort of literary penetration. He remarks, in an otherwise commonplace review, that George Moore, the half-forgotten English novelist of the late nineteenth century, enjoyed the advantage of 'not having an over-developed sense of pity; hence he could resist the temptation to make his characters more sensitive than they would have been in real life.' In 'Bookshop Memories,' never before in a book, Orwell shows the peculiar sand-papery humor that would emerge in his later writings:

Seen in the mass, five or ten thousand at a time, books were boring and even slightly sickening. . . . The sweet smell of decaying paper appeals to me no longer. It is too closely associated in my mind with paranoiac customers and dead bluebottles.

In another early piece, not otherwise notable, there suddenly leaps out a sentence carrying Orwell's deepest view of life, his faith in the value and strength of common existence: 'The fact to which we have got to cling, as to a life-belt, is that it *is* possible to be a normal decent person and yet to be fully alive.' Let that be inscribed on every blackboard in the land!

---

[1] Murray Kempton, liberal political columnist of the *New York Post*.

Orwell's affectionate sense of English life, its oddities, paradoxes, and even outrages, comes through in an anecdote he tells:

... the other day I saw a man—Communist, I suppose—selling the *Daily Worker*, & I went up to him & said, 'Have you the DW?'—He: 'Yes, sir.' Dear Old England!

There are even a few early poems, slightly this side of *Weltschmerz*,[1] which I rather like:

> I know, not as in barren thought,
> But wordlessly, as the bones know,
> What quenching of my brain, what
>    numbness,
> Wait in the dark grave where I go.

Orwell's first fully achieved piece of writing appears in 1936: 'Shooting an Elephant,' a mixture of reminiscence and reflection. The essay takes off from his experience as a minor British official in Burma who, in the half-jeering half-respectful presence of a crowd of 'natives,' must destroy a maddened elephant, and then it moves on to larger issues of imperialism and the corruption of human nature by excessive power. For the first time, his characteristic fusion of personal and public themes is realized, and the essay as a form—vibrant, tight-packed, nervous—becomes a token of his meaning. The evocation of brutality is brought to climax through one of those symbolic moments he would employ brilliantly in his later pieces: 'The elephant's mouth was wide and open—I could see far down into caverns of pale pink throat.'

During these years, the late Thirties, Orwell went through a rapid political development. He kept assaulting the deceits of Popular Frontism, and this brought him even more intellectual loneliness than it would have in America. He tried to find a tenable basis for his anti-Stalinist leftism, a task at which he encountered the same difficulties other intellectuals did—these, after all, were intrinsic to a worldwide crisis of socialist thought. For a while he fought in Spain with the militia of the POUM, a left-wing anticommunist party, and suffered a throat wound; back in England he spoke some painful truths about the Stalinist terror launched against dissident leftists on the Loyalist side, and for this he was cordially hated by the *New Statesman* and

[1] World weariness.

most of the liberal intellectuals. He published one of his most valuable and neglected books, *Homage to Catalonia*, the record of his experience in Spain. He went through a brief interval in which he put forward a semi-Trotskyist line, denying that the bourgeois West could successfully oppose Hitlerism and declaring that the prerequisite for destroying fascism was a socialist revolution in England. But when the war broke out, he had the good sense—not all his co-thinkers did—to see that his earlier views on combating fascism had been abstract, unreal, ultimatistic. He supported the war yet remained a radical, steadily criticizing social privilege and snobbism. Here is a passage from his previously unpublished 'War-Time Diary,' breathing his ingrained plebeian distaste for the English upper classes:

From a letter from Lady Oxford to the *Daily Telegraph*:
'Since most London houses are deserted there is little entertaining . . . in any case, most people have to part with their cooks and live in hotels.'

Apparently nothing will ever teach these people that the other 99% of the population exists.

The high plateau of Orwell's career as essayist—and it is as essayist he is likely to be remembered best—begins around 1940. He had by then perfected his gritty style; he had settled into his combative manner (sometimes the object of an unattractive kind of self-imitation); and he had found his subjects: the distinctive nature of English life and its relation to the hope for socialism, a number of close examinations of popular culture, a series of literary studies on writers ranging from Dickens to Henry Miller, and continued social reportage on the life of the poor. His productivity during the next five or six years is amazing. He works for the BBC, he writes a weekly column for the socialist *Tribune*, he sends regular London Letters to *Partisan Review* in New York, he keeps returning to his fiction, and he still manages to produce such extraordinary essays as the appreciation of Dickens, the piquant investigation of boys' magazines, the half-defense half-assault on Kipling, the brilliant 'Raffles and Miss Blandish,' the discussion of Tolstoi's hatred for Shakespeare—to say nothing of such gems, rescued from little magazines, as a short piece on Smollett and a long one on George Gissing.

We see him now in his finished, his mature, public role. There is something irascible about Orwell, even pugnacious, which both conventional liberals and literary aesthetes find unnerving. He is constantly getting into fights, and by no means always with good judgment. But meanwhile his curiosity also keeps growing. In Volume III one finds a neat little set of essays, previously unknown to American readers, about such native institutions as the London pub, tea-drinking, and English cooking, as well as the ambitious short book called *The Lion and the Unicorn* in which he tries to anchor socialist values in a realistic apprehension of English custom.

My sense of Orwell, as it emerges from reading him in bulk, is rather different from that which became prevalent in the Fifties: the 'social saint' one of his biographers called him, the 'conscience of his generation' V. S. Pritchett declared him to be, or the notably good man Lionel Trilling saw in him. The more I read of Orwell, the more I doubt that he was particularly virtuous or good; but why should that worry anyone? Neither the selflessness nor the patience of the saint, certainly not the indifference to temporal passion that would seem a goal of sainthood, can be found in Orwell. He himself wrote in his essay on Gandhi: 'No doubt alcohol, tobacco and so forth are things a saint must avoid, but sainthood is a thing that human beings must avoid.'

As a 'saint' Orwell would not trouble us, for by now we have learned how to put up with saints: we canonize them and are rid of them. Orwell, however, stirs us by his all too human, his truculent example. He stood in basic opposition to the modes and assumptions that have since come to dominate our cultural life. He rejected the rituals of Good Form which had been so deeply ingrained among the English and took on a brief popularity among us in the Fifties; he knew how empty, and often how filled with immoderate aggression, the praise of moderation could be; he turned away from the pretentiousness of the 'literary.' He wasn't a Marxist or even a political revolutionary. He was something better: a revolutionary personality. He turned his back on his own caste; he tried to discover what was happening beyond the provincial limits of highbrow life. If he was a good man, it was mainly in the sense that he had measured his desperation and come to accept it as a mode of honor. And he possessed an impulse essential to a serious writer: he was prepared to take chances, even while continuing to respect the heritage of the past.

Orwell had serious faults, both as writer and thinker. He liked to indulge himself in a pseudo-tough anti-intellectualism, some of it pretty damned nasty, as in his sneers at 'pansy-pinks'—though later he was man enough to apologize to those he had hurt. He was less than clear-sighted or generous on the subject of the Jews, sharing something of the English impatience with what he regarded—in the 1940s!—as their need for special claims. He could be mean in polemics. During the war he was, by one standard, quite outrageous in attacking English anarchists and pacifists like Alex Comfort, Julian Symons, and George Woodcock for lending 'objective' comfort to the Nazis. Yet it speaks well for Orwell that in a short time at least two of these men became his friends, and it isn't at all clear to me that, despite their manifest good will, Orwell wasn't, in his angry and overstated denunciation, making a point against them and all other pacifists which must be seriously considered.

Meanwhile, reading through these volumes from remarkable essay to essay, one suddenly comes to a stop and notices that Orwell's letters are not, as letters, particularly interesting or distinguished. At first, this comes as a surprise, for one might have expected the same pungency, the same verbal thrust, as in the public writing. There is, however, nothing to be found of the qualities that make for great letter writing: nothing of the brilliant rumination of Keats in his letters, or the profound self-involvement of Joyce in his, or the creation of a dramatic persona such as T. E. Lawrence began in his. He seems to have poured all his energies into his published work and used his letters simply as a convenience for making appointments, conveying information, rehearsing opinion. Perhaps it's just as well, for he had a horror of exposing his private life and asked that no biography be written about him. In these days of instant self-revelation, there is something attractive about a writer who throws up so thick a screen of reticence.

One reason these uninteresting letters do finally, however, prove interesting is that they put to rest the notion that Orwell's prose was an achievement easily come by. The standard formula is that he wrote in a 'conversational' style, and he himself is partly responsible for this simplification. I think, however, that Yvor Winters[1] was right in saying that human conversation is a sloppy form of communication and seldom a good model for prose. What we call colloquial or conversational prose is the result of cultivation, and can be written only by a disciplined refusal of the looseness of both the colloquial and the conversational. If you compare the charged lucidity of Orwell's prose in his best essays with the merely adequate and often flat writing of his letters, you see at once that the style for which he became famous was the result of artistry and hard work. It always is.

[1] Yvor Winters (1900–68), American poet, critic and teacher.

In an essay called 'Why I Write,' Orwell ends with a passage at once revealing and misleading:

All writers are vain, selfish and lazy, and at the very bottom of their motives there lies a mystery. Writing a book is a horrible, exhausting struggle, like a long bout of some painful illness. . . . Good prose is like a window pane. I cannot say with certainty which of my motives are the strongest, but I know which of them deserve to be followed. And looking back through my work, I see that it is invariably where I lacked a *political* purpose that I wrote lifeless books and was betrayed into purple passages. . . .

Orwell is saying something of great importance here, but saying it in a perverse way. (After a time he relished a little too much his self-image as embattled iconoclast.) He does *not* mean what some literary people would gleefully suppose him to mean: that only tendentiousness, only propaganda, makes for good prose. He deliberately overstates the case, as a provocation to the literary people he liked to bait. But a loyal reader, prepared to brush aside his mannerisms, would take this passage to mean that, once a minimal craftsmanship has been reached, good writing is the result of being absorbed by an end greater than the mere production of good writing. A deliberate effort to achieve virtuosity or beauty or simplicity usually results in mannerism, which is often a way of showing off.

In his best work Orwell seldom allowed himself to show off. He was driven by a passion to clarify ideas, correct error, persuade readers, straighten things out in the world and in his mind. Somewhere Hemingway speaks of 'grace under pressure,'[1] and many of his critics have used this marvelous phrase to describe the excellence of his style. What I think you get in Orwell at his best is something different: 'pressure under grace.' He achieves a state of 'grace' as a writer through having sloughed off the usual vanities of composition, and thereby he speaks not merely for himself but as a voice of moral urgency. His prose becomes a prose of pressure: the issue at stake being too important to allow him to slip into fancies or fanciness. Moral pressure makes for verbal compression, a search like Flaubert's for *le mot juste*, but not at all to achieve aesthetic nicety, rather to achieve a stripped speech. And the result turns out to be aesthetically pleasing: the Christians, with much more to be risked, understood all this when they spoke of 'dying into life.'

Good prose, says Orwell, should be 'like a window pane.' He is

[1] Not Hemingway's phrase, but Dorothy Parker's famous description of Hemingway.

both right and wrong. Part of his limitation as a literary critic is that he shows little taste for the prose of virtuosity: one can't easily imagine him enjoying Sir Thomas Browne. If some windows should be clear and transparent, why may not others be stained and opaque? Like all critics who are also significant writers themselves, Orwell developed standards that were largely self-justifying: he liked the prose that's like a window pane because that's the kind of prose he wrote.

His style doesn't seem to change much from early essays to late, but closely watched it shows significant modulations. At the outset his effort to be clear at all costs does involve him in heavy costs: a certain affectation of bluntness, a tendency to make common sense into an absolute virtue. But by the end, as in the superb prose of 'Such, Such Were the Joys,' there has occurred a gradual increase of control and thereby suppleness.

'Pressure under grace' brings rewards. Orwell learns to mold the essay into a tense structure, learns to open with a strong thrust ('Dickens is one of those writers who are well worth stealing'), and above all, to end with an earned climax, a release of the tension that has been accumulating and can now be put to the service of lucidity. I think a useful critical study could be made of the way he ends his essays. Here is the last paragraph on Dickens:

When one reads any strongly individual piece of writing, one has the impression of seeing a face somewhere behind the page. It is not necessarily the actual face of the writer. . . . What one sees is the face that the writer *ought* to have. Well, in the case of Dickens I see a face that is not quite the face of Dickens' photographs, though it resembles it. It is the face of a man about forty, with a small beard and a high color. He is laughing, with a touch of anger in his laughter, but no triumph, no malignity. It is the face of a man who is always fighting against something, but who fights in the open and is not frightened, the face of a man who is *generously angry*—in other words, of a nineteenth-century liberal, a free intelligence, a type hated with equal hatred by all the smelly little orthodoxies which are now contending for our souls.

The passage is marvelous, but if a criticism is to be made, it is that Orwell has composed a set piece too easily lifted out of context, and that in the final sentence he has allowed himself to turn away from his subject in order to take a smack at fanatics of left and right. Yet this self-indulgence, if it is one, works pretty well, mainly because Orwell has by now so thoroughly persuaded his readers that the qualities he admires in Dickens *are* indeed admirable.

Here is another Orwell ending, this time from the essay on Swift,

'Politics vs. Literature,' published some seven years after the one on Dickens. Orwell makes some important observations on the problem of 'belief' in literature:

In so far as a writer is a propagandist, the most one can ask of him is that he shall genuinely believe in what he is saying, and that it shall not be something blazingly silly. Today . . . one can imagine a good book being written by a Catholic, a Communist, a Fascist, a Pacifist, an Anarchist, perhaps by an old-styled Liberal or an ordinary Conservative; one cannot imagine a good book being written by a spiritualist, a Buchmanite or a member of the Ku Klux Klan. The views that a writer holds must be compatible with sanity, in the medical sense, and with the power of continuous thought: beyond that what we ask of him is talent, which is probably another name for conviction. Swift did not possess ordinary wisdom, but he did possess a terrible intensity of vision. . . . The durability of *Gulliver's Travels* goes to show that, if the force of belief is behind it, a world-view which only just passes the test of sanity is sufficient to produce a great work of art.

What grips our attention here is the ferocity with which Orwell drives home his point—by reaction, we almost see old Tolstoi rising from his grave to thunder against this heresy. Rhetorically, the passage depends on the sudden drop of the last sentence, with its shocking reduction of the preceding argument—so that in the movement of his prose Orwell seems to be enacting the curve of his argument. It is a method he picked up from Swift himself.

And finally, here is the ending of his great essay, 'How the Poor Die':

The dread of hospitals probably still survives among the very poor and in all of us it has only recently disappeared. It is a dark patch not far beneath the surface of our minds. I have said earlier that, when I entered the ward at the Hospital X, I was conscious of a strange feeling of familiarity. What the scene reminded me of, of course, was the reeking, pain-filled hospitals of the nineteenth century, which I had never seen but of which I had a traditional knowledge. And something, perhaps the black-clad doctor with his frowsy black bag, or perhaps only the sickly smell, played the queer trick of unearthing from my memory that poem of Tennyson's, 'The Children's Hour,' which I had not thought of for twenty years. It happened that as a child I had had it read aloud to me by a sick-nurse. . . . Seemingly I had forgotten it. Even its name would probably have recalled nothing to me. But the first glimpse of the ill-lit, murmurous room, with the beds so close together, suddenly roused the train of thought to which it belonged, and in the night that followed I found myself remembering the whole story and atmosphere of the poem, with many of its lines complete.

This ending seems to me a triumph of composition. All that has been detailed with such gruesome care about the terribleness of a French hospital is brought to imaginative climax through the anecdote at the end. Proust could hardly have done better.

Orwell died, in 1950, at the age of forty-six, stricken by tuberculosis. It is depressing to think that if he had lived, he would today be no more than sixty-five years old. How much we have missed in these two decades! Imagine Orwell ripping into one of Harold Wilson's mealy speeches, imagine him examining the thought of Spiro Agnew, imagine him dissecting the ideology of Tom Hayden,[1] imagine him casting a frosty eye on the current wave of irrationalism in Western culture!

The loss seems enormous. . . . He was one of the few heroes of our younger years who remains untarnished. Having to live in a rotten time was made just a little more bearable by his presence.

# 106. Malcolm Muggeridge, *Esquire*

March 1969, pp. 12–14

The four volumes of George Orwell's collected essays, journalism and letters, impeccably edited by his widow Sonia Orwell and Ian Angus, are wonderfully readable, wonderfully illuminating, and a rare treasure for any aspiring writer. I have always thought that Orwell, apart from anything else, was the perfect twentieth-century stylist. His dry sentences with their splendid clarity and smoldering indignation convey better than any other contemporary writer the true mood of our times. He stood alone in every sense, but especially in the temper of his mind, avoiding alike the incoherence (Joyce, Beckett), the pedantry (Eliot, Sartre, Pound), the false rhetoric (Hemingway, Céline), the hysteria (D. H. Lawrence, John Osborne), and other devices for evading an all too overwhelmingly tragic reality. As a

[1] Tom Hayden, radical American student leader.

novelist he was unsatisfactory, as a thinker he was often confused, illogical and prejudiced, but as an essayist and journalist he was incomparable. Thus these volumes show him at his very best—and his best is uniquely good.

Many of the pieces appeared originally in *Tribune*, a weekly organ of the independent Left. It was partly owing to Orwell's influence that *Tribune* kept its head about the U.S.S.R. in the years of wartime cooperation when all the weightiest Establishment voices—notably *The Times* of London—were fulsomely sycophantic about Stalin and his monstrous policies at home and abroad. Historians will note as a curious and significant circumstance that it was in this obscure publication that the only effective protests appeared at the time against Roosevelt's and Churchill's sellout at Teheran and Yalta. Orwell's pen lent them an extra force and sharpness. He was possessed of that sort of implacable honesty which I like to think of as an English characteristic—an honesty which is humorous, obstinate if not pigheaded, and, above all, somehow *sweet*. It's the only word I can use. Though he was a dry old stick in many ways, and sometimes, I have to confess, tedious (though more in conversation than in the written word), there was always this abiding sweetness which made his company invariably enjoyable and uplifting. Perceptive readers will readily sense what I mean.

May I, egotistically, cite by way of illustration a review Orwell wrote of *The Thirties*, a book of mine, in *The New English Weekly* of April 25, 1940. As it happens, I had never read the review before coming upon it in the first of these four volumes of occasional pieces; *The Thirties* appeared when I was serving as a private in the army and expecting the world to come to an end any moment, so circumstances were not propitious for looking at press cuttings or otherwise familiarizing myself with the book's reception. Reading the review now, nearly thirty years later, with Orwell dead and myself old and grey and full of years, was oddly moving. I could hear that corncracking voice of his speaking it; see that weird, deadpan face of his—a Woeful Countenance like Don Quixote's, I often used to reflect when in his company. And what a brilliant review it is—absolutely bang-on-target, and as fresh and clear and true today as when it was written. I only wish this or any other review of mine might seem as relevant and as readable in years to come.

I had various interests in common with Orwell. We both as young men had been to India in the days of the British Raj—he to serve in the

Burma Police, and I to teach in an Indian Christian college in what was then Travancore, in South India, and is now Kerala. While Orwell was, in his own estimation, doing the Raj's dirty work for it—suppressing subversion and maintaining the supremacy of the white man, or Sahib—I, ludicrously attired in Indian costume made of the home-spun cloth decreed by Gandhi and prone to torture my stiff European limbs by trying to sit cross-legged on the ground, was urging my students to shake off the fetters of imperialism and demand their independence. We often used to talk about India, having that obsessive interest in the country which no Englishman who has lived there ever wholly shakes off.

Orwell, of course, reacted very strongly against the Burma Police and the Raj, but it is interesting to note in his writings on the subject—notably, in *Burmese Days* and his brilliant essay on Kipling, but scattered throughout his occasional pieces as well—a certain sympathy with the mystique of British rule in India. In many ways he admired Kipling very much, and told me once that he considered 'Mandalay' the finest poem in the English language—an endearingly preposterous critical judgment. The truth is that there was in Orwell—as, again, perceptive readers will detect—a strong strain of deep, romantic conservatism; a passionate, even boyish, love for England's past, a detestation of the present, and a dread of a future in which, as he feared, all the most English habits of thought, feeling and behavior would be obliterated.

Again one thinks of Cervantes' original Knight of the Woeful Countenance, Don Quixote. Orwell had the correct lanky and creaky figure; his long thin legs would easily have drooped over Rosinante's flanks. He was also, like the Don, in the most enchanting conceivable manner rather crazy, and, as such crazed ones usually are, capable of deeds of inconceivable heroism, as well as of an obstinacy so unshakable, so impregnable, that it became exceedingly funny. The best example of this last characteristic was given me by Orwell's delightful sister, Avril; he remarked to her on one occasion, she told me, that all tobacconists were Fascists. His conversation was studded with such gems, and they crop up fairly frequently in his writings: I well remember him insisting once that in the old days plowmen developed one shoulder higher than the other, and that coats appropriately cut to meet this deformity used to be on sale in the shops in country districts—a rather pleasing notion for which there is not the smallest evidence. Were such remarks an expression of a weird sense of humor? It is quite possible; a sort of low chuckle sometimes accompanied them, meant, I daresay, to reassure all those nice, kindly tobacconists labeled Fascists that no harm was meant. At the same time, a word of caution is in order. It is dangerous to take Orwell *au pied de la lettre*,[1] though he was by nature the most truthful man who ever lived, he often described what he expected to see and thought he saw rather than what he actually saw. Thus, for instance, his numerous accounts of working-class life, on which he regarded himself as an expert, were culled more from popular newspapers and magazines than from reality —a kindly, conscientious Etonian's picture of a proletarian interior.

What is superlative about Orwell's journalism is not its objective accuracy but its total integrity. In an age of ideological conflict he managed to avoid being in any sense an ideologue. He belonged to the Left, but the Left hated him; he exposed, as no one else has, the fraudulence of what purported to be Leftish regimes in Spain, in the U.S.S.R., in Welfare England, thereby delighting the Right, but his distaste for the Right was unabated. In *Animal Farm*, in *Nineteen Eighty-Four*, in piece after piece included in this collection, one may observe with admiration and delight the workings of a wholly honest mind confronted with a world given over more even than is usual to chicanery of every kind. Orwell was never a mere partisan; when the Left-wing weekly, the *New Statesman*, declined his articles on the Spanish Civil War (he used some of the material in *Homage to Catalonia*, and, in my opinion, the best thing of its kind in the English language) on the ground that in the middle of a civil war it would be wrong to prejudice the Republican cause by telling the truth about it, his indignation knew no bounds. Such an attitude was utterly alien to him. He, too, remained on the Republican side and a hater of Franco, but not to the point of hiding the truth—that Stalin had found in the Civil War an opportunity to move his whole vile terrorist *apparat* into Spain, and that its first victims were the Spaniards who most truly loved freedom and were prepared most heroically to defend it.

Any journalist must share a little in the glory of these four volumes; take a vicarious pride in the excellence of work knocked off in a hurry for a meager financial reward often desperately needed. Orwell cherished the dream that he would retire to the country and write great literary masterpieces; nevermore sit in anguish over a typewriter with a deadline to meet. That dream so often dreamed within sound of the printing presses! Well, he had his house, remote enough, God

[1] Literally.

knows—on the island of Jura off the coast of Scotland—and went there; in view of his dangerous tubercular condition, it was a disastrous move. Everything came true for him when it was too late; he fell sick, managed to finish *Nineteen Eighty-Four* in a feverish state, and then came south. When I saw him a few days before he died he was talking eagerly about going to Switzerland and taking his fishing rod with him. Of course, he never went. Had it come off; had he, now comfortably off, settled down in some delightful spot free from financial worry and the deadline pressure, would he then have produced great works of literature? I doubt it. I think his journalism was his best work and when I say *his* best I mean *the* best.

# 107. George Steiner, *New Yorker*

## March 1969, pp. 139–51

George Steiner (b. 1929 in France), critic and Fellow of Churchill College, Cambridge; author of *Tolstoy or Dostoyevsky* (1958) and *The Death of Tragedy* (1960).

To me, the notion of 'reviewing' George Orwell is mildly impertinent. Anyone who earns his living writing about books and politics, who tries to get the words on the page aligned cleanly, so that the light can get through, finds himself in a special relationship to Orwell. Partly, there is exasperation—a feeling that Orwell did the job so much better, that in him style was not laborious métier but a way of drawing breath. Mostly, however, there is a sense of insurance. One might get things right because he did, because he kept his balance under continuous political and psychological stress, because he wrote, and wrote voluminously, under pressure of need and journalistic occasion, and did so with almost unfailing justice and vivacity; because there was in his personal and professional life a comeliness—unobtrusive yet to everyone who came in contact with it oddly penetrating, like one of those spells of sun and light mist in England at winter's end. (Orwell loved England with an abrupt, embarrassed ardor.)

In one of his last essays, the 'Reflections on Gandhi,' Orwell remarked that 'saints should always be judged guilty until they are proved innocent.' This is a characteristic gambit, wry and beautifully to the point, Gandhi's so efficacious sanctity having been so full of shrewd tactics. It also applies to Orwell. Where are the covert byways in all this plain going, where the compromises, the failures of nerve? Orwell would have been the first to ask. He detested the monumental; he had the sharpest nose for humbug since Swift. But ferret as we will in a life, in a body of work at every moment vulnerable to the temptations of cynicism, of merely professional competence, and our indebtedness deepens. 'The thing that frightens me about the modern intelligentsia,' wrote Orwell in the black April of 1940, 'is their inability to see that human society must be based on common decency.' 'Common decency' uncommonly argued, uncommonly enacted toward enemies, toward his foster child, toward his own body, whose racked condition he held in a dry, amused respect, was Orwell's politics of being. He added, in the same letter, 'My chief hope for the future is that the common people have never parted company with their moral code.' Another who never did was Eric Blair, the man who became Orwell. This companionship makes of the nineteen hundred-odd pages of *The Collected Essays, Journalism, and Letters* something larger, more needed than good writing. These four volumes are a place of renewal for the moral imagination.

The strength of Orwell is manual. He had a carpenter's grip on jagged particularities. His work exhibits unswerving attention to detail, to the loose ends and broken edges which in fact make up the fabric of human behavior. He was a formidable reporter. That is where his art begins—in the memorable ordures of *Down and Out in Paris and London*, in that close witness of heat and sullen dust, of the scratch in the white man's voice, which makes *Burmese Days* a classic. In a short essay on Marrakech, written in 1939, Orwell commented wryly on the invisibility of the oppressed: 'People with brown skins are next door to invisible. Anyone can be sorry for the donkey with its galled back, but it is generally owing to some kind of accident if one even notices the old woman under her load of sticks.' Orwell made it his job to see where others had merely blinked and passed by. He paid the compliment of total attention to aspects of society and culture ordinarily under the carpet—to the broken men and women on the edge of an industrial society, to the dirty postcards in the tobacconist's shop, to the 'good bad books' and outright pulp which the vast majority of one's fellow-men read, if they read at all. And because Orwell made of the act of observation a harsh test of integrity, because he never allowed himself to patronize, to focus from 'above,' the objects of his notice—grim, commonplace as they so often are—acquire a fierce insistence. The diary Orwell kept when he was preparing *The Road to Wigan Pier* (material here published for the first time) shows his technique:

One woman had a face like a death's head. She had a look of absolutely intoler-able misery and degradation. I gathered that she felt as I would feel if I were coated all over with dung. . . . Passing up a horrible squalid side-alley, saw a woman, youngish but very pale and with the usual draggled exhausted look, kneeling by the gutter outside a house and poking a stick up the leaden waste-pipe, which was blocked. I thought how dreadful a destiny it was to be kneeling in the gutter in a back-alley in Wigan, in the bitter cold, prodding a stick up a blocked drain.

In each of the snapshots we get the same movement of spirit, from naked sight to identification.

Orwell persistently took journalism to the pitch of literature be-cause he despised generality. It was the specific, local truth which mattered. He knew that honesty is the art of the obvious: 'To see what is in front of one's nose needs a constant struggle.' The charlatan levels at eternity and falls short; an honest writer is never afraid to date. Indeed, as Orwell assured a correspondent in the summer of 1934, 'anything worth reading always "dates." '

He was wary of blueprints, of any design from which the smudge of actual human behavior is absent. Reflecting on Stalinism and Nazism, and on the nature of wartime government in England, he noted, 'I admit to having a perfect horror of a dictatorship of theorists.' This horror goes a long way toward explaining his polemics against the intelligentsia. 'During the past twenty-five years the activities of what are called "intellectuals" have been largely mischievous. I do not think it an exaggeration to say that if the "intellectuals" had done their work a little more thoroughly, Britain would have surrendered in 1940.'

The quarrel involves the center of Orwell's vision—a stringent discrimination between detachment and fairness. Detachment, the purported objectivity of the mandarin and intellectual inquirer, seemed to him a betrayal of the responsible life of the mind. It is 'fairness' we must strive for. The word is complex in Orwell. It carries echoes of Eric Blair's public-school background. It is, of course, a profoundly English-Victorian term. Reading Orwell's reporting and letters, one comes to see just what it signifies—imaginative scruple, a refusal to judge without taking risks. A 'fair' account of a social conflict, of an individual predicament, is one in which the observer has put himself on the line. Orwell spent time in the doss houses of East London and the common wards of the Hôpital Cochin, in Paris. He had watched the poor die within reach of his own bedsheet. At Alcubierre, he was in the front trenches. Too often the intellectuals were waiting in the hotel.

Though he savaged them in his famous memoir 'Such, Such Were the Joys'—a text hitherto unavailable in England—Orwell owed much to the snobberies and physical harshness of his schooling at St Cyprian's and Eton. Those who survive more or less whole carry with them an ascetic elegance, a talent for taking the world as it comes. In the midst of the grime and mendacity he made it his business to explore, George Orwell maintained a natural poise. This curious mixture of grit and fastidiousness accounts for a distinct strain in English letters. It relates a Tory such as Swift to a Jacobin such as Hazlitt. We see it in Bunyan and in Wilde, who for all his dandyism was as thoroughly at home in the refuse of the modern city as was Orwell. I know of no exact counterpart to this tradition in any other literature.

In the fall of 1922, Orwell chose not to go to university but to join the Indian Imperial Police. The episode remains obscure, but there may lie behind it an early addiction to realism, a desire to test the power relations that were to govern 'an age like this.' There is an illuminating concession in Orwell's attack on Kipling in 1942: 'He identified himself with the ruling power and not with the opposition. In a gifted writer this seems to us strange and even disgusting, but it did have the advantage of giving Kipling a certain grip on reality. The ruling power is always faced with the question, "In such and such circumstances, what would you *do*?," whereas the opposition is not obliged to take responsibility or make any real decisions.' As assistant district superintendent in Burma, Orwell found himself having to decide. When the mad elephant appeared on the street in Moulmein, police officer Blair took careful aim and shot him.

Burma and the 'black lands' of England during the Depression educated Orwell's eye and made it obvious—to him, at least—that writing and politics were inseparable. But it was in Spain that he hammered out his personal creed and first struck the notes of sadness and of lucid rage which were to shape his brief life. (The man whose work is in so many respects a representative, summarizing statement of the twentieth-century condition died at forty-six.)

Orwell was in Spain from late December of 1936 to the end of June of 1937. He went out to fight the Fascist junta and left a step ahead of the Stalinist police, who would, on orders from the Republican Government in Madrid, have arrested and probably killed him. *Homage to Catalonia*, which seems to me a flawless book, tells the cruel, ironic tale. Now, with the aid of the letters, articles, book reviews he wrote from and about Spain, we can follow the entire development of Orwell's awareness. Much more is at stake than the record of an exceptionally acute mind. It was in Barcelona during the murderous Communist betrayal of the Socialist, Trotskyite, and Anarchist allies that Orwell, with a Fascist bullet lodged in his throat, realized where the only possible decency lay. It was there that he chose the impossible middle, equidistant from the lies and raptures of totalitarianism, be it of the right or of the left. Like Arthur Koestler, waiting to be shot in a prison in Málaga, like Victor Serge and Franz Borkenau, both on the run from the G.P.U., Orwell joined the handful of men—that small, harried club of conscience—who knew as early as 1936 that Fascism and Communism are antagonistic but profoundly related inhumanities. From that point on—Victor Serge called it 'the zero of the century'— an honest man could be defined as one whom both the Gestapo and Stalin's hoodlums wanted dead. In fact, the two packs were already collaborating. In September of 1937, Orwell stated the acid conclusion which was to govern his politics: 'The logical end is a régime in which every opposition party and newspaper is suppressed and every dis-sentient of any importance is in jail. Of course, such a régime will be Fascism. . . . Only, being operated by Communists and Liberals, it will be called something different.'

The inclusion of 'Liberals' is important. When he returned from Spain, undermined in health and literally possessed by his insight into the common hideousness of Stalinism and Fascism, Orwell had an ugly awakening. The so-called radicals and leftist intellectuals who had only months before acclaimed him as one of theirs, as a hero fighting for democracy on the Aragon front, found the truth unpalatable. Victor Gollancz, whose Left Book Club had honored *The Road to Wigan Pier*, turned down *Homage to Catalonia* before it was even written. (Years later, on similar grounds of political expediency, T. S.

Eliot was to turn down *Animal Farm*.) In his review of Borkenau's *The Spanish Cockpit*, Orwell stated that 'the Communist Party is now (presumably for the sake of Russian foreign policy) an anti-revolutionary force,' and characterized Barcelona, with its 'ceaseless arrests, the censored newspapers, and the prowling hordes of armed police,' as a nightmare. The *New Statesman* refused to print the piece. From the foxholes of their typewriters, stalwarts of the liberal intelligentsia termed Orwell a crypto, a Trotskyite unwittingly playing the Fascist game. The two experiences—his actual encounter with Fascism and Communism in northern Spain, and the cowardice and falsehood of the intellectual, academic-journalistic left at home—stamped Orwell's genius. Against despair—and, like other clairvoyants in the late nineteen-thirties, Orwell must at moments have been near to it—he set two things: an article of faith and a strategy. The faith he proclaimed to his old school chum Cyril Connolly in a letter he wrote when he was lying gravely wounded in Spain: 'I have seen wonderful things and at last really believe in Socialism.' He gave a characteristic reason when he joined the Independent Labour Party—'the only régime which, in the long run, will dare to permit freedom of speech is a Socialist régime.' The strategy was henceforth to fight on two fronts, to occupy the beleaguered middle of truth at whatever cost. Orwell put it simply: 'I hold the outmoded opinion that in the long run it does not pay to tell lies.'

I see no escape from Orwell's position and the obligations of untimeliness and tactlessness which it imposes. Moreover, its present relevance is equally inescapable. The failure of the 'new left' (why 'new'?) to link its critique of the Vietnam war with any responsible plan for an alternative policy would have drawn Orwell's fire. To orate fluently about American atrocities and pass over those of the Vietcong, to advocate withdrawal without tackling such political, human realities as the fate of several million refugees from the North— these postures would have struck Orwell with ironic familiarity. The divorcement between mental agility and a capacity to take political action seemed to him the besetting sin of the liberal conscience, as did the habit of abstraction, of simplification, in the face of realities which are messy and irrational. One can hear him saying, the day after the Soviet invasion of Prague, that this latest spasm of the Stalinist terror, which he fought his whole life, might never have happened had the West not rearmed NATO Germany or had we dealt, using a minimum of common sense, with the problem of the status of East Germany.

What need there is, just now, of an Orwell essay on the wholly understandable but probably self-betraying and self-defeating course of
Israeli politics and policy! Everywhere, since Guernica[1] and Madrid,
the lies have thickened and barbarism has drawn closer. Orwell fore-
saw what lay ahead and set himself a job: to defend 'a conception of
right and wrong, and of intellectual decency, which has been responsible
for all true progress for centuries past, and without which the very
continuance of civilized life is by no means certain.' This defense led
to his two most interesting achievements—a critique of language and,
at the very last, the most telling use of allegory in English literature
after Bunyan and Swift.

Orwell's profile of a book reviewer is disenchanted: he sits 'in a cold
but stuffy bed-sitting room littered with cigarette ends and half-
empty cups of tea,' cursing as the next 'wad of ill-assorted, unappetizing
books' lands on his desk. He himself reviewed perpetually, but a
remarkable portion of his journalistic criticism lasts, and is vital
beyond the book he happened to be reviewing. This is because a sustained argument is implicit. Like de Maistre,[2] a brilliant Catholic
conservative, Orwell arrived at the conviction that language is a sort
of organism, that it has its own strength of being, that it can be damaged
or destroyed. Like de Maistre, whom he probably never read, Orwell
came to believe that the health of language and that of society are
connected by strong strands. To abuse, inflate, or falsify the meaning
of words is to devalue the political process. Political sanity, the ability
of a community to view and communicate issues clearly, are closely
dependent on the integrity of syntax. The lies, the nauseating propaganda and hate slogans of Fascism and Communism, corrupt language
deliberately. Less deliberately, but sometimes to comparable effect, the
mendacities of advertisement and the semiliteracy of a consumer
society do likewise. The fight for meaningful speech is a fight for
moral and political life. Orwell's fullest statement of the case came in
1946, in his famous essay on "Politics and the English Language':

In our time, political speech and writing are largely the defence of the indefen-
sible. . . . Thus political language has to consist largely of euphemism, question-
begging, and sheer cloudy vagueness. Defenceless villages are bombarded from
the air, the inhabitants driven out into the countryside, the cattle machine-
gunned, the huts set on fire with incendiary bullets: this is called *pacification*.

[1] Basque town bombed by the Nazis during the Spanish Civil War. It became the subject
of Picasso's greatest painting.
[2] Joseph de Maistre (1753–1821), French diplomat and philosopher.

Millions of peasants are robbed of their farms and sent trudging along the roads with no more than they can carry: this is called *transfer of population* or *rectification of frontiers*. People are imprisoned for years without trial, or shot in the back of the neck, or sent to die of scurvy in Arctic lumber camps: this is called *elimination of unreliable elements*. . . . When there is a gap between one's real and one's declared aims, one turns as it were instinctively to long words and exhausted idioms, like a cuttlefish squirting out ink. . . . All issues are political issues, and politics itself is a mass of lies, evasions, folly, hatred, and schizophrenia.

Toward the close of his indictment, Orwell gives a set of rules for lucid writing. He concludes splendidly: 'Break any of these rules sooner than say anything outright barbarous,' in which prescription 'barbarous' carries both its human and its grammatical weight. This view of language as the essential, the threatened locale of truth and political freedom determined Orwell's literary opinions. It inspired his extension of serious criticism to such marginal forms as thrillers, pulp fiction, boys' magazines, and best-sellers. Any linguistic statement which could reach millions and shape their fantasy lives seemed to Orwell far too important to patronize or omit from serious scrutiny. Intent on the *Realpolitik* which underlies middle-class speech, alert to the evasions behind the humanitarian pathos of the Victorians, Orwell was both wonderfully perceptive and unjust on Dickens. He missed the tough ironies in Cyril Connolly's *Unquiet Grave* and was uninformative and bad-humored about the *Four Quartets*. But then Orwell always held prose to be more important, more akin to the pulse of responsible thought, than verse. He condemned Carlyle, who 'had not even the wit to write in plain straightforward English,' and found D. H. Lawrence's major novels 'difficult to get through.' Seeking to justify this bit of myopia, Orwell got out of his depth; demanding probability and cold-blooded construction, he totally failed to recognize the deeply organized genius of Lawrence's fiction. On the other hand, and surprisingly, he was humbly responsive to Joyce: 'When I read a book like that,' he said of *Ulysses* in 1934, 'and then come back to my own work, I feel like a eunuch who has taken a course in voice production.' Orwell saw virtues in Kipling and wrote vigorously in defense of Henry Miller, though the attitude of the first struck him as imperialist and that of the second as infantile. In the last analysis, literature did not matter all that much. Not even Shakespeare, about whom Tolstoy had said such obtuse, madly pejorative things. (Orwell's commentary on Tolstoy's attack, 'Lear,

Tolstoy, and the Fool,' is one of the classics of the Puritan sensibility.) What mattered was the use of language to make human beings more humane, to impel them to right action. Indeed, too much of literature was sophisticated tinsel designed to make social injustice less visible. Orwell's canons are unmistakable: 'There are music-hall songs which are better poems than three-quarters of the stuff that gets into the anthologies. . . . And by the same token I would back *Uncle Tom's Cabin* to outlive the complete works of Virginia Woolf.'

This populist, Puritan commitment makes it surprising that Orwell's most famous writing should have been allegory. Neither *Animal Farm* nor *1984* is a simple book; in fact, both are oblique and highly artful. That it was the Book-of-the-Month-Club edition of *Animal Farm* in 1946—with its sale of half a million—which for the first time in his life freed Orwell from financial anxiety is of itself a bit of complex irony. Here was no tract for the oppressed, no radical flysheet posted in the night. To understand these two books (neither has until now been thoroughly placed), we have to keep in focus a set of contradictory, partly undeclared motives. By the end of the war, Orwell may have had a fairly distinct premonition of his own fatal illness. He may have been fiercely intent on giving his political views a stable form, an expression unrelated to the force and the chaos of daily events. At the same time, the positive role of Stalinism in the overthrow of Hitler and the new expansiveness of American policy had made Orwell's position more isolated, more difficult to proclaim directly. His loathing of Communism had in no way been altered by Stalingrad. But new dangers were now pressing on Socialism—dangers which arose from the strength of capitalism and the subtler inhumanities of a consumer culture. And even graver was the menace of nuclear war—a ruin of mankind so drastic that the very possibility of a future Socialism would disappear. Seeking to dramatize these insights, compelled to do so in a way that would get through the barriers of pro-Russian and pro-American reflexes, Orwell wrote allegory. In this he joined the company of his masters, of those other Puritans whom complexity of mood and fear of repression had led to *Pilgrim's Progress* and to *Gulliver's Travels*.

I can see the virtuosity of *Animal Farm*, the cunning of the fable (how much ambivalence and suggestive indirection lie just below the surface of its lapidary style). But as an analysis of Communist dictatorship, of Stalinist mental processes, it seems to me thin and, understandably, desperate. The interplay between man and quadruped in Part IV of

*Gulliver* on which Orwell based his parable is a bleaker yet more comprehensive act of imagination. *Nineteen Eighty-Four* can be grasped only, I think, if one realizes that it was written under sentence of death. Orwell must have known, be it unconsciously, that his time was out. It seems to have been an attempt to pull together everything he knew of language, of politics, of the slim chances of love. As early as January of 1939, he wrote, 'It is quite possible that we are descending into an age in which two and two will make five when the Leader says so.' The notion of Newspeak goes back to an article written in 1940. But it was, of course, Zamyatin's *We* that provided Orwell with his immediate model. He came across this anti-utopian satire, by one of the most gifted of Russian Symbolists, in February of 1944. He remarked, 'I am interested in that kind of book, and even keep making notes for one myself that may get written sooner or later.' Two years later, Orwell reviewed *We*. Though superior to *Brave New World*, said Orwell, Zamyatin's was 'not a book of the first order.' Yet his article, and the passages he chose for comment, show how deeply Orwell was inspired. *Nineteen Eighty-Four* is a close imitation, and Zamyatin's seems to me the subtler, more inventive fiction. Big Brother derives from The Benefactor; the bell lowered over Winston's head is that under which 1-330 is tortured. Orwell's review, moreover, picks up a decisive clue: 'What Zamyatin seems to be aiming at is not any particular country but the implied aims of industrial civilization.' Both the strength and the ambiguity of Orwell's fantasia stem from a latent identification between Stalinist terror and the inhumanity of a supertechnology. The result is a harrowing but somewhat forced and unsteady parable. The domestic aspects of *Nineteen Eighty-Four* go back to Orwell's early novels, to *A Clergyman's Daughter* and *Keep the Aspidistra Flying*. The politics are those of the Moscow purge trials and the nuclear-arms race. It is a desolate book, and very nearly posthumous.

A word needs to be said about this new collection. It is a model of unobtrusive learning, of editorial tact. Sonia Orwell and Ian Angus have presented the material chronologically; the letters thus serve as a constant illumination and inner critique of the articles and essays. Each volume has its particular chronology and index. The general index alone is worth the price of the set. In March of 1933, Eric Blair published a poem in the *Adelphi*. It ends:

> And we will live, hand, eye, and brain,
> Piously, outwardly, ever-aware,

Till all our hours burn clear and brave
Like candle flames in windless air;

So shall we in the rout of life
Some thought, some faith, some meaning
    save,
And speak it once before we go
In silence to the silent grave.

These volumes insure that there need be no silence. George Orwell's voice rings clear.

# 108. Jeffrey Meyers, *Philological Quarterly*

## October 1969, pp. 526–33, 549

Jeffrey Meyers (b. 1939), American author of *The Wounded Spirit* (1973), *Painting and the Novel* (1975) and *Fever at the Core: The Idealist in Politics* (1976). The footnotes were published with the article.

When I look back upon resolutions of improvement and amendments, which have year after year been made and broken, either by negligence, forgetfulness, vicious idleness, casual interruption, or morbid infirmity, I find that so much of my life has stolen unprofitably away, and that I can descry by retrospection scarcely a few single days properly and vigorously employed.

(Samuel Johnson, *Diary*, April 1775)

There has literally been not one day in which I did not feel that I was idling, that I was behind with the current job, & that my total output was miserably small. Even at the periods when I was working 10 hours a day on a book, or turning out 4 or 5 articles a week, I have never been able to get away from this neurotic feeling.

(George Orwell, *Diary*, early 1949)

These entries are remarkably similar in the fervor of their unjustified self-torment, and they suggest Orwell's close resemblance to Johnson as well as his place as the last of the English moralists—Johnson, Blake and Lawrence—whose passionate intensity is nearly prophetic. Both Johnson and Orwell had unhappy childhoods, struggled long with severe illness and bitter poverty, spent many years as hack journalists and did not achieve fame until their mid-forties. Both men were independent, combative, harsh on themselves and others, and often wrong-headed in a fascinating way. Both had limited imaginations but great critical faculties; and their satire was an expression of high principle, integrity and compassion. Both were pessimistic, patriotic, pragmatic, courageous, commonsensical, intellectually curious, scrupulously honest, fundamentally decent, oddly humorous and quintessentially English.

The new edition of Orwell's *Collected Essays, Journalism and Letters* enables us to sharpen our appreciation of Orwell and to place his life and works in a more precise perspective. Reviewing Orwell's posthumous essays in 1954, John Wain wrote, 'It is clear enough that this will be the last volume of barrel-scrapings from the Orwell stock, so that anything not included here will have small chance of emerging in the future.' In fact, only one third of Orwell's short articles and reviews have even here been included (about 230 out of 700) so that a definitive edition may still appear in the future. Orwell too would have been surprised by the existence of this collection, in which the majority of items are very short pieces, for he firmly stated, 'I would never reprint in book form anything of less than 2000 words' (IV, 233); and he would have been amazed by the price (and royalties) of these four large volumes, for the ten dollars he received for each 'London Letter' was probably his highest fee for a short article and he rarely earned more than four or five pounds a week until the success of *Animal Farm* in 1946. Nevertheless, we now have two thousand more pages of Orwell's writing, a quarter of it published for the first time, and it is first appropriate to state what has been omitted and what included.

The editors give no indication of exactly how much unpublished material has been excluded; two unpublished letters I remember are to Humphrey Slater in September 1946 mentioning a draft of *1984* and to Leonard Moore in July (?) 1947 giving a chronology of his life. The BBC material and many trivial notes have been rightly omitted; and though Mrs Orwell writes, somewhat unclearly, 'there is nothing either concealed or spectacularly revealed in his letters' (I, xvi), the unpublished letters and papers in the Archive at London University are not available to scholars, while those in the New York Public

Library and the University of Texas can be read but not quoted. Only selections from the last Notebook are published, so that Orwell's notes for a projected essay on Evelyn Waugh are printed while those for an essay on Conrad and a long short story are not.

Though Mrs Orwell writes, 'Anything he would have considered as an essay is certainly included' (I, xvii), the long political essays in *The Betrayal of the Left* and *Victory or Vested Interests?*, and the Introduction to *British Pamphleteers* (which is better than 'Pamphlet Literature') have been omitted. The following published though uncollected writings have considerable value and deserve to be printed in a fifth volume: the sixteen film and drama reviews for *Time and Tide* (1940–1941); the fourteen war reports from France and Germany for *The Observer* and *The Manchester Evening News* (early 1945) which (*pace* Mrs Orwell, I, xviii) are much more like straight reporting than his wartime 'London Letters'; the very important book reviews on Dostoyevsky, Baudelaire, Butler, Edmund Wilson and F. R. Leavis; the other interesting reviews of Milton, Byron, Balzac, Stendhal, Gogol, Chekhov, Rilke, Mann, Hardy, Hopkins, Joyce, Silone and Richard Wright; and finally the shorter reviews on the subjects of his major essays in which he first worked out his ideas on novelists who influenced him: Dickens, Gissing and Koestler, and on those whom he criticized for their reactionary political views: Swift, Tolstoy, Kipling, Wells, Wodehouse and Henry Miller.*

The most interesting unpublished material printed in these volumes includes 284 letters (relatively few of them before Orwell became

* The editing and the index have been highly praised and they deserve commendation. I would like to mention the following errors so that they can be corrected in future printings: the editors claim the 'War-time Diaries' have never been published; actually about half the 1940–41 Diary was published in *World Review*, XVI (June 1950), pp. 21–44; the book jacket says Orwell wrote ten books (excluding essays) during his lifetime while the Introduction says he wrote nine (which is correct); 'said' in III, 31, 'there' in IV, 146.n.1 are both misspelled; in III, 358 'José' lacks an accent; in IV, 48–49 the quotaton from Herbert Read is garbled. The references to Dr Johnson in III, 6 and to D. H. Lawrence in III, 166 are missing from the index; and the index references to *Talking to India* in III, 428 are incorrect.

The annotations seem at times inconsistent. R. H. Tawney and William Empson get explanatory footnotes but Frank Buchman and Lord Rothermere do not. The lines in Orwell's footnote on II, 4 from Marvell's 'The Garden' are not identified, nor is the mysterious reference to '18b' in III, 80. The note on Rayner Heppenstall in II, 18, 'their friendship continued until Orwell's death,' is misleading in view of the denigrating and destructive portrait of Orwell in Heppenstall's *Four Absentees* (1960). And the 'backward boy' (I, 546) that Orwell took care of in 1930 is called a 'congenital imbecile' in *Down and Out in Paris and London* (New York: Berkeley, 1961), p. 84 and is probably the subject of his lost short story, 'An Idiot.'

famous in his last years), the War Diaries (1940–2), the brief Manuscript Notebook (1949) and the Preface to the Ukrainian edition of *Animal Farm* where he describes the original creative impulse of that book. . . .

Of less interest are 'Clink,' 'Hop Picking,' '*The Road to Wigan Pier* Diary' and 'Notes on the Spanish Militias,' which are very similar to material already published in Orwell's early books. The remaining 1500 pages of previously published material consists of the 32 major essays (autobiographical, literary, sociological and political), 77 short articles and reviews, 73 (nearly all) of the 'As I Please' column and all the 15 'London Letters.'

The most striking thing about this occasional journalism, produced in Grub Street fashion at the rate of three or four pieces a week, is how readable and interesting it still is, for Orwell is the great master of colloquial ease. His style is extremely flexible and far-ranging, from very close observation:

A few rats running slowly though the snow, very tame, presumably weak with hunger (I, 177)

and witty aphorisms:

Poetry on the air sounds like the Muses in striped trousers (II, 334)

Nine times out of ten a revolutionary is merely a climber with a bomb in his pocket (I, 400)

to a strange Swiftian presentation of the seemingly familiar:

All our food springs ultimately from dung and dead bodies, the two things which of all others seem to us the most horrible (VI, 222)

and the startling, almost Donne-like openings of his major essays:

As I write, highly civilised human beings are flying overhead, trying to kill me (II, 56)

Autobiography is only to be trusted when it reveals something disgraceful (III, 156).

The only writer who approaches Orwell in both highbrow political analysis and intelligent literary criticism is Edmund Wilson, though D. H. Lawrence's *Phoenix* essays and Dwight Macdonald's political polemics are also comparable to Orwell's. His best characteristics are a Conradian concern with human solidarity; generosity of spirit that extends to enemy prisoners, French collaborators and Fascist war criminals; intellectual honesty in admitting his own mistakes; balanced judgment;* and courage to speak out against any mean or cowardly attitude and to defend dangerous and unpopular views. As Orwell says, 'To write in plain, vigorous language one has to think fearlessly, and if one thinks fearlessly one cannot be politically orthodox' (IV, 66).

The dullest and most dated of the journalism are the 'London Letters' and some of the more heavy-handed and repetitive political articles that often contain plodding uncharacteristic sentences like this one:

Though a collectivised economy is bound to come, those countries will know how to evolve a form of Socialism which is not totalitarian, in which freedom of thought can survive the disappearance of economic individualism (II, 137).

The literary articles are much livelier and more original than the political ones; and the delightful 'As I Please' column exhibits the uniquely random and miscellaneous quality of Orwell's mind (with some curious gaps—he has virtually no philosophical or psychological interests), as he ranges from the New Year's Honours List to the ugliest building in the world, and seems to resemble his own description of Charles Reade: 'a man of what one might call penny-encyclo-paedic learning. He possessed vast stocks of disconnected information with a lively narrative gift' (II, 34).

The volumes also have very considerable biographical interest, especially since no life of Orwell exists. I believe one is now being written, and it will certainly be welcome despite Mrs Orwell's assertion that 'there was so little that could be written about his life—except for "psychological interpretation"—which he had not written himself. . . . With these present volumes the picture is as complete as it can be' (I, xix). This is hardly true, for there is a vast difference between a mere factual chronology of a life and a full-scale interpretive biography of a man and his age, especially a man like Orwell who was deeply involved in all the political controversies of his time and whose life of art and action was equalled only by T. E. Lawrence, Malraux and Hemingway. Though the books and autobiographical essays ('Such, Such Were the Joys,' 'Shooting an Elephant,' 'A Hanging,' 'How the Poor Die,' 'Bookshop Memories,' 'Marrakech,' 'Confessions of a Book

* But not always balanced. In a letter of July 1940, he writes rather perversely: 'I actually rather hope that the [German] invasion will happen. The local morale is extremely good, and if we are invaded we shall at any rate get rid once and for all of the gang that got us into this mess' (II, 34).

Reviewer' and 'Why I Write') tell us a good deal about certain periods in his life, there are many large lacunae.

We know virtually nothing about Orwell's birthplace and earliest years. Like Kipling, he was born in India, spent his first years there, had an unhappy childhood,* and was sent to school in England; and Orwell is undoubtedly thinking of himself when he writes of Kipling, 'Much in his development is traceable to his having been born in India and having left school early' (II, 188). The first chapters of Kipling's *Something of Myself* describe an Indian childhood while 'Baa Baa Black Sheep' portrays the horrors of early youth. Cyril Connolly's *Enemies of Promise* gives a rather different and more pleasant picture of their prep school, St Cyprian's, than Orwell does, and he also describes their later life at Eton.

The Burmese period is the next obscure phase of Orwell's life, and exactly why he chose the Burmese police instead of Cambridge or at least the political section of the Indian or West African Civil Service is, as Mr Angus says, 'not known.' Mr A. S. F. Gow, Orwell's classical tutor at Eton, whom Orwell visited after Burma in 1927 and later corresponded with, has written to me (in a letter of 1 January 1969) that Orwell's father said he 'could not go to a University unless he got a scholarship and . . . there was not the faintest hope of his getting one. . . . He had shown so little taste or aptitude for academic subjects that I doubted whether in any case a University would be worth while for him.' (Orwell had won scholarships to both St Cyprian's and Eton but resolved to 'slack off and cram no longer' after prep school. He writes of Eton, 'I did no work there and learned very little, and I don't feel that Eton has been much of a formative influence in my life' II, 23.)† Mr. Gow also writes that Orwell's father then 'spoke of the Burmese police'; and the job was undoubtedly secured through personal connections which, writes Orwell, his family had 'with the country over three generations. My grandmother lived forty years in Burma' (IV, 114). His statement that when he was there 'nationalist feelings in Burma were not very marked, and relations between the English and the Burmese were not particularly bad' (III, 403) is very

* 'My early childhood had not been altogether happy. . . . I knew very well that I merely disliked my own father, whom I had barely seen before I was eight and who appeared to me simply as a gruff-voiced elderly man forever saying "Don't"' (IV, 334, 360).
† See Orwell's *Keep the Aspidistra Flying* (London: Penguin, 1962), p. 13, where Gordon attacks the 'Snooty, refined books on safe painters and safe poets by those moneyed young beasts who glide so gracefully from Eton to Cambridge and from Cambridge to the literary reviews.'

different from the atmosphere portrayed in *Burmese Days*. Leonard Woolf's *Growing* and Philip Woodruff's *The Men Who Ruled India* describe the social and political background of Orwell's Burmese period.

Another obscure phase of his life is his decision in 1946 to live the extremely arduous and exhausting existence on the remote island of Jura in the Hebrides. Mr Angus' explanation that he had gone to Jura 'to find some peace away from journalism, the telephone, etc' (IV, 518) is clearly unsatisfactory since an equally quiet place could be found in a more salubrious climate, closer to medical assistance and away from the country that Orwell professed to dislike (see IV, 357–58 and *Keep the Aspidistra Flying*, p. 42). The terminal phase of Orwell's very serious illness (he could speak, like Pope, of 'this long disease, my Life') dates from the winter of 1946, part of which he spent on Jura.

One pattern that emerges from these volumes is the terrible state of Orwell's health. Like D. H. Lawrence, he seems to have had defective lungs since boyhood—'after about the age of ten, I was seldom in good health. . . . I had defective bronchial tubes and a lesion in one lung that was not discovered till many years later' (IV, 345–46)—which tormented him for the rest of his life. The Burmese climate ruined his health (II, 23), he had pneumonia in February 1929 (see 'How the Poor Die'), was shot through the throat in Spain in May 1937, had tuberculosis in March 1938, was unfit for service in the Second World War due to bronchiectasis and was gravely ill during the last three years of his life.

Orwell's published letters, like Conrad's, are strangely impersonal, rather pedestrian and unvarying with each correspondent, but they become extraordinarily moving during the last months of his life when he faces the gravity of his disease with a Keatsian courage. He was deeply devoted to his adopted son, Richard, and poignantly writes,

I am so afraid of his growing away from me, or getting to think of me as just a person who is always lying down & can't play. Of course children can't understand illness. He used to come to me & say 'Where have you hurt yourself?' (IV, 479)

In May 1949 he admits,

I am in most ghastly health. . . . When the picture is taken I am afraid there is not much doubt it will show that both lungs have deteriorated badly. I asked the doctor recently whether she thought I would survive, & she wouldn't go further than saying she didn't know. . . . Don't think I am making up my mind to peg out. On the contrary, I have the strongest reasons for wanting to stay alive. But I want to get a clear idea of *how long* I am likely to last, & not just be jollied along the way doctors usually do. (IV, 500)

In August he announces, rather surprisingly,

I intend getting married again (to Sonia) when I am once again in the land of he living, if I ever am. I suppose everyone will be horrified. (IV, 505–06)

And in October he writes,

I am still very weak & ill, but I think better on the whole. I am getting married very unobtrusively this week. It will probably be a long time before I can get out of bed. (IV, 508)

He died three months later, in January 1950.

Future biographers will certainly be interested in Orwell's unusual second marriage, just as Orwell, in discussing Carlyle's marriage, was interested in 'the frame of mind in which people get married, and the astonishing selfishness that exists in the sincerest love' (I, 36).

The other dominant pattern in Orwell's life (closely related to his illness) is the series of masochistic impulses for a higher cause that testifies to his compulsive need for self-punishment: in school; in the Burmese Police; among scullions and beggars; in squalid doss houses and inside mines; with the ragged, weaponless army of the Republic in Spain; in propagandistic drudgery for the wartime BBC (a 'whore-shop and lunatic asylum'); in thankless and exhausting political polemics; and finally in that mad and suicidal sojourn amidst the damp, bleak and isolated wastes of Jura. In *Wigan Pier* Orwell states, 'I was conscious of an immense weight of guilt that I had got to expiate' and explains that this guilt derives from his experience as a colonial oppressor. But it seems that the source of this guilt, which he could never extinguish (see his *Diary* on p. 526), was both earlier and deeper than Orwell suggests ('Such, Such Were the Joys' describes his deep-rooted childhood guilt). Though no specific evidence yet exists, it is possible to imagine an early Lord Jim syndrome, a kind of moral self-betrayal or dishonorable fall from self-esteem that is a truer source of his masochistic guilt. But whatever the source, Orwell's writing is manifest proof of his ability to transcend this personal guilt by channeling it into effective social and political thought and action. . . . The words that provide the theoretical basis of Orwell's life were inscribed in his diary during the grim days of June 1940, and they express, perhaps more than anything else he wrote, his personal courage and high moral principle:

Both E and G* insistent that I should go to Canada if the worst comes to the worst, in order to stay alive and keep up propaganda. I will go if I have some function, e.g. if the government were transferred to Canada and I had some kind of a job, but not as a refugee, not as an expatriate journalist squealing from a safe distance. There are too many of these exiled 'anti-Fascists' already. Better to die if necessary, and maybe even as propaganda one's death might achieve more than going abroad and living more or less unwanted on other people's charity.

* 'E' is his wife Eileen, 'G' his sister-in-law, Gwen O'Shaughnessy.

# Select Bibliography

MEYERS, JEFFREY, 'George Orwell: A Bibliography,' *Bulletin of Bibliography*, XXXI (July–September 1974), pp. 117–21 and 'George Orwell: A Selected Checklist,' *Modern Fiction Studies*, XXI (Spring 1975), pp. 133–6. The most complete bibliographies on Orwell list virtually every important article and book that has been written about him in English and in foreign languages.

MEYERS, JEFFREY, *A Reader's Guide to George Orwell* (London: Thames & Hudson, 1975). Analyzes Orwell's books and major essays in the context of his life and historical background, and places him in the English and French literary traditions.

PRYCE-JONES, DAVID, 'Orwell's Reputation,' in *The World of George Orwell*, ed. Miriam Gross (London: Weidenfeld & Nicolson, 1971), pp. 144–52. A brief but interesting survey of the critics' response to Orwell.

RANKIN, DAVID, 'The Critical Reception of the Art and Thought of George Orwell,' Dissertation, University College, London University, 1965. A useful survey of Orwell's literary reputation.

STANSKY, PETER and WILLIAM ABRAHAMS, *The Unknown Orwell* (London: Constable, 1972). This first biography considers Orwell's life up to 1933.

WILLISON, IAN, 'George Orwell: Some Materials for a Bibliography,' Librarian Thesis, London University, 1953. Provides a great many facts about the publication of Orwell's works.

WOODCOCK, GEORGE, *The Crystal Spirit: A Study of George Orwell* (London: Cape, 1967). A biographical discussion of Orwell and careful analysis of his works.

# Index

## DATE DUE

# THE CRITICAL HERITAGE SERIES

GENERAL EDITOR: B. C. SOUTHAM

---

*Volumes published and forthcoming*